GS

Glouc

Items should be returned to a
on or before the date stamped.
be renewed in perso
0845

CW01376635

993176939 4

CALLOW PUBLISHING

Land Registration Manual

by Stephen R Coveney, LL.B, Solicitor
Land Registrar at Kingston-upon-Hull

London
Callow Publishing
2003

ISBN 1 898899 66 5

First published 2003

All rights reserved

Every care is taken in the preparation of this publication, but the author and publishers cannot accept responsibility for the consequences of any error,

Gloucestershire County Council	

Published by Callow Publishing Limited,
4 Shillingford Street, London N1 2DP
www.callowpublishing.com

Preface

The coming into force of the Land Registration Act 2002 and the Land Registration Rules 2003 on 13 October 2003 brings about the biggest changes in land law since 1926. All previous Land Registration Acts and Rules are repealed, although there are certain transitional provisions which are dealt with in this Manual.

My aim has been to provide busy conveyancers with the answers to their questions on the law and practice of land registration and dispositions of registered estates, within a logical and straightforward format.

No mention is made of land certificates or charge certificates, as these have been abolished. No existing certificate need be lodged with an application and no new certificates will be issued. Where the Land Registry completes an application, a title information document may be issued to show the amended register and, if necessary, the title plan. The title information document is not proof of ownership and does not need to be lodged with any application.

References in this Manual to a "conveyancer" are to be read as to a solicitor, or a licensed conveyancer, or a fellow of the Institute of Legal Executives. The Land Registration Rules 2003 and the forms prescribed by those Rules are to be read similarly.

The text of the Land Registration Act 2002 is available at www.legislation.hmso.gov.uk/acts/acts2002/20020009.htm

The text of the Land Registration Rules 2003 is available at www.legislation.hmso.gov.uk/si/si2003/2003.htm

All land registry forms may be freely downloaded from the Land Registry's website at www.landregistry.gov.uk

The law is stated as at 13 October 2003.

SRC

To Di, who made everything possible.

Contents

Access to neighbouring land
   orders... 1
Accretion and diluvion....................... 3
Administration orders........................ 4
Administrative receivers.................... 6
Adverse possession............................ 8
Advowsons.. 21
Agreement for lease.......................... 21
Agreement for mortgage................... 23
Agreement to pay further
   consideration............................... 25
Airspace.. 26
Alteration of the register.................. 26
Amalgamation of registered titles....28
Annuities... 29
Assents.. 30

Bankruptcy.. 34
Bare trusts... 47
Beneficial interests of joint
   proprietors of land....................... 49
Bona vacantia and escheat............... 50
Boundaries.. 51

Cautions against conversion............. 55
Cautions against dealings................. 56
Cautions against first registration.... 59
Chancel repair................................... 66
Charging orders................................ 66
Charities... 69
Children.. 79
Church of England............................ 81
Classes of title.................................. 86
Coal... 90
Collective enfranchisement............. 91
Commons... 99
Companies.. 102
Compulsory purchase...................... 104
Constructive, implied and
   resulting trusts........................... 108
Contracts for sale (including
   sub-sale)..................................... 109

Copyhold... 111
Correction of mistakes in an
   application or accompanying
   document.................................... 113
Costs.. 114
Credit unions.................................. 116
Death of applicant for registration.116
Debentures...................................... 117
Deeds of arrangement..................... 118
Demesne land.................................. 119
Disputes.. 120
Division of registered titles........... 122

Embankments or sea or river
   walls.. 123
Enlargement of long leases............ 124
Equitable charges........................... 126
Equitable easements....................... 130
Estate right and interest................. 131
European Economic Interest
   Groupings................................... 131
Exclusive use.................................. 133

First registration............................. 133
Floating charges............................. 140
Flying freeholds............................. 141
Foreshore.. 142
Franchises....................................... 143
Fraud... 145
Freezing orders............................... 147
Friendly societies........................... 148

Gifts.. 150

Historical information.................... 153
Housing action trusts..................... 154
Housing associations..................... 155

Implied covenants.......................... 157
Indemnity.. 161
Indemnity covenants...................... 163
Industrial and provident societies.. 164
Inhibitions...................................... 164
Internal waters................................ 165

Joint proprietors......................... 166
Land Registry Act 1862................. 167
Leasehold enfranchisement........... 167
Leases.. 169
Legal charges................................ 184
Legal easements............................ 190
Licences.. 193
Limited liability partnerships......... 194
Limited owner's charge................. 195
Limited partnerships..................... 197
Liquidators................................... 197
Local land charges........................ 200
Lost deeds..................................... 201

Manors.. 202
Matrimonial home occupation rights.. 204
Mental Health Act 1983 patients... 205
Mere equities................................ 206
Mines and minerals....................... 207

Notices.. 209
Notices of deposit......................... 214

Official copies............................... 214
Official searches............................ 217
Official searches of the index........ 219
Options... 220
Outline applications...................... 222
Overriding interests...................... 223
Overseas insolvency proceedings.. 228

Partnerships.................................. 229
Pending land actions..................... 229
Personal representatives................ 231
Plans... 233
Positive covenants........................ 234
Powers of attorney........................ 236
PPP leases relating to transport in London.. 238
Priorities....................................... 239
Profits a prendre........................... 242
Property adjustment orders............ 246
Proprietary estoppel...................... 248

Receivers...................................... 249
Receivers appointed by order of the court.. 251
Rectification................................. 253
Registered social landlords............ 254

Rentcharges.................................. 255
Restraint orders............................. 260
Restrictions................................... 262
Restrictive covenants.................... 273
Right to buy and right to acquire under the Housing Acts............. 274
Rights of light and air................... 278
Rights of pre-emption................... 278
Rights of reverter under the School Sites Acts................................... 280

Sequestrators................................ 281
Settlements................................... 282
Severance of a beneficial joint tenancy....................................... 286
Shared ownership leases............... 286
Souvenir land............................... 288
Special powers of appointment...... 290
Sporting rights.............................. 290
Statutory charges.......................... 292
Subrogation.................................. 293
Supervisor of an individual voluntary arrangement............................... 294

Time share.................................... 295
Town or village greens................. 295
Transfers....................................... 298
Trusts of land............................... 300

Unincorporated associations.......... 303
Upgrading titles............................ 304

Vendor's lien................................ 307

Writs or orders affecting land........ 308

Index.. 311

Table of Cases

Alpenstow Ltd v Regalian Properties Plc [1985] 1 WLR 721,
 [1985] 2 All ER 545 (Ch D) 59
Armstrong & Holmes Ltd v Holmes [1993] 1 WLR 1482,
 [1994] 1 All ER 826 (Ch D) 220
Ashburn Anstalt v W J Arnold and Co [1989] Ch 1, [1988] 2 WLR 706,
 [1988] 2 All ER 147 (CA) 1, 108, 193
Aston Cantlow and Wilmcote with Billesley Parochial Church Council v
 Wallbank [2001] EWCA Civ 713, [2001] 3 WLR 1323,
 [2001] 3 All ER 393 (CA) 66
Banque Financière de la Cité v Parc (Battersea) Ltd [1999] 1 AC 221,
 [1998] 2 WLR 475, [1998] 1 All ER 737 (HL) 293
Barclays Bank v Taylor [1974] Ch 137, [1973] 2 WLR 293,
 [1973] 1 All ER 752 (CA) 57
Beaufort, Duke of v John Aird and Co (1904) 20 TLR 602 291
Bennington Road, 51, Aston, Re [1993] The Times 21 July (Ch D) 124, 167
Bettison v Langton [2002] 1 AC 27, [2001] 2 WLR 1605,
 [2001] 3 All ER 417 (HL) 99
Binions v Evans [1972] Ch 359, [1972] 2 WLR 729, [1972] 2 All ER 70
 (CA) 108
Boscawen v Bajwa [1996] 1 WLR 328, [1995] 4 All ER 769 (CA) 293
Bradford City Council v McMahon [1994] 1 WLR 52,
 [1993] 4 All ER 237 (CA) 274
Brandwood v Bakewell Management Limited [2003] EWCA Civ 23,
 [2003] All ER (D) 302 (Jan) (CA) 191
Brightlife Ltd, Re [1987] Ch 200, [1987] 2 WLR 197, [1986] 3 All ER 673 4
Bromley LBC v Morritt [1999] EWCA Civ 1631, (1999) 78 P&CR D37 (CA). 13

Carlton v Goodman [2002] EWCA Civ 545, [2002] 2 FLR 259 (CA) 49, 50
Carroll v Manek (2000) 79 P & CR 173 (Ch D) 17
Celsteel Ltd v Alton House Holdings Ltd [1985] 1 WLR 204,
 [1985] 2 All ER 562 130
Clark v Chief Land Registrar, Chancery plc v Ketteringham [1994] Ch 370,
 [1994] 3 WLR 593, [1994] 4 All ER 96 (CA) 57
Clayhope Properties Ltd v Evans and Jennings [1986] 1 WLR 1223,
 [1986] 2 All ER 795 (CA) 252
Clearbrook Property Holdings v Verrier [1974] 1 WLR 243,
 [1973] 3 All ER 614 .... 57, 61
Costello v Costello [1996] 1 FLR 805 (CA) 282
Cottage Holiday Associates Limited v Customs and Excise Commissioners
 [1983] QB 735, [1983] 2 WLR 861 (VAT Tr) 295

ix

Crabb v Arun District Council [1976] Ch 179, [1975] 3 WLR 487,
 [1975] 3 All ER 865 (CA)..248
Dean v Walker (1997) 73 P & CR 366 (CA).. 1
Dennis v Malcolm [1934] Ch 244... 86
Elias v Mitchell [1972] Ch 652, [1972] 2 WLR 740, [1972] 2 All ER 153..........57
Fairweather v St Marylebone Property Co Ltd [1963] AC 510,
 [1962] 2 WLR 1020, [1962] 2 All ER 288 (HL).......................................20, 90
Ferrishurst Ltd v Wallcite Ltd [1999] Ch 355, [1999] 2 WLR 667,
 [1999] 1 All ER 977 (CA)..224
Friends' Provident Life Office v British Railways Board [1996] 1 All ER 336
 (CA)...172, 180
Gillett v Holt [2001] Ch 210, [2000] 3 WLR 315, [2000] 2 All ER 289 (CA)..248
Gissing v Gissing [1971] AC 886, [1970] 3 WLR 255,
 [1970] 2 All ER 780 (HL)...108
Gorman (a Bankrupt), Re [1990] 1 WLR 616, [1990] 1 All ER 717 (DC)....49–50
Hanbury v Jenkins [1901] 2 Ch 401..291
Hanning v Top Deck Travel Group Ltd (1994) 68 P & CR 14 (CA).................191
Hayling v Harper [2003] All ER (D) 41 (Apr) (CA)..192
Huntingford v Hobbs [1993] 1 FLR 736, [1992] Fam Law 437 (CA)...........49, 50
IDC Group Ltd v Clark (1993) 65 P & CR 179, [1992] 49 EG 103 (CA)......... 108
Kemmis v Kemmis [1988] 1 WLR 1307 (CA).. 246
Leigh v Jack (1879) 5 Ex D 264...13
Lloyd v Dugdale [2001] EWCA Civ 1754, [2001] All ER (D) 306 (Nov),
 [2002] 2 P&CR 13 (CA)... 108
Lyus v Prowsa Developments Ltd [1982] 1 WLR 1044,
 [1982] 2 All ER 953 (Ch D).. 108
McClymont v Primecourt Property Management Ltd [2000] All ER (D) 1871
 (Ch D)..133
Melbury Road Properties 1995 Ltd v Kreidi [1999] 3 EGLR 108,
 [1999] 43 EG 157.. 108
Metropolitan Railway Company v Fowler [1893] AC 416 (HL)........................133
Oceanic Village Ltd v United Attractions Ltd [2000] Ch 234,
 [2000] 2 WLR 476, [2000] 1 All ER 975 (Ch D)..178
Overseas Investment Services Ltd v Simcobuild Construction Ltd
 (1995) 70 P & CR 322, [1996] 1 EGLR 49 (CA)..225
Perez-Adamson v Perez Rivas [1987] Fam 89, [1987] 2 WLR 500,
 [1987] 3 All ER 20 (CA)..246
Pettitt v Pettitt [1970] AC 777, [1969] 2 WLR 966,
 [1969] 2 All ER 385 (HL)..50
Phillips v Phillips (1861) 4 De GF & J 208..206
Pinekerry Ltd v Needs (Kenneth) Contractors Ltd (1992) 64 P & CR 245
 (CA)...99, 296

Table of Cases

Powell v McFarlane (1979) 38 P & CR 452 (Ch D)... 12
Pritchard v Briggs [1980] Ch 338, [1979] 3 WLR 868, [1980] 1 All ER 294
  (CA)..278
Pye, J A, (Oxford) Ltd v Graham [2002] UKHL 30, [2003] 1 AC 347,
  [2002] 3 WLR 221, [2002] 3 All ER 865 (HL)..12, 13

R v Oxfordshire County Council ex parte Sunningwell Parish Council
  [2000] 1 AC 335, [1999] 3 WLR 160, [1999] 3 All ER 385 (HL).............. 296
R v Whixley Inhabitants (1786) 1 Term Rep 137.. 100
Rawlplug Co Ltd, The v Kamvale Properties Ltd (1968) 20 P & CR 32.............59
Reilly v Booth (1890) 44 Ch D 12 (CA).. 133
Rhone v Stephens [1994] 2 AC 310, [1994] 2 WLR 429,
  [1994] 2 All ER 65 (HL)... 235

Secretary of State for the Environment, Transport and the Regions v
  Baylis (Gloucester) Ltd [2000] All ER(D) 563, (2000) 80 P & CR 324..... 225
Smith v Colbourne [1914] 2 Ch 533 (CA)... 278
Southern Centre of Theosophy Inc v State of South Australia [1982] AC 706,
  [1982] 2 WLR 544, [1982] 1 All ER 283 (PC).. 3
Spook Erection Ltd v Secretary of State for the Environment [1989] QB 300,
  [1988] 3 WLR 291, [1988] 2 All ER 667 (CA).. 143
Springette v Defoe [1992] 2 FLR 388, (1993) 65 P & CR 1 (CA)...................... 50
Stockler v Fourways Estates Limited [1984] 1 WLR 25, [1983] 3 All ER 501
  (QBD)... 147

Taylor Fashions v Liverpool Victoria Friendly Society [1981] QB 133,
  [1981] 2 WLR 576, [1981] 1 All ER 897 (Ch D).. 248

United Bank of Kuwait v Sahib [1997] Ch 107, [1996] 3 WLR 372,
  [1996] 3 All ER 215 (CA)...214

Walker v Hall [1984] FLR 126, [1984] Fam Law 21 (CA)................................. 50
Whittingham v Whittingham [1979] Fam 19, [1978] 2 WLR 936,
  [1978] 3 All ER 805 (CA)...246
Wibberley, Alan, Building Ltd v Insley [1999] 1 WLR 894,
  [1999] 2 All ER 897 (HL)...52, 233
Woolf Project Management v Woodtrek Limited (1988) 56 P & CR 134...........25

Table of Legislation

Access to Justice Act 1999, s 10(7)....... 292
Access to Neighbouring Land Act
   1992.. 211
   ss 1, 5(5), 5(6), 6, 8(3)............................ 1
Banking and Financial Dealings Act
   1971, s 1........... 10, 54, 62, 64, 115, 142,
   185–186, 213, 218, 222, 241, 257, 264
Bankruptcy Act 1914, s 42........................ 44
Cathedrals Measure 1999, 1999 No. 1..... 84
   s 9(1)(a).. 84
   s 15, (4), (5).. 85
Charitable Trusts Acts 1853–1939............ 70
Charities Act 1960..................................... 70
Charities Act 1993..................... 81, 84, 85
   Part V... 69
   Part VII..................................... 71, 73, 79
   s 16... 71
   s 18.. 71, 72, 74, 77
   s 19... 74
   s 21(1).. 71
   s 22(3)... 72, 265
   s 36..................... 70, 72, 74, 75, 76, 265
   s 36(9)................................. 70, 74, 75, 76
   s 36(9)(a)... 77
   s 37... 73
   s 37(1).. 74
   s 37(2)........................... 72, 74, 78, 265
   s 37(5)................................. 69, 83, 156
   s 38...................... 72, 75, 76, 265
   s 38(2).. 75
   s 38(5)... 75, 76
   s 39(1).. 75
   s 39(2).. 72, 75, 265
   s 40... 76
   s 50.. 71, 78
   s 51... 78
   s 60... 73
   s 61... 78
   ss 68(1)(d), 82....................................... 73
   s 83.. 77, 78
   s 96... 69
   s 96(2).. 81
Church of England (Miscellaneous
   Provisions) Measure 2000, 2000
   No. 1... 82, 85

Civil Procedure Rules 1998, SI 1998
   No. 3132, Practice Direction 56,
   para 13.. 169
Coal Industry Act 1994–
   s 38....... 5, 8, 19, 31, 33, 38, 90, 91, 101,
      105, 106, 107, 125, 137, 139, 151,
      152, 171, 210, 251, 297, 299
   s 49....... 5, 8, 19, 31, 33, 38, 90, 91, 101,
      105, 106, 107, 125, 137, 139, 151,
      152, 171, 210, 251, 297, 299
   s 51....... 5, 8, 19, 31, 33, 38, 90, 91, 101,
      105, 106, 107, 125, 137, 139, 151,
      152, 171, 210, 251, 297, 299
   Sch 9... 90
Commonhold and Leasehold Reform
   Act 2002... 91
   s 121... 91
   s 132... 174
   s 142... 167
Commons Land (Rectification of Registers)
   Act 1989....................................... 100, 297
Commons Registration Act 1965........... 5, 8,
      19, 31, 33, 38, 99, 100, 101, 105,
      106, 107, 125, 137, 139, 150, 152,
      171, 209, 227, 243, 244, 245, 251,
      295, 296, 297, 298, 299
   s 1... 99
   s 8... 296, 298
   s 11... 100, 296
Commons Registration (New Land)
   Regulations 1969, SI 1969 No
   1843.. 100, 296
Companies (N.I.) Order 1986, SI 1986
   No. 1032 (N. 16), arts 403, 409........ 103,
      117, 184
Companies Act 1985...... 102, 117, 132, 140
   s 395................. 103, 117, 184, 195, 250
   ss 401, 410, 418......... 103, 117, 184, 195
   s 654... 50
Compulsory Purchase Act 1965, s 9,
   (3), (4)... 104
Compulsory Purchase (Vesting
   Declarations) Act 1981..................... 135
   s 1.. 106
   s 6.. 107

Compulsory Purchase (Vesting Declarations) Act 1981, continued–
s 12 106
Compulsory Purchase of Land (Vesting Declarations) Regulations 1990, SI 1990 No. 497 106
Sch 107
Copyhold Act 1852, s 48 .... 111, 291
Copyhold Act 1894, s 23 .... 111, 291
Council Regulation (EEC) No 2137/85 of 25 July 1985 on the European Economic Interest Group, OJ L 199 31/7/85 p. 1, art 25 132
Council Regulation (EC) No 1346/2000 of 29 May 2000 on insolvency proceedings, OJ L 160 3/6/00, p. 1, art 3(1) 228
Countryside and Rights of Way Act 2000, s 68 192
Credit Unions Act 1979, s 12 116
Criminal Justice Act 1988 165
s 78 66

Deeds of Arrangement Act 1914 118
Drug Trafficking Act 1994 165
s 27 66
Duchy of Cornwall Management Act 1863, s 30 119

Endowments and Glebe Measure 1976, 1976 No. 4 69
s 15 .... 85, 86
s 15(1)(b), (2) 86
s 20, (1), (10), (11) 85
Enduring Powers of Attorney Act 1985 236
s 7(3) 236
European Convention for the Protection of Human Rights and Fundamental Freedoms 1950 66
European Economic Interest Grouping Regulations 1989 (SI 1989 No 638) . 132
regs 3, 5 131
reg 8(2) 133
reg 19(1) 132
Evidence and Powers of Attorney Act 1940, s 4 236

Family Law Act 1996 .... 44, 45
s 31(10)(a), s 32 188
s 33 .... 44, 45
s 56 188
s 31(10) (a) 204
s 33(5) 204, 205

Sch 4 para 4(3)(a) 188, 205
Sch 4 para 4(3)(b) 188, 204
Friendly Societies Act 1974 148–149
s 53(1) 149
Friendly Societies Act 1992 .... 148, 149

Greater London Authority Act 1999,
s 218 .... 5, 8, 19, 31, 33, 38, 101, 105, 106, 107, 125, 134, 137, 139, 151 152, 171, 210, 238, 251, 298, 300

Housing Act 1985 274
Part 5 .. 134–135, 154, 155, 169, 170, 224
s 37 .... 269, 276
s 136 274
ss 143, 156 275
s 157 .... 269, 276
s 160 275
s 171A 134, 135, 169, 170, 224, 276
s 171D(2) 269, 277
Sch 1 para 2–12 155
Sch 6 para 2, 20, 21, 21(3), 23(1), 23(3), Sch 6A 275
Sch 9A para 4 269
Housing Act 1988, Part I 155
s 79(2) 153
s 81, 81(8) 154, 269, 277
s 81(10) 154
s 133 .... 269, 277
Sch 1 para 48 155
Housing Act 1996 .... 102, 155, 157, 274
Part I 154, 155
ss 1, 2(2), 9 254
s 10 255
s 11 .... 287, 288
s 13 .... 255, 269, 271
s 17 155
Housing Associations Act 1985 ..... 102, 155
s 1 155
s 9 .... 156, 157
Sch 1 .... 102, 155
Sch 1 para 2 155–156
Sch 1 para 3 156
Housing (Preservation of Right to Buy) Regulations 1993, SI 1993 No. 2241 .... 269, 277
Housing (Right to Acquire) Regulations 1997, SI 1997 No 619, Sch 1, para 41(g) 275
Human Rights Act 1998, Sch 1 66

Inclosure Act and Award 207

Table of Legislation

Industrial and Provident Societies
Act 1965.................................. 116, 164
s 3.. 116
s 30, (1)(a)................................... 164
Inheritance Tax Act 1984, ss 237, (6),
238...241
Insolvency Act 1986............ 35, 36, 39, 151
Part III...132
s 14(1), (6)...................................... 4
s 15... 5
s 15(1).. 4
s 15(2).. 5
s 15(3).. 4
ss 15(4), (5), 29(2).......................... 6
ss 42(3), 43..................................... 7
ss 89, 178.................................... 198
s 181.. 199
ss 238, 244, 245.......................... 250
s 251... 4
s 252 – 263................................. 294
s 282.. 42
s 283(3)... 37
ss 284, 306(2).............................. 36
ss 307, 309............................. 42, 43
s 313.. 45
s 320....................................... 46, 47
s 336(1), (4), (5)........................... 44
s 337....................................... 44, 45
s 337(3)...45
s 339........................... 43, 44, 153, 250
s 340..................................... 44, 153
s 343............................. 44, 153, 250
s 423............................. 43, 44, 153
Sch 1... 4, 7
International Criminal Court Act
2001................................... 147, 148
Interpretation Act 1978–
s 16.. 112
Sch 1... 165

Land Charges Act 1972......... 34, 35, 41, 62
s 6(1)(a)....................................... 308
Land Registration Act 1925........ 86, 88, 91,
143, 147, 170, 200, 202, 242, 273, 295
s 33...................................... 127, 137
s 53...60, 61
s 54.. 56, 214
s 56(3)... 61
s 57.. 164
s 61... 36
s 70... 90
s 70(1)(c)....................................... 66
s 70(1)(f).. 20

s 70(1)(g)..................................... 227
s 70(1)(k)..................................... 224
s 75(1)............................... 18, 21, 228
s 99.. 82
s 123...................................... 99, 296
s 137(1).......................................167
Land Registration Act 2002–
s 3.................... 143, 202, 242, 256
s 3(1).. 133
s 3(2)............................... 20, 87, 90, 131
s 3(4)..295
s 3(5), 6)...................................... 134
s 4............................... 31, 150, 295
s 4(1)(b)....................................... 276
s 4(1)(d), (e)................................224
s 4(1)(f)................................ 224, 276
s 4(1)(g)... 75
s 4(6)..134
s 6(5)................ 31, 99, 136, 150, 296
s 7... 31, 150
s 7(1), (3)..................................... 136
s 8............................... 31, 136, 150
s 9(2)......................................86, 138
s 9(3)............................... 86, 131, 138
s 9(4)... 87
s 9(5)......................................20, 87
s 10(2)..88
s 10(3)..89
s 10(4)............................... 88, 89, 131
s 10(5)..89
s 10(6)......................................20, 89
s 11................... 27, 112, 123, 224
s 11(3).................. 86, 141, 190, 208, 242
s 11(4)..87
s 11(4)(a)........................... 190, 242
s 11(5), (6)................................... 87
s 11(7)..88
s 12..................... 27, 112, 123, 224
s 12(3).................. 88, 141, 190, 208, 242
s 12(4)..88
s 12(4)(a), (b)........................... 190, 242
s 12(5), (6), (7)............................. 89
s 12(8)..90
s 15................... 59, 60, 61, 120
s 15(3)..60
s 16..................................... 143, 203
s 16(3).. 62
s 18.. 63, 120
s 18(2)..63
s 21, (1), (3).................................. 65
s 23.. 184
s 23(2)(b), (3).............................. 189
s 26... 303

Land Registration Act 2002, continued–

s 27.............. 50, 104, 129, 184, 292, 299
s 27(1)...32, 152
s 27(2)...169, 295
s 27(2)(c).................................... 145, 204
s 27(2)(d)...................... 99, 130, 191, 243
s 27(3)(a).. 190
s 27(3)(b).. 189
s 27(5).. 36
s 27(5)(b).. 50
s 27(7)...191, 243
s 28........................ 129, 152, 239, 240
s 29................ 21, 23, 109, 112, 123, 209
   220, 226, 239, 240, 241, 277, 278, 293
s 29(1)...307
s 29(3)...200
s 29(4)...240
s 30............... 21, 23, 109, 112, 123, 209,
   220, 226, 240, 241, 278
s 30(3)...200
s 31.. 241
s 32............... 21, 23, 109, 209, 220, 278
s 32(3)...273
s 33.......... 5, 7, 19, 29, 31, 33, 38, 47–48,
   67, 91, 101, 105, 106, 107, 125,
   138, 150, 152, 171, 196, 209, 250,
   297, 299
s 33(a)............................... 109, 282, 300
s 33(c).. 178
s 33(d)...99, 243
s 33(e)...209
s 34.. 57, 210
s 34(3)(c)......... 2, 22, 24, 67, 92, 96, 110,
   129, 147, 175, 221, 230, 246, 261
s 36... 120, 213
s 37....................................... 192, 244
s 38.. 210
s 41... 262
s 41(2)..165, 263
s 41(3)..263, 271
s 42(1)(a)... 154
s 42(1)(c)........... 93, 94, 97, 98, 118, 176,
   177, 252, 281
s 42(2)....................23, 24, 111, 221, 279
s 42(3)...............93, 94, 97, 98, 118, 176,
   177, 230, 247, 252, 261, 262, 281, 309
s 43.. 57–58
s 43(1)...263
s 43(1)(c)......... 40, 68, 69, 128, 280, 294
s 43(3)................3, 7, 23, 25, 26, 29, 111,
   222, 230, 247, 249, 280, 290, 309
s 44(1)............49, 72, 197, 229, 271, 303
s 44(2)..255, 276

s 45...................... 40, 68, 128, 196, 264
s 45(1)..294
s 46(1), (3)... 241
s 48(1)..186
s 49(1)..185
s 49(3), (4), (6)................................. 186
s 50... 161
s 51... 184
s 52(1)..187
s 54... 188
s 55... 200
s 58... 145
s 59(1)..191, 242
s 60... 55
s 61... 51
s 61(1).. 3
s 61(2)... 4, 51
s 62................................... 56, 161, 304
s 62(1)...87, 88
s 62(2)...55, 89
s 62(3)...89, 90
s 62(4)...304
s 62(5).......................................194, 304
s 62(6)..56, 304
s 63... 305
s 64... 183
ss 66, 67(1)....................................... 214
s 72(2)..241
s 72(6)(a)............................. 21, 23, 110
s 73.................. 11, 58, 62, 64, 213, 254
s 73(1), (2), (3), (5)........................... 120
s 73(5)(a).. 58
s 73(6)..120
s 73(7)..............................58, 63, 64, 120
s 76(4), (5)... 116
s 77... 61
s 77(1), (2)................... 61, 210, 212, 263
s 78...................... 49, 108, 166, 300
s 79, (2), (5)..................................... 119
s 81.. 119, 120
s 84... 119
s 86(1)..39
s 86(2), (3).. 34
s 86(4)..35, 271
s 86(5), (7)...39
s 87(1)........ 118, 229, 246, 252, 281, 308
s 87(2).............................. 118, 251, 281
s 87(3).......92, 93, 96, 97, 118, 175, 176,
   230, 246, 252, 281, 308
s 90... 223
s 90(1).......................................134, 238
s 90(2)..238
s 90(3)..239

Table of Legislation

Land Registration Act 2002, continued–
s 90(4).......5, 7, 19, 31, 33, 38, 101, 105, 107, 125, 137, 138, 150, 152, 171, 209, 239, 250, 297, 299
s 90(5)..239
s 96.. 9, 14
s 96(2)..187
s 98, (1), (2), (3)................................ 17
s 98(4)..18
s 108.. 122
s 110(1)....................................121, 214
s 110(4)..121
s 111....................................... 121, 214
ss 111(3), 112................................... 121
s 115.. 278
s 116...................................... 206, 248
s 117.. 112
s 117(1).............. 123, 143, 203, 225, 226
s 117(2)...... 112, 143, 144, 203, 225, 226
s 119.. 202
s 120.. 215
s 121.. 117
s 122.. 167
s 130.. 165
s 131................................... 194, 253, 304
s 132(1)..217
s 132(2)..50
Sch 1............. 19, 31, 66, 86, 87, 88, 101, 106, 125, 130, 137, 150, 167–168, 173, 202, 223, 297
Sch 1 para 1.......... 19, 31, 101, 106, 125, 137, 151, 170, 298
Sch 1 para 2............. 1, 21, 91, 92, 93, 96, 97, 118, 174, 175, 176, 204, 230, 246, 252, 281, 282, 308
Sch 1 para 3....................... 191, 194, 243
Sch 1 para 6.. 200
Sch 1 para 7.. 90
Sch 1 para 10...................................... 143
Sch 1 para 13...................................... 123
Sch 2 para 4............................... 145, 204
Sch 2 para 5............................... 145, 204
Sch 2 para 6....................................... 243
Sch 2 para 7....................... 130, 191, 243
Sch 2 para 10...................................... 190
Sch 2 para 11...................................... 189
Sch 3............. 1, 5, 7, 21, 33, 38, 66, 105, 107, 130, 152, 167–168, 171, 173, 202, 223, 226, 227, 228, 239, 240, 250, 277, 299, 308
Sch 3 para 1............. 5, 8, 22, 33, 38, 105, 107, 152, 170, 171, 251, 300

Sch 3 para 2................21, 22, 91, 92, 93, 96, 97, 118, 174, 175, 176, 204, 230, 246, 248, 252, 281, 282
Sch 3 para 3............. 130, 193, 194, 227, 244, 245
Sch 3 para 6................................ 200, 256
Sch 3 para 7.. 90
Sch 3 para 10...................................... 143
Sch 3 para 13...................................... 123
Sch 4 para 1........................... 26–27, 253
Sch 4 para 2(1)..................................... 27
Sch 4 para 3(2).................................... 194
Sch 4 para 3(3).................................... 253
Sch 4 para 5(d).................................... 272
Sch 4 para 6(2).................................... 194
Sch 6................................ 16, 257, 258
Sch 6 para 1........... 13–15, 121, 258–259
Sch 6 para 1(2)............................ 13, 258
Sch 6 para 1(3)..................................... 14
Sch 6 para 2.. 9
Sch 6 para 5................. 10, 14, 17, 259
Sch 6 para 5(4).................................... 11
Sch 6 para 6................. 15–16, 259–260
Sch 6 para 6(2)............................ 16, 260
Sch 6 para 8.................. 14, 16, 258, 259
Sch 6 para 8(2), (3), (4)....................... 206
Sch 6 para 11................................ 14, 15
Sch 6 para 13...................................... 142
Sch 8................. 114, 162, 163, 209, 256, 258, 259, 260
Sch 8 para 2.. 209
Sch 8 para 5.. 153
Sch 8 para 5(2), para 6.......................162
Sch 8 para 10...................................... 163
Sch 8 para 11...................................... 161
Sch 10 para 29...................................... 69
Sch 11 para 26(4).................................... 1
Sch 11 para 34(2)................................ 204
Sch 12 para 2(1).................................... 36
Sch 12 para 2(2)................... 82, 36, 147
Sch 12 para 2(3)............................ 56, 57
Sch 12 para 4.. 61
Sch 12 para 7....................... 21, 226, 228
Sch 12 para 8....................................... 227
Sch 12 para 9..... 130, 193, 227–228, 245
Sch 12 para 10................. 193, 228, 245
Sch 12 para 11............................ 18, 228
Sch 12 para 12................. 170, 224, 295
Sch 12 para 13.................................... 200
Sch 12 para 14(1).................................. 60
Sch 12 para 15(1)................................ 119
Sch 12 para 17...................................... 58
Sch 12 para 18...................................... 18

LAND REGISTRATION MANUAL

Land Registration Act 2002, continued–
  Sch 12 para 18(1)................. 17, 18, 228
  Sch 12 para 20..................................... 159
  Sch 12 para 20(3), (4)................ 179, 180
Land Registration Act 2002 (Transitional Provisions) Order 2003–
  art 11, (4), (5)..................................... 289
  art 15.. 56
  arts 22(5), 25..................................... 214
Land Registration and Land Charges Act 1971, s 4(5)................................. 289
Land Registration (Referral to the Adjudicator to HM Land Registry) Rules 2003, r 5................................. 121
Land Registration Rules 1925, SR&O 1925 No. 1093............................. 74, 75
  r 215(2).. 55
  r 251... 141
  r 258... 130, 228
  r 278... 51, 52
Land Registration Rules 1995, SI 1995 No. 140... 214
Land Registration Rules 2003, SI 2003 No. 1417–
  Part 1... 95
  r 3... 190
  r 3(5).. 29, 122
  r 5... 51
  r 5(a)............................... 29, 122, 208
  r 6(2)... 172
  r 8(2)... 138
  r 11... 220
  r 13(2)... 166
  r 15... 223
  r 17.............................. 14, 16, 259, 260
  r 18... 116
  r 19.............................. 62, 64, 120, 213
  r 21... 135
  r 22... 139
  r 23(2)... 119
  r 26.. 26, 137
  r 26(1)... 141
  r 27... 201
  r 28............. 19, 31, 32, 66, 101, 105, 106, 125, 136, 137, 144, 150, 151, 191, 208, 239, 243, 287, 297
  r 28(2)(d)... 200
  r 29... 138
  r 30................. 20, 32, 101, 138, 151, 298
  r 31, (1)... 142
  r 32... 208
  r 33... 242
  r 34... 139

r 35............. 138, 139, 140, 191, 243, 256
r 36... 139, 278
rr 37, 38... 139
r 45... 63
r 47... 60, 63
rr 48(1), 49, 50(2)................................ 65
r 51(1).. 64
r 51(2).. 65
r 52... 120
r 53... 62, 64
r 53(3).. 64
r 54... 222
r 55... 242
r 56... 298
r 57........... 5, 6, 7, 8, 33, 38, 66, 104, 105, 107, 152, 171, 172, 193, 239, 245, 250, 287, 299, 300, 302, 303
r 57(2)(c)... 200
r 58... 298
r 59... 299
r 60(1), (2), (3)................................. 179
r 62... 236
r 63... 238
r 64... 234
r 64(3).. 235
r 65, (3)... 163
r 66... 160
r 67(1).. 157
r 67(6).. 159
r 68... 158
r 69... 160
r 69(4).. 161
r 70... 29, 122
r 71... 208
r 72... 299
r 76... 278
rr 77, 78... 172
r 80................................... 1, 204, 210
r 84(4).. 140
r 86... 213
r 86(7).. 120, 213
r 89............................... 192, 193, 210, 244
r 92... 185
r 93... 263, 264
r 93(a).. 30, 40, 48, 68, 69, 128, 247, 280
r 93(b).. 302
r 93(c)...................................... 48, 232, 301
r 93(d).. 232, 301
r 93(e).. 290
r 93(f).. 69
r 93(g).. 84
r 93(h), (i)................................. 147, 148
r 93(j).. 40

xviii

Table of Legislation

Land Registration Rules 2003, continued–

r 93(k)	68, 69
r 93(l)	262
r 93(m)	261
r 93(n)	98
r 93(o)	97
r 93(p)	94, 177
r 93(q)	93, 176
r 93(r)	147, 148
r 93(s)	252, 281
r 93(t)	118
r 93(u)	262
r 93(v)	261
r 94	30, 72, 264, 273
r 94(1)	48, 300
r 94(1)(b)	286
r 94(2)	48, 300
r 94(3)	301
r 94(4)	48, 232, 301
r 94(7)	232
r 95(2)(a)	271
r 95(2)(b), (c)	276
r 95(2)(h)	255
rr 98, 99	272
r 100	271
rr 101, 102	186
r 104	200
r 105	292
r 105(1)	201
r 108	186
r 111(1), (2)	103, 184, 195
r 113	187
r 114	189
r 117	53
r 118	10
r 118(1)	53
r 119	10
r 119(1), (6), (7)	53
r 120	10
r 121	10, 54
r 122	10, 55
r 123(1)	3
r 125(1)	183
r 126(1), (2)	27
r 128	28, 126, 254
r 130	113
r 136	215
r 136(6)	215, 216
rr 137, 139	217
r 145	144, 219
r 147	217
rr 150, 151	218
r 153	241
rr 154, 155	218
r 161	104
r 162	32, 232
r 163(3), (5)	231
r 164	166
r 165(1)	34
r 166(1)	35
r 167(2)	34
r 167(2)	35–36
r 172	230, 308
r 173	51
r 174	83
r 175	84
r 176, (3)	72
r 177	71
r 178(3)	72
r 179	69, 83, 156
r 180(1)	74, 76, 83
r 180(2)	75, 76, 84
r 180(3)	75
r 181	156
r 181(1)	102, 156
r 181(2)	102, 254
r 181(3)	102, 156
r 181(4)	194
r 182	156
r 182(1)	71, 81, 156
r 182(2)	254
r 182(3)	156
r 182(4)	71, 81
r 183(1)	102, 156, 164
r 183(2)	102, 156
r 183(3)	102, 254
r 183(4)	102, 156
r 184(2)	4
r 185	50
rr 192, 193	258
r 194	9
r 195	114, 162
r 196(1)	95
r 196(2)	174
r 198	61
r 202	115
r 213	298
rr 216, 217	214
r 217(1)	60
r 218	56, 58, 214
r 219	214
r 220(2)	56, 58
r 221(3), (5)	58
r 221(6)	59
r 223	58
r 223(3)	58, 59

Land Registration Rules 2003, continued–
r 232..82
r 278..51
Sch 4... 3, 7, 23, 25, 26, 27, 28, 111, 114, 145, 222, 230, 247, 249, 264, 279, 309
Sch 7 para 3(2)................................. 196
Sch 7 para 7.. 29
Sch 7 para 7(2)................................. 282
Sch 8... 257
Sch 8 para 1(2)(b)............................ 146
Sch 8 para 5.............................. 146, 257
Sch 9.. 103, 195
Sch 12 para 2(2)...................... 146, 164
Land Registration (Souvenir Land) Rules 1972, SI 1972 No. 985............ 288
Land Registry Act 1862................... 52, 167
Land Transfer Act 1875, s 125.............. 167
Land Transfer Rules 1898, r 213............. 51
Land Transfer Rules 1903, r 274............. 51
Landlord and Tenant (Covenants) Act 1995, s 1..................................... 159, 180
Landlord and Tenant Act 1954............... 182
Landlord and Tenant Act 1987–
s 28.. 96, 97–98
s 28(5)..96
s 30(6)..97
s 35... 172
ss 38, 39(4)................................ 173, 211
Law of Property Act 1922......................112
Part V...202
s 1(2)...239
s 128... 111, 112
Sch 12..................................111, 112, 291
Law of Property Act 1925–
s 1(6)...79
s 1(7)...290
s 2(2), (3)...................................... 30, 195
s 27............. 40, 48, 57, 68, 109,128, 286
s 34... 166
s 36... 166
s 36(2)...286
s 53(2)...108
s 55(1)...59
s 56(2)...56
s 56(3), (4)..57
s 62.................................... 141, 191, 243
s 76... 159
s 77... 160
s 77(1)(A), (B)................................... 161
s 84... 274
s 90... 129
s 105... 188
s 109... 249

s 153.. 124, 167
s 153(4)...124
s 153(8)...126
s 162... 1
Law of Property (Amendment) Act 1926.. 30
Law of Property (Miscellaneous Provisions) Act 1989–
s 2... 214
s 2(5)..108
Law of Property (Miscellaneous Provisions) Act 1994–
Part I.......................... 157, 158, 159, 160
s 7... 153
s 8(1)..158
s 11(1)..159
Leasehold Reform Act 1967......... 124, 157, 167–169, 173–174
s 5(2), (5)..................................... 168, 173
ss 10, (2), (3), (4), 13......................... 169
s 14... 174
Leasehold Reform, Housing and Urban Development Act 1993.....................91, 157, 167, 174–178, 22
s 13.. 91–92
s 18(1), (2).. 95
s 24(4), (6)..................................... 94, 95
s 26(1)...92–94, 95
s 32(2)..95, 307
ss 32(2)(a), (b), (c), 33, 34(10), 35...... 95
s 36... 96
s 42... 174, 175
s 50(1).............................175, 176, 177
s 56... 174
s 58(1), (2), (5), (6)............................ 178
s 97(1)...91–92, 174
s 97(2)(a)....................................... 93, 176
s 97(2)(b)....................................... 92, 175
s 107... 287
s 117... 275
Sch 9, paras 4(1), 8..............................96
Sch 13... 174
Legal Aid Act 1988, s 16(6)................. 292
Limitation Act 1980................8, 20, 86, 87, 90, 131, 163, 226, 228
s 15... 9, 14, 15
s 16... 9, 188
s 17... 9, 18
ss 18, 22(3).. 19
ss 28, 32, 38... 18
Sch 1 para 6... 15
Limitation (Enemies and War Prisoners) Act 1945................. 11, 14, 16, 258, 260

xx

Table of Legislation

Limited Liability Partnerships Act
2000.....61, 117, 164, 194, 195, 197, 229
Limited Partnership Act 1907................197
Literary and Scientific Institutions
Act 1854.. 280
Local Government Act 1972, ss 1, 20....165
Local Government and Housing Act
1989, s 173................................. 269, 277
Local Land Charges Act 1975, s 19(3)..200

Matrimonial Homes Act 1967,–
s 2(7)...188
s 5(3)(b... 188
Matrimonial Homes Act 1983–
s 2(8)...188
s 5(3)(b).. 188
Mental Health Act 1983.205, 206, 249, 251

New Parishes Measure 1943, 6 & 7
Geo VI No. 1................................ 82, 265

Parsonages Measure 1938, 1 & 2
Geo VI No. 3................................ 82, 265
s 1(3)(iii)..83
s 9(2), (2A).. 82
s 9(2B).. 83
Party Wall etc Act 1996...........................53
Pastoral Measure 1983, 1983 No. 1.......... 84
Patronage (Benefices) Measure
1986, s 6... 21
Places of Worship Registration
Act 1955, s 9...70
Places of Worship Sites Act 1873...........280
Powers of Attorney Act 1971, s 3...........236
Proceeds of Crime Act 2002, ss 41,
246.. 260
Property Misdescriptions Act 1991....... 234

Rentcharges Act 1977–
s 2, (4), (5)..255
ss 8, 9,10..76
Repair of Benefice Buildings Measure
1972, 1972 No. 2................................. 82
s 1(1)...83
Reverter of Sites Act 1987, s 1, (4)........280

School Sites Acts 1841, 1844, 1849,
1852...280
Settled Land Act 1925......... 5, 8, 19, 29, 31,
33, 38, 101, 105, 106, 107, 125, 137,
138, 150, 152, 171, 196, 209, 224, 251,
266, 282, 283, 284, 285, 297, 299, 300
s 17... 285
s 65... 283
s 72(3)...30, 195

Statute Law (Repeals) Act 1969............ 112
Statutory Declarations Act 1835....237, 238
Terrorism Act 2000................................165
Sch 4 para 5(1), (2)............................260
Trade Union and Labour Relations
(Consolidation) Act 1992, ss 13,
129... 304
Trustee Act 1925–
s 34... 166
s 34(3)...72
s 40... 77, 302
s 40(4)... 302
Trusts of Land and Appointment of
Trustees Act 1996........................47, 109
s 1.. 108, 300
s 2.. 282
s 2(2)...284
s 6(6), (8).. 302
s 8.. 48, 232, 301
s 9... 237, 238
s 23(2)...80
Sch 1 para 1.. 80
Sch 1 para 1(1).................................... 79
Sch 1 para 1(2).................................... 80

Vehicular Access Across Common and
Other Land (England) Regulations
2002, SI 2002 No. 1711.....................192

Wild Creatures and Forest Laws Act
1971, s 1(1)................................ 143, 291

Access to Neighbouring Land Orders

A person who wishes, for the purpose of carrying out works to land, to enter on adjoining or adjacent land and who needs, but does not have, the consent of some other person, may apply to the court for an access order (Access to Neighbouring Land Act 1992 ("ANLA 1992") section 1). "Land" for this purpose does not include a highway (ANLA 1992 section 8(3)), but does include a party wall (*Dean v Walker* (1997) 73 P & CR 366 (CA)). The application must be commenced in the county court and constitutes a pending land action (ANLA 1992 section 5(6)). The priority of the pending land action may be protected by the entry on the register of a notice, or a restriction, or both. In practice, an application for an agreed notice will be the usual course of action.

Where the result of the application is that the court makes an access order, this should be protected by an agreed notice. The entry made on the register will give details of the interest protected. It is not possible to protect such an access order by a unilateral notice (Land Registration Rules 2003 ("LRR 2003") rule 80).

The rights conferred by the access order are not capable of falling within paragraph 2 of Schedule 1 or Schedule 3 to the Land Registration Act 2002 ("LRA 2002"), which deal with the overriding status of interests of persons in actual occupation (ANLA 1992 section 5(5) as substituted by LRA 2002 Schedule 11 paragraph 26(4)).

The court may make an order, under ANLA 1992 section 6, varying the access order. The variation should also be protected by an agreed notice. The entry made on the register will give details of the variation. It is not possible to protect such a variation by a unilateral notice (LRR 2003 rule 80).

Where access to neighbouring land is allowed under a licence from the registered proprietor, it is not possible to protect this by way of notice in the register. Even a contractual licence does not bind successors in title (*Ashburn Anstalt v W J Arnold and Co* [1989] Ch 1; [1988] 2 WLR 706; [1988] 2 All ER 147 (CA)). If the registered proprietor is prepared to consent, a restriction may be entered in the register of the servient title. A restriction does not confer any priority; it simply prevents an entry being made in the register if it is not permitted under the wording of the restriction.

It is also possible to have an easement to enter on another's land for the purpose of carrying out work on one's own land. The perpetuity rule does not apply to such an easement (Law of Property Act 1925 section 162). See *Equitable Easements*, page 130 and *Legal Easements*, page 190.

Notice in Respect of a Pending Action
An applicant should deliver to the registry:
- (a) an application in form AN1;
- (b) the sealed claim form and notice of issue; and
- (c) the fee payable. A fee calculator for all types of application is on the Land Registry's website at www.landregistry.gov.uk/fees.

This is likely to be sufficient to satisfy the registrar as to the validity of the applicant's claim in accordance with LRA 2002 section 34(3)(c). Where the applicant wishes to apply for a unilateral notice he should deliver to the registry:
- (a) an application in form UN1;
- (b) a plan of the affected land (where the pending action affects only part of the land in the registered title); and
- (c) the fee payable. A fee calculator for all types of application is on the Land Registry's website at www.landregistry.gov.uk/fees.

Form UN1 should be completed on the following lines to show the interest of the applicant:

"applicant in an application under section 1 of the Access to Neighbouring Land Act 1992 in the ... County Court [*set out full court reference and parties*]."

The unilateral notice will give brief details of the interest protected and identify the beneficiary of that notice.

Agreed Notice of the Access Order
An applicant should deliver to the registry:
- (a) an application in form AN1;
- (b) the access order or a certified copy of it; and
- (c) the fee payable. A fee calculator for all types of application is on the Land Registry's website at www.landregistry.gov.uk/fees.

Agreed Notice of an Order Varying the Access Order
An applicant should deliver to the registry:
- (a) an application in form AN1;
- (b) the order varying the access order or a certified copy of it; and
- (c) the fee payable. A fee calculator for all types of application is on the Land Registry's website at www.landregistry.gov.uk/fees.

Restriction in Respect of a Licence
An applicant should deliver to the registry:
- (a) an application in form RX1;
- (b) the consent of the registered proprietor of the land (unless this is given in panel 15 of form RX1 or the applicant's conveyancer certifies that he holds such consent. The certificate may be given in panel 11 of form RX1); and

(c) the fee payable. A fee calculator for all types of application is on the Land Registry's website at www.landregistry.gov.uk/fees.

A possible form of restriction based on Form N in Schedule 4 to LRR 2003 is:

"No disposition of the registered estate (other than a charge) by the proprietor of the registered estate is to be registered without a written consent signed by [*licensee*] of [*address*] or his conveyancer."

A restriction in this form does not require the approval of the registrar under LRA 2002 section 43(3).

Accretion and Diluvion

Where land has a boundary with water, the title of the owner of the land normally extends to any land added by accretion. Equally where there is erosion, or diluvion, title to the land affected is lost. This doctrine of accretion and diluvion applies only where the changes are gradual and imperceptible (*Southern Centre of Theosophy Inc v State of South Australia* [1982] AC 706, [1982] 2 WLR 544, [1982] 1 All ER 283 (PC)). The doctrine can be excluded if this is the intention of the parties.

The fact that a registered estate in land is shown in the register as having a particular boundary does not affect the operation of accretion or diluvion (Land Registration Act 2002 section 61(1)). This applies whether the registered title has a general boundary or a determined boundary.

An agreement about the operation of accretion or diluvion in relation to registered land has effect only if it is registered. An application to register such an agreement must be made by, or accompanied by the consent of, the registered proprietor of the land and of any registered charge, but no such consent is required from a person who is party to the agreement (Land Registration Rules 2003 rule 123(1)).

Registration of Agreement

An applicant should deliver to the registry:
(a) an application in form AP1;
(b) the agreement about the operation of accretion or diluvion;
(c) a certified copy of the agreement (if the original agreement is to be returned);
(d) the consent(s) of the registered proprietor(s) of the land and of any registered charge, where such person or persons are not party to the agreement;
(e) the fee payable. A fee calculator for all types of application is on the Land Registry's website at www.landregistry.gov.uk/fees.

On registration of the agreement, a note is made in the property register that the agreement is registered for the purposes of section 61(2) of the Land Registration Act 2002.

Administration Orders

A court may make an order under the Insolvency Act 1986 which has the effect that the affairs, business and property of a company are managed by an administrator appointed by the court so long as that order is in force (section 8(2)). The administrator can apply for the administration order and his appointment to be noted in the register (Land Registration Rules 2003 ("LRR 2003") rule 184(2)).

Notice
The administrator should deliver to the registry:
 (a) an application in form AP1;
 (b) an office copy of the administration order;
 (c) the fee payable. A fee calculator for all types of application is on the Land Registry's website at www.landregistry.gov.uk/fees.

Where the court appoints a new administrator in place of the existing administrator, a similar application is required. In that case an office copy of the court order appointing the new administrator should be delivered to the registry.

The notice entered in the proprietorship register should be on the following lines:

"By an Order of the court dated ... an administration order was made in respect of [*name of company*] and [*name of administrator*] of [*administrator's address*] was appointed administrator of the company."

Sale by the Administrator
An administrator may sell the company's property and execute any deed or other document in the name and on behalf of the company (Insolvency Act 1986 section 14(1) and Schedule 1). Any person dealing with the administrator for value and in good faith does not need to ascertain whether he is acting within his powers (Insolvency Act 1986 section 14(6)).

An administrator may dispose of property that is subject to a floating charge as though it was not subject to that charge (Insolvency Act 1986 section 15(1) and (3)). This extends to any charge which, as created, was a floating charge. It is irrelevant that the charge has, under its terms, crystallised on the service of notice by the administrator (Insolvency Act 1986 section 251; *Re Brightlife Ltd* [1987] Ch 200, [1987] 2 WLR 197, [1986] 3 All ER 673).

An administrator may also apply to the court for an order authorising him to dispose of the property free from a charge which, as created, was not a floating charge (Insolvency Act 1986 section 15(2)).

A person applying to register a disposition of a registered estate must provide information to the registrar in form DI about any of the overriding interests (other than local land charges or public rights) set out in Schedule 3 to LRA 2002 that affect the estate to which the application relates and are within the actual knowledge of the applicant. For details see *Overriding Interests*, page 223. The applicant must produce to the registrar any documentary evidence of the overriding interest that is under his control (LRR 2003 rule 57). The registrar may enter a notice in the register in respect of any such interest.

The applicant is not required, however, to provide information about interests that, under LRA 2002 section 33 or 90(4), cannot be protected by notice. Such interests are:
   (a) interests under a trust of land or under a Settled Land Act 1925 settlement;
   (b) a leasehold estate in land granted for three years or less from the date of the grant and which is not required to be registered;
   (c) a restrictive covenant between lessor and lessee, so far as relating to the demised premises;
   (d) an interest which is capable of being registered under the Commons Registration Act 1965;
   (e) an interest in any coal or coal mine, or the rights attached to any such interest, or the rights of any person under the Coal Industry Act 1994 section 38, 49 or 51; and
   (f) leases created for public-private partnerships relating to transport in London, within the meaning given by the Greater London Authority Act 1999 section 218.

The applicant is also not required to provide information about a leasehold estate in land which falls within paragraph 1 of Schedule 3 to LRA 2002 but, at the time of the application, has one year or less to run.

A transferee of a registered title from an administrator should deliver to the registry:
   (a) an application in form AP1;
   (b) a transfer by the administrator;
   (c) an office copy of the administration order (where this has not been noted in the register);
   (d) releases in respect of any charges appearing on the title and not dealt with under (e) or (f) below;
   (e) where a floating charge is noted in the register (other than by way of unilateral notice), form CN1 signed by the administrator with panel 12 stating that the registered title has been transferred pursuant to the Insolvency Act 1986 section 15;
   (f) where the court has made an order allowing the administrator to

dispose of the registered title free from a fixed charge, an office copy of that order;
(g) form DI giving the information as to overriding interests required by LRR 2003 rule 57, including any documentary evidence of the interests; and
(h) the fee payable. A fee calculator for all types of application is on the Land Registry's website at www.landregistry.gov.uk/fees.

Acquisition by Company Subject to an Administration Order
Where a company's property has been disposed of free from a charge, the chargee has the same priority in respect of any property of the company directly or indirectly representing the property disposed of as he would have had in respect of the property subject to the security (Insolvency Act 1985 section 15(4)). Accordingly, where a company subject to an administration order is registered as proprietor of a registered estate, the following entry is made in the charges register:

"The registered estate is subject to such security or securities as may exist and affect the same by virtue of the provisions of section 15(5) of the Insolvency Act 1986."

This entry is not made if the administrator certifies that there are no such securities or that such securities as affected have been discharged.

Administrative Receivers

An administrative receiver is defined as a receiver or manager of the whole (or substantially the whole) of a company's property appointed by or on behalf of the holders of any debentures of the company secured by a charge which, as created, was a floating charge, or by such a charge and one or more other securities; or a person who would be such a receiver or manager but for the appointment of some other person as the receiver of part of the company's property (Insolvency Act 1986 section 29(2)).

The appointment of an administrative receiver is not capable of being noted on the register of any title of which the company is registered proprietor.

Address for Service
The administrative receiver should ensure that the company's address for service shown in the register is such as will allow notices to be received. If an additional address for service (up to three are permitted), or an amended address for service, is required, the administrative receiver should deliver to the registry:
(a) an application in form AP1;

(b) a certified copy of the appointment of the receiver; and
(c) a certified copy of the debenture (if not already noted or registered).
No fee is payable.

Restriction
An administrative receiver may wish to apply for a restriction in respect of a registered title owned by the company. A restriction does not confer any priority; it simply prevents an entry being made in the register if it is not permitted under the wording of the restriction.

The administrative receiver should deliver to the registry:
(a) an application in form RX1;
(b) a statement signed by the administrative receiver or his conveyancer that the applicant is the administrative receiver of the registered proprietor company (this may be given in panel 13 of form RX1); and
(c) the fee payable. A fee calculator for all types of application is on the Land Registry's website at www.landregistry.gov.uk/fees.

A possible form of restriction based on Form N in Schedule 4 to the Land Registration Rules 2003 ("LRR 2003") is:

"No disposition of the registered estate by the proprietor of the registered estate is to be registered without a written consent signed by [*administrative receiver*] of [*address*] or his conveyancer."

A restriction in this form does not require the approval of the registrar under the Land Registration Act 2002 ("LRA 2002") section 43(3).

Sale by Administrative Receiver
An administrative receiver may sell the company's property and execute any deed or other document in the name and on behalf of the company (Insolvency Act 1986, Schedule 1). Any person dealing with the administrative receiver for value and in good faith does not need to ascertain whether he is acting within his powers (Insolvency Act 1986 section 42(3)).

An administrative receiver may apply to the court for an order authorising him to dispose of the property free from charges that have priority to the debenture under which he was appointed (Insolvency Act 1986 section 43).

A person applying to register a disposition of a registered estate must provide information to the registrar in form DI about any of the overriding interests (other than local land charges or public rights) set out in Schedule 3 to LRA 2002 that affect the estate to which the application relates and are within the actual knowledge of the applicant. For details see *Overriding Interests*, page 223. The applicant must produce to the registrar any documentary evidence of the interest that is under his control (LRR 2003 rule 57). The registrar may enter a notice in the register in respect of any such interest.

The applicant is not required, however, to provide information about interests that, under LRA 2002 section 33 or 90(4), cannot be protected by

notice. Such interests are:
- (a) interests under a trust of land or under a Settled Land Act 1925 settlement;
- (b) a leasehold estate in land granted for three years or less from the date of the grant and which is not required to be registered;
- (c) a restrictive covenant between lessor and lessee, so far as relating to the demised premises;
- (d) an interest which is capable of being registered under the Commons Registration Act 1965;
- (e) an interest in any coal or coal mine, or the rights attached to any such interest, or the rights of any person under the Coal Industry Act 1994 section 38, 49 or 51; and
- (f) leases created for public-private partnerships relating to transport in London, within the meaning given by the Greater London Authority Act 1999 section 218.

The applicant is also not required to provide information about a leasehold estate in land which falls within paragraph 1 of Schedule 3 to LRA 2002 but, at the time of the application, has one year or less to run.

A transferee of a registered title from an administrative receiver should deliver to the registry:
- (a) an application in form AP1;
- (b) a transfer;
- (c) a certified copy of the receiver's appointment;
- (d) a certified copy of the debenture under which the receiver was appointed (unless already noted on the register of the title being sold);
- (e) releases in respect of any charges appearing on the title and not dealt with under (f) below;
- (f) where the court has made an order allowing the administrative receiver to dispose of the registered title free from charges, an office copy of that order;
- (g) details of any challenge to the validity of the debenture by a liquidator of the company;
- (h) form DI, giving the information as to overriding interests required by LRR 2003 rule 57, including any documentary evidence of the interest(s); and
- (i) the fee payable. A fee calculator for all types of application is on the Land Registry's website at www.landregistry.gov.uk/fees.

Adverse Possession

The Land Registration Act 2002 ("LRA 2002") lays down rules for obtaining a title to registered land under the Limitation Act 1980, such that the position relating to registered land differs from that relating to unregistered land. No period of limitation under section 15 of the Limitation Act 1980 is to run against any person, other than a chargee, in relation to an estate in land or rentcharge the title to which is registered. No period of limitation under section 16 of the Limitation Act 1980 is to run against any person in relation to such an estate in land or rentcharge. Accordingly, section 17 of the 1980 Act does not operate to extinguish the title of any person where, by virtue of this, a period of limitation does not run against him (LRA 2002 section 96).

For adverse possession in relation to rentcharges, see *Rentcharges*, page 255.

A person may apply to be registered as proprietor of a registered estate in land if he has been in adverse possession of the estate for the period of ten years ending on the date of the application. The estate need not have been registered throughout the period of adverse possession. A person may also apply for registration if he has, in the period of six months prior to the application, ceased to be in adverse possession of the estate because of eviction by the registered proprietor or a person claiming under the registered proprietor; and on the day before his eviction he had been in adverse possession for the period of ten years; and the eviction was not pursuant to a judgment for possession. A person may not make such an application if he is a defendant in proceedings which involve asserting a right to possession of the land, or if judgment for possession of the land has been given against him in the last two years.

The registrar must give notice of the application to the proprietor of the estate and the proprietor of any registered charge on the estate. Where the estate is leasehold the registrar must also give notice to the proprietor of any superior registered estate. Any person who can satisfy the registrar that he has an interest in a registered estate in land which would be prejudiced by the registration of any other person as proprietor consequent upon an adverse possession application may apply to be registered as a person to be notified of such application (Land Registration Rules 2003 ("LRR 2003") rule 194).

Registration as a Person Entitled to be Notified of an Adverse Possession Application

An applicant should deliver to the registry:
  (a) an application in form ADV2;
  (b) the fee payable. A fee calculator for all types of application is on the Land Registry's website at www.landregistry.gov.uk/fees.

The interest of the applicant is shown in his statutory declaration in panel 10 or in his conveyancer's certificate in panel 11. If the application is in order, the registrar must enter the name of the applicant in the proprietorship register as a person entitled to be notified under paragraph 2 of Schedule 6 to LRA 2002.

Notice of an Application Based on Adverse Possession

The notice of the application to be registered as proprietor of the registered estate includes notice that, if the application is not required to be dealt with under LRA 2002 Schedule 6 paragraph 5, the applicant is entitled to be entered in the register as the new proprietor of the estate. The period allowed for reply is the period ending at 12 noon on the sixty-fifth business day after the date of issue of the notice. A business day is a day when the Land Registry is open to the public, that is, every day except Saturdays, Sundays, Christmas Day, Good Friday or any other day either specified or declared by proclamation under section 1 of the Banking and Financial Dealings Act 1971 or appointed by the Lord Chancellor.

A person given notice of such an application may require that it is dealt with under LRA 2002, Schedule 6 paragraph 5. He must do this by giving notice to the registrar in Form NAP, a copy of which would have accompanied any notice of the application based on adverse possession. When notice in Form NAP has been given to the registrar requiring that the application be dealt with under paragraph 5, the applicant is entitled to be registered as the new proprietor only if any of the following three conditions is met.

The first condition is that it would be unconscionable, because of an equity by estoppel, for the registered proprietor to seek to dispossess the applicant and the circumstances are such that the applicant ought to be registered as the proprietor. An example might be where a person built on the registered land under the mistaken belief that he was the owner and the registered proprietor acquiesced in that belief, and the person in possession applied for registration after ten years, having then learnt the true position.

The second condition is that the applicant is for some other reason entitled to be registered as the proprietor of the estate; for example, where a person entered into a valid contract to purchase and paid the purchase money over ten years before, but the registered title has never been transferred to him.

The third condition is the one most likely to be met with in practice. It is that:
  (a) the land to which the application relates is adjacent to land belonging to the applicant;
  (b) the exact line of the boundary between the two has not been determined under LRR 2003, rules 118 to 122;
  (c) for at least ten years of the period of adverse possession ending on the date of the application, the applicant (or any predecessor in title) reasonably believed that the land to which the application relates belonged to him; and
  (d) the estate to which the application relates was registered more than one year prior to the date of the application.

Where an application is made after the applicant has been evicted by the registered proprietor or a person claiming under him, the period referred to in (c) of the third condition is to be treated as the period ending on the day before the date of the applicant's eviction.

The Law Commission Report *Land Registration for the Twenty-First Century: A Conveyancing Revolution* (Law Com No 271) indicates that this third condition, in LRA 2002 Schedule 6 paragraph 5(4), is to come into force one year after the rest of the Act. This will allow registered proprietors one year from 13 October 2003 to commence proceedings against any squatter who might come within paragraph 5(4), or regularise the position in some other way so as to end the adverse possession.

It is also possible for the registered proprietor to use form NAP to object to the registration on grounds set out in panel 6, for example that the acts of adverse possession had not happened or that those acts did not constitute adverse possession. Such an objection would be dealt with in accordance with LRA 2002 section 73; see *Disputes*, page 120. In addition to objecting on form NAP the registered proprietor may also require on that form that the application is dealt with under paragraph 5. By doing so he retains the option of proceeding under paragraph 5 if his objection is not successful.

Right to Make Further Application for Registration
When the application of a person who has been in adverse possession of a registered estate is rejected, he may make a further application to be registered as the proprietor of the estate if he is in adverse possession of the estate from the date of the application until the last day of the period of two years beginning with the date of its rejection. If a person makes such an application, he is entitled to be entered in the register as the new proprietor of the estate. A person may not, however, make such an application if:
  (a) he is a defendant in proceedings which involve asserting a right to possession of the land;
  (b) judgment for possession of the land has been given against him in the last two years; or
  (c) he has been evicted from the land pursuant to a judgment for possession.

Restrictions on Applications
No one who has been in adverse possession of a registered estate may apply to be registered as proprietor of that estate during, or before the end of twelve months after the end of, any period in which the existing registered proprietor is, for the purposes of the Limitation (Enemies and War Prisoners) Act 1945, an enemy or detained in enemy territory. Where it appears to the registrar that this applies, he may include a note to that effect in the register.

No one who has been in adverse possession of a registered estate may apply to be registered as proprietor of that estate during any period in which the existing registered proprietor is unable, because of mental disability, to make decisions about issues of the kind to which such an application would give rise, or unable to communicate such decisions because of mental disability or physical impairment. Where it appears to the registrar that this applies, he may include a note to that effect in the register. For these purposes "mental disability" means a disability or disorder of the mind or brain, whether permanent or temporary, which results in an impairment or disturbance of mental functioning.

Meaning of "Adverse Possession"
In *J A Pye (Oxford) Ltd v Graham* [2002] UKHL 30, [2003] 1 AC 347, [2002] 3 WLR 221, [2002] 3 All ER 865 (HL), Lord Browne-Wilkinson said:
> "In my judgment much confusion and complication would be avoided if reference to adverse possession were to be avoided so far as possible and effect given to the clear words of the [Limitation] Acts. The question is simply whether the defendant squatter has dispossessed the paper owner by going into ordinary possession of the land for the requisite period without the consent of the owner."

He went on to say:
> "There are two elements necessary for legal possession:
> 1. a sufficient degree of physical custody and control ('factual possession');
> 2. an intention to exercise such custody and control on one's behalf and for one's own benefit ('intention to possess')."

In *Powell v McFarlane* (1979) 38 P & CR 452, Slade J said:
> "Factual possession signifies an appropriate degree of physical control. It must be a single and [exclusive] possession, though there can be a single possession exercised by or on behalf of several persons jointly. Thus an owner of land and a person intruding on that land without his consent cannot both be in possession of the land at the same time. The question what acts constitute a sufficient degree of exclusive physical control must depend on the circumstances, in particular the nature of the land and the manner in which land of that nature is commonly used or enjoyed. ... Everything must depend on the particular circumstances, but broadly, I think what must be shown as constituting factual possession is that the alleged possessor has been dealing with the land in question as an occupying owner might have been expected to deal with it and that no-one else has done so."

This statement of the law by Slade J was approved by the House of Lords in *J A Pye (Oxford) Ltd v Graham*. In that case the House of Lords also approved the following statement by Slade J in *Powell v McFarlane* that "intention to possess" requires an:
> "intention, in one's own name and on one's own behalf, to exclude the world at large, including the owner with the paper title if he be not himself

the possessor, so far as is reasonably practicable and so far as the processes of the law will allow."

Leigh v Jack (1879) 5 Ex D 264 was often cited in the past as authority for the proposition that in order to defeat a title by dispossessing the former owner, acts must be done which are inconsistent with his enjoyment of the land for the purposes for which he intended to use it. This has now been laid to rest by the House of Lords in *J A Pye (Oxford) Ltd v Graham*, where Lord Browne-Wilkinson said:

"The suggestion that the sufficiency of the possession can depend on the intention not of the squatter but of the true owner is heretical and wrong. ... The highest it can be put is that, if the squatter is aware of a special purpose for which the paper owner uses or intends to use the land and the use made by the squatter does not conflict with that use, that may provide some support for a finding as a question of fact that the squatter had no intention to possess the land in the ordinary sense but only an intention to occupy it until needed by the paper owner. For myself I think there will be few occasions in which such inference could be properly drawn in cases where the true owner has been physically excluded from the land. But it remains a possible, if improbable, inference in some cases."

In *Bromley LBC v Morritt* [1999] EWCA Civ 1631, Mummery LJ stated:

"As a matter of law, an adverse possession or squatter's title cannot be acquired to land over which a public right of way exists."

Application under LRA 2002 Schedule 6 paragraph 1 for Registration by Person in Adverse Possession of Registered Land

Where an applicant has not previously had an application under LRA 2002 Schedule 6 paragraph 1 rejected, he should deliver to the registry:

(a) an application in form ADV1;
(b) a statutory declaration made by the applicant not more than one month before the application, together with any necessary supporting statutory declarations, to provide evidence of adverse possession of the land against which the application is made for a period of not less than ten years ending on the date of application;
(c) a plan enabling the extent of the land to be fully identified on the Ordnance Survey map; this plan should be an exhibit to the applicant's statutory declaration;
(d) any additional evidence which the applicant considers necessary to support the claim; and
(e) the fee payable. A fee calculator for all types of application is on the Land Registry's website at www.landregistry.gov.uk/fees.

The statutory declaration by the applicant must also contain:

(a) if reliance is placed on LRA 2002 Schedule 6 paragraph 1(2), the facts relied upon with any appropriate exhibits. Paragraph 1(2) allows a person to apply for registration if he has, in the period of six months

prior to the application, ceased to be in adverse possession of the estate because of eviction by the registered proprietor or a person claiming under the registered proprietor, and on the day before his eviction he had been in adverse possession for the period of ten years and the eviction was not pursuant to a judgment for possession;
(b) confirmation that LRA 2002 Schedule 6 paragraph 1(3) does not apply. Paragraph 1(3) provides that a person may not make an application under Schedule 6 paragraph 1 if he is a defendant in proceedings which involve asserting a right to possession of the land, or if judgment for possession of the land has been given against him in the last two years;
(c) confirmation that to the best of his knowledge the restriction on applications in LRA 2002 Schedule 6 paragraph 8 does not apply. Paragraph 8 provides that no one who has been in adverse possession of a registered estate may apply to be registered as proprietor of that estate during, or before the end of twelve months after the end of, any period in which the existing registered proprietor is for the purposes of the Limitation (Enemies and War Prisoners) Act 1945 an enemy or detained in enemy territory. It also provides that no one who has been in adverse possession of a registered estate may apply to be registered as proprietor of that estate during any period in which the existing registered proprietor is unable, because of mental disability, to make decisions about issues of the kind to which such an application would give rise, or unable to communicate such decisions because of mental disability or physical impairment;
(d) confirmation that to the best of his knowledge the estate is not, and has not been during any of the period of alleged adverse possession, subject to a trust (other than one where the interest of each of the beneficiaries is an interest in possession); and
(e) if, should a person given notice of the application require that it be dealt with under LRA 2002 Schedule 6 paragraph 5, it is intended to rely on one or more of the conditions set out in that paragraph, the facts supporting such reliance. Paragraph 5 and its three conditions are dealt with under *Notice of an application based on adverse possession*, page 10.

The applicant must also supply such additional evidence as the registrar directs after the application has been considered (LRR 2003 rule 17).

Although LRA 2002 section 96 provides that no period of limitation under section 15 of the Limitation Act 1980 is to run against any person, other than a chargee, in relation to an estate in registered land, a person is treated as being in adverse possession of an estate in registered land if, but for section 96, a period of limitation under the Limitation Act 1980 section 15 would run in his favour in relation to the estate (LRA 2002 Schedule 6 paragraph 11). In determining whether for the purposes of paragraph 11 a period of limitation would run under section 15 of the Limitation Act 1980, the commencement of any legal proceedings is disregarded.

The Limitation Act 1980 Schedule 1 paragraph 6 provides that where a person is in possession under a lease in writing that reserves a rent of at least ten pounds and the rent is wrongfully received by some person claiming to be entitled to the immediate reversion, the right of action to recover the land is deemed to have accrued on the date when the rent was first wrongfully received, not on the date of the determination of the lease. In determining whether, for the purposes of LRA 2002 Schedule 6 paragraph 11, a period of limitation would run under section 15 of the Limitation Act 1980, however, the Limitation Act 1980 Schedule 1 paragraph 6 is disregarded.

A person is also to be regarded as having been in adverse possession of an estate in land where he is the successor in title during any period of adverse possession by a predecessor in title to that estate. He is also to be regarded as having been in adverse possession during any period of adverse possession by another person which comes between, and is continuous with, periods of adverse possession of his own.

When an estate in registered land is subject to a trust, a person is not to be regarded as being in adverse possession of that estate unless the interest of each of the beneficiaries is an interest in possession.

Where the registered land consists of foreshore belonging to the Queen in right of the Crown or the Duchy of Lancaster or to the Duchy of Cornwall, the period of adverse possession required before an application may be made is sixty years rather than ten years.

Where a person is registered as a result of a successful application based on adverse possession of registered land, the title by virtue of adverse possession which he had at the time of the application is extinguished. The estate is normally vested in him free of any registered charge affecting the estate immediately before registration, but otherwise his registration does not affect the priority of any interest affecting the estate.

Application under LRA 2002 Schedule 6 paragraph 6 for Registration by Person in Adverse Possession of Registered Land

Where an applicant has had an application under LRA 2002 Schedule 6 paragraph 1 rejected, he may be able to make a further application under LRA 2002 Schedule 6 paragraph 6 if he has been in adverse possession for a further two years from the date of rejection. See *Right to make further application for registration* (above, page 11) for details of when such an application may be made.

The applicant should deliver to the registry:
(a) an application in form ADV1;
(b) a statutory declaration made by the applicant not more than one month before the application, together with any necessary supporting statutory declarations, to provide evidence of adverse possession of

the land against which the application is made for a period of not less than two years beginning with the date of rejection of the original application and ending on the date of application;
(c) a plan enabling the extent of the land to be fully identified on the Ordnance Survey map; this plan should be an exhibit to the applicant's statutory declaration. A plan is not needed if the extent is the same as in the previous rejected application;
(d) any additional evidence which the applicant considers necessary to support the claim; and
(e) the fee payable. A fee calculator for all types of application is on the Land Registry's website at www.landregistry.gov.uk/fees.

The statutory declaration by the applicant must also contain:
(a) full details of the previous rejected application;
(b) confirmation that to the best of his knowledge the restriction on applications in LRA 2002 Schedule 6 paragraph 8 does not apply. Paragraph 8 provides that no one who has been in adverse possession of a registered estate may apply to be registered as proprietor of that estate during, or before the end of twelve months after the end of, any period in which the existing registered proprietor is for the purposes of the Limitation (Enemies and War Prisoners) Act 1945 an enemy or detained in enemy territory. It also provides that no one who has been in adverse possession of a registered estate may apply to be registered as proprietor of that estate during any period in which the existing registered proprietor is unable because of mental disability to make decisions about issues of the kind to which such an application would give rise, or unable to communicate such decisions because of mental disability or physical impairment;
(c) confirmation that to the best of his knowledge the estate is not, and has not been during any of the period of alleged adverse possession, subject to a trust (other than one where the interest of each of the beneficiaries is an interest in possession); and
(d) confirmation that LRA 2002 Schedule 6 paragraph 6(2) does not apply. Paragraph 6(2) provides that a person may not make an application under paragraph 6 if he is a defendant in proceedings which involve asserting a right to possession of the land, or judgment for possession of the land has been given against him in the last two years, or he has been evicted from the land pursuant to a judgment for possession.

The applicant must also supply such additional evidence as the registrar directs after the application has been considered (LRR 2003 rule 17).

Registered Charges

Where a person is registered as proprietor under LRA 2002 Schedule 6, the application having been determined other than by reference to whether any of the conditions in paragraph 5 applies, the estate is vested in him free of any registered charge affecting the estate immediately before his registration. If the application proceeded only because one of the three conditions in LRA 2002 Schedule 6 paragraph 5 was met, the estate remains subject to any registered charges. Where such a charge affects other property as well as the registered estate, the proprietor of the estate may require the chargee to apportion the amount secured by the charge at that time between the estate and the other property on the basis of their respective values. The person requiring the apportionment is entitled to a discharge of his estate from the charge on payment of the amount apportioned to the estate and the costs incurred by the chargee as a result of the apportionment. Thus LRA 2002 has had the effect of overturning the decision in *Carroll v Manek* (2000) 79 P & CR 173 so far as registered land is concerned where an application is made under Schedule 6. Where an application is made under LRA 2002 Schedule 12 paragraph 18(1), the applicant takes subject to any registered charge in existence when he commenced adverse possession. See *Transitional Provisions* (below, page 18) as to paragraph 18(1).

Additional Defences to Actions for Possession
LRA 2002 section 98 contains various defences to an action for possession of land. Those defences are additional to any other defences a person may have. That section also sets out when a judgment for possession of land ceases to be enforceable. Where in any proceedings a court determines that a person is entitled to a defence under that section, or that a judgment for possession has ceased to be enforceable against a person by virtue of section 98(4), the court must order the registrar to register that person as the proprietor of the registered estate in respect of which he is entitled to make an application based on adverse possession.

A person has a defence to an action for possession of land if, on the day immediately preceding that on which the action was brought, he was entitled to make an application to be registered as the proprietor of registered land having been in adverse possession for ten years and, had he made such an application on that day, the third condition in LRA 2002 Schedule 6 paragraph 5 would have been satisfied (LRA 2002 section 98(1)).

A judgment for possession of land ceases to be enforceable at the end of the period of two years beginning with the date of the judgment if the proceedings in which the judgment is given were commenced against a person who at that time had been in adverse possession for ten years (LRA 2002 section 98(2)).

A person has a defence to an action for possession of land if, on the day immediately preceding that on which the action was brought, he was entitled to make a further application to be registered as proprietor having been in adverse possession for a period of two years from the date of the rejection of his prior application (LRA 2002 section 98(3)).

A judgment for possession of land ceases to be enforceable at the end of the period of two years beginning with the date of the judgment if, at the end of that period, the person against whom the judgment was given is entitled to make a further application to be registered as proprietor having been in adverse possession for a period of two years from the date of the rejection of his prior application (LRA 2002 section 98(4)).

Transitional Provisions
Where a registered estate in land was held in trust for a person by virtue of the Land Registration Act 1925 section 75(1) immediately before the coming into force of LRA 2002, he is entitled to be registered as the proprietor of the estate (LRA 2002 Schedule 12 paragraph 18(1)). The position under the Land Registration Act 1925 was that where a registered proprietor's title had been extinguished by adverse possession, it was open to the squatter to apply for the closure of the registered proprietor's title which was deemed, in the meantime, to be held on trust for the squatter by the registered proprietor (Land Registration Act 1925 section 75(1)).

For the period of three years beginning with 13 October 2003, the right to be registered under LRA 2002 Schedule 12 paragraph 18(1) is an interest overriding a registered disposition (LRA 2002 Schedule 12 paragraph 11).

A person has a defence to any action for the possession of land (in addition to any other defence he may have) if he is entitled to be registered as the proprietor of an estate in the land under LRA 2002 Schedule 12 paragraph 18. Where in an action for possession of land a court determines that a person is entitled to such a defence, the court must order the registrar to register him as the proprietor of the estate in question.

An application to be registered as proprietor under these transitional provisions should be made using application form AP1, not form ADV1. Form AP1 should show that the applicant is applying to be registered as proprietor in accordance with the Land Registration Act 2002 Schedule 12 paragraph 18(1). Evidence of adverse possession by way of statutory declarations should be lodged in support of the application.

Application for First Registration
Where a person has been in adverse possession of unregistered land for the appropriate period of limitation, the documentary title owner's paper title is extinguished (Limitation Act 1980 section 17). The normal period of limitation for recovery of land is twelve years but this period is extended to thirty years for the Crown and any spiritual or eleemosynary corporation sole. In the case of foreshore owned by the Crown the period is sixty years. The normal period may also be extended where there has been fraud or deliberate concealment of a cause or action, or mistake (Limitation Act 1980 section 32), or where the person entitled to recover the land is under the age of eighteen or is of unsound mind (Limitation Act 1980 sections 28 and 38).

Adverse Possession

Where the land is held on trust or is settled land, the legal estate is not extinguished until the rights of action of all the beneficiaries to recover the land have been barred (Limitation Act 1980 section 18).

An applicant who can show adverse possession for the appropriate limitation period should deliver to the registry:
 (a) an application in form FR1;
 (b) sufficient details, by plan or otherwise, so that the land can be clearly identified on the Ordnance Survey map;
 (c) all deeds and documents relating to the title that are in the control of the applicant, including statutory declaration evidence as to the adverse possession;
 (d) a list in duplicate in form DL of all the documents delivered;
 (e) form DI giving the information as to overriding interests required by LRR 2003 rule 28; and
 (f) the fee payable. A fee calculator for all types of application is on the Land Registry's website at www.landregistry.gov.uk/fees.

In the case of a leasehold estate, the lease, if in the control of the applicant, and a certified copy must also be lodged.

Rule 28 of the LRR 2003 provides that a person applying for first registration must provide information to the registrar in form DI about any of the overriding interests (other than local land charges or public rights) set out in Schedule 1 to LRA 2002 that affect the estate to which the application relates and are within the actual knowledge of the applicant but are not apparent from the deeds and documents accompanying the application. The registrar may enter a notice in the register in respect of any such interest.

The applicant is not required, however, to provide information about interests that, under LRA 2002 section 33 or 90(4), cannot be protected by notice. Such interests are:
 (a) interests under a trust of land or under a Settled Land Act 1925 settlement;
 (b) a leasehold estate in land granted for three years or less from the date of the grant and which is not required to be registered;
 (c) a restrictive covenant between lessor and lessee, so far as relating to the demised premises;
 (d) an interest which is capable of being registered under the Commons Registration Act 1965;
 (e) an interest in any coal or coal mine, or the rights attached to any such interest, or the rights of any person under the Coal Industry Act 1994 section 38, 49 or 51; and
 (f) leases created for public-private partnerships relating to transport in London, within the meaning given by the Greater London Authority Act 1999 section 218.

The applicant is also not required to provide information about a leasehold estate in land which falls within paragraph 1 of Schedule 1 to LRA 2002 but at the time of the application has one year or less to run.

In examining the title the registrar has regard to any examination by a conveyancer prior to the application and to the nature of the property. He may make searches and enquiries and give notice to other persons, direct that searches and enquiries be made by the applicant, and advertise the application (LRR 2003 rule 30).

The applicant may be registered with absolute title if the registrar is of the opinion that the applicant's title is such as a willing buyer could properly be advised by a competent professional adviser to accept. In the case of a leasehold title this suffices for a good leasehold title; for an absolute title the registrar must in addition approve the lessor's title to grant the lease. In considering the applicant's title, the registrar may disregard the fact that the title appears to him to be open to objection if he is of the opinion that the defect would not cause the holding under the title to be disturbed.

An applicant may be registered with qualified title if the registrar is of the opinion that the person's title to the estate, or in the case of a leasehold the lessor's title to the reversion, has been established only for a limited period or subject to certain reservations which cannot be disregarded. Qualified titles are rare in practice.

An applicant may be registered with possessory title if the registrar is of the opinion that the applicant is in actual possession of the land, or in receipt of the rents and profits of the land, by virtue of the estate, and that there is no other class of title with which he may be registered (LRA 2002 sections 9(5) and 10(6)). LRA 2002 section 3(2) provides that a person may apply for first registration if the legal estate is vested in him or he is entitled to require the legal estate to be vested in him. Accordingly, if an applicant has not been in adverse possession for the requisite period under the Limitation Act 1980, no class of title can be granted.

The House of Lords, in *Fairweather v St Marylebone Property Co Ltd* [1963] AC 510, [1962] 2 WLR 1020, [1962] 2 All ER 288, held that when the title to a leasehold estate is unregistered and the lessee has been ousted by a squatter for the full period of limitation, the lessee may still surrender to the lessor who can then take action to recover possession from the squatter. This must be taken into consideration where a squatter is seeking a possessory title of a leasehold estate.

Overriding Interests

Prior to the coming into force of LRA 2002, rights acquired, or in the course of being acquired, under the Limitation Acts were overriding interests (Land Registration Act 1925 section 70(1)(f)). Although this particular category of overriding interest is not reproduced in LRA 2002, for the period of three years from 13 October 2003 there is included in the list of unregistered interests which override first registration a right acquired under the Limitation Act 1980 before the coming into force of LRA 2002. For this period therefore, a person who has acquired title by adverse possession but is no longer in actual occupation continues to have an interest which overrides first registration (LRA 2002 Schedule 12 paragraph 7). If that person is in actual occupation then his interest may be protected under paragraph 2 of Schedule 1 and Schedule 3 to LRA 2002.

For the overriding status of the right to be registered as proprietor where a registered estate in land was held in trust for a person by virtue of the Land Registration Act 1925 section 75(1) immediately before the coming into force of the Land Registration Act 2002, see *Transitional Provisions,* above.

Advowsons

It has not been possible to register advowsons at the Land Registry after 1 October 1986. On 1 January 1989 all existing registrations of advowsons were deemed to be closed and removed from the register of title without any entry being made in the register (Patronage (Benefices) Measure 1986 section 6).

Agreement for Lease

An agreement for lease of registered land may be protected by the entry in the register of an agreed notice, a unilateral notice, and/or by a restriction. A notice does not necessarily mean that the agreement for lease is valid but does mean that the priority of the agreement for lease is protected on any registered disposition (Land Registration Act 2002 ("LRA 2002") sections 32, 29 and 30). A restriction does not confer any priority; it simply prevents an entry being made in the register if it is not permitted under the wording of the restriction.

LRA 2002 section 72(6)(a) provides that rules may make provision for priority periods in connection with the noting in the register of a contract for the making of a registrable disposition of a registered estate or charge. At October 2003, no such rules have been made.

Where the agreement for lease of registered land is not protected by a notice, it may still override a later registered disposition for value if, at the time of that later disposition, the person having the benefit of the agreement for lease is in actual occupation of the land to which the agreement for lease relates. If he is in actual occupation of only part of the land to which the agreement relates, he has an overriding interest only in respect of the part he is occupying (LRA 2002 sections 29 and 30 and Schedule 3 paragraph 2).

The interest of the person in actual possession does not override a registered disposition if enquiry was made of him before the disposition and he failed to disclose the agreement for lease when he could reasonably have been expected to do so. Nor does the agreement for lease override a registered disposition if it belongs to a person whose occupation would not have been obvious on a reasonably careful inspection of the land at the time of the disposition, and if the person to whom the disposition is made does not have actual knowledge of the agreement for lease at the time of the disposition (LRA 2002 Schedule 3 paragraph 2).

Although a leasehold estate in land granted for a term not exceeding seven years from the date of the grant is usually an overriding interest under LRA 2002 Schedule 3 paragraph 1, an agreement to create such a lease is not itself an overriding interest and should be protected by a notice.

Agreed Notice

An applicant should deliver to the registry:
  (a) an application in form AN1;
  (b) the agreement for lease or a certified copy of it;
  (c) the consent of the registered proprietor of the land where this is not contained in form AN1; and
  (d) the fee payable. A fee calculator for all types of application is on the Land Registry's website at www.landregistry.gov.uk/fees.

Where the consent of the registered proprietor is not available but the original agreement for lease is signed by him, this is likely to be sufficient to satisfy the registrar as to the validity of the applicant's claim in accordance with LRA 2002 section 34(3)(c).

The entry made in the register will give details of the interest protected.

A unilateral notice may be preferred where the applicant does not wish the terms of the agreement to be open to public scrutiny.

Unilateral Notice

An applicant should deliver to the registry:
  (a) an application in form UN1;
  (b) a plan of the affected land (where the agreement for lease affects only part of the land in the registered title); and
  (c) the fee payable. A fee calculator for all types of application is on the Land Registry's website at www.landregistry.gov.uk/fees.

Form UN1 should be completed on the following lines to show the interest of the applicant:

"intending lessee under an agreement for lease dated ... made between [*registered proprietor*] and [*purchaser*]."

The unilateral notice will give brief details of the interest protected and identify the beneficiary of that notice.

Agreement for Lease

Restriction
As a result of LRA 2002 section 42(2), no restriction may be entered for the purpose of protecting the priority of an interest which is, or could be, the subject of a notice. This does not necessarily prevent a restriction being entered in addition to the notice of the contract. Although the notice protects the priority of the agreement, a restriction may be used to ensure that any conditions in relation to another disposition by the registered proprietor are complied with. The consent of the registered proprietor to the entry of the restriction is required.

An applicant should deliver to the registry:
(a) an application in form RX1;
(b) the consent of the registered proprietor of the land (unless this is given in panel 15 of form RX1 or the applicant's conveyancer certifies that he holds such consent. The certificate may be given in panel 11 of form RX1); and
(c) the fee payable. A fee calculator for all types of application is on the Land Registry's website at www.landregistry.gov.uk/fees.

A possible form of restriction based on Form N in Schedule 4 to the Land Registration Rules 2003 is:

"No disposition of the registered estate by the proprietor of the registered estate is to be registered without a written consent signed by [*intending lessee*] of [*address*] or his conveyancer."

A restriction in this form does not require the approval of the registrar under LRA 2002 section 43(3).

Agreement for Mortgage

An agreement for mortgage of registered land may be protected by the entry in the register of an agreed notice, a unilateral notice and/or by a restriction. A notice does not necessarily mean that the agreement for mortgage is valid but does mean that the priority of that agreement is protected on any registered disposition (Land Registration Act 2002 ("LRA 2002") sections 32, 29 and 30). A restriction does not confer any priority; it simply prevents an entry being made in the register if it is not permitted under the wording of the restriction.

LRA 2002 section 72(6)(a) provides that rules may make provision for priority periods in connection with the noting in the register of a contract for the making of a registrable disposition of a registered estate or charge. At October 2003, no such rules have been made.

Agreed Notice
An applicant should deliver to the registry:

(a) an application in form AN1;
(b) the agreement or a certified copy of it;
(c) the consent of the registered proprietor of the land where this is not contained in form AN1; and
(d) the fee payable. A fee calculator for all types of application is on the Land Registry's website at www.landregistry.gov.uk/fees.

Where the agreement is by an intending purchaser who has the benefit of a contract for sale, that contract or a certified copy of it should be included with the application. This is not necessary if there is already a notice of that contract in the register.

Where the consent of the registered proprietor is not available but the original agreement for mortgage is signed by him, this is likely to be sufficient to satisfy the registrar as to the validity of the applicant's claim in accordance with LRA 2002 section 34(3)(c).

The entry made in the register will give details of the interest protected.

A unilateral notice may be preferred where the applicant does not wish the terms of the agreement to be open to public scrutiny.

Unilateral Notice

An applicant should deliver to the registry:
(a) an application in form UN1;
(b) a plan of the affected land (where the agreement for mortgage affects only part of the land in the registered title); and
(c) the fee payable. A fee calculator for all types of application is on the Land Registry's website at www.landregistry.gov.uk/fees.

Form UN1 should be completed on the following lines to show the interest of the applicant:

"intending mortgagee under an agreement for mortgage dated ... made between [*registered proprietor*] and [*mortgagee*]."

In the case of an agreement for mortgage given by an intending purchaser who has the benefit of a contract for sale, form UN1 should be completed on the following lines:

"intending mortgagee under an agreement for mortgage dated ... made between [*purchaser*] and [*mortgagee*], [*purchaser*] being the purchaser under a contract for sale dated ... made between [*registered proprietor*] and [*purchaser*]."

The wording must establish the link between the registered proprietor and the person who is to be shown as the beneficiary of the notice. The unilateral notice will give brief details of the interest protected and identify the beneficiary of that notice.

Restriction

As a result of LRA 2002 section 42(2) no restriction may be entered for the purpose of protecting the priority of an interest which is, or could be, the subject of a notice. This does not necessarily prevent a restriction being entered in addition to the notice of the agreement for mortgage. Although the notice protects the priority of the agreement for mortgage, a restriction may be used to ensure that any conditions in relation to another disposition by the registered proprietor are complied with. The consent of the registered proprietor to the entry of the restriction is required.

An applicant should deliver to the registry:
(a) an application in form RX1;
(b) the consent of the registered proprietor of the land (unless this is given in panel 15 of form RX1 or the applicant's conveyancer certifies that he holds such consent. The certificate may be given in panel 11 of form RX1); and
(c) the fee payable. A fee calculator for all types of application is on the Land Registry's website at www.landregistry.gov.uk/fees.

A possible form of restriction based on Form N in Schedule 4 to the Land Registration Rules 2003 is:

"No disposition of the registered estate by the proprietor of the registered estate is to be registered without a written consent signed by [*mortgagee*] of [*address*] or his conveyancer."

A restriction in this form does not require the approval of the registrar under LRA 2002 section 43(3).

Agreement to Pay Further Consideration

A vendor may impose a covenant or provision under which the purchaser is required to pay a further sum or sums. This is sometimes referred to as overage. A common example is where a vendor of undeveloped land is to be paid further sums if planning permission is granted in the future. Another example is where a payment will become due if the use of the land is changed.

Such sums may be secured by a legal charge or an equitable charge; see *Legal Charges,* page 184, and *Equitable Charges*, page 126.

Where the vendor does not take some form of charge to secure payment, the question arises as to whether he can claim that a vendor's lien has arisen. Although this depends on the particular facts, in the main the requirement to pay overage does not give rise to a vendor's lien (*Woolf Project Management v Woodtrek Limited* (1988) 56 P & CR 134). For the situation where a vendor's lien has arisen, see *Vendor's Lien*, page 307.

If the registered proprietor consents, a restriction can be entered on the register. This does not confer any priority but prevents an entry being made in the register if it is not permitted under the wording of the restriction.

Restriction

An applicant should deliver to the registry:
- (a) an application in form RX1;
- (b) the consent of the registered proprietor of the land (unless this is given in panel 15 of form RX1 or the applicant's conveyancer certifies that he holds such consent. The certificate may be given in panel 11 of form RX1); and
- (c) the fee payable. A fee calculator for all types of application is on the Land Registry's website at www.landregistry.gov.uk/fees.

A possible form of restriction based on Form N in Schedule 4 to the Land Registration Rules 2003 is:

"No disposition of the registered estate by the proprietor of the registered estate is to be registered without a written consent signed by [*vendor*] of [*address*] or his conveyancer."

A restriction in this form does not require the approval of the registrar under the Land Registration Act 2002 section 43(3).

Airspace

Unless an entry to the contrary appears in the property register of a registered title, that title includes the airspace above the land identified on the title plan.

In an application for first registration, unless all of the land above the surface is included in that application, the applicant must provide a plan of the surface on, under or over which the land to be registered lies. He must also provide sufficient information to define the vertical and horizontal extents of the land (Land Registration Rules 2003 rule 26). On completion of the registration this information is reflected by an appropriate entry in the property register.

Alteration of the Register

In considering applications for alteration of the register it is necessary to distinguish between those applications that involve rectification and those that do not. It is also necessary to distinguish alterations pursuant to a court order from those not pursuant to a court order.

Rectification in this context is an alteration which involves the correction of a mistake and which prejudicially affects the title of a registered proprietor (Land Registration Act 2002 ("LRA 2002") Schedule 4 paragraph 1). For applications involving rectification see *Rectification*, page 253.

Alteration Pursuant to a Court Order
Where in any proceedings the court decides that:
    (a) there is a mistake in the register,
    (b) the register is not up to date, or
    (c) there is an estate, right or interest excepted from the effect of registration that should be given effect to,
it must make an order for alteration of the register (LRA 2002 Schedule 4 paragraph 2(1) and Land Registration Rules 2003 ("LRR 2003") rule 126(1)). Rule 126(1) does not apply to an alteration of the register that amounts to rectification. The court is not, however, obliged to make an order if there are exceptional circumstances that justify not doing so (LRR 2003 rule 126(2)).

    An estate, right or interest may be excepted from the effect of registration by registration with qualified, possessory or good leasehold title (LRA 2002 sections 11 and 12). Such an estate, right or interest could be the subject of a court order for alteration of the register even though the class of title was not itself changed.

    The court order for alteration of the register must state the title number of the title affected and the alteration that is to be made. It must also direct the registrar to make the alteration.

    An applicant should deliver to the registry:
    (a) an application in form AP1;
    (b) the court order for alteration of the register or a sealed copy of that court order; and
    (c) the fee (if any) payable. A fee calculator for all types of application is on the Land Registry's website at www.landregistry.gov.uk/fees.

If the register is altered under LRA 2002 Schedule 4 in a case not involving rectification, the registrar may pay such amount as he thinks fit in respect of any costs or expenses reasonably incurred by a person in connection with the alteration which have been incurred with the consent of the registrar. Even where the registrar has not consented to the costs or expenses being incurred, he may still make a payment if it appears to him that the costs or expenses had to be incurred urgently and it was not reasonably practicable to apply for his consent. He may also still make a payment if he has subsequently approved the incurring of the costs or expenses.

Alteration not Pursuant to a Court Order
The registrar may alter the register for the purpose of:
    (a) correcting a mistake,
    (b) bringing the register up to date,
    (c) giving effect to any estate, right or interest excepted from the effect of

registration, or

(d) removing a superfluous entry.

The alteration may be made as the result of an application or by the registrar without an application having been made. The registrar may make such enquiries as he thinks fit and must give notice of the proposed alteration to any person who would be affected by it, unless he is satisfied that such notice is unnecessary (LRR 2003 rule 128). Rule 128 does not, however, apply to alteration of the register in the specific circumstances covered by any other rule.

An applicant for an alteration of the register not pursuant to a court order should deliver to the registry:

(a) an application in form AP1;
(b) a statement of the alteration being applied for;
(c) all relevant evidence held by the applicant which is pertinent to the application to alter the register; and
(d) the fee (if any) payable. A fee calculator for all types of application is on the Land Registry's website at www.landregistry.gov.uk/fees.

If the register is altered under LRA 2002 Schedule 4 in a case not involving rectification, the registrar may pay such amount as he thinks fit in respect of any costs or expenses reasonably incurred by a person in connection with the alteration which have been incurred with the consent of the registrar. Even where the registrar has not consented to the costs or expenses being incurred, he may still make a payment if it appears to him that the costs or expenses had to be incurred urgently and it was not reasonably practicable to apply for his consent. He may also still make a payment if he has subsequently approved the incurring of the costs or expenses.

Amalgamation of Registered Titles

The registrar may amalgamate two or more registered titles to form one registered title. He may also add an estate which is being registered for the first time to an existing registered title. In either case the estates must be of the same kind and vested in the same proprietor. Accordingly a freehold title cannot be amalgamated with a leasehold title, nor can a possessory title be amalgamated with an absolute title.

Amalgamation may be as the result of an application by the proprietor of the registered estate and of any registered charge over it, or because the registrar considers it desirable for the keeping of the register of title. An application by the proprietor should be made in Form AP1 listing the relevant title numbers in panel 2. For the fee (if any) payable, see the fee calculator for all types of application on the Land Registry's website at www.landregistry.gov.uk/fees.

Where the proprietor has not made an application but amalgamation is effected because the registrar considers it desirable for the keeping of the register of title, the registrar must notify the proprietor of the registered estate and any registered charge, unless they have agreed to the amalgamation. In these circumstances the registrar may make a new edition of any individual register or make entries on any individual register to reflect the amalgamation (Land Registration Rules 2003 ("LRR 2003") rule 3(5)).

LRR 2003 rule 70 applies on amalgamation where a registered estate in land includes any mines or minerals but there is no note on the register that they are included, and it is appropriate when describing the amalgamated registered estate to do so by reference to the land where the mines or minerals are or may be situated. In such circumstances the registrar may make an entry in the property register to the effect that such description is an entry made under LRR 2003 rule 5(a), and is not a note that the registered estate includes the mines or minerals for the purposes of extending the payment of indemnity to such mines or minerals. LRR 2003 rule 5(a) provides that the property register must contain a description of the registered estate.

Annuities

Strictly, an annuity is not secured on land and so does not require protection at the Land Registry. The term "annuity" is, however, sometimes used to describe a rentcharge for life, which is an interest under a trust of land or a settlement under the Settled Land Act 1925. No notice may be entered on the register in respect of any such interest (Land Registration Act 2002 ("LRA 2002") section 33).

In the case of settled land, restrictions are entered on the register for the protection of persons interested in the settled land. The proprietor, or (if there is no proprietor) the personal representatives of a deceased proprietor, must apply in Form RX1 for the entry of such restrictions (in addition to a restriction in Form G, H or I) as may be appropriate. The applicant must state that the restrictions applied for are required for the protection of the beneficial interests and powers under the settlement. The registrar must enter such restrictions without inquiry as to the terms of the settlement (Land Registration Rules 2003 ("LRR 2003") Schedule 7 paragraph 7). Even so, if it does not appear to the registrar that the terms of the proposed restriction are reasonable and that applying the proposed restriction would be straightforward and not place an unreasonable burden on him, he may not approve the application for the restriction (LRA 2002 section 43(3)). For the various restrictions appropriate to settled land, see *Settlements*, page 282.

Where the annuity is an interest under a trust of land, the proprietor of the registered land must apply for a restriction in Form A, unless there is already one on the register (LRR 2003 rule 94). Form A is:

"No disposition by a sole proprietor of the registered estate (except a trust corporation) under which capital money arises is to be registered unless authorised by an order of the court."

Where a restriction in Form A is required but the proprietor of the registered land has not applied for it, any person who has an interest in a registered estate held under a trust of land may apply for that restriction to be entered in the register of that registered estate (LRR 2003 rule 93(a)).

An annuity which is a rentcharge for life or lives, or determinable on the dropping of a life, and not arising under a settlement or trust of land, can be overreached by a disposition under the Settled Land Act 1925 section 72(3) or the Law of Property Act 1925 section 2(2) and (3) (as amended by the Law of Property (Amendment) Act 1926). A settlement restriction or Form A restriction would again be appropriate.

Restriction

The trustee should deliver to the registry:
 (a) an application in form RX1 (setting out full details of the restriction required in panel 10);
 (b) (where applicable) the consent of the registered proprietor of the land (unless this is given in panel 15 of form RX1 or the applicant's conveyancer certifies that he holds such consent. The certificate may be given in panel 11 of form RX1);
 (c) (where applicable) a statement signed by the applicant or his conveyancer that the applicant has an interest as specified in LRR 2003 rule 93(a) (this may be given in panel 13 of form RX1); and
 (d) the fee payable. A fee calculator for all types of application is on the Land Registry's website at www.landregistry.gov.uk/fees.

Assents

The personal representative of a deceased owner of land may vest the legal estate of that land in the person entitled by way of an assent rather than a transfer or conveyance. Although the assent must be in writing and signed by all the personal representatives, it does not have to be drawn as a deed.

Unregistered Land

When the title to land is unregistered, an application for first registration must be made after an assent has transferred a legal freehold estate in the land, or a legal leasehold estate in the land for a term which, at the time of the assent, has more than seven years to run (Land Registration Act 2002

("LRA 2002") section 4). The requirement to apply for first registration does not apply to mines and minerals held apart from the surface.

The person taking under the assent must apply for first registration within two months of the assent. He may apply to the registrar for an order that the period for registration ends on a later date, which date will be specified in the order. The registrar will make such an order if he is satisfied that there is good reason for doing so (LRA 2002 section 6(5)).

If the requirement of registration is not complied with following the assent, the legal estate reverts to the personal representative who holds it on a bare trust for the assentee (LRA 2002 section 7). Where an order is made under LRA 2002 section 6(5), this reverter of the legal estate is treated as not having occurred.

If there has to be a further assent because of the failure to apply for first registration following the original assent, the assentee is liable for the proper costs of the personal representative in respect of the new assent (LRA 2002 section 8).

A person applying for first registration must provide information to the registrar in form DI about any of the overriding interests (other than local land charges or public rights) set out in Schedule 1 to LRA 2002 that affect the estate to which the application relates and are within the actual knowledge of the applicant, but are not apparent from the deeds and documents accompanying the application (Land Registration Rules 2003 ("LRR 2003") rule 28). For details see *Overriding Interests*, page 223. The registrar may enter a notice in the register in respect of any such interest.

The applicant is not required, however, to provide information about interests that, under LRA 2002 section 33 or 90(4), cannot be protected by notice. Such interests are:
  (a) interests under a trust of land or under a Settled Land Act 1925 settlement;
  (b) a leasehold estate in land granted for three years or less from the date of the grant and which is not required to be registered;
  (c) a restrictive covenant between lessor and lessee, so far as relating to the demised premises;
  (d) an interest which is capable of being registered under the Commons Registration Act 1965;
  (e) an interest in any coal or coal mine, or the rights attached to any such interest, or the rights of any person under the Coal Industry Act 1994 section 38, 49 or 51; and
  (f) leases created for public-private partnerships relating to transport in London, within the meaning given by the Greater London Authority Act 1999 section 218.

The applicant is also not required to provide information about a leasehold estate in land which falls within paragraph 1 of Schedule 1 to LRA 2002 but, at the time of the application, has one year or less to run.

An assentee applying for first registration should deliver to the registry:
(a) an application in form FR1;
(b) sufficient details, by plan or otherwise, so that the land can be clearly identified on the Ordnance Survey map;
(c) all deeds and documents relating to the title that are in the control of the applicant;
(d) a list in duplicate in form DL of all the documents delivered;
(e) form DI giving the information as to overriding interests required by LRR 2003 rule 28; and
(f) the fee payable. A fee calculator for all types of application is on the Land Registry's website at www.landregistry.gov.uk/fees.

In the case of a leasehold estate, the lease, if in the control of the applicant, and a certified copy must also be lodged.

In examining the title the registrar may have regard to any examination by a conveyancer prior to the application and to the nature of the property. He may make searches and enquiries and give notice to other persons, direct that searches and enquiries be made by the applicant, and advertise the application (LRR 2003 rule 30).

The applicant may be registered with absolute title if the registrar is of the opinion that the applicant's title is such as a willing buyer could properly be advised by a competent professional adviser to accept. In the case of a leasehold title this suffices for a good leasehold title; for an absolute title the registrar must in addition approve the lessor's title to grant the lease. In considering the applicant's title, the registrar may disregard the fact that the title appears to him to be open to objection if he is of the opinion that the defect will not cause the holding under the title to be disturbed.

Registered Land

Where a sole proprietor or the last surviving joint proprietor has died, his personal representative may transfer the deceased's registered estate or registered charge without himself becoming registered as proprietor. The registrar is not under a duty to investigate the reasons why any transfer by such a personal representative is made, nor to consider the contents of the Will. Provided the terms of any restriction on the register are complied with, the registrar must assume, whether or not he knows the terms of the Will, that the personal representative is acting correctly and within his powers (LRR 2003 rule 162).

If the transfer from the personal representative to the beneficiary is to be by an assent, this must be in form AS1 (for whole of land in registered title), AS2 (for registered charge), or AS3 (for part of land in registered title). Until the transfer of the registered estate or registered charge is completed by registration, it does not operate at law (LRA 2002 section 27(1)).

The assentee is not able to apply for an official search with priority using form OS1 or OS2 but is able to reserve a period of priority by an outline application. See the *Outline Applications*, page 222.

A person applying to register a disposition of a registered estate must provide information to the registrar in form DI about any of the overriding interests (other than local land charges or public rights) set out in Schedule 3 to LRA 2002 that affect the estate to which the application relates and are within the actual knowledge of the applicant. For details see *Overriding Interests*, page 223. The applicant must produce to the registrar any documentary evidence of the interest that is under his control (LRR 2003 rule 57). The registrar may enter a notice in the register in respect of any such interest.

The applicant is not required, however, to provide information about interests that, under LRA 2002 section 33 or 90(4), cannot be protected by notice. Such interests are:
 (a) interests under a trust of land or under a Settled Land Act 1925 settlement;
 (b) a leasehold estate in land granted for three years or less from the date of the grant and which is not required to be registered;
 (c) a restrictive covenant between lessor and lessee, so far as relating to the demised premises;
 (d) an interest which is capable of being registered under the Commons Registration Act 1965;
 (e) an interest in any coal or coal mine, or the rights attached to any such interest, or the rights of any person under the Coal Industry Act 1994 section 38, 49 or 51; and
 (f) leases created for public-private partnerships relating to transport in London, within the meaning given by the Greater London Authority Act 1999 section 218.

The applicant is also not required to provide information about a leasehold estate in land which falls within paragraph 1 of Schedule 3 to LRA 2002 but at the time of the application has one year or less to run.

A person applying to register an assent of registered land should deliver to the registry:
 (a) an application in form AP1;
 (b) form AS1, AS2 or AS3 (as appropriate);
 (c) the original or an office copy or certified copy of the grant of probate or letters of administration (this is not required if the personal representative is already registered as proprietor);
 (d) form DI giving the information as to overriding interests required by LRR 2003 rule 57, including any documentary evidence of the interest; and
 (e) the fee payable. A fee calculator for all types of application is on the Land Registry's website at www.landregistry.gov.uk/fees.

Bankruptcy

Petition in Bankruptcy
Once a petition in bankruptcy has been filed in the court, the court registrar must apply to the Land Charges Department for registration of the petition in the register of pending actions. As soon as practicable after registration of a petition in bankruptcy as a pending action under the Land Charges Act 1972, the registrar must enter in the register, in relation to any registered estate or charge which appears to him to be affected, a notice in respect of the pending action (Land Registration Act 2002 ("LRA 2002") section 86(2)). This notice is designated a "bankruptcy notice" (Land Registration Rules 2003 ("LRR 2003") rule 165(1)). No fee is payable.

The bankruptcy notice in relation to a registered estate is entered in the proprietorship register in the following form:

"BANKRUPTCY NOTICE entered under section 86(2) of the Land Registration Act 2002 in respect of a pending action, as the title of the proprietor of the registered estate appears to be affected by a petition in bankruptcy against [*name of debtor*], presented in the [*name*] Court (Court Reference Number ...) (Land Charges Reference Number PA ...)."

The bankruptcy notice in relation to a registered charge is entered in the charges register in the following form:

"BANKRUPTCY NOTICE entered under section 86(2) of the Land Registration Act 2002 in respect of a pending action, as the title of the proprietor of the charge dated ... referred to above appears to be affected by a petition in bankruptcy against [*name of debtor*], presented in the [*name*] Court (Court Reference Number ...) (Land Charges Reference Number PA ...)."

The registrar must give notice of the entry of a bankruptcy notice to the proprietor of the registered estate or registered charge to which it relates.

The registrar must enter the bankruptcy notice where it *appears* to him that the registered estate or charge is affected by a pending action in respect of a petition in bankruptcy. Occasionally therefore a bankruptcy notice may be entered where the proprietor is not the debtor but has a name similar to that of the debtor. Where it appears to the registrar that there is doubt whether the debtor is the same person as the proprietor, he must as soon as practicable take such action as he considers necessary to resolve the doubt (LRR 2003 rule 167(2)). Where the proprietor is not the debtor, he should provide a written statement or statutory declaration to that effect.

Unless the bankruptcy notice is cancelled by the registrar, it continues in force until a bankruptcy restriction is entered in the register or the trustee in bankruptcy is entered as proprietor (LRA 2002 section 86(3)). The registrar will cancel any bankruptcy notice when he is satisfied that:

  (a) the bankruptcy order made pursuant to the proceedings to which the bankruptcy notice relates has been annulled;

(b) the bankruptcy petition to which the bankruptcy notice relates has been dismissed or withdrawn with the court's permission; or
(c) the bankruptcy proceedings do not affect or have ceased to affect the registered estate or registered charge in relation to which the bankruptcy notice has been entered in the register.

Bankruptcy Order
Once the bankruptcy order has been made, the court registrar applies to the Land Charges Department for registration of that order. As soon as practicable after registration of a bankruptcy order under the Land Charges Act 1972, the registrar must enter in the register, in relation to any registered estate or charge which appears to him to be affected, a restriction reflecting the effect of the Insolvency Act 1986 (LRA 2002 section 86(4)). This restriction is designated a "bankruptcy restriction" (LRR 2003 rule 166(1)). No fee is payable.

The bankruptcy restriction in relation to a registered estate is entered in the proprietorship register in the following form:

"BANKRUPTCY RESTRICTION entered under section 86(4) of the Land Registration Act 2002, as the title of the proprietor of the registered estate appears to be affected by a bankruptcy order made by the [*name*] Court (Court Reference Number ...) against [*name of debtor*] (Land Charges Reference Number WO ...).

No disposition of the registered estate is to be registered until the trustee in bankruptcy of the property of the bankrupt is registered as proprietor of the registered estate."

The bankruptcy restriction in relation to a registered charge is entered in the charges register in the following form:

"BANKRUPTCY RESTRICTION entered under section 86(4) of the Land Registration Act 2002, as the title of the proprietor of the charge dated ... referred to above appears to be affected by a bankruptcy order made by the [*name*] Court (Court Reference Number ...) against [*name of debtor*] (Land Charges Reference Number WO ...).

No disposition of the charge is to be registered until the trustee in bankruptcy of the property of the bankrupt is registered as proprietor of the charge."

The registrar must give notice of the entry of a bankruptcy restriction to the proprietor of the registered estate or registered charge to which it relates.

The registrar must enter the bankruptcy restriction where it *appears* to him that the registered estate or charge is affected by the bankruptcy order. Occasionally therefore a bankruptcy restriction may be entered where the proprietor is not the bankrupt but has a name similar to that of the bankrupt. Where it appears to the registrar that there is doubt whether the bankrupt is the same person as the proprietor, he must as soon as practicable take such action as he considers necessary to resolve the doubt (LRR 2003 rule

167(2)). Where the proprietor is not the bankrupt, he should provide a written statement or statutory declaration to that effect.

The bankruptcy restriction reflects the position under the Insolvency Act 1986. Section 284 of that Act provides that where a person is adjudged bankrupt, any disposition of property made by him between the presentation of the petition and the time at which the property vests in the trustee in bankruptcy is void, except to the extent that it is or was made with the consent of the court, or is or was subsequently ratified by the court.

A bankruptcy restriction appearing in the proprietorship register does not prevent a disposition by the proprietor of a registered charge under the power of sale.

Bankruptcy Entries under the Land Registration Act 1925

Under the Land Registration Act 1925 section 61, a creditors' notice was entered in the register following the petition in bankruptcy, much as a bankruptcy notice is now entered. Following the making of the bankruptcy order, a bankruptcy inhibition was entered on the register.

Where a creditors' notice appears on a registered title, it has the same effect as a bankruptcy notice. A bankruptcy inhibition has the same effect as a bankruptcy restriction (LRA 2002 Schedule 12 paragraph 2(1) and (2)).

The form of entry in the register of a creditors' notice was:

"Creditors' Notice in respect of a petition in bankruptcy presented in the ... Court (Court Reference Number ...) (Land Charges Reference Number PA ...)".

The form of entry of a bankruptcy inhibition was:

"Bankruptcy Inhibition in pursuance of a bankruptcy order made by the ... Court (Court Reference Number ...). No disposition by the proprietor of the land or transmission is to be registered until a trustee in bankruptcy is registered. (Land Charges Reference Number WO ...)."

In the case of the bankruptcy of the proprietor of a registered charge, the inhibition referred to the proprietor of the charge rather than the proprietor of the land.

Registration of the Trustee in Bankruptcy

Although the usual rule is that the disposition of a registered estate does not operate at law until the relevant registration requirements are met, this does not apply to a transfer on the bankruptcy of an individual proprietor (LRA 2002 section 27(5)). The legal estate of a bankrupt individual proprietor vests automatically in the trustee in bankruptcy immediately his appointment as trustee takes effect (Insolvency Act 1986 section 306(2)). The legal estate vests in the official receiver when he becomes trustee.

A trustee in bankruptcy may apply for the register to be altered by the registration of the trustee in place of the bankrupt proprietor where an individual proprietor has had a bankruptcy order made against him and the bankrupt's registered estate or registered charge has vested in the trustee in bankruptcy. The registered estate or registered charge does not, however, vest in the trustee in bankruptcy where that property is held by the bankrupt on trust for any other person (Insolvency Act 1986 section 283(3)).

An applicant should deliver to the registry:
(a) an application in form AP1;
(b) an office copy of the bankruptcy order relating to the bankrupt;
(c) a certificate signed by the trustee that the registered estate or registered charge is comprised in the bankrupt's estate;
(d) (i) where the official receiver is the trustee, a certificate by him to that effect, or
(ii) the trustee's certificate of appointment as trustee by the meeting of the bankrupt's creditors, or
(iii) the trustee's certificate of appointment as trustee by the Secretary of State, or
(iv) an office copy of the order of the court appointing the trustee; and
(e) the fee payable. A fee calculator for all types of application is on the Land Registry's website at www.landregistry.gov.uk/fees.

Where the official receiver is registered as proprietor, the words "Official Receiver and trustee in bankruptcy of [*name*]" are added to the register. Where another trustee in bankruptcy is registered as proprietor, the words "Trustee in bankruptcy of [*name*]" are added to the register.

On registration of the trustee in bankruptcy, any bankruptcy notice or bankruptcy restriction appearing against the replaced bankrupt proprietor is cancelled.

Vacating of Office by Trustee in Bankruptcy

Where a trustee in bankruptcy, who has been registered as proprietor, vacates his office and the official receiver or some other person has been appointed as trustee in bankruptcy, the official receiver or that person may apply to be registered as proprietor in place of the former trustee.

An applicant should deliver to the registry:
(a) an application in form AP1;
(b) (i) where the official receiver is the new trustee, a certificate by him to that effect, or
(ii) the new trustee's certificate of appointment as trustee by the meeting of the bankrupt's creditors, or
(iii) the new trustee's certificate of appointment as trustee by the Secretary of State, or
(iv) an office copy of the order of the court appointing the new trustee;
(c) the fee payable. A fee calculator for all types of application is on the Land Registry's website at www.landregistry.gov.uk/fees.

Where the official receiver is registered as proprietor, the words "Official Receiver and trustee in bankruptcy of [*name*]" are added to the register.

Where another trustee in bankruptcy is registered as proprietor, the words "Trustee in bankruptcy of [*name*]" are added to the register.

Sale by Trustee in Bankruptcy
A trustee in bankruptcy may sell the registered title without having himself been entered in the register as proprietor. A person applying to register a disposition of a registered estate must provide information to the registrar in form DI about any of the overriding interests (other than local land charges or public rights) set out in Schedule 3 to LRA 2002 that affect the estate to which the application relates and are within the actual knowledge of the applicant. For details see *Overriding Interests*, page 223. The applicant must produce to the registrar any documentary evidence of the interest which is under his control (LRR 2003 rule 57). The registrar may enter a notice in the register in respect of any such interest.

The applicant is not required, however, to provide information about interests that, under LRA 2002 section 33 or section 90(4), cannot be protected by notice. Such interests are:
 (a) interests under a trust of land or under a Settled Land Act 1925 settlement;
 (b) a leasehold estate in land granted for three years or less from the date of the grant and which is not required to be registered;
 (c) a restrictive covenant between lessor and lessee, so far as relating to the demised premises;
 (d) an interest which is capable of being registered under the Commons Registration Act 1965;
 (e) an interest in any coal or coal mine, or the rights attached to any such interest, or the rights of any person under the Coal Industry Act 1994 section 38, 49 or 51; and
 (f) leases created for public-private partnerships relating to transport in London, within the meaning given by the Greater London Authority Act 1999 section 218.

The applicant is also not required to provide information about a leasehold estate in land which falls within paragraph 1 of Schedule 3 to LRA 2002 but, at the time of the application, has one year or less to run.

The purchaser should deliver to the registry:
 (a) an application in form AP1;
 (b) a transfer in form TR1 (or TR3, TR4, or TR5, as appropriate);
 (c) form DI giving the information as to overriding interests required by LRR 2003 rule 57, including any documentary evidence of the interest;
 (d) an office copy of the bankruptcy order relating to the bankrupt proprietor;
 (e) a certificate signed by the trustee that the registered estate or registered charge was comprised in the bankrupt's estate;

(f) (i) where the official receiver is the trustee, a certificate by him to that effect; or
(ii) the trustee's certificate of appointment as trustee by the meeting of the bankrupt's creditors; or
(iii) the trustee's certificate of appointment as trustee by the Secretary of State; or
(iv) an office copy of the order of the court appointing the trustee; and
(g) the fee payable. A fee calculator for all types of application is on the Land Registry's website at www.landregistry.gov.uk/fees.

On registration of the transfer, any bankruptcy notice or bankruptcy restriction is cancelled.

Protection of Purchaser from Bankrupt

For the purposes of the Land Registration Act 2002, references to an estate or charge do not include a petition in bankruptcy or bankruptcy order (LRA 2002 section 86(1)). Instead section 86(5) of that Act provides for the protection of purchasers in relation to such petitions and orders. This follows the scheme of the Insolvency Act 1986, even though this brings in the concept of notice. A person to whom a registrable disposition is made is not required to make any search under the Land Charges Act 1972 (LRA 2002 section 86(7)).

Where the proprietor of a registered estate or charge is adjudged bankrupt, the title of his trustee in bankruptcy is void against a person to whom a registrable disposition of the estate or charge is made if:
(a) the disposition is made for valuable consideration;
(b) the person to whom the disposition is made acts in good faith; and
(c) at the time of the disposition:
(i) no bankruptcy notice or bankruptcy restriction is entered in relation to the registered estate or charge; and
(ii) the person to whom the disposition is made has no notice of the bankruptcy petition or the adjudication.

Although this protection applies only if the relevant registration requirements are met in relation to the disposition, as and when they are met it has effect from the date of the disposition.

Bankruptcy of a Joint Proprietor

Where one of two or more joint registered proprietors becomes bankrupt neither a bankruptcy notice nor a bankruptcy restriction is entered in the register. Since the bankrupt is holding the legal estate as trustee, the legal estate does not automatically vest in the trustee in bankruptcy. The bankruptcy order does, however, have the effect of severing a beneficial joint tenancy and the bankrupt's beneficial share vests in the trustee in bankruptcy.

If there is no restriction in Form A on the register, the trustee in bankruptcy has a sufficient interest for the purposes of LRA 2002 section 43(1)(c) to apply for a restriction in Form A to ensure that a survivor of the joint proprietors (unless a trust corporation) is not able to give a valid receipt for capital money (LRR 2003 rule 93(a)). Form A is:

"No disposition by a sole proprietor of the registered estate (except a trust corporation) under which capital money arises is to be registered unless authorised by an order of the court."

The trustee in bankruptcy also has a sufficient interest for the purposes of LRA 2002 section 43(1)(c) to apply for a restriction in Form J to ensure that he receives notice of a disposition (LRR 2003 rule 93(j)). Form J is:

"No disposition of the registered [estate] [charge] is to be registered without a certificate signed by the applicant for registration or his conveyancer that written notice of the disposition was given to [*name of trustee in bankruptcy*] (the trustee in bankruptcy of [*name of bankrupt*]) at [*address for service*]".

This restriction does not of itself prevent a disposition, provided it is complied with. This is because the interest of the trustee in bankruptcy will be overreached where the requirements of Form A have been met (Law of Property Act 1925 section 27).

The registrar must give notice of an application for a restriction to the proprietor of the registered estate or charge concerned (LRA 2002 section 45).

A restriction does not confer any priority; it simply prevents an entry being made in the register if it is not permitted under the wording of the restriction.

If applying for a restriction in Form A, the trustee in bankruptcy should deliver to the registry an application in form RX1. No fee is payable where the application is in respect of a restriction in Form A only.

Panel 13 of RX1 should be completed on the following lines:

"The interest is that specified in rule 93(a) of the Land Registration Rules 2003."

Panel 10 should be completed as to Form A set out above.

If applying for a restriction in Form J, the trustee in bankruptcy should deliver to the registry:

(a) an application in form RX1; and
(b) the fee payable. A fee calculator for all types of application is on the Land Registry's website at www.landregistry.gov.uk/fees.

Panel 13 of RX1 should be completed on the following lines:

"The interest is that specified in rule 93(j) of the Land Registration Rules 2003."

Panel 10 should be completed as to Form J set out above.

Administration of Insolvent Estate

When an insolvency administration petition is registered as a pending action under the Land Charges Act 1972, a bankruptcy notice is entered in the register of any title where the deceased appears as proprietor of the land or of a registered charge. Following registration of the insolvency administration order in the register of writs and orders under the Land Charges Act 1972, a bankruptcy restriction is entered in the proprietorship register or charges register as appropriate.

Where, as a result of an insolvency administration order, the deceased's registered estate or registered charge has vested in the trustee in bankruptcy, the trustee may apply for the alteration of the register by registering the trustee in place of the deceased proprietor.

An applicant should deliver to the registry:
(a) an application in form AP1;
(b) an office copy of the insolvency administration order relating to the deceased debtor's estate;
(c) a certificate signed by the trustee that the registered estate or registered charge is comprised in the deceased debtor's estate;
(d) (i) where the official receiver is the trustee, a certificate by him to that effect; or
(ii) the trustee's certificate of appointment as trustee by the meeting of the deceased debtor's creditors; or
(iii) the trustee's certificate of appointment as trustee by the Secretary of State; or
(iv) an office copy of the order of the court appointing the trustee; and
(e) the fee payable. A fee calculator for all types of application is on the Land Registry's website at www.landregistry.gov.uk/fees.

Where the official receiver is registered as proprietor, the words "Official Receiver and trustee in bankruptcy of [*name*]" are added to the register. Where another trustee in bankruptcy is registered as proprietor, the words "Trustee in bankruptcy of [*name*]" are added to the register.

On registration of the trustee in bankruptcy, any bankruptcy notice or bankruptcy restriction appearing against the deceased proprietor is cancelled.

Discharge from Bankruptcy

A discharge from bankruptcy releases the bankrupt from his bankruptcy debts, but does not have the effect of revesting in him any property which has vested in the trustee in bankruptcy. A certificate of discharge does not allow any bankruptcy notice or bankruptcy restriction to be cancelled.

If, unusually, the trustee in bankruptcy is prepared to revest registered land in the discharged bankrupt, this should be carried out by a transfer in form TR1.

Where the trustee in bankruptcy has not been registered as proprietor, the applicant should deliver to the registry:
(a) an application in form AP1;
(b) a transfer in form TR1;

(c) an office copy of the bankruptcy order relating to the discharged bankrupt;
(d) a certificate signed by the trustee that the registered estate or registered charge was comprised in the discharged bankrupt's estate;
(e) (i) where the official receiver is the trustee, a certificate by him to that effect; or
(ii) the trustee's certificate of appointment as trustee by the meeting of the bankrupt's creditors; or
(iii) the trustee's certificate of appointment as trustee by the Secretary of State; or
(iv) an office copy of the order of the court appointing the trustee; and
(f) the fee payable. A fee calculator for all types of application is on the Land Registry's website at www.landregistry.gov.uk/fees.

On registration of the transfer, any bankruptcy notice or bankruptcy restriction relating to the bankruptcy is cancelled.

Annulment of Bankruptcy Order
A court may annul the bankruptcy order (Insolvency Act 1986 section 282). Where the registrar is satisfied that the bankruptcy order has been annulled, he must as soon as practicable cancel any bankruptcy notice or bankruptcy restriction which relates to that bankruptcy order. An applicant for such entries to be cancelled should deliver to the registry:
(a) an application in form AP1;
(b) an office copy of the court order of annulment.

No fee is payable.

On annulment, any of the bankrupt's estate which is vested in the official receiver or trustee in bankruptcy vests in such person as the court appoints. If no other person is appointed, it will vest in the former bankrupt on such terms as the court may direct. Where the official receiver or trustee in bankruptcy has been registered as proprietor, an applicant for the former bankrupt to be registered should deliver to the registry:
(a) an application in form AP1;
(b) an office copy of the court order of annulment;
(c) the fee payable. A fee calculator for all types of application is on the Land Registry's website at www.landregistry.gov.uk/fees.

After-acquired Property
A trustee in bankruptcy may claim property which has been acquired by, or has devolved on, the bankrupt after the commencement of the bankruptcy and before his discharge. The trustee does this by the service of notice within forty-two days beginning on the day when it came to his knowledge that the property had been acquired by, or had devolved on, the bankrupt (Insolvency Act 1986 sections 307 and 309). This period may be extended by the court.

Where, before or after service of such a notice by the trustee in bankruptcy, a person acquires the property in good faith for value and without notice of the bankruptcy, the trustee has no remedy against the purchaser.

When the trustee has served notice on the bankrupt, he may apply to be registered as proprietor of the after-acquired property in place of the bankrupt. He should deliver to the registry:
(a) an application in form AP1;
(b) an office copy of the bankruptcy order relating to the bankrupt;
(c) a certified copy of the notice served by the trustee under the Insolvency Act 1986 section 307;
(d) an office copy of any order made under the Insolvency Act 1986 section 309;
(e) a certificate signed by the trustee that the registered estate or registered charge is comprised in the bankrupt's estate and that the notice(s) under the Insolvency Act 1986 section 307 was served within the period prescribed by section 309;
(f) (i) where the official receiver is the trustee, a certificate by him to that effect; or
(ii) the trustee's certificate of appointment as trustee by the meeting of the bankrupt's creditors; or
(iii) the trustee's certificate of appointment as trustee by the Secretary of State; or
(iv) an office copy of the order of the court appointing the trustee; and
(g) the fee payable. A fee calculator for all types of application is on the Land Registry's website at www.landregistry.gov.uk/fees.

Where the official receiver is registered as proprietor, the words "Official Receiver and trustee in bankruptcy of [*name*]" are added to the register. Where another trustee in bankruptcy is registered as proprietor, the words "Trustee in bankruptcy of [*name*]" are added to the register.

Where the bankrupt holds the after-acquired property as joint proprietor and the trustee in bankruptcy has served the notice under the Insolvency Act 1986 section 307, the trustee in bankruptcy may apply for a restriction in Form J and, where it is not already on the register, Form A. See *Bankruptcy of a Joint Proprietor,* page 39.

Voidable Transactions

Where there has been a transaction at an undervalue for the purposes of the Insolvency Act 1986 section 339, or a preference for the purposes of section 340 of that Act, the trustee in bankruptcy may apply to the court for an order. The court may make such order as it thinks fit for restoring the position to what it would have been had the relevant transaction not taken place. Where the court is satisfied that a transaction at an undervalue constitutes a transaction defrauding creditors for the purposes of the Insolvency Act 1986 section 423, it may make such order as it thinks fit for restoring the position to what it would have been if the transaction had not been entered into and protecting the interests of victims of the transaction.

If the bankrupt has entered into an extortionate credit transaction within the three years before the commencement of the bankruptcy, the trustee in bankruptcy may apply to the court for an order (Insolvency Act 1986 section 343). The court has wide powers to vary or set aside the transaction.

Where an order of the court under section 339, 340, 343 or 423 requires the register to be altered, the applicant should deliver to the registry:
(a) an application in form AP1;
(b) the court order or a sealed copy of the court order; and
(c) the fee payable. A fee calculator for all types of application is on the Land Registry's website at www.landregistry.gov.uk/fees.

It was previously the practice of the Land Registry to make an entry on the register referring to the Insolvency Act 1986 on first registration where the title deduced revealed a possible transaction at undervalue. That practice was discontinued in 2000. When next updating a register, the Land Registry will cancel automatically any existing entries relating to the Insolvency Act 1986 section 339 or to the Bankruptcy Act 1914 section 42.

Bankruptcy and the Matrimonial Home
Nothing occurring in the period between the presentation of the petition for the bankruptcy order and the vesting of the bankrupt's estate in the trustee is to be taken as having given rise to any matrimonial home rights under the Family Law Act 1996 in relation to a dwelling house comprised in the bankrupt's estate (Insolvency Act 1986 section 336(1)).

Where a spouse's matrimonial home rights under the Family Law Act 1996 are a charge on the estate or interest of the other spouse and the other spouse is adjudged bankrupt, the charge continues and binds the trustee in bankruptcy, but any application for an order under the Family Law Act 1996 section 33 must be made to the court having jurisdiction in relation to the bankruptcy. On such application the court may make such order as it thinks just and reasonable having regard to the matters set out in the Insolvency Act 1986 section 336(4). Where such an application is made more than a year after the property vested in the trustee in bankruptcy, however, the court must assume, unless the circumstances of the case are exceptional, that the interests of the bankrupt's creditors outweigh all other considerations (Insolvency Act 1986 section 336(5)).

A bankrupt may have rights equivalent to matrimonial home rights under the Family Law Act 1996 against the trustee in bankruptcy if he was entitled to occupy a dwelling house, and any persons under the age of eighteen with whom he occupied the house had their home with him when the bankruptcy petition was presented and at the commencement of the bankruptcy (Insolvency Act 1986 section 337). Such rights are a charge having the same priority as an equitable interest created immediately before the commencement of the bankruptcy, on so much of his estate or interest in the dwelling house as vests in the trustee in bankruptcy. That charge is treated as if it were a charge under the Family Law Act 1996 on the estate or interest of a spouse (Insolvency Act 1986 section 337(3) as substituted by the Family Law Act 1996).

A bankrupt applying to register an agreed notice in respect of a charge under the Insolvency Act 1986 section 337 should deliver to the registry application form AN1 rather than form MH1, together with the fee payable.

Panel 9 of form AN1 should be completed to show "charge on the legal estate registered under the title number mentioned in panel 2 arising under section 337 of the Insolvency Act 1986".

Charging Order in Favour of Trustee in Bankruptcy
Where the trustee in bankruptcy is unable to realise a dwelling house which forms part of the bankrupt's estate and which is occupied by the bankrupt or his spouse or former spouse, the trustee may apply to the court for a charging order on that dwelling house (Insolvency Act 1986 section 313). In the order the court also vests the legal estate in the bankrupt. Such an order allows a bankruptcy notice or bankruptcy restriction to be cancelled.

The trustee in bankruptcy may apply for the entry in the register of a notice in respect of the charging order. The application may be for the registration of an agreed notice or a unilateral notice. In the case of an application for an agreed notice, the registrar may approve the application without the consent of the proprietor where he is satisfied of the validity of the applicant's claim. Normally the production of the charging order enables the registrar to be so satisfied.

Agreed Notice of the Charging Order
An applicant should deliver to the registry:
 (a) an application in form AN1;
 (b) the charging order or a certified copy of it; and
 (c) the fee payable. A fee calculator for all types of application is on the Land Registry's website at www.landregistry.gov.uk/fees.
The entry made in the register will give details of the interest protected.

Unilateral Notice of the Charging Order
An applicant should deliver to the registry:
 (a) an application in form UN1; and
 (b) the fee payable. A fee calculator for all types of application is on the Land Registry's website at www.landregistry.gov.uk/fees.
Form UN1 should be completed on the following lines to show the interest of the applicant:
"chargee under a charging order of the ... Court [*set out full court reference and parties*]."

The unilateral notice will give brief details of the interest protected and identify the beneficiary of that notice.

Disclaimer by Trustee in Bankruptcy
A trustee in bankruptcy may disclaim any onerous property comprised in the bankrupt's estate. In the case of land it is normally a leasehold estate which is disclaimed. The disclaimer is not effective unless a copy of it has been served on any underlessee or mortgagee claiming under the bankrupt. In the case of a dwelling house a copy of the disclaimer must also be served on every person who is in occupation or claims a right to occupy. Any person claiming an interest in the disclaimed property may apply to the court for a vesting order vesting the property in him or in a trustee on his behalf (Insolvency Act 1986 section 320). An application for a vesting order may also be made by any person who, at the time the bankruptcy petition was presented, was in occupation of, or entitled to occupy, a disclaimed dwelling house. A person who is under a liability in respect of a disclaimed property, which liability will not be discharged by the disclaimer, may also apply for a vesting order.

If no vesting order is made, a lease which has been disclaimed vests in the lessor and so will determine. If no vesting order is made, a freehold which has been disclaimed vests in the Crown by escheat.

Where the trustee in bankruptcy has disclaimed a registered lease, an applicant should deliver to the registry:
 (a) an application in form AP1 showing the application as "Disclaimer of lease"; if the lease is noted on a superior title the application should also be made in respect of that title so that the notice of the lease may be cancelled;
 (b) the lease;
 (c) a certificate signed by the trustee in bankruptcy that all notices required to be served under the Insolvency Act 1986 have been served and that he is not aware of any application to the court for a vesting order under the Insolvency Act 1986 section 320;
 (d) an office copy of the notice of disclaimer; and
 (e) the fee payable. A fee calculator for all types of application is on the Land Registry's website at www.landregistry.gov.uk/fees.

Where the trustee in bankruptcy has not already been registered as proprietor of the leasehold title, the applicant should also deliver to the registry:
 (f) an office copy of the bankruptcy order relating to the bankrupt;
 (g) a certificate signed by the trustee that the registered lease is comprised in the bankrupt's estate; and
 (h) (i) where the official receiver is the trustee, a certificate by him to that effect; or
 (ii) the trustee's certificate of appointment as trustee by the meeting of the bankrupt's creditors; or

(iii) the trustee's certificate of appointment as trustee by the Secretary of State; or

(iv) an office copy of the order of the court appointing the trustee.

Where the disclaimed lease has not been registered but has been noted against a registered title, an applicant should deliver to the registry:
- (a) an application in form CN1, panel 9 being completed by entering details of the lease and placing an "X" against "disclaimer";
- (b) the lease;
- (c) the deeds and documents relating to the leasehold title;
- (d) a certificate signed by the trustee in bankruptcy that all notices required to be served under the Insolvency Act 1986 have been served and that he is not aware of any application to the court for a vesting order under the Insolvency Act 1986 section 320;
- (e) an office copy of the notice of disclaimer;
- (f) an office copy of the bankruptcy order relating to the bankrupt;
- (g) a certificate signed by the trustee that the registered lease is comprised in the bankrupt's estate;
- (h) the fee payable. A fee calculator for all types of application is on the Land Registry's website at www.landregistry.gov.uk/fees.; and
- (i) (i) where the official receiver is the trustee, a certificate by him to that effect; or
  (ii) the trustee's certificate of appointment as trustee by the meeting of the bankrupt's creditors; or
  (iii) the trustee's certificate of appointment as trustee by the Secretary of State; or
  (iv) an office copy of the order of the court appointing the trustee.

Where the property has been disclaimed and an order has been made by the court vesting the property in some other person, an applicant should deliver to the registry:
- (a) an application in form AP1;
- (b) an office copy of the court order; and
- (c) the fee payable. A fee calculator for all types of application is on the Land Registry's website at www.landregistry.gov.uk/fees.

Bare Trusts

A bare trust arises where a trustee holds property for a single beneficiary who is of full age and under no legal disability. Where the property consists of or includes land, the trust is a trust of land for the purposes of the Trusts of Land and Appointment of Trustees Act 1996. No notice may be entered in the register in respect of an interest under a trust of land (Land Registration

Act 2002 section 33).

Where the trustee is, or becomes, the registered proprietor of property held on a bare trust, he must apply for a restriction in Form A (Land Registration Rules 2003 ("LRR 2003") rule 94(1) and (2)). Where the declaration of trust imposes limitations on the powers of the trustee under the Trusts of Land and Appointment of Trustees Act 1996 section 8, the trustee must also apply for a restriction in Form B (LRR 2003 rule 94(4)). For example, the declaration of trust may require the obtaining of consent to any sale of the property.

If the trustee did not apply for the necessary restrictions, the beneficiary is able to do so (LRR 2003 rule 93(a) and (c)).

Form A is:

"No disposition by a sole proprietor of the registered estate (except a trust corporation) under which capital money arises is to be registered unless authorised by an order of the court."

Form B is:

"No disposition [*or specify details*] by the proprietors of the registered estate is to be registered unless they make a statutory declaration, or their conveyancer gives a certificate, that the disposition [*or specify details*] is in accordance with [*specify the disposition creating the trust*] or some variation thereof referred to in the declaration or certificate."

This restriction does not of itself prevent a disposition, provided it is complied with. This is because the interest of the beneficiary will be overreached where the requirements of Form A have been met (Law of Property Act 1925 section 27).

A restriction does not confer any priority; it simply prevents an entry being made in the register if it is not permitted under the wording of the restriction.

If applying for a restriction in Form A, the applicant should deliver to the registry an application in form RX1. No fee is payable where the application is in respect of a restriction in Form A only.

Panel 10 should be completed as to Form A set out above.

If applying for a restriction in Form B, the applicant should deliver to the registry:

(a) an application in form RX1; and
(b) the fee payable. A fee calculator for all types of application is on the Land Registry's website at www.landregistry.gov.uk/fees.

Panel 10 should be completed as to Form B set out above.

Beneficial Interests of Joint Proprietors of Land

In *Carlton v Goodman* [2002] EWCA Civ 545 (CA), [2002] 2 FLR 259, Ward LJ said:

"I ask in despair how often this court has to remind conveyancers that they would save their clients a great deal of later difficulty if only they would sit the purchasers down, explain the difference between a joint tenancy and a tenancy in common, ascertain what they want and then expressly declare in the conveyance or transfer how the beneficial interest is to be held because that will be conclusive and save all argument. When are conveyancers going to do this as a matter of invariable standard practice? This court has urged that time after time. Perhaps conveyancers do not read the law reports. I will try one more time: ALWAYS TRY TO AGREE ON AND THEN RECORD HOW THE BENEFICIAL INTEREST IS TO BE HELD. It is not very difficult to do."

The prescribed forms of transfer of registered land (TR1, TR2, TR5, TP1, TP2 and TP3) all contain a panel headed "Declaration of trust" containing the alternatives:

(a) The Transferees are to hold the Property on trust for themselves as joint tenants.
(b) The Transferees are to hold the Property on trust for themselves as tenants in common in equal shares.
(c) The Transferees are to hold the Property *(complete as necessary)*.

Where there is more than one transferee the declaration of trust should be completed to reflect the agreement of the transferees and they should execute the transfer.

Unless the transferees are holding the property on trust for themselves as joint tenants, the registrar enters a restriction in Form A (Land Registration Act 2002 ("LRA 2002") section 44(1)). Form A is:

"No disposition by a sole proprietor of the registered estate (except a trust corporation) under which capital money arises is to be registered unless authorised by an order of the court."

Despite the fact that a declaration of trust appears in a transfer, the registrar is not affected with notice of the trust (LRA 2002 section 78).

Transfers often formerly contained the statement:

"The transferees declare that the survivor of them can/cannot give a valid receipt for capital money arising on a disposition of the land."

In the light of the majority judgments in the Court of Appeal in *Huntingford v Hobbs* [1993] 1 FLR 736, [1992] Fam Law 437, this statement does not constitute a declaration of trust; neither is the entry or lack of a restriction conclusive as to how the parties hold the beneficial interests.

Where the transfer contains a declaration of trust but has not been executed by the transferees, it may still be effective. In *Re Gorman (a Bankrupt)* [1990] 1 WLR 616, [1990] 1 All ER 717, Vinelott J said:

" ... the transfer, if signed by the transferees, would have constituted them beneficial joint tenants, However, even though unsigned, it is still evidence of the parties' intentions of an agreement that they would be joint tenants, and in the context of this case it is my judgment conclusive evidence of their intention."

Clearly it is preferable for the transferees to execute the transfer and so avoid the need for any such considerations.

Where there is no declaration of trust the beneficial interests of joint proprietors fall to be decided, in case of dispute, according to the principles set out in cases such as *Pettitt v Pettitt* [1970] AC 777, [1969] 2 WLR 966, [1969] 2 All ER 385 (HL); *Walker v Hall* [1984] FLR 126, [1984] Fam Law 21 (CA); *Re Gorman* (above); *Springette v Defoe* [1992] 2 FLR 388, (1993) 65 P & CR 1 (CA); *Huntingford v Hobbs* (above); and *Carlton v Goodman* (above).

A beneficial joint tenancy which has been properly constituted may still be severed at a later date: see *Severance of a Beneficial Joint Tenancy*, page 286.

Bona Vacantia and Escheat

Where a company is dissolved, its property (other than that held on trust for another person) vests as *bona vacantia* in the Crown, under the jurisdiction of the Treasury Solicitor, or in the Duchy of Lancaster or Duchy of Cornwall, under the jurisdiction of the solicitor of the duchy (Companies Act 1985 section 654). If the Treasury Solicitor disclaims a freehold estate passing as *bona vacantia*, it passes on escheat to the Crown and comes under the management of the Crown Estate Commissioners. In neither case does this constitute a disposition requiring to be registered under the Land Registration Act 2002 ("LRA 2002") section 27 (LRA 2002 section 27(5)(b)).

For the purposes of LRA 2002 "demesne land" does not include land in relation to which a freehold estate in land has determined, but in relation to which there has been no act of entry or management by the Crown (LRA 2002 section 132(2)).

Where a corporation shown as the proprietor of a registered estate or registered charge has been dissolved, the registrar may enter a note of that fact in the proprietorship register or charges register, as appropriate (Land Registration Rules 2003 ("LRR 2003") rule 185).

Where a registered estate in land has determined on escheat, the registrar may enter a note of that fact in the property register and in the property register of any inferior registered title. If the registrar considers that there is doubt whether a registered freehold title in land has determined, the entry must be modified by a statement to that effect (LRR 2003 rule 173). Where an entry is made under LRR 2003 rule 173, the registrar need not close that registered title until a freehold estate has been registered in respect of the land in which the former estate subsisted.

Boundaries

The boundary of registered land shown on the title plan, or otherwise on the register, is a general boundary unless it is shown as determined under the Land Registration Act 2002 ("LRA 2002") section 61. A general boundary does not determine the exact line of the boundary (LRA 2002 section 61(2)).

There is no definition of a general boundary in the Land Registration Act 2002. The Law Commission Report, *Land Registration for the Twenty-First Century: A Conveyancing Revolution* (Law Com No 271) indicates that it was the intention to retain the so-called "general boundaries rule", that is rule 278 of the Land Registration Rules 1925. Rule 213 of the Land Transfer Rules 1898 and rule 274 of the Land Transfer Rules 1903 also provided for general boundaries. Rule 278 of the 1925 Rules stated:

(1) Except in cases in which it is noted in the Property Register that the boundaries have been fixed, the filed plan shall be deemed to indicate the general boundaries only.
(2) In such cases the exact line of the boundary will be left undetermined – as, for instance, whether it includes a hedge or wall and ditch, or runs along the centre of a wall or fence, or its inner or outer face, or how far it runs within or beyond it; or whether or not the land registered includes the whole or any portion of an adjoining road or stream.
(3) When a general boundary only is desired to be entered in the register, notice to the owners of the adjoining lands need not be given.
(4) This rule shall apply notwithstanding that a part or the whole of a ditch, wall, fence, road, stream, or other boundary is expressly included in or excluded from the title or that it forms the whole of the land comprised in the title.

All registered estates in land, registered rentcharges and registered franchises which are affecting franchises have a title plan. That title plan is based on the Ordnance Survey Map (Land Registration Rules 2003 ("LRR 2003") rule 5). A registered franchise is an affecting franchise if it relates to a defined area of land and is an adverse right affecting, or capable of affecting, the title to an estate or charge.

Prior to the coming into force of LRA 2002, the title plan was known as the filed plan.

The title plan usually shows the extent of the registered estate by red edging, although other means may be used in particular circumstances. However, because the boundary shown is a general boundary, the legal boundary of the land does not necessarily follow the red edging on the title plan. So, for example, the so-called "hedge and ditch rule" may apply. This is a rebuttable presumption that arises when a boundary comprises a hedge and a man-made ditch. It is presumed that the owner of the hedge also owns the ditch beyond it, although this may be rebutted on the facts. The House of Lords applied this presumption in the case of *Alan Wibberley Building Ltd v Insley* [1999] 1 WLR 894, [1999] 2 All ER 897. Lord Hope of Craighead said:

> "Any boundary dispute which leads to litigation as protracted as the dispute has been in this case is regrettable. But no workable system of conveyancing can be expected to eliminate entirely the opportunity for disputes to arise about boundaries. In most cases neighbours are content to accept that absolute precision is unattainable. They recognise that a certain amount of latitude must be given to whatever method has been used to fix the boundaries of their land. That also is the view which has been taken by the legislature. The original system of precise guaranteed boundaries under the Land Registry Act 1862 gave rise to considerable difficulty. It had to be abandoned in view of the expense which was involved in a survey of the precise boundaries and the many disputes which arose between neighbours who had been content until then to accept a certain amount of vagueness as to the precise line of their common boundary. The result was the introduction of the general boundaries rule now contained in rule 278 of the Land Registration Rules 1925.
>
> The use of maps or plans such as those published by the Ordnance Survey is now widespread and has obvious advantages. Ordnance Survey maps are prepared to a high standard of accuracy and are frequently and appropriately used to fix boundaries by reference, for example, to Ordnance Survey field numbers. But like all maps they are subject to limitations. The most obvious are those imposed by scale. No map can reproduce to anything like the same scale of detail every feature which is found on the ground. Furthermore the Ordnance Survey does not fix private boundaries. The purpose of the survey is topographical, not taxative. Even the most detailed Ordnance Survey map may not show every feature on the ground which can be used to identify the extent of the owner's land. In the present case the Ordnance Survey map shows the hedge, but it does not show the ditch. So there is no reason in principle in this case for preferring the line on the map to other evidence which may be relevant to identify the boundary."

Where, on first registration or on the registration of a transfer of part, an agreement or declaration as to the ownership of boundary structures appears in the relevant deeds, an entry is made in the register reflecting this. Commonly, for example, this may be an agreement that a particular wall is a party wall. Where the entry refers to T marks, these are reproduced on the title plan or otherwise described in the register. But neither a party wall notice, nor a party wall award under the Party Wall etc Act 1996, may be the subject of a notice in the register.

Determination of the Exact Line of a Boundary

A proprietor of a registered estate may apply to the registrar for the exact line of the boundary of that registered estate to be determined. The application may be in respect of part only of such a boundary (LRR 2003 rules 117 and 118(1)).

A person applying for the exact line of a boundary to be determined should deliver to the registry:
  (a) an application in form DB;
  (b) a plan, or a plan and a verbal description, identifying the exact line of the boundary claimed and showing sufficient surrounding physical features to allow the general position of the boundary to be drawn on the Ordnance Survey map;
  (c) the documents on which the applicant relies as evidence to establish the exact line of the boundary; and
  (d) the fee payable. A fee calculator for all types of application is on the Land Registry's website at www.landregistry.gov.uk/fees.

Where the registrar is satisfied that:
  (a) the plan, or plan and verbal description, supplied identifies the exact line of the boundary claimed;
  (b) the applicant has shown an arguable case that the exact line of the boundary is in the position shown on that plan, or plan and verbal description; and
  (c) he can identify all the owners of the land adjoining the boundary to be determined and has an address at which each owner may be given notice;

he must give such adjoining owners notice of the application (LRR 2003 rule 119(1)). For these purposes "owner" means the proprietor of any registered estate or charge affecting land, a person who holds an unregistered legal estate in land which he could apply to register, and, if the land is demesne land, Her Majesty.

Where the evidence supplied in support includes an agreement in writing as to the exact line of the boundary with an owner of the land adjoining the boundary, the registrar need not give notice of the application to that owner.

Where the registrar is not satisfied as to (a), (b) and (c) above, he must cancel the application (LRR 2003 rule 119(7)).

If no recipient of a notice of the application objects within the relevant period of time, the registrar must complete the application (LRR 2003 rule 119(6)). The time for objection fixed by the notice is the period ending at 12 noon on the twentieth business day after the date of issue of the notice, or such longer period as the registrar may decide before the issue of the notice. A business day is a day when the Land Registry is open to the public, that is every day except Saturdays, Sundays, Christmas Day, Good Friday or any other day either specified or declared by proclamation under the Banking and Financial Dealings Act 1971 section 1 or appointed by the Lord Chancellor.

Before the period set in the notice has expired, a recipient of the notice may apply to the registrar for an extension of the period, setting out why an extension should be allowed. On receipt of such a request, the registrar may, if he considers it appropriate, seek the views of the applicant. If, after considering any such views and all other relevant matters, he is satisfied that a longer period should be allowed, he may allow such period as he considers appropriate, whether or not the period is the same as any period requested by the recipient of the notice.

On completion of an application to determine a boundary, there is added to the title plan of the applicant's registered title and, if appropriate, to the title plan of any superior or inferior registered title, and any registered title affecting the other land adjoining the determined boundary, such particulars of the exact line of the boundary as the registrar considers appropriate. An entry of the fact of determination of the boundary is also made in the property register of the applicant's registered title. If appropriate, similar entries are made in the property register of any superior or inferior registered title, and any registered title affecting the other land adjoining the determined boundary.

Where the exact line of only part of the boundary of a registered estate has been determined, the ends of that part of the boundary are not to be treated as determined for the purposes of adjoining parts of the boundary the exact line of which has not been determined (LRR 2003 rule 121). By way of example, figure 1 shows a rectangular piece of land, where A–B is the northern boundary. The part of the boundary between points C and D has been determined but not the rest of the boundary. The determined position for points C and D shown on the title plan determines those points for the boundary C–D but not for the boundaries A–C and B–D. Notice of the application will have been served on the owners of the land adjoining on the south of C–D, but not on the owners of the land adjoining on the east of B–D nor on the owners of the land adjoining on the west of A–C.

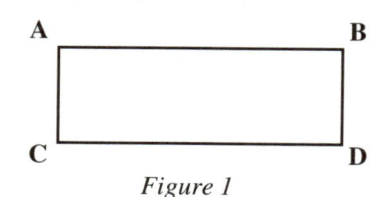

Figure 1

The registrar may determine the exact line of a common boundary without an application being made where there is a transfer of part of a registered estate in land and there is sufficient information in the transfer to enable him to do so. The same applies on a grant of a lease which is a registrable disposition of part of a registered estate in land. A common boundary in this context is any boundary of the land disposed of by the transfer of part or lease of part which adjoins land in which the transferor or lessor, at the date of the transfer or lease, had a registered estate in land or of which such transferor or lessor was entitled to be registered as proprietor (LRR 2003 rule 122).

Where the registrar does determine the exact line of the common boundary without an application, he must make an entry in the property registers of the affected registered titles stating that the exact line of the common boundary is determined under LRA 2002 section 60. The registrar must also add to the title plan of the transferor's or lessor's affected registered title (whether or not the transferor or lessor is still the proprietor of that title, or still entitled to be registered as proprietor of that title) and to the title plan of the registered title under which the transfer or lease is being registered, such particulars of the exact line of the common boundary as he considers appropriate. Instead of, or as well as, adding such particulars to the title plans, the registrar may make an entry in the property registers of the affected registered titles referring to the description of the common boundary in the transfer or lease.

Cautions Against Conversion

Where a proprietor was registered with possessory, qualified, or good leasehold title, it was possible under the Land Registration Rules 1925 rule 215(2) for a caution against conversion to be entered on the register. This has the effect of preventing the title being converted to qualified, good leasehold, or absolute (as appropriate) until notice of the application has been served on the cautioner, allowing him an opportunity to object to the conversion. It is not possible to register a caution against conversion under the Land Registration Act 2002 ("LRA 2002").

If a caution against conversion has been entered in the register and an application is made to upgrade the title, the registrar, before determining the application, gives notice of it to the person named in the caution. Where the cautioner responds to the notice by claiming any estate, right or interest in the land in the title, then, to the extent such estate right or interest subsists and is otherwise enforceable, the claim is treated for the purposes of LRA 2002 section 62(6) as one for an estate, right or interest whose enforceability is preserved by virtue of the existing entry about the class of title (Land

Registration Act 2002 (Transitional Provisions) Order 2003 article 15).

LRA 2002 section 62(6) provides that none of the powers to upgrade the title contained in section 62 is exercisable if there is outstanding any claim adverse to the title of the registered proprietor which is made by virtue of an estate, right or interest whose enforceability is preserved by virtue of the existing entry about the class of title.

Cautions Against Dealings

The Land Registration Act 1925 ("LRA 1925") section 54 provided that any person interested in any land or charge registered in the name of any person might lodge a caution to the effect that no dealing with such land or charge is to be registered until notice has been served upon the cautioner.

It is not possible to register a caution against dealings under the Land Registration Act 2002. Any existing caution against dealings continues to have effect (Land Registration Act 2002 ("LRA 2002") Schedule 12 paragraph 2(3)).

Where a caution has been registered, no registration of any dealing will be completed until notice of it has been served on the cautioner by the registrar. The notice may be by post to the address for service (whether within or outside the United Kingdom), by leaving the notice at the address for service in the United Kingdom, by directing the notice to a DX number entered as the address for service, by electronic transmission to an electronic address for service, or by fax where the cautioner has informed the registrar in writing that he is willing to accept service by fax and of the fax number to which it should be sent. The registrar may also serve the notice by post to an address, other than an address for service, where the registrar believes the addressee is likely to receive it. The same applies to DX to, or leaving the notice at, an address other than an address for service. Whatever method of service is used, the notice period is the period ending at 12 noon on the fifteenth business day, or ending at 12 noon on such later business day as the registrar may allow, after the date of issue of the notice (Land Registration Rules 2003 ("LRR 2003") rules 220(2) and 218). A business day is a day when the Land Registry is open to the public, that is every day except Saturdays, Sundays, Christmas Day, Good Friday or any other day either specified or declared by proclamation under the Banking and Financial Dealings Act 1971 section 1 or appointed by the Lord Chancellor.

The notice warns the cautioner that the caution will cease to have effect at the expiry of the notice period (or such longer period as the registrar may allow), unless an order to the contrary is made by the registrar. That is the only effect of a caution. It does not provide any form of priority or confer validity upon any claim (LRA 1925 section 56(2) which continues to have effect in respect of existing cautions against dealings as a result of LRA 2002 Schedule 12 paragraph 2(3)). See also *Barclays Bank v Taylor* [1974] Ch 137, [1973] 2 WLR 293, [1973] 1 All ER 752 (CA) and *Clark v Chief Land Registrar* [1994] Ch 370, [1994] 3 WLR 593, [1994] 4 All ER 96 (CA)).

Where the caution is registered against the proprietor of the land, this does not allow the cautioner to prevent a registered chargee selling under his power of sale (*Chancery plc v Ketteringham* [1994] Ch 370, [1994] 3 WLR 593, [1994] 4 All ER 96 (CA)). The cautioner will be informed that his caution has been cancelled. This possibility should be borne in mind when a cautioner consents to the registration of a charge.

Although an interest under a trust of land may have been protected by a caution against dealings (*Elias v Mitchell* [1972] Ch 652, [1972] 2 WLR 740, [1972] 2 All ER 153), a disposition by two or more trustees or a trust corporation which overreaches that interest under the Law of Property Act 1925 section 27 prevents an objection by a cautioner being sustained, although he will have received notice of the application to register the dealing.

If a caution was lodged without reasonable cause, then the cautioner is liable to make, to any person who may have sustained damage by the lodging of the caution, such compensation as may be just. Such compensation is recoverable as a debt by the person who has sustained damage from the person who lodged the caution (LRA 1925 section 56(3), which continues to have effect in respect of existing cautions against dealings as a result of LRA 2002 Schedule 12 paragraph 2(3)). In practice the prospects of a successful claim under section 56(3) may be more limited than would appear at first sight. In *Clearbrook Property Holdings v Verrier* [1974] 1 WLR 243, [1973] 3 All ER 614, Templeman J said:

"It is at least arguable that a person who genuinely believes he is entitled to specific performance and issues a writ for that purpose under legal advice may say that he lodged his caution with reasonable cause."

Where a cautioner has died, his personal representatives may proceed in the same manner as the cautioner (LRA 1925 section 56(4), which continues to have effect in respect of existing cautions against dealings as a result of LRA 2002 Schedule 12 paragraph 2(3)). The personal representatives should always consider the need to amend the address for service.

The cautioner may apply at any time for the cancellation of the caution. The application must be in Form WCT and signed by the cautioner or his conveyancer. If the cautioner has died the application should be made by his personal representatives and a copy of the grant enclosed. Where the cautioner is applying to withdraw the caution as to part only, a plan defining the relevant land should be attached to Form WCT. No fee is payable.

A cautioner may make an application for the entry of a notice under LRA 2002 section 34, or for the entry of a restriction under LRA 2002 section 43 in relation to that estate, right, interest or claim in respect of which the caution was lodged only if he also applies for the withdrawal of the caution (LRA 2002 Schedule 12 paragraph 17).

The proprietor of the registered estate or charge to which the caution relates may apply for the cancellation of the caution. Such an application may also be made by a person who, but for the existence of the caution, would be entitled to be registered as the proprietor of that estate of charge. The application must be in Form CCD. No fee is payable. The registrar must give the cautioner notice of the application (LRR 2003 rule 223(3)). The notice period is the period ending at 12 noon on the fifteenth business day, or ending at 12 noon on such later business day as the registrar may allow, after the date of issue of the notice (LRR 2003 rules 220(2) and 218).

Cautioner Showing Cause

When the cautioner has received a notice (whether as the result of an application to register a dealing or an application to cancel a caution under LRR 2003 rule 223), he may at any time before the expiry of the notice period show cause why the registrar should not give effect to that application. If he does not reply to the notice, or consents unconditionally, the caution will be cancelled.

To show cause, the cautioner must deliver to the registrar a written statement setting out the grounds relied upon and show that he has a fairly arguable case for the registrar not to give effect to the application in question (LRR 2003 rule 221(3)). The written statement must be signed by the cautioner or his conveyancer.

If, after reading the written statement, and making any enquiries he thinks necessary, the registrar is satisfied that cause has been shown, he must order that the caution is to continue until withdrawn or otherwise disposed of under LRA 2002 or LRR 2003. The registrar must then give notice to the applicant and the cautioner that he has made the order and that the cautioner is to be treated as having objected under LRA 2002 section 73 to the application that resulted in notice being served (LRR 2003 rule 221(5)). The notice give by the registrar under rule 221(5) is treated as notice under LRA 2002 section 73(5)(a).

The cautioner and the applicant may still resolve their dispute by agreement. If, however, it is not possible to dispose of the objection by agreement, the registrar must refer the matter to the adjudicator (LRA 2002 section 73(7)). See *Disputes*, page 120.

Agreement might be reached, for example, that the dealing be registered but the caution remain on the register, or that the caution be cancelled and the dealing completed with the interest to which the caution related being noted in priority to the dealing. The latter course of action is possible only where the interest is one capable of being protected by a notice.

Where a cautioner is considering agreeing to the registration of a charge on condition that his caution remains in the proprietorship register, he should bear in mind that his caution could be overreached subsequently if the proprietor of the charge sells under his power of sale.

If after service of the notice under LRA 1925 section 55(1) or LRR 2003 rule 223(3) the application that resulted in the notice being served is cancelled, withdrawn or otherwise does not proceed, the registrar must make an order that the caution will continue to have effect, unless he has already done so or the caution has been cancelled (LRR 2003 rule 221(6)).

The High Court has an inherent jurisdiction to order the vacation of a caution, which it may exercise on motion. In *Alpenstow Ltd v Regalian Properties Plc* [1985] 1 WLR 721, [1985] 2 All ER 545, Nourse J said:

"An order vacating a caution or an estate contract can and ought to be made on motion if there is no fair arguable case in support of the registration which ought to go to trial. In this respect a certain robustness of approach is permissible. If the issues are defined and their resolution depends only on the ascertained documents and affidavit evidence, they can and ought to be decided, even if they involve difficult questions of construction or law."

In *The Rawlplug Co Ltd v Kamvale Properties Ltd* (1968) 20 P & CR 32, Megarry J dealt with this robustness of approach in the following passage:

"Accordingly, it seems to me that the speedy form of remedy by way of motion ought to be available to a land owner in all cases where there are no substantial grounds for supporting registration. I would thus favour a certain robustness of approach. If there is a firmer arguable case in support of the registration the matter must stand over until the trial. But if, although not cloudless, the sky has in it no more than a cloud the size of a man's hand, I would clear the registration and leave the purchaser to such remedies as he may be advised to take by way of specific performance or damages."

Cautions Against First Registration

A person claiming to be the owner of a qualifying estate or entitled to an interest affecting a qualifying estate may lodge an application for a caution against first registration. For these purposes a qualifying estate is a legal estate which relates to land to which the caution relates and is an estate in land, a rentcharge, a franchise, or a *profit a prendre* in gross (Land Registration Act 2002 ("LRA 2002") section 15). A caution against first registration cannot be entered in the cautions register, however, where the application is by virtue of the applicant's ownership of a freehold estate in land or a leasehold estate in land where more than seven years of the term are unexpired. The limitation on the leaseholder applies equally to a caution in respect of his leasehold estate and a caution in respect of the lessor's estate (LRA 2002 section 15(3)).

Section 53 of the Land Registration Act 1925 contained no limitation equivalent to that in LRA 2002 section 15(3). For the period of two years from 13 October 2003 the limitation in section 15(3) will not have effect (LRA 2002 Schedule 12 paragraph 14(1)). Any caution lodged under paragraph 14(1), however, will cease to have effect at the end of that period of two years, except in relation to applications for first registration made before the end of that period.

Different rules apply to cautions against first registration lodged by the Queen where the land is demesne land; see *Demesne Land,* page 119.

A caution against first registration which was lodged under the Land Registration Act 1925 section 53 continues to have effect, and the provisions of LRA 2002, other than the limitation in LRA 2002 section 15(3) on an owner applying for a caution against first registration, apply to such a caution.

A person applying for a caution against first registration should deliver to the registry:
(a) an application in form CT1;
(b) a plan allowing the extent of the land to which the caution relates to be identified clearly on the Ordnance Survey map, unless this can be clearly identified from the description in panel 2 on form CT1; and
(c) the fee payable. A fee calculator for all types of application is on the Land Registry's website at www.landregistry.gov.uk/fees.

Either one of the cautioners, or someone authorised by the cautioners, must make the statutory declaration in panel 9 of form CT1, or the cautioner's conveyancer must complete the certificate in panel 10. In either case no documents should be exhibited.

The interest stated in the form CT1 will appear in the caution property register of the individual caution register, together with a description of the legal estate to which the caution relates. The description of the legal estate will refer to a caution plan based on the Ordnance Survey map, unless the legal estate is a relating franchise. A relating franchise is a franchise which is not an affecting franchise. An affecting franchise is a franchise which relates to a defined area of land and is an adverse right affecting, or capable of affecting, the title to an estate or charge (Land Registration Rules 2003 ("LRR 2003") rule 217(1)).

The other part of an individual caution register, other than the caution property register, is the cautioner's register. This contains the name of the cautioner, an address for service and, where appropriate, details of any person consenting to the lodging of the caution. A person consents to the lodging of a caution if, before the caution is entered in the cautions register, he has confirmed in writing that he consents to the lodging of the caution and that consent is produced to the registrar (LRR 2003 rule 47).

Where the cautioner is a company registered under the Companies Acts, or a limited liability partnership incorporated under the Limited Liability Partnerships Act 2000, its registered number also appears in the cautioner's register.

The cautioner must supply at least one and not more than three addresses for service to which all notices are to be sent. One address must be a postal address, whether or not in the United Kingdom. The other one or two additional addresses may be postal addresses but may also be a box number at a United Kingdom document exchange or an e-mail address. The box number referred to must be at a United Kingdom document exchange to which delivery can be made on behalf of the Land Registry under arrangements already in existence between the Land Registry and a service provider at the time the box number details are provided to the registrar (LRR 2003 rule 198). A cautioner may at any time apply for a replacement or additional address, subject to there being, after the application, no more than three addresses, at least one of which is a postal address. No fee is payable for such an application, which should be made in form AP1.

If a caution against first registration was lodged under the Land Registration Act 1925 section 53 without reasonable cause, then the cautioner is liable to make, to any person who may have sustained damage by the lodging of the caution, such compensation as may be just. Such compensation is recoverable as a debt by the person who has sustained damage from the person who lodged the caution (LRA 1925 section 56(3), which continues to have effect in relation to cautions against first registration lodged under that Act as a result of LRA 2002 Schedule 12 paragraph 4).

A person must not exercise the right to lodge a caution against first registration under LRA 2002 section 15 without reasonable cause (LRA 2002 section 77(1)). This duty to act reasonably is owed to any person who suffers damage in consequence of its breach (LRA 2002 section 77(2)).

In practice, when considering the prospects of a claim under the Land Registration Act 1925 section 56(3) or LRA 2002 section 77 the following statement by Templeman J in *Clearbrook Property Holdings v Verrier* [1974] 1 WLR 243, [1973] 3 All ER 614 should be borne in mind:

"It is at least arguable that a person who genuinely believes he is entitled to specific performance and issues a writ for that purpose under legal advice may say that he lodged his caution with reasonable cause."

Effect of a Caution Against First Registration

Where an application for first registration relates to a legal estate which is subject to a caution against first registration, the registrar gives the cautioner notice of the application and of his right to object to it. The period in which the cautioner can object is a period ending at 12 noon on the fifteenth business day after the date of issue of the notice or such longer period as the registrar may allow following a request, provided that the longer period never exceeds a period ending at 12 noon on the thirtieth business day after the date of issue of the notice (LRR 2003 rule 53). The request referred to is one by the cautioner to the registrar setting out why the longer period should be allowed. This request must be made before the period ending at 12 noon on the fifteenth business day after the date of issue of the notice has expired. After receiving such a request the registrar may, if he considers it appropriate, seek the views of the applicant for first registration; if, after considering any such views and all other relevant matters, he is satisfied that a longer period should be allowed, he may allow such period (not exceeding a period ending at 12 noon on the thirtieth business day after the date of issue of the notice) as he considers appropriate, whether or not the period is the same as any period requested by the cautioner (LRR 2003 rule 53(3)). A business day is a day when the Land Registry is open to the public, that is every day except Saturdays, Sundays, Christmas Day, Good Friday or any other day either specified or declared by proclamation under the Banking and Financial Dealings Act 1971 section 1 or appointed by the Lord Chancellor.

The application for first registration cannot be completed within the notice period unless the cautioner has given notice to the registrar that he does not intend to object or unless the cautioner has objected and the objection has been disposed of in the notice period. An example of the latter is where the cautioner objected on the grounds that he had an easement over the land sought to be registered and, still within the notice period, the applicant consented to the making of an entry on the register in respect of the easement.

The above is the only effect of a caution against first registration. In particular a caution against first registration has no effect on the validity or priority of any interest of the cautioner in the legal estate to which the caution relates (LRA 2002 section 16(3)). Registration of a caution against first registration can therefore never supersede the need to register a land charge under the Land Charges Act 1972 in appropriate cases.

Objection by Cautioner

Where the cautioner objects to the application for first registration, he must deliver to the registrar at the address indicated in the notice a written statement signed by himself or his conveyancer. That statement must state that he objects and set out the grounds for the objection (LRR 2003 rule 19). If he wishes communications to be sent to an address other than his address for service, this should be stated.

Unless the registrar is satisfied that the objection is groundless, he must give notice of the objection to the applicant for first registration and may not complete the application for first registration until the objection has been disposed of (LRA 2002 section 73). The cautioner and the applicant may still resolve their dispute by agreement. If, however, it is not possible to dispose of the objection by agreement, the registrar must refer the matter to the adjudicator (LRA 2002 section 73(7)). See *Disputes*, page 120.

Withdrawal of a Caution against First Registration
The cautioner may withdraw the caution against first registration at any time. The cautioner should deliver to the registry:
  (a) an application in form WCT; and
  (b) if the withdrawal relates to part only of the land to which the caution relates, a plan or other sufficient details to allow the extent in question to be clearly identified on the Ordnance Survey map.
No fee is payable.

Cancellation of a Caution Against First Registration
The owner of the legal estate to which the caution against first registration relates may apply to the registrar for cancellation of the caution (LRA 2002 section 18). In addition the owner of a legal estate which derives out of the legal estate to which the caution against first registration relates may also apply to the registrar for cancellation of the caution (LRR 2003 rule 45). If, however, the owner of the legal estate to which the caution against first registration relates has consented to the lodging of the caution in accordance with LRR 2003 rule 47, he may make an application for cancellation only if the interest claimed by the cautioner has come to an end or if he claims that the consent was induced by fraud, misrepresentation, mistake or undue influence or given under duress. The same limitation on applying for cancellation affects a person who derives title to the legal estate by operation of law from a person who has consented (LRA 2002 section 18(2) and LRR 2003 rule 47).

The applicant for cancellation of a caution against first registration should deliver to the registry:
  (a) an application in form CCT;
  (b) if the application relates to part only of the land to which the caution relates, a plan or other sufficient details to allow the extent in question to be clearly identified on the Ordnance Survey map;
  (c) evidence that the applicant is the owner of the legal estate to which the caution relates, where he is applying as such owner;
  (d) evidence that the applicant is the owner of a legal estate derived out of the legal estate to which the caution relates, where he is applying as such owner; and
  (e) where the applicant, or a person from whom the applicant derives title to the legal estate by operation of law, has consented to the lodging of the caution, evidence that the interest claimed by the cautioner has come to an end or that the consent was induced by fraud, misrepresentation, mistake or undue influence or given under duress.

No fee is payable.

When such an application is received the registrar gives the cautioner notice of the application and notice that if he does not object to the application within the prescribed period the registrar must cancel the caution. The period in which the cautioner can object is a period ending at 12 noon on the fifteenth business day after the date of issue of the notice or such longer period as the registrar may allow following a request, provided that the longer period never exceeds a period ending at 12 noon on the thirtieth business day after the date of issue of the notice (LRR 2003 rule 53). The request referred to is one by the cautioner to the registrar setting out why the longer period should be allowed. This request must be made before the period ending at 12 noon on the fifteenth business day after the date of issue of the notice has expired. After receiving such a request the registrar may, if he considers it appropriate, seek the views of the applicant for cancellation; if, after considering any such views and all other relevant matters, he is satisfied that a longer period should be allowed, he may allow such period (not exceeding a period ending at 12 noon on the thirtieth business day after the issue of the notice) as he considers appropriate, whether or not the period is the same as any period requested by the cautioner (LRR 2003 rule 53(3)). A business day is a day when the Land Registry is open to the public, that is every day except Saturdays, Sundays, Christmas Day, Good Friday or any other day either specified or declared by proclamation under the Banking and Financial Dealings Act 1971 section 1 or appointed by the Lord Chancellor.

Where the cautioner objects to the application for cancellation, he must deliver to the registrar at the address indicated in the notice a written statement signed by himself or his conveyancer. That statement must state that he objects and set out the grounds for the objection (LRR 2003 rule 19). If he wishes communications to be sent to an address other than his address for service, this should be stated.

Unless the registrar is satisfied that the objection is groundless, he must give notice of the objection to the applicant for cancellation and may not complete the application for cancellation until the objection has been disposed of (LRA 2002 section 73). The cautioner and the applicant may still resolve their dispute by agreement. If, however, it is not possible to dispose of the objection by agreement, the registrar must refer the matter to the adjudicator (LRA 2002 section 73(7)). See *Disputes*, page 120.

Alteration of the Cautions Register
There was no machinery under the Land Registration Act 1925 allowing a successor by operation of law to the cautioner to be shown on the register in place of the cautioner. In such circumstances a new application for a caution against first registration was required. LRR 2003 rule 51(1) provides that a person who claims that the whole of the relevant interest recorded in an

individual cautions register is vested in him by operation of law as successor to the cautioner may apply for the register to be altered to show him as cautioner in the cautioner's register, in place of the cautioner. The applicant should deliver to the registry:
(a) an application in form AP1;
(b) written details of the grounds on which he claims that the whole of the relevant interest recorded in the cautions register is vested in him by operation of law as successor to the cautioner;
(c) any supporting documents; and
(d) the fee payable. A fee calculator for all types of application is on the Land Registry's website at www.landregistry.gov.uk/fees.

Before the registrar alters the cautioner's register to show the new cautioner he must serve a notice on the existing cautioner giving details of the application, unless the registrar is satisfied that service of the notice is unnecessary (LRR 2003 rule 50(2)). If the registrar does not serve notice or if the existing cautioner does not object within the time specified in the notice, the registrar alters the cautioner's register to show the new cautioner in place of the existing cautioner. The new cautioner is then treated as "the cautioner" for the purposes of LRA 2002.

The registrar may also alter the cautions register for the purpose of bringing it up to date in some other manner, or for the purpose of correcting a mistake (LRA 2002 section 21). A person who wishes to apply for an alteration under LRA 2002 section 21 should deliver to the registry:
(a) an application in form AP1;
(b) written details of the alteration required and of the grounds on which the application is made;
(c) any supporting documents; and
(d) the fee payable. A fee calculator for all types of application is on the Land Registry's website at www.landregistry.gov.uk/fees.

Before the registrar alters the cautions register he must serve a notice on the cautioner giving details of the application, unless the registrar is satisfied that service of the notice is unnecessary (LRR 2003 rule 50(2)). If the registrar is satisfied that the cautioner does not own the relevant interest, or owns only part, or that such interest did not exist or has come to an end wholly or in part, he alters the cautions register under LRA 2002 section 21(1) (LRR 2003 rule 49). Where an alteration is made under LRA 2002 section 21, the registrar may pay such amount as he thinks fit in respect of any costs reasonably incurred by a person in connection with the alteration (LRA 2002 section 21(3)). This is most likely to arise where there has been a mistake in the cautions register.

If, in any proceedings, the High Court or a county court decides that a cautioner does not own the interest claimed by the cautioner, or owns only part, or that such interest either wholly or in part did not exist or has come to an end, the court must make an order for the alteration of the cautions

register (LRR 2003 rule 48(1)). The court may make an order for alteration of the cautions register for the purpose of correcting a mistake or bringing the register up to date. The order must state the caution title number of the individual cautions register affected, describe the alteration that is to be made, and direct the registrar to make the alteration. The order must be served on the registrar by making an application for him to give effect to the order. The applicant should deliver to the registry:
  (a) an application in form AP1;
  (b) the order; and
  (c) the fee payable. A fee calculator for all types of application is on the Land Registry's website at www.landregistry.gov.uk/fees.

Chancel Repair

The liability for chancel repair was an overriding interest under the Land Registration Act 1925 section 70(1)(c). In *Aston Cantlow and Wilmcote with Billesley Parochial Church Council v Wallbank* [2001] EWCA Civ 713, [2001] 3 WLR 1323, [2001] 3 All ER 393, the Court of Appeal held that the modern liability of lay owners of what was once the glebe lands of a rectory to defray the unmet cost of repairs to the chancel of the parish church was a form of taxation which operated arbitrarily. This was held to have breached the defendants' right to peaceful enjoyment of their possessions under article 1 of the First Protocol to the European Convention for the Protection of Human Rights and Fundamental Freedoms 1950 (as set out in Schedule 1 to the Human Rights Act 1998), and so was unenforceable.

As a result of this decision, the liability for chancel repair is not included in the list of unregistered interests which override first registration set out in Schedule 1 to the Land Registration Act 2002, nor in the list of unregistered interests which override registered dispositions set out in Schedule 3 to that Act. There is therefore no duty to disclose a liability for chancel repair under rule 28 or 57 of the Land Registration Rules 2003.

Charging Orders

A person who has obtained a charging order against the legal estate in registered land may apply for the entry in the register of a notice in respect of the charging order. This is so whether the order is an interim charging order or a charging order absolute, including a charging order made under the Criminal Justice Act 1988 section 78 or the Drug Trafficking Act 1994 section 27. The applicant is not able to apply for an official search with priority using form OS1 or OS2 but is able to reserve a period of priority by an outline application. See *Outline Applications*, page 222.

Where the charging order is over a beneficial interest in registered land held under a trust of land, a notice cannot be entered in the register (Land Registration Act 1925 ("LRA 2002") section 33). In that case it is possible to apply for the entry of a restriction.

An application for a notice may be for an agreed notice or a unilateral notice. In the case of an application for an agreed notice, the registrar may approve the application without the consent of the proprietor where he is satisfied of the validity of the applicant's claim. Normally the production of the charging order enables the registrar to be so satisfied.

Where an application for a charging order is pending before the court, the priority of the pending action is usually protected by an agreed notice.

Notice in Respect of a Pending Action
An applicant should deliver to the registry:
   (a) an application in form AN1;
   (b) the sealed claim form and notice of issue; and
   (c) the fee payable. A fee calculator for all types of application is on the Land Registry's website at www.landregistry.gov.uk/fees.

This is likely to be sufficient to satisfy the registrar as to the validity of the applicant's claim in accordance with LRA 2002 section 34(3)(c). Where the applicant wishes to apply for a unilateral notice he should deliver to the registry:
   (a) an application in form UN1; and
   (b) the fee payable. A fee calculator for all types of application is on the Land Registry's website at www.landregistry.gov.uk/fees.

Form UN1 should be completed on the following lines to show the interest of the applicant:

"applicant in an application for a charging order in the ... Court [*set out full court reference and parties*]."

The unilateral notice will give brief details of the interest protected and identify the beneficiary of that notice.

Agreed Notice of the Charging Order
An applicant should deliver to the registry:
   (a) an application in form AN1;
   (b) the charging order or a certified copy of it; and
   (c) the fee payable. A fee calculator for all types of application is on the Land Registry's website at www.landregistry.gov.uk/fees.

The entry made in the register will give details of the interest protected.

Unilateral Notice of the Charging Order
An applicant should deliver to the registry:

(a) an application in form UN1; and
(b) the fee payable. A fee calculator for all types of application is on the Land Registry's website at www.landregistry.gov.uk/fees.

Form UN1 should be completed on the following lines to show the interest of the applicant:

"chargee under a charging order of the ... Court dated ... [*set out full court reference and parties*]."

The unilateral notice will give brief details of the interest protected and identify the beneficiary of that notice.

Restriction Where the Charging Order is over a Beneficial Interest

If there is no restriction in Form A on the register, a person having the benefit of a charging order over a beneficial interest under a trust of land has a sufficient interest for the purposes of LRA 2002 section 43(1)(c) to apply for a restriction in Form A to ensure that a survivor of the joint proprietors (unless a trust corporation) will not be able to give a valid receipt for capital money (LRR 2003 rule 93(a)). Form A is:

"No disposition by a sole proprietor of the registered estate (except a trust corporation) under which capital money arises is to be registered unless authorised by an order of the court."

The person having the benefit of a charging order over a beneficial interest under a trust of land also has a sufficient interest for the purposes of LRA 2002 section 43(1)(c) to apply for a restriction in Form K to ensure that he receives notice of a disposition (LRR 2003 rule 93(k)). Form K is:

"No disposition of the registered [estate] [charge] is to be registered without a certificate signed by the applicant for registration or his conveyancer that written notice of the disposition was given to [*name of person with the benefit of the charging order*] at [*address for service*], being the person with the benefit of [an interim charging order] [a charging order absolute] on the beneficial interest of [*name of judgment debtor*] made by the ... Court on [*date*] (Court reference...)."

This restriction does not of itself prevent a disposition, provided it is complied with. This is because the interest of the person having the benefit of a charging order will be overreached where the requirements of Form A have been met (Law of Property Act 1925 section 27).

The registrar must give notice of an application for a restriction to the proprietor of the registered estate or charge concerned (LRA 2002 section 45).

A restriction does not confer any priority; it simply prevents an entry being made in the register if it is not permitted under the wording of the restriction.

If applying for a restriction in Form A, the person having the benefit of a charging order over a beneficial interest under a trust of land should deliver to the registry an application in form RX1. No fee is payable where the

application is in respect of a restriction in Form A only.
   Panel 13 of RX1 should be completed on the following lines:
"The interest is that specified in rule 93(a) of the Land Registration Rules 2003."
Panel 10 should be completed as to Form A set out above.
   If applying for a restriction in Form K, the person having the benefit of a charging order over a beneficial interest under a trust of land should deliver to the registry:
   (a) an application in form RX1; and
   (b) the fee payable. A fee calculator for all types of application is on the Land Registry's website at www.landregistry.gov.uk/fees.
Panel 13 of RX1 should be completed on the following lines:
"The interest is that specified in rule 93(k) of the Land Registration Rules 2003."
Panel 10 should be completed as to Form K set out above.

Charities

The disposition of land by charities is dealt with by Part V of the Charities Act 1993 (which is amended by the Land Registration Act 2002 ("LRA 2002") Schedule 10 paragraph 29). For the purposes of the Charities Act 1993, a charity is any institution, corporate or not, which is established for charitable purposes and is subject to the control of the High Court in the exercise of the court's jurisdiction with respect to charities (Charities Act 1993 section 96). "Charity" has the same meaning in the Land Registration Rules 2003 ("LRR 2003"). The Charities Act 1993 does not apply to land held by corporations in the Church of England in cases where such corporations are not subject to the control of the High Court, for example where they hold land for ecclesiastical purposes, or where a Diocesan Board of Finance is holding glebe land in accordance with the Endowments and Glebe Measure 1976. See *Church of England*, page 81.
   The Charity Commissioners are regarded as having a sufficient interest to apply for a restriction in relation to registered land held on charitable trusts (LRA 2002 section 43(1)(c) and LRR 2003 rule 93(f)).

Dispositions in Favour of Charities
Any disposition of registered land in favour of a charity which requires to be registered, and any disposition in favour of a charity which triggers first registration, must contain a statement in one of the following forms (Charities Act 1993 section 37(5) and LRR 2003 rule 179):
   (a) "The land transferred (*or as the case may be*) will, as a result of this

transfer (*or as the case may be*) be held [by] [in trust for] (*name of charity*), an exempt charity."
(b) "The land transferred (*or as the case may be*) will, as a result of this transfer (*or as the case may be*) be held [by] [in trust for] (*name of charity*), a non-exempt charity, and the restrictions on disposition imposed by section 36 of the Charities Act 1993 will apply to the land (subject to section 36(9) of that Act)."

The appropriate statement should be made in the contract as well as in the document effecting the disposition.

None of the above applies to a mortgage in favour of a charity, nor do any of the restrictions discussed below need to be entered where a charity is registered as proprietor of a charge.

Exempt charities are:
(a) any charity which, if the Charities Act 1960 had not been passed, would be exempted from the jurisdiction of the Charity Commissioners or the Minister of Education by the terms of any Act not contained in the Charitable Trusts Acts 1853 to 1939, other than by the Places of Worship Registration Act 1855 section 9;
(b) the universities of Oxford, Cambridge, London, Durham and Newcastle, the colleges and halls in universities of Oxford, Cambridge, Durham and Newcastle, Queen Mary and Westfield Colleges in the University of London and the colleges of Winchester and Eton;
(c) any university, university college, or institution connected with a university or university college, declared an exempt charity by Order in Council;
(d) a grant-maintained school;
(e) the National Curriculum Council, the Curriculum Council for Wales and the School Examinations and Assessment Council;
(f) a higher education corporation;
(g) a successor company to a higher education corporation;
(h) a further education corporation;
(i) the Board of Trustees of the Victoria and Albert Museum;
(j) the Board of Trustees of the Science Museum;
(k) the Board of Trustees of the Armouries;
(l) the Board of Trustees of the Royal Botanic Gardens, Kew;
(m) the Board of Trustees of the National Museums and Galleries on Merseyside;
(n) the Trustees of the British Museum and the Trustees of the Natural History Museum;
(o) the Board of Trustees of the National Gallery;
(p) the Board of Trustees of the Tate Gallery;
(q) the Board of Trustees of the National Portrait Gallery;
(r) the Board of Trustees of the Wallace Collection;

(s) the Trustees of the Imperial War Museum;
(t) the Trustees of the National Maritime Museum;
(u) any institution administered by or on behalf of an institution included above and established for the general purposes of, or for any special purpose of or in connection with, the last-mentioned institution;
(v) the Church Commissioners and any institution which is administered by them;
(w) any registered industrial and provident society and any registered friendly society;
(x) the Board of Governors of the Museum of London;
(y) the British Library Board;
(z) the National Lottery Charities Board; and
(aa) the Royal College of Art.

The application to register the disposition does not require to be in any special form merely because the applicants are charity trustees. The trust deed of the charity does not need to be produced in the case of a non-exempt charity. Where a corporation or body of trustees holding on charitable, ecclesiastical or public trusts applies to be registered as proprietor of a registered estate or registered charge, the application must be accompanied by the document creating the trust or a certified copy of it (LRR 2003 rule 182(1)). It may be necessary to enter a restriction to reflect any limitations on the power of disposition contained in that trust document. This requirement in LRR 2003 rule 182(1) does not apply in the case of an estate or a charge held by or in trust for a non-exempt charity (LRR 2003 rule 182(4)).

If the disposition is in favour of charity trustees incorporated under Part VII of the Charities Act 1993, they must be described as "a body corporate under Part VII of the Charities Act 1993" and the application to register the disposition must be accompanied by the certificate granted by the Charity Commissioners under the Charities Act 1993 section 50 (LRR 2003 rule 177). These requirements apply equally to a disposition of a registered charge in favour of charity trustees.

Where the application is to register the official custodian for charities as proprietor of a registered estate or registered charge, the application must be accompanied by:

(a) an application in form RX1 for a restriction in Form F; and
(b) an order of the court made under the Charities Act 1993 section 21(1); or
(c) an order of the Charity Commissioners made under the Charities Act 1993 section 16 or 18.

Form F is:

"No disposition executed by the trustees of [*name of charity*] in the name and on behalf of the proprietor shall be registered unless the transaction is authorised by an order of the court or of the Charity Commissioners, as

required by section 22(3) of the Charities Act 1993."
Where the official custodian for charities is registered as proprietor of a registered estate or a registered charge, except where the estate or charge is vested in him by virtue of an order under the Charities Act 1993 section 18, the address of the charity trustees or, where the registered estate or charge is held on behalf of a charity which is a corporation, the address of the charity, must be entered on the register as his address for service (LRR 2003 178(3)).

There is no limit to the number of trustees of a charity who can be registered as proprietors (Trustee Act 1925 section 34(3)). The names of the trustees in the proprietorship register may be followed by an appropriate description such as:

"the trustees of the charity known as [*name of charity*]".

Where the charity being registered as proprietor is an exempt charity, it is not compulsory for any restriction to be entered in the register. In the case of an application to register a non-exempt charity, or trustees of a non-exempt charity, as proprietor, it must be accompanied by an application for the appropriate restriction (LRR 2003 rule 176). The application may be in form RX1 or set out in the additional provisions panel of Form TP1, TP2, TP3, TR1, TR2, TR3, TR4, TR5, AS1, AS2 or AS3. No additional fee is payable for the application for the restriction.

The appropriate restriction is usually Form E, which is:

"No disposition by the proprietor of the registered estate to which section 36 or section 38 of the Charities Act applies is to be registered unless the instrument contains a certificate complying with section 37(2) or section 39(2) of the Charities Act 1993 as appropriate."

Where the estate is vested in the official custodian for charities under the Charities Act 1993 section 18, in addition to a restriction in Form E, a restriction in Form F is required.

In all cases where two or more trustees of the charity are registered as proprietors a restriction in Form A is entered in the register (LRA 2002 section 44(1)). Where a sole or last surviving trustee of the charity applies to be registered as proprietor of the land held on a trust of land, he must apply for a restriction in Form A in addition to any charity restriction (LRR 2003 rule 94).

Form A is:

"No disposition by a sole proprietor of the registered estate (except a trust corporation) under which capital money arises is to be registered unless authorised by an order of the court."

Corporation Becoming a Non-exempt Charity

Where a registered estate is held by or in trust for a corporation and the corporation becomes a non-exempt charity, the charity trustees must apply for a restriction in Form E (LRR 2003 rule 176(3)).

The charity trustees should deliver to the registry:

(a) an application in form RX1; and
(b) the fee payable. A fee calculator for all types of application is on the Land Registry's website at www.landregistry.gov.uk/fees.

Dispositions by Charities
Any disposition of registered land by a charity which requires to be registered must comply with the restrictions which appear on the register. The deed effecting the disposition and the contract for such disposition must contain an appropriate statement (Charities Act 1993 section 37).

Subject to the trusts of the charity, charity trustees may confer on two or more of their number authority to execute deeds and instruments in the names and on behalf of the trustees (Charities Act 1993 section 82). This also allows execution on behalf of the official custodian for charities, unless a contrary intention appears. Where a deed is expressed to be executed under the Charities Act section 82 and the disposition is in favour of a person acquiring in good faith for money or money's worth an interest in or charge on land, it is not necessary to deliver to the registry evidence of the authority to execute under that section.

Where the registered proprietor is a charitable company and its name does not include the words "charity" or "charitable", the deed effecting the disposition must contain a statement that the company is a charity (Charities Act 1993 section 68(1)(d)).

Where the charity is an incorporated body under Part VII of the Charities Act 1993, it can execute deeds using its common seal if it has one. Whether or not it has a common seal, a document may be executed by it either:
(a) by being signed by a majority of the trustees of the charity and expressed to be executed by the incorporated body; or
(b) by being executed by two or more of the trustees authorised to execute in the name and on behalf of the incorporated body.

This also allows execution on behalf of the official custodian for charities, unless a contrary intention appears. In favour of a purchaser (including a lessee or mortgagee) in good faith for valuable consideration, a document is deemed to be duly executed by an incorporated body which is a charity if it purports to be signed:
(a) by a majority of the trustees of the charity; or
(b) by such of the trustees of the charity as are authorised by the trustees of that charity to execute it in the name and on behalf of that body
(Charities Act 1993 section 60).

Where this applies, no evidence that the trustees are a majority, or of their authority, needs be delivered to the registry.

Where the official custodian for charities is the registered proprietor, any deed is executed by the charity trustees, either by all of them, or under the provisions of section 82 or 60 referred to above.

If the Charity Commissioners have appointed a receiver and manager under the Charities Act 1993 sections 18 and 19, a certified copy of the order must accompany any application in respect of a deed executed by him.

Transfers on Sale or Leases by Non-exempt Charities

The restriction in Form E appearing in the proprietorship register requires the deed to contain a certificate complying with the Charities Act 1993 section 37(2). A restriction in Form 12 under the Land Registration Rules 1925 is to like effect. A transfer on sale or lease requiring to be registered should therefore include one or other of the following certificates, as appropriate:
- (a) "The [transferors] [lessors] certify that this disposition has been sanctioned by an order of [the court] [the Charity Commissioners]."; or
- (b) "The [transferors] [lessors] certify that as charity trustees they have power under the trusts of the charity to effect this disposition and that they have complied with the provisions of section 36 of the Charities Act 1993 so far as applicable to it."

The certificate must be given by the charity trustees. If they are not the registered proprietors, the certificate should be amended so as to be made by the charity trustees. In that event the charity trustees should be party to the deed and should execute it.

In addition to containing the appropriate certificate, the transfer or lease must also contain the statement required by the Charities Act 1993 section 37(1). This is one of the following statements, as appropriate (LRR 2003 rule 180(1)):
- (a) "The land [transferred] [leased] is held by [(*proprietors*) in trust for] (*charity*), a non-exempt charity, but this [transfer] [lease] is one falling within paragraph [(a), (b) *or* (c) *as the case may be*] of section 36(9) of the Charities Act 1993."; or
- (b) "The land [transferred] [leased] is held by [(*proprietors*) in trust for] (*charity*), a non-exempt charity, and this [transfer] [lease] is not one falling within paragraph (a), (b) or (c) of section 36(9) of the Charities Act 1993, so that the restrictions on disposition imposed by section 36 of that Act apply to the land."

The restrictions on dispositions imposed by the Charities Act 1993 section 36 apply notwithstanding anything in the trusts of the charity. Section 36(9) provides, however, that nothing in section 36 applies:
- (a) to any disposition for which general or special authority is expressly given (without the authority being made subject to the sanction of an order of the court) by any statutory provision contained in or having effect under an Act of Parliament or by any scheme legally established; or
- (b) to any disposition of land held by or in trust for a charity which–
    - (i) is made to another charity otherwise than for the best price that can

reasonably be obtained, and
(ii) is authorised to be so made by the trusts of the first-mentioned charity; or
(c) to the granting, by or on behalf of a charity and in accordance with its trusts, of a lease to any beneficiary under those trusts where the lease–
(i) is granted otherwise than for the best rent that can reasonably be obtained, and
(ii) is intended to enable the demised premises to be occupied for the purposes, or any particular purposes, of the charity.

Where the statement contained in the transfer or lease shows that it falls within paragraph (a), (b) or (c) of the Charities Act 1993 section 36(9), the certificate mentioned in the Form E restriction is not required.

Charges by Non-exempt Charities

The restriction in Form E appearing in the proprietorship register requires the charge to contain a certificate complying with the Charities Act 1993 section 39(2). A restriction in Form 12 under the Land Registration Rules 1925 is to like effect. A charge should therefore include one of the following certificates, as appropriate:
(a) "The chargors certify that this charge has been sanctioned by an order of [the court] [the Charity Commissioners]."; or
(b) "The chargors certify that as charity trustees they have power under the trusts of the charity to effect this charge and that they have obtained and considered such advice as is mentioned in section 38(2) of the Charities Act 1993."

The certificate must be given by the charity trustees. If they are not the registered proprietors, the certificate should be amended so as to be made by the charity trustees. In that event the charity trustees should be party to the charge and should execute it.

In addition to containing the appropriate certificate, the charge must also contain the statement required by the Charities Act 1993 section 39(1). This is one of the following, as appropriate (LRR 2003 rule 180(2)):
(a) "The land charged is held [by] [in trust for] (*charity*), a non-exempt charity, but this [charge] [mortgage] is one falling within section 38(5) of the Charities Act 1993."; or
(b) "The land charged is held [by] [in trust for] (*charity*), a non-exempt charity, but this [charge] [mortgage] is not one falling within section 38(5) of the Charities Act 1993, so that the restrictions imposed by section 38 of that Act apply."

Where the land being charged is unregistered but the charge triggers compulsory first registration under LRA 2002 section 4(1)(g), in addition to the appropriate statement as above, the charge must also contain the following statement (LRR 2003 rule 180(3)):

"The restrictions on disposition imposed by section 36 of the Charities Act

1993 also apply to the land (subject to section 36(9) of that Act)."

The restrictions on charges imposed by the Charities Act 1993 section 38 apply notwithstanding anything in the trusts of a charity. That section provides that no charge of charity land shall be granted without an order of the court or of the Charity Commissioners. Such an order is not required where the charity trustees have, before executing the charge, obtained and considered proper written advice on the following:

(a) whether the proposed loan is necessary in order for the charity trustees to be able to pursue the particular course of action in connection with which the loan is sought by them;
(b) whether the terms of the proposed loan are reasonable having regard to the status of the charity as a prospective borrower; and
(c) the ability of the charity to repay on those terms the sum proposed to be borrowed.

As a result of the Charities Act 1993 section 38(5), nothing in section 38 applies to any charge for which general or special authority is expressly given (without the authority being made subject to the sanction of an order of the court) by any statutory provision or by any scheme legally established. Where the statement contained in the charge shows that it falls within section 38(5), the certificate mentioned in the Form E restriction is not required.

Dispositions by Exempt Charities

No charity restriction is required to be entered on the registration of a disposition by an exempt charity. Any restriction which does appear in the proprietorship register must, however, be complied with in the usual way.

Even where there is no restriction, an appropriate statement must be included in the charge or in any contract for the sale, lease or other disposition, or in the conveyance, transfer, lease or other instrument effecting such disposition by the exempt charity.

The statement required in the case of a disposition which is not a charge is (LRR 2003 rule 180(1)):

"The land transferred (*or as the case may be*) is held by [(*proprietors*) in trust for] (*charity*), an exempt charity."

The statement required in the case of a charge is (LRR 2003 rule 180(2)):

"The land charged is held [by] [in trust for] (*charity*), an exempt charity."

Rentcharge Titles

Where there is a transfer by way of release of a registered rentcharge under the Charities Act 1993 section 40 or a redemption of a registered rentcharge under the Rentcharges Act 1977 sections 8 to 10, no certificate as to compliance with the Charities Act 1993 section 36 is required. In either of these situations the statement required in the instrument effecting the release of the registered rentcharge is (LRR 2003 rule 180(1)):

(a) in the case of an exempt charity:
"The rentcharge released is held by [(*proprietors*) in trust for] (*charity*), an exempt charity."
(b) in the case of a non-exempt charity:
"The rentcharge released is held by [(*proprietors*) in trust for] (*charity*), a non-exempt charity, but this release is one falling within paragraph (a) of section 36(9) of the Charities Act 1993."

Any other disposition of a rentcharge title should be dealt with in the same way as a disposition of registered land, as set out above.

Dispositions of Land Vested in the Official Custodian for Charities under the Charities Act 1993 section 18

Where the land has vested in the official custodian for charities under the Charities Act 1993 section 18, in addition to the usual charity restriction in Form E, Form F will appear in the proprietorship register. Form F is:

"No disposition executed by the trustees of (*charity*) in the name and on behalf of the proprietor shall be registered unless the transaction is authorised by an order of the court or of the Charity Commissioners, as required by section 22(3) of the Charities Act 1993."

Any application in respect of a disposition lodged where this restriction appears should be accompanied by a copy of the order of the court or of the Charity Commissioners authorising the transaction.

Appointment of New Trustees

Where under the trusts of a charity its trustees may be appointed or discharged by resolution of a meeting of the charity trustees, members or other persons, a memorandum declaring a trustee to have been so appointed or discharged operates as a vesting declaration under the Trustee Act 1925 section 40, provided:
  (a) the memorandum is executed as a deed;
  (b) the execution is effected either at the meeting by the person presiding or in some other manner directed by the meeting; and
  (c) the memorandum is attested by two persons present at the meeting

(Charities Act 1993 section 83).

The exclusions relating to charges and leases referred to in the Trustee Act 1925 section 40 also apply to this procedure under the Charities Act 1993 section 83.

Where an application is made to register the new trustees as proprietors and this procedure has been used, the applicant should deliver to the registry:
  (a) an application in form AP1;
  (b) the memorandum;
  (c) a certificate from the charity's conveyancer that it has power to use the procedure set out in the Charities Act 1993 section 83;
  (d) evidence of the death of any deceased trustee; and

(e) the fee payable. A fee calculator for all types of application is on the Land Registry's website at www.landregistry.gov.uk/fees.

Where the appropriate restriction does not appear in the register, this should be applied for using Form RX1.

In addition to the method set out in the Charities Act 1993 section 83, all the methods set out under the heading *Appointment of New Trustees*, page 77, are available. Where the appropriate restriction does not appear in the register, this should be applied for using Form RX1. A transfer merely vesting the estate in new trustees does not need to contain a certificate under the Charities Act 1993 section 37(2).

The Charity Commissioners have the same powers as the High Court of appointing, discharging or removing a trustee of a charity. Where such powers are exercised and affect the registered proprietors, the applicant should deliver to the registry:

(a) an application in form AP1;
(b) a certified copy of the order of the Charity Commissioners; and
(c) the fee payable. A fee calculator for all types of application is on the Land Registry's website at www.landregistry.gov.uk/fees.

Where the appropriate restriction does not appear in the register, this should be applied for using Form RX1.

Incorporation of Trustees of a Charity

Where the Charity Commissioners grant a certificate of incorporation to the trustees of a charity under the Charities Act 1993 section 50, the property of the charity, other than any vested in the official custodian for charities, vests in the body corporate (Charities Act 1993 section 51). An application should be made to amend the register of all affected titles. The applicant should deliver to the registry:

(a) an application in form AP1;
(b) a certified copy of the certificate of incorporation; and
(c) the fee payable (if any). A fee calculator for all types of application is on the Land Registry's website at www.landregistry.gov.uk/fees.

Where the appropriate restriction does not appear in the register, this should be applied for using Form RX1.

Where an incorporated body is dissolved under the Charities Act 1993 section 61, a similar application is required and the applicant should deliver to the registry:

(a) an application in form AP1;
(b) a certified copy of the order of the Charity Commissioners;
(c) where the order does not state in whom the land is vested, a certificate by the charity's conveyancer as to who are the trustees of the charity; and
(d) the fee payable (if any). A fee calculator for all types of application is on the land Registry's website at www.landregistry.gov.uk/fees.

Where the appropriate restriction does not appear in the register, this should be applied for using Form RX1.

Change of Status of Charity
Where an exempt charity ceases to be exempt or a non-exempt charity becomes exempt, an application must be made to ensure the appropriate restriction is shown in the register. An application to register a restriction should be made using Form RX1. An application to cancel a restriction should be made in Form RX3 accompanied by evidence of the change of status.

Change of Name of Charity
Where a charity changes its name, whether of its own volition or at the direction of the Charity Commissioners, an application to change the name of the charity or its description on the register should be made. The applicant should deliver to the registry:
  (a) an application in form AP1; and
  (b) a new certificate of incorporation (where the charity is incorporated under Part VII of the Charities Act 1993), or a certificate by the charity's conveyancer as to its new name.

No fee is payable for reflecting a change in the name, address or description of a registered proprietor.

Children

A person under the age of eighteen cannot hold a legal estate in land (Law of Property Act 1925 section 1(6)). He may hold an equitable interest only. Nevertheless situations do arise where, through inadvertence, a legal estate or legal charge is purported to be vested in a minor.

Transfer of Land to a Minor
After 1996 a purported transfer to one or more minors is not effective to pass the legal estate but operates as a declaration that the land is held in trust for the minor or minors (or if it purports to transfer it to the minors in trust for any persons, for those persons) (Trusts of Land and Appointment of Trustees Act 1996 Schedule 1 paragraph 1(1)). An application should be made in Form RX1 for a restriction in Form A, if this is not already on the register. Form A is:

"No disposition by a sole proprietor of the registered estate (except a trust corporation) under which capital money arises is to be registered unless authorised by an order of the court."

Since no evidence of the age of an applicant is required to be produced to the

registry, a conveyancer may discover that a person is under the age of eighteen only after he has been registered as proprietor. An application for alteration of the register should be made to reinstate the previous proprietor and enter a Form A restriction. The applicant should deliver to the registry:
  (a) an application in form AP1;
  (b) a statement by the conveyancer briefly summarising the facts and stating the alteration sought;
  (c) evidence of minority (for example a birth certificate); and
  (d) the fee payable (if any). A fee calculator for all types of application is on the Land Registry's website at www.landregistry.gov.uk/fees.

Transfer of Land to a Minor Jointly with an Adult

After 1996 a purported transfer to one or more minors and an adult or adults operates to vest the land in the adult or adults in trust for the minor or minors and the adult or adults (or if it purports to convey it to them in trust for any persons, for those persons) (Trusts of Land and Appointment of Trustees Act 1996 Schedule 1 paragraph 1(2)). An application should be made in Form RX1 for a restriction in Form A, if this is not already on the register. Form A is:

"No disposition by a sole proprietor of the registered estate (except a trust corporation) under which capital money arises is to be registered unless authorised by an order of the court."

Since no evidence of the age of an applicant is required to be produced to the registry, a conveyancer may discover that a person is under the age of eighteen only after he has been registered as one of the proprietors. An application for alteration of the register should be made to remove the minor as proprietor and enter a Form A restriction, if this is not already in the proprietorship register. The applicant should deliver to the registry:
  (a) an application in form AP1;
  (b) a statement by the conveyancer briefly summarising the facts and stating the alteration sought;
  (c) evidence of minority (for example a birth certificate); and
  (d) the fee payable (if any). A fee calculator for all types of application is on the Land Registry's website at www.landregistry.gov.uk/fees.

Charge in Favour of a Minor or to a Minor Jointly with an Adult

After 1996 any purported grant or transfer of a charge to one or more minors (or to one or more minors and one or more adults) operates in the same way as a purported transfer of land (Trusts of Land and Appointment of Trustees Act 1996 section 23(2) and Schedule 1 paragraph 1). Where the grant of a charge is to a minor it cannot be registered, nor, since it is an interest under a trust of land, can a notice be entered in the register, but a Form A restriction should be entered. Where the grant of a charge or transfer of a charge is to a minor and an adult, the charge may be registered showing the adult as proprietor of the charge.

Where a minor has been registered as proprietor inadvertently, an application for alteration of the register should be made on the same lines as explained above in respect of a transfer of land.

Church of England

The Charities Act 1993 does not apply to:
  (a) any corporation sole or corporation aggregate in the Church of England which is established for spiritual purposes in respect of its corporate property;
  (b) a Diocesan Board of Finance (or any subsidiary thereof) in respect of glebe land; or
  (c) any trust of property for purposes for which the property has been consecrated

(Charities Act 1993 section 96(2)).

Where a corporation aggregate in the Church of England has some purposes which are ecclesiastical and some which are not, the Charities Act 1993 applies in respect of its corporate property held for non-ecclesiastical purposes. For example, where land is vested in the incumbent and churchwardens of a parish for the purposes of an educational trust, the Charities Act 1993 applies. Equally, where an ecclesiastical corporation such as a bishop is an *ex officio* trustee of a charity, the trust property is not corporate property of the ecclesiastical corporation and the Charities Act 1993 applies. The Central Board of Finance of the Church of England and the Church of England Pensions Board are charities to which the Charities Act 1993 applies. That Act also applies where land which is not glebe land is vested in a Diocesan Board of Finance and where a diocesan authority is holding land on behalf of a parochial church council. For the position where the Charities Act 1993 applies, see *Charities*, page 69.

Where a corporation or body of trustees holding on charitable, ecclesiastical or public trusts applies to be registered as proprietor of a registered estate or registered charge, the application must be accompanied by the document creating the trust or a certified copy of it (Land Registration Rules 2003 ("LRR 2003") rule 182(1)). It may be necessary to enter a restriction to reflect any limitations on the power of disposition contained in that trust document. This requirement in LRR 2003 rule 182(1) does not apply in the case of an estate or a charge held by or in trust for a non-exempt charity (LRR 2003 rule 182(4)).

Incumbent of a Benefice

The incumbent of a benefice usually has the parsonage house and grounds,

the church and churchyard vested in him. Prior to 13 October 2003 an inhibition was entered in the proprietorship register when the incumbent was registered (Land Registration Rules 1925 rule 232). The inhibition was:
> "No disposition of the land shall be registered except on production of a certificate from the Church Commissioners in accordance with section 99 of the Land Registration Act 1925."

The Land Registration Act 2002 ("LRA 2002") applies to inhibitions entered under the Land Registration Act 1925 as it applies to restrictions entered under LRA 2002 Schedule 12 paragraph 2(2)).

The certificate required should be in the following form, endorsed on the deed and signed by or on behalf of the Church Commissioners:
> "(*Date*) This is to certify that the within-written [transfer] [charge] [*other deed as appropriate*] is made under the provisions of [*state the statute or other authority under which it is made*] and is authorised thereby, and may be registered."

The same certificate is required if it is the bishop selling land vested in the incumbent during a vacancy in the benefice.

Where an incumbent applies for registration as proprietor under LRA 2002 he should also apply in form RX1 for a restriction in Form D. The application may alternatively be set out in the additional provisions panel of Form TP1, TP2, TP3, TR1, TR2, TR3, TR4, TR5, AS1, AS2 or AS3. Form D is:
> "No disposition of the registered estate is to be registered unless made in accordance with [the Parsonages Measure 1938 *(in the case of parsonage land)*] [the New Parishes Measure 1943 *(in the case of church or churchyard land)*] or some other Measure or authority."

On a disposition, a certificate by the Church Commissioners on the same lines as outlined above will meet the requirements of the restriction.

The amendments to the Parsonages Measure 1938 made by the Church of England (Miscellaneous Provisions) Measure 2000 allow certain dispositions of parsonage land to be made without the consent of the Church Commissioners. The sealing by the Parsonages Board of any transfer or conveyance executed under the Parsonages Measure 1938 is conclusive evidence that all the requirements of that measure with respect to the transaction carried out by such transfer or conveyance have been complied with (Parsonages Measure 1938 section 9(2)). Where the Diocesan Board of Finance has been designated for the purposes of the Repair of Benefice Buildings Measure 1972, sealing by that Board has the same effect.

A statement in a document, signed by the secretary or other duly authorised officer of the Church Commissioners, that the Commissioners have consented to the terms of any transaction under the Parsonages Measure 1938 affecting property specified in the document is conclusive evidence that they have consented to those terms (Parsonages Measure 1938 section 9(2A)).

A statement in a document giving effect to any transaction under the Parsonages Measure 1938 that the consent of the Church Commissioners or the Board or both to the terms of the transaction is not required under the Parsonages Measure 1938 section 1(3)(iii) is, if the document is sealed by the seal of the Board or sealed on behalf of the Board or signed on behalf of the Board by a person duly authorised by the Board, conclusive evidence of that fact (Parsonages Measure 1938 section 9(2B)). The Board referred to is the Parsonages Board or (if designated as such under the Repair of Benefice Buildings Measure 1972 section 1(1)) the Diocesan Board of Finance.

Where by virtue of any Act or Measure a transfer to the Church Commissioners has the effect, subject only to being completed by registration, of vesting any registered land either immediately or at a subsequent time in an incumbent (or any other ecclesiastical corporation sole), the application to register the incumbent (or other appropriate corporation sole) must be accompanied by the transfer to the Commissioners and a certificate in Form 4 (LRR 2003 rule 174). The certificate may be given either in the transfer or in a separate document. Form 4, which should be sealed by the Church Commissioners, is:

"(*Date*) This is to certify that [the registered estate] [the registered charge] [that part of the registered estate] comprised in a Transfer [*date and parties*] under the provisions of [*state the statute or Measure*] (if such transfer were a conveyance under such Act or Measure), vests in [the Incumbent of ...] [Bishop of ...] and his successors [immediately] [upon the happening of the following event, namely, the ...]."

The Church Commissioners

The Church Commissioners and any institution which is administered by them are exempt charities. Any disposition of registered land in favour of such a charity which requires to be registered, and any disposition in favour of such a charity which triggers first registration, must contain a statement in the following form (Charities Act 1993 section 37(5) and LRR 2003 rule 179):

"The land transferred (*or as the case may be*) will, as a result of this transfer (*or as the case may be*) be held [by] [in trust for] (*name of charity*), an exempt charity."

This statement should be made in the contract as well as in the document effecting the disposition, but is not required in a mortgage in favour of a charity.

Where the Church Commissioners or an exempt charity administered by them effect a disposition which is not a charge, the following statement must be included in any contract for the sale, lease or other disposition, or in the conveyance, transfer, lease or other instrument effecting such disposition (LRR 2003 rule 180(1)):

"The land transferred (*or as the case may be*) is held by [(*proprietors*) in trust for] (*charity*), an exempt charity."

Where the Church Commissioners (or an exempt charity administered by them) effect a charge, the statement required in the charge is (LRR 2003 rule 180(2)):

"The land charged is held [by] [in trust for] (*charity*), an exempt charity."

The Church Commissioners are regarded as having sufficient interest to apply for the entry of a restriction where they are not the registered proprietor if the restriction is:

- (a) to give effect to any arrangement which is made under any enactment or Measure administered by or relating to the Church Commissioners; or
- (b) to protect any interest in registered land arising under any such arrangement or statute

(LRR 2003 rule 93(g)).

When registered land is transferred to or (subject only to completion by registration) vested in the Church Commissioners, any ecclesiastical corporation, aggregate or sole, or any other person by a scheme of the Church Commissioners, LRR 2003 rule 175 applies. Rule 175 also applies where the land is so transferred or vested by an instrument taking effect on publication in the *London Gazette* made pursuant to any Act or Measure relating to or administered by the Church Commissioners, or any transfer authorised by any such Act or Measure. Rule 175 provides that the application to register the Church Commissioners (or other appropriate party) must be accompanied by a certificate in Form 5 and the transfer (if any). If there is no transfer, a copy of the *London Gazette* publishing the instrument is required in place of the transfer. The certificate may be given either in the transfer or in a separate document. Form 5, which should be sealed by the Church Commissioners, is:

"(*Date*) This is to certify that the [*describe scheme, instrument or conveyance or otherwise as appropriate*] operates to vest [immediately] [on publication in the London Gazette] [*at some subsequent period as the case may be*], the [registered estate] [registered charge] [that part of the registered estate (*include description by reference to a plan or to the register if possible*)] in the [Church Commissioners] [*other corporation or person as appropriate*]."

Am example of where this might apply is a scheme made under the Pastoral Measure 1983.

Cathedrals

The Charities Act 1993 does not apply to land vested in a cathedral as part of its corporate property. Where a corporate body established in accordance with the Cathedrals Measure 1999 section 9(1)(a) is to be registered as proprietor of such land an appropriate restriction is:

"No disposition by the proprietor of the registered estate is to be registered unless made in accordance with the Cathedrals Measure 1999 or some other Measure or authority."

The Chapter has power to acquire and dispose of land on behalf of the Cathedral but this is subject to the need to obtain consents in accordance with the Cathedrals Measure 1999 section 15. The sealing by the Church Commissioners of any document to which the Cathedrals Measure 1999 section 15 relates is conclusive evidence that all the requirements of that section with respect to the transaction to which the document relates have been complied with (Cathedrals Measure 1999 section 15(4)). A statement in a document sealed by the Chapter that the consent to that document of the Church Commissioners is not required under the Cathedrals Measure 1999 is sufficient evidence of that fact (Cathedrals Measure 1999 section 15(5)).

Glebe Land

Since 1 April 1978 glebe land has been vested in the Diocesan Board of Finance of the appropriate diocese (Endowments and Glebe Measure 1976 section 15). The Charities Act 1993 does not apply to glebe land. Dispositions of glebe land by a Diocesan Board of Finance require the consent of the Church Commissioners (Endowments and Glebe Measure 1976 section 20). A statement in a document, signed by the secretary or other duly authorised officer of the Commissioners, that the Commissioners have consented to the terms of any transaction under the Endowments and Glebe Measure 1976 section 20(1) which is specified in the document, is conclusive evidence that such consent has been obtained (Endowments and Glebe Measure 1976 section 20(10)).

The amendments to the Endowments and Glebe Measure 1976 made by the Church of England (Miscellaneous Provisions) Measure 2000 allow certain dispositions of glebe land to be made without the consent of the Church Commissioners. A statement in a document giving effect to a transaction made by a Diocesan Board of Finance (or any subsidiary of the Board) under the Endowments and Glebe Measure 1976 section 20 that all the requirements of that Measure with respect to that transaction have been complied with is, if the document is sealed with the seal of the Board or the subsidiary or is signed on behalf of the Board by a person duly authorised by the Board or the subsidiary to act in its behalf, conclusive evidence of that fact (Endowments and Glebe Measure 1976 section 20(11)).

Where a Diocesan Board of Finance is to be registered as proprietor of glebe land an appropriate form of restriction is:

"No disposition by the proprietor of the registered estate is to be registered unless made in accordance with the Endowments and Glebe Measure 1976 or some other Measure or authority."

When glebe land was vested in a Diocesan Board of Finance under the Endowments and Glebe Measure 1976 section 15, it was vested subject to all such rights in the nature of easements as were necessary for the reasonable enjoyment of any parsonage land belonging to the benefice or any church land and which had been previously exercisable by the incumbent in right of his benefice (Endowments and Glebe Measure 1976 section 15(1)(b)). Such rights became legal easements appurtenant to the parsonage or church land (Endowments and Glebe Measure 1976 section 15(2)). Where title devolved under section 15, the following entry may therefore appear in the charges register:

"The land is subject to such easements as affect the same by virtue of section 15(1)(b) of the Endowments and Glebe Measure 1976."

Classes of Title

Titles to Freehold Estates
There are three classes of title with which a proprietor of a freehold estate may be registered: absolute title, qualified title and possessory title.

Under the Land Registration Act 1925 the court had no jurisdiction to overrule the registrar if he was not prepared to register a title as absolute, or indeed to register it with any class of title (*Dennis v Malcolm* [1934] Ch 244). Similarly there is no provision under the Land Registration Act 2002 ("LRA 2002") for an appeal to either a court or the adjudicator in respect of such a decision of the registrar. Presumably any wrongful action or inaction by the registrar could be the subject of an application for judicial review.

Absolute Title
A person may be registered with absolute title if the registrar is of the opinion that the person's title to the freehold estate is such as a willing buyer could properly be advised by a competent professional adviser to accept (LRA 2002 section 9(2)). In applying LRA 2002 section 9(2), the registrar may disregard the fact that a person's title appears to him to be open to objection if he is of the opinion that the defect will not cause the holding under the title to be disturbed (LRA 2002 section 9(3)).

First registration of a proprietor with absolute title has the following effects:
  (a) the estate is vested in the proprietor together with all interests subsisting for the benefit of the estate (LRA 2002 section 11(3)); and
  (b) the estate is vested in the proprietor subject to the following interests affecting the estate at the time of registration:
    (i) interests which are the subject of an entry in the register in relation to the estate,
    (ii) unregistered interests falling within Schedule 1 to LRA 2002, and
    (iii) interests acquired under the Limitation Act 1980 of which the proprietor has notice

(LRA 2002 section 11(4)).

For details of the types of unregistered interest which fall within Schedule 1 to LRA 2002, see *Overriding Interests*, page 223.

If, on first registration, the proprietor is not entitled to the estate for his own benefit, or not entitled solely for his own benefit, then, as between himself and the persons beneficially entitled to the estate, the estate is vested in him subject to such of their interests as he has notice of (LRA 2002 section 11(5)).

Qualified Title

A person may be registered with qualified title if the registrar is of the opinion that the person's title to the estate has been established for a limited period only, or is subject to certain reservations which cannot be disregarded as defects which will not cause the holding under the title to be disturbed (LRA 2002 section 9(4)). Qualified titles are rarely met with in practice. A qualified title might be given, for example, where the conveyance to the applicant for first registration constituted a breach of trust.

Registration with qualified title has the same effect as registration with absolute title, except that it does not affect the enforcement of any estate, right or interest which appears from the register to be excepted from the effect of registration (LRA 2002 section 11(6)).

It is possible for a qualified title to be upgraded to absolute under LRA 2002 section 62(1), if the registrar is satisfied as to the title to the estate; see *Upgrading Titles*, page 304.

Possessory Title

A person may be registered with possessory title if the registrar is of the opinion:
  (a) that the person is in actual possession of the land, or in receipt of the rents and profits of the land, by virtue of the estate; and
  (b) that there is no other class of title with which he may be registered
(LRA 2002 section 9(5)).

The most common examples of situations where the registrar may register with a possessory title are where the applicant has been in adverse possession for twelve years or more, and where the applicant has lost the deeds and documents to prove his title. For further details as to such applications see *Adverse Possession*, page 8, and *Lost Deeds*, page 201. With regard to applications based on adverse possession, LRA 2002 section 3(2) provides that a person may apply for first registration if the legal estate is vested in him or he is entitled to require the legal estate to be vested in him. Accordingly, if an applicant has not been in adverse possession for the requisite period under the Limitation Act 1980, no class of title can be granted.

Registration with possessory title has the same effect as registration with absolute title, except that it does not affect the enforcement of any estate, right or interest adverse to, or in derogation of, the proprietor's title subsisting at the time of registration or then capable of arising (LRA 2002 section 11(7)).

It is possible for a possessory title to be upgraded to absolute under LRA 2002 section 62(1), if the registrar is satisfied as to the title to the estate; see *Upgrading Titles*, page 304.

Titles to Leasehold Estates
There are four classes of title with which a proprietor of a leasehold estate may be registered: absolute title, good leasehold title, qualified title and possessory title.

Under the Land Registration Act 1925 the court had no jurisdiction to overrule the registrar if he was not prepared to register a title as absolute, or indeed to register it with any class of title (*Dennis v Malcolm* [1934] Ch 244). Similarly there is no provision under LRA 2002 for an appeal to either a court or the adjudicator in respect of such a decision of the registrar. Presumably any wrongful action or inaction on the part of the registrar could be the subject of an application for judicial review.

Absolute Title
A person may be registered with absolute title if the registrar is of the opinion that the person's title to the leasehold estate is such as a willing buyer could properly be advised by a competent professional adviser to accept and the registrar approves the lessor's title to grant the lease (LRA 2002 section 10(2)). In applying LRA 2002 section 10(2), the registrar may disregard the fact that a person's title appears to him to be open to objection if he is of the opinion that the defect will not cause the holding under the title to be disturbed (LRA 2002 section 10(4)).

First registration of a proprietor with absolute title has the following effects:
(a) the estate is vested in the proprietor together with all interests subsisting for the benefit of the estate (LRA 2002 section 12(3)); and
(b) the estate is vested subject only to the following interests affecting the estate at the time of registration:
   (i) implied and express covenants, obligations and liabilities incident to the estate,
   (ii) interests which are the subject of an entry in the register in relation to the estate,
   (iii) unregistered interests falling within Schedule 1 to LRA 2002, and
   (iv) interests acquired under the Limitation Act 1980 of which the proprietor has notice (LRA 2002 section 12(4)).
For details of the types of unregistered interest which fall within Schedule 1 to LRA 2002, see *Overriding Interests*, page 223.

If, on first registration, the proprietor is not entitled to the estate for his own benefit, or not entitled solely for his own benefit, then, as between himself and the persons beneficially entitled to the estate, the estate is vested in him subject to such of their interests as he has notice of (LRA 2002 section 12(5)).

Good Leasehold Title
A person may be registered with good leasehold title if the registrar is of the opinion that the person's title to the leasehold estate is such as a willing buyer could properly be advised by a competent professional adviser to accept (LRA 2002 section 10(3)). In applying section 10(3), the registrar may disregard the fact that a person's title appears to him to be open to objection if he is of the opinion that the defect will not cause the holding under the title to be disturbed (LRA 2002 section 10(4)).

Registration with good leasehold title has the same effect as registration with absolute title, except that it does not affect the enforcement of any estate, right or interest affecting, or in derogation of, the title of the lessor to grant the lease (LRA 2002 section 12(6)).

It is possible for a good leasehold title to be upgraded to absolute under LRA 2002 section 62(2), if the registrar is satisfied as to the superior title; see *Upgrading Titles*, page 304.

Qualified Title
A person may be registered with qualified title if the registrar is of the opinion that the person's title to the estate, or the lessor's title to the reversion, has been established only for a limited period or subject to certain reservations which cannot be disregarded as defects which will not cause the holding under the title to be disturbed (LRA 2002 section 10(5)). Qualified titles are rarely met with in practice. A qualified title might be given, for example, where the assignment to the applicant for first registration constituted a breach of trust.

Registration with qualified title has the same effect as registration with absolute title, except that it does not affect the enforcement of any estate, right or interest which appears from the register to be excepted from the effect of registration (LRA 2002 section 12(7)).

It is possible for a qualified title to be upgraded to good leasehold under LRA 2002 section 62(3), if the registrar is satisfied as to the title to the estate; and to absolute if he is satisfied both as to the title to the estate and as to the superior title; see *Upgrading Titles*, page 304.

Possessory Title
A person may be registered with possessory title if the registrar is of the opinion:
   (a) that the person is in actual possession of the land, or in receipt of the rents and profits of the land, by virtue of the estate; and
   (b) that there is no other class of title with which he may be registered (LRA 2002 section 10(6)).

The most common examples of situations where the registrar may register with a possessory title are where the applicant has been in adverse possession for twelve years or more, and where the applicant has lost the deeds and documents to prove his title. For further details as to such applications see *Adverse Possession*, page 8, and *Lost Deeds*, page 201. With regard to applications based on adverse possession, LRA 2002 section 3(2) provides that a person may apply for first registration if the legal estate is vested in him or he is entitled to require the legal estate to be vested in him. Accordingly, if an applicant has not been in adverse possession for the requisite period under the Limitation Act 1980, no class of title can be granted.

The House of Lords, in *Fairweather v St Marylebone Property Co Ltd* [1963] AC 510, [1962] 2 WLR 1020, [1962] 2 All ER 288, held that when the title to a leasehold estate is unregistered and the lessee has been ousted by a squatter for the full period of limitation, the lessee may still surrender to the lessor, who can then take action to recover possession from the squatter. This should be taken into consideration where a squatter is seeking a possessory title of a leasehold estate.

Registration with possessory title has the same effect as registration with absolute title, except that it does not affect the enforcement of any estate, right or interest adverse to, or in derogation of, the proprietor's title subsisting at the time of registration or then capable of arising (LRA 2002 section 12(8)).

It is possible for a possessory title to be upgraded to good leasehold under LRA 2002 section 62(3), if the registrar is satisfied as to the title to the estate; and to absolute if he is satisfied both as to the title to the estate and as to the superior title; see *Upgrading Titles*, page 304.

Coal

An interest in any coal or coal mine, the rights attached to any such interest and the rights of any person under the Coal Industry Act 1994 section 38, 49 or 51 are unregistered interests which override both first registration and registered dispositions (Land Registration Act 2002 ("LRA 2002") Schedule 1 paragraph 7 and Schedule 3 paragraph 7). Such interests are therefore protected without any entry on the register. Section 38 deals with rights to withdraw support after the service of notices, section 49 with rights to work coal in land that was formerly copyhold land after the service of notices, and section 51 with rights attaching to underground land.

These interests were similarly overriding interests under the Land Registration Act 1925 section 70 as amended by the Coal Industry Act 1994 Schedule 9.

It is not possible to enter a notice in the register in respect of an interest in any coal or coal mine, the rights attached to any such interest and the rights of any person under the Coal Industry Act 1994 section 38, 49 or 51 (LRA 2002 section 33). It was similarly not possible to register or lodge any notice or caution relating to such interests under the Land Registration Act 1925.

Collective Enfranchisement

The Leasehold Reform, Housing and Urban Development Act 1993 ("LRHUDA 1993"), as amended by the Commonhold and Leasehold Reform Act 2002, confers on qualifying tenants of flats the right to have the freehold of the building containing the flats acquired on their behalf by their nominee. When the Commonhold and Leasehold Reform Act 2002 section 121 comes into force, the nominee will have to be an RTE company for the purposes of that Act.

Notice under LRHUDA 1993 Section 13
Any right of a tenant arising from a notice under LRHUDA 1993 section 13 claiming to exercise the right of collective enfranchisement is not capable of being an overriding interest within the Land Registration Act 2002 ("LRA 2002") Schedule 1 paragraph 2 or Schedule 3 paragraph 2 (LRHUDA 1993 section 97(1)). It may be the subject of a notice as if it were an estate contract. Where the registered proprietor of the freehold estate is prepared to consent to the entry of a notice on his title, application may be made for the entry of an agreed notice. Where the registered proprietor does not consent, an application for entry of a unilateral notice may still be made.

Agreed Notice
An applicant should deliver to the registry:
   (a) an application in form AN1;
   (b) a certified copy of the notice under LRHUDA 1993 section 13;
   (c) the consent of the registered proprietor of the land where this is not contained in form AN1; and
   (d) the fee payable. A fee calculator for all types of application is on the Land Registry's website at www.landregistry.gov.uk/fees.
The entry made in the register will give details of the interest protected.

Unilateral Notice
An applicant should deliver to the registry:
   (a) an application in form UN1;
   (b) a plan of the affected land (where the notice under LRHUDA 1993 section 13 affects part only of the land in the registered title); and

(c) the fee payable. A fee calculator for all types of application is on the Land Registry's website at www.landregistry.gov.uk/fees.

Form UN1 should be completed on the following lines to show the interest of the applicant:

"[nominee] [RTE company], notice of collective enfranchisement under section 13 of the Leasehold Reform, Housing and Urban Development Act 1993 having been given on [*date*] to [*name and address of the landlord*]."

The unilateral notice will give brief details of the interest protected and identify the beneficiary of that notice.

Application for Vesting Order under LRHUDA 1993 Section 26(1)

If the qualifying tenants wish to exercise their right to collective enfranchisement but the landlord cannot be found or his identity cannot be ascertained, the court may make a vesting order (LRHUDA 1993 section 26(1)). An application for such a vesting order is treated as a pending land action (LRHUDA 1993 section 97(2)(b)) and cannot therefore be an overriding interest within LRA 2002 Schedule 1 paragraph 2 or Schedule 3 paragraph 2 (LRA 2002 section 87(3)). Such an application may be protected by a notice, a restriction, or both.

Notice

The applicants for an agreed notice should deliver to the registry:

(a) an application in form AN1;
(b) the application to the court for the vesting order; and
(c) the fee payable. A fee calculator for all types of application is on the Land Registry's website at www.landregistry.gov.uk/fees.

This is likely to be sufficient to satisfy the registrar as to the validity of the applicants' claim in accordance with LRA 2002 section 34(3)(c). Where the applicants wish to apply for a unilateral notice they should deliver to the registry:

(a) an application in form UN1;
(b) a plan of the affected land (where the vesting order is sought in respect of part only of the land in the registered title); and
(c) the fee payable. A fee calculator for all types of application is on the Land Registry's website at www.landregistry.gov.uk/fees.

Form UN1 should be completed on the following lines to show the interest of the applicants:

"qualifying tenants in an application under section 26(1) of the Leasehold Reform, Housing and Urban Development Act 1993 in the [… County Court] [… Division of the High Court of Justice] [*state full court reference and parties*]."

The unilateral notice will give brief details of the interest protected and identify the beneficiaries of that notice.

Restriction

The applicants for a vesting order under the LRHUDA 1993 section 26(1) may be treated as having a right or claim in relation to a registered estate or charge for the purposes of LRA 2002 section 42(1)(c) if they are applying for a restriction in Form N (Land Registration Rules 2003 ("LRR 2003") rule 93(q)). The registrar must give notice of the application for a restriction to the proprietor of the registered estate or charge concerned (LRA 2002 section 42(3)).

A restriction does not confer any priority; it simply prevents an entry being made in the register if it is not permitted under the wording of the restriction.

The applicants should deliver to the registry:
  (a) an application in form RX1; and
  (b) the fee payable. A fee calculator for all types of application is on the Land Registry's website at www.landregistry.gov.uk/fees.

Panel 10 should be completed as to the appropriate restriction. Form N is:

"No disposition [*or specify details*] of the registered estate [(other than a charge)] by the proprietor of the registered estate [or by the proprietor of any registered charge] is to be registered without a written consent signed by [*name*] of [*address*] (or [his conveyancer] [*or specify appropriate details, for example* signed on behalf of [*name*] of [*address*] by its secretary or conveyancer])."

Vesting Order under LRHUDA 1993 Section 26(1)

Where the court makes a vesting order under LRHUDA 1993 section 26(1), LRA 2002 applies in relation to that order as it applies in relation to an order affecting land which is made by the court for the purpose of enforcing a judgment or recognisance (LRHUDA 1993 section 97(2)(a)). Such a vesting order cannot be an overriding interest within LRA 2002 Schedule 1 paragraph 2 or Schedule 3 paragraph 2 (LRA 2002 section 87(3)), but it may be protected by a notice, a restriction, or both.

(a) Notice

The applicants for an agreed notice should deliver to the registry:
  (a) an application in form AN1;
  (b) the vesting order or a certified copy of it; and
  (c) the fee payable. A fee calculator for all types of application is on the Land Registry's website at www.landregistry.gov.uk/fees.

The entry made in the register will give details of the interest protected.

The applicants for a unilateral notice should deliver to the registry:
  (a) an application in form UN1;
  (b) a plan of the affected land (where the vesting order is sought in respect of part only of the land in the registered title); and
  (c) the fee payable. A fee calculator for all types of application is on the

Land Registry's website at www.landregistry.gov.uk/fees.
Form UN1 should be completed on the following lines to show the interest of the applicants:

"[qualifying tenants] [nominee] [RTE company] having the benefit of an order under section 26(1) of the Leasehold Reform, Housing and Urban Development Act 1993 made by the [... County Court] [... Division of the High Court of Justice] [*state full court reference and parties*]."

The unilateral notice will give brief details of the interest protected and identify the beneficiaries of that notice.

(b) Restriction

A person who has obtained a vesting order under LRHUDA 1993 section 26(1) may be treated as having a right or claim in relation to a registered estate or charge for the purposes of LRA 2002 section 42(1)(c) if he is applying for a restriction in Form L or Form N (LRR 2003 rule 93(p)). The registrar must give notice of the application for a restriction to the proprietor of the registered estate or charge concerned (LRA 2002 section 42(3)).

A restriction does not confer any priority; it simply prevents an entry being made in the register if it is not permitted under the wording of the restriction.

The applicants should deliver to the registry:
(a) an application in form RX1; and
(b) the fee payable. A fee calculator for all types of application is on the Land Registry's website at www.landregistry.gov.uk/fees.

Panel 10 should be completed as to the appropriate restriction. Form L is:

"No disposition [*or specify details*] of the registered estate [(other than a charge)] by the proprietor of the registered estate [or by the proprietor of any registered charge] is to be registered without a certificate signed by [*name*] of [*address*] (*or* [his conveyancer] [*or specify appropriate details, for example* signed on behalf of [*name*] of [*address*] by its secretary or conveyancer]) that the provisions of [*specify clause, paragraph or other particulars*] of [*specify details*] have been complied with."

Form N is:

"No disposition [*or specify details*] of the registered estate [(other than a charge)] by the proprietor of the registered estate [or by the proprietor of any registered charge] is to be registered without a written consent signed by [*name*] of [*address*] (or [his conveyancer] [*or specify appropriate details, for example* signed on behalf of [*name*] of [*address*] by its secretary or conveyancer])."

Vesting Order under LRHUDA 1993 Section 24(4) or 25(6)

Although there is no provision in LRHUDA 1993 relating to the protection of vesting orders under section 24(4) or 25(6), such orders may be protected in a manner similar to that relating to vesting orders under section 26(1).

Transfer or Conveyance to RTE Company

Once the nominee or RTE company has taken a transfer or conveyance of the freehold estate, an application for registration should be made in the normal way: see *Transfers,* page 298, or *First Registration,* page 133, as appropriate. Where the acquisition is made under the provisions of the LRHUDA 1993, the transfer or conveyance must contain a statement in the following terms (LRHUDA 1993 section 34(10) and LRR 2003 rule 196(1)):

"This [conveyance] [transfer] is executed for the purposes of Chapter 1 of Part 1 of the Leasehold Reform, Housing and Urban Development Act 1993."

Where the court has made a vesting order under LRHUDA 1993 section 24(4), 25(6) or 26(1), a certified copy of the order should accompany the application for registration.

Unless there is a contrary agreement, the transfer or conveyance is effective to discharge the property from any mortgage and from the operation of any order made by a court for the enforcement of the mortgage, and to extinguish any term of years created for the purpose of the mortgage (LRHUDA 1993 section 35).

Vendor's Lien

The vendor's lien for the price payable extends to amounts which, at the time of the transfer or conveyance, are due to him from his tenants in respect of their leases or any collateral agreements. The lien also extends to sums payable to the vendor under LRHUDA 1993 section 18(2) (increases in the price where the nominee or RTE company has not disclosed the existence of agreements in accordance with section 18(1)) and to any costs of the enfranchisement payable to him under LRHUDA 1993 section 33 (LRHUDA 1993 section 32(2)).

For the protection of a vendor's lien by an agreed notice see *Vendor's Lien,* page 307. Since the items referred to in the last paragraph (other than the price payable) do not arise under the contract, it would seem that the vendor could apply for a notice in respect of the lien in respect of those items after the transfer had been completed. In that case the vendor could apply for a unilateral notice rather than an agreed notice. If applying for a unilateral notice the vendor should deliver to the registry:

(a) an application in form UN1; and
(b) the fee payable. A fee calculator for all types of application is on the Land Registry's website at www.landregistry.gov.uk/fees.

Form UN1 should be completed on the following lines to show the interest of the applicant:

"having the benefit of a vendor's lien in respect of sums falling within section 32(2)[*(a) (b) or (c) as appropriate*] of the Leasehold Reform, Housing and Urban Development Act 1993 following a Transfer dated ... made between [*parties*]."

The unilateral notice will give brief details of the interest protected and identify the beneficiary of that notice.

Lease Back by Nominee or RTE Company

Under certain circumstances, set out in Schedule 9 to LRHUDA 1993, the nominee or RTE company is required to grant a lease back to the person from whom the freehold has been acquired (LRHUDA 1993 section 36). For example, a lease back is required where the former freeholder was the immediate landlord of a tenant of a flat let under a secure tenancy. The lease back will be for 999 years at a peppercorn rent (LRHUDA 1993 Schedule 9 paragraph 8), unless the nominee or RTE company and the freeholder have agreed otherwise with the approval of a leasehold valuation tribunal (LRHUDA 1993 Schedule 9 paragraph 4(1)). Such a lease itself requires registration; see *Leases*, page 169.

Application for Acquisition Order under Landlord and Tenant Act 1987 Section 28

An application for an acquisition order under the Landlord and Tenant Act 1987 section 28 is treated as a pending land action (Landlord and Tenant Act 1987 section 28(5)) and cannot therefore be an overriding interest within LRA 2002 Schedule 1 paragraph 2 or Schedule 3 paragraph 2 (LRA 2002 section 87(3)). Such an application may be protected by a notice, a restriction, or both.

Notice

The applicants for an agreed notice should deliver to the registry:
  (a) an application in form AN1;
  (b) the application to the court for the acquisition order; and
  (c) the fee payable. A fee calculator for all types of application is on the Land Registry's website at www.landregistry.gov.uk/fees.

This is likely to be sufficient to satisfy the registrar as to the validity of the applicants' claim in accordance with LRA 2002 section 34(3)(c). Where the applicants wish to apply for a unilateral notice they should deliver to the registry:
  (a) an application in form UN1;
  (b) a plan of the affected land (where the acquisition order is sought only in respect of part of the land in the registered title); and
  (c) the fee payable. A fee calculator for all types of application is on the Land Registry's website at www.landregistry.gov.uk/fees.

Form UN1 should be completed on the following lines to show the interest of the applicant:

"qualifying tenants in an application under section 28 of the Landlord and Tenant Act 1987 in the ... Court [*state full court reference and parties*]."

The unilateral notice will give brief details of the interest protected and

Collective Enfranchisement

identify the beneficiaries of that notice.

Restriction

The applicants for an acquisition order under the Landlord and Tenant Act 1987 section 28 may be treated as having a right or claim in relation to a registered estate or charge for the purposes of LRA 2002 section 42(1)(c) if they are applying for a restriction in Form N (LRR 2003 rule 93(o)). The registrar must give notice of the application for a restriction to the proprietor of the registered estate or charge concerned (LRA 2002 section 42(3)).

A restriction does not confer any priority; it simply prevents an entry being made in the register if it is not permitted under the wording of the restriction.

The applicants should deliver to the registry:
(a) an application in form RX1; and
(b) the fee payable. A fee calculator for all types of application is on the Land Registry's website at www.landregistry.gov.uk/fees.

Panel 10 should be completed as to the appropriate restriction. Form N is: "No disposition [*or specify details*] of the registered estate [(other than a charge)] by the proprietor of the registered estate [or by the proprietor of any registered charge] is to be registered without a written consent signed by [*name*] of [*address*] (or [his conveyancer] [*or specify appropriate details, for example* signed on behalf of [*name*] of [*address*] by its secretary or conveyancer])."

Acquisition Order under Landlord and Tenant Act 1987 Section 28

Where the court makes an acquisition order under the Landlord and Tenant Act 1987 section 28, LRA 2002 applies in relation to that order as it applies in relation to an order affecting land which is made by the court for the purpose of enforcing a judgment or recognisance (Landlord and Tenant Act 1987 section 30(6)). Such an order cannot be an overriding interest within LRA 2002 Schedule 1 paragraph 2 or Schedule 3 paragraph 2 (LRA 2002 section 87(3)), but it may be protected by a notice, a restriction, or both.

Notice

The applicants for an agreed notice should deliver to the registry:
(a) an application in form AN1;
(b) the acquisition order or a certified copy of it; and
(c) the fee payable. A fee calculator for all types of application is on the Land Registry's website at www.landregistry.gov.uk/fee

The entry made in the register will give details of the interest protected.

The applicants for a unilateral notice should deliver to the registry:
(a) an application in form UN1;
(b) a plan of the affected land (where the acquisition order is sought only in respect of part of the land in the registered title); and
(c) the fee payable. A fee calculator for all types of application is on the

Land Registry's website at www.landregistry.gov.uk/fees.

Form UN1 should be completed on the following lines to show the interest of the applicant:

"qualifying tenants having the benefit of an acquisition order under section 28 of the Landlord and Tenant Act 1987 made by the ... Court [*state full court reference and parties*]."

The unilateral notice will give brief details of the interest protected and identify the beneficiaries of that notice.

Restriction

A person who has obtained an acquisition order under the Landlord and Tenant Act 1987 section 28 may be treated as having a right or claim in relation to a registered estate or charge for the purposes of LRA 2002 section 42(1)(c) if he is applying for a restriction in Form L or Form N (LRR 2003 rule 93(n)). The registrar must give notice of the application for a restriction to the proprietor of the registered estate or charge concerned (LRA 2002 section 42(3)).

A restriction does not confer any priority; it simply prevents an entry being made in the register if it is not permitted under the wording of the restriction.

The applicants should deliver to the registry:

(a) an application in form RX1; and
(b) the fee payable. A fee calculator for all types of application is on the Land Registry's website at www.landregistry.gov.uk/fees.

Panel 10 should be completed as to the appropriate restriction. Form L is:

"No disposition [*or specify details*] of the registered estate [(other than a charge)] by the proprietor of the registered estate [or by the proprietor of any registered charge] is to be registered without a certificate signed by [*name*] of [*address*] (*or* [his conveyancer] [*or specify appropriate details, for example* signed on behalf of [*name*] of [*address*] by its secretary or conveyancer]) that the provisions of [*specify clause, paragraph or other particulars*] of [*specify details*] have been complied with."

Form N is:

"No disposition [*or specify details*] of the registered estate [(other than a charge)] by the proprietor of the registered estate [or by the proprietor of any registered charge] is to be registered without a written consent signed by [*name*] of [*address*] (*or* [his conveyancer] [*or specify appropriate details, for example* signed on behalf of [*name*] of [*address*] by its secretary or conveyancer])."

Commons

As a result of the Commons Registration Act 1965, all common land in England and Wales was required to be registered with the appropriate council specified in that Act during a period expiring on 31 July 1970. After that date no land capable of being registered under the Commons Registration Act 1965 is deemed to be common land unless so registered. Common land is defined in that Act as land subject to rights of common and waste land of a manor not subject to rights of common.

Registration under the Commons Registration Act 1965 was of land which is common land, the rights of common over that land, and of the persons claiming to be or found to be owners of that land. No person was to be registered as owner of any land already registered at the Land Registry. Once the ownership had been registered under the 1965 Act, the land was subject to compulsory registration at the Land Registry on sale, even in areas which at that time were not compulsory areas. The application had to be made within two months of the sale. Where this requirement has been overlooked, an application may be made to the registrar for an order under the Land Registration Act 2002 ("LRA 2002") section 6(5) extending the period for registration. The application may be made by letter and should explain the reasons why the period for registration should be extended. See *Pinekerry Ltd v Needs (Kenneth) Contractors Ltd* (1992) 64 P & CR 245 (CA) (a case referring to the similar section 123 of the Land Registration Act 1925) as to the inability of a purchaser to show a good title to a sub-purchaser when an application for first registration had not been made within two months and no order under section 123 had been made.

Once common land is registered at the Land Registry, the registrar notifies the appropriate council accordingly. The council then deletes the registration of ownership and indicates that the land is registered at the Land Registry.

Rights of common, subject to the exceptions stated below, ceased to exist if they were not registered under the Commons Registration Act 1965. Section 1 of that Act provides that no rights of common over land which is capable of being registered under that Act may be registered in the register of title at the Land Registry. The express grant or reservation of a right which is capable of being registered under the Commons Registration Act 1965 is not required to be completed by registration at the Land Registry (LRA 2002 section 27(2)(d)). No notice may be entered in the register at the Land Registry in respect of any interest which is capable of being registered under the Commons Registration Act 1965 (LRA 2002 section 33(d)). Accordingly it is not possible to register or enter a notice in respect of any right of common at the Land Registry. This applies whether the right is in gross or appurtenant to land (including where an appurtenant right of pasture is severable, as in *Bettison v Langton* [2002] 1 AC 27, [2001] 2 WLR 1605,

[2001] 3 All ER 417 (HL)) and whether the right was registered under the Commons Registration Act 1965 or the Commons Registration (New Land) Regulations 1969.

The Commons Registration Act 1965 section 11 exempts from the effect of that Act the New Forest, Epping Forest and the Forest of Dean and any land exempted by an order of the Minister. Such orders were made in respect of the following areas:

Austenwood Common (Amersham), Brooks Hill Common (Esher), Cassiobury Common (Watford), Cippenham Village Green Common (Slough), Coleshill Common (Amersham), Coulsdon Common (Croydon), Downside Common (Esher), Farthing Down Common (Croydon), Gold Hill Common (Amersham), Gosford Green (Coventry), Greyfriars Green (Coventry), Hearsall Common (Coventry), Hyde Heath (Amersham), Kenley Common (Croydon), Keresley Common (Coventry), Leigh Hill Common (Esher), Ley Hill Common (Amersham), Little Heath Common (Esher), Lower Tilt Common (Esher), Micklegate Stray (York), Mitcham Common (Merton), Old Common (Esher), Otterbourne Hill Common (Hampshire), Oxshott Heath (Esher), Radford Common (Coventry), Riddlesdown Common (Croydon), Shenfield Common (Brentwood), Sowe Common (Coventry), Spring Park (Bromley), Stivichall Common (Coventry), Stoke Commons (Coventry),The Links Common (Whitley Bay), The Stray (Harrogate), Thorpe Green (Egham), Top Green (Coventry), Upper Tilt Common (Esher), Victoria Gardens (Portland), West End Road Recreation Ground (Southampton), West Wickham Common (Bromley), and Whitley Common (Coventry).

A right of common is usually a *profit a prendre*, but land affected by cattlegates is sometimes vested in the cattlegate owners as tenants in common (*R v Whixley Inhabitants* (1786) 1 Term Rep 137). Where a *profit* affects land exempted from the Commons Registration Act 1965, it should be dealt with in the usual way; see *Profits a prendre*, page 242.

The Common Land (Rectification of Registers) Act 1989 made provision for removal from the register of common land, on application by the owner, of dwellinghouses and land ancillary to dwellinghouses. Any such application had to be made by 22 July 1992. A copy of any order made under that Act should be lodged with any application for first registration of the land in question.

First Registration of Common Land
An applicant should deliver to the registry:
  (a) an application in form FR1;
  (b) sufficient details, by plan or otherwise, so that the land can be clearly identified on the Ordnance Survey map;
  (c) all deeds and documents relating to the title that are in the control of the applicant;

(d) a copy of the entries in the commons register;
(e) a list in duplicate in form DL of all the documents delivered;
(f) form DI giving the information as to overriding interests required by the Land Registration Rules 2003 ("LRR 2003") rule 28; and
(g) the fee payable. A fee calculator for all types of application is on the Land Registry's website at www.landregistry.gov.uk/fees.

Rule 28 of LRR 2003 provides that a person applying for first registration must provide information to the registrar in form DI about any of the overriding interests (other than local land charges or public rights) set out in Schedule 1 to LRA 2002 that affect the estate to which the application relates and are within the actual knowledge of the applicant, but are not apparent from the deeds and documents accompanying the application. The registrar may enter a notice in the register in respect of any such interest.

The applicant is not required, however, to provide information about interests that, under section 33 or 90(4) of LRA 2002, cannot be protected by notice. Such interests are:

(a) interests under a trust of land or under a Settled Land Act 1925 settlement;
(b) a leasehold estate in land granted for three years or less from the date of the grant and which is not required to be registered;
(c) a restrictive covenant between lessor and lessee, so far as relating to the demised premises;
(d) an interest which is capable of being registered under the Commons Registration Act 1965;
(e) an interest in any coal or coal mine, or the rights attached to any such interest, or the rights of any person under the Coal Industry Act 1994 section 38, 49 or 51; and
(f) leases created for public-private partnerships relating to transport in London, within the meaning given by the Greater London Authority Act 1999 section 218.

The applicant is also not required to provide information about a leasehold estate in land which falls within paragraph 1 of Schedule 1 to LRA 2002 but, at the time of the application, has one year or less to run.

In examining the title the registrar has regard to any examination by a conveyancer prior to the application and to the nature of the property. He may make searches and enquiries and give notice to other persons, direct that searches and enquiries be made by the applicant, and advertise the application (LRR 2003 rule 30).

Any discrepancy between the commons registration ownership register and the deeds must be accounted for. Registration as owner under the Commons Registration Act 1965 is not conclusive proof of ownership; a good documentary title must be produced to the Land Registry in the normal way.

Companies

In addition to the material below, reference should be made, as appropriate, to *Administration Orders*, page 4; *Administrative Receivers*, page 6; *Bona Vacantia and Escheat*, page 50; *Debentures*, page 117; *Floating Charges*, page 140; *Liquidators*, page 197 and *Receivers*, page 249.

Companies not Registered under the Companies Acts

Where a company (or other corporation aggregate) which is not registered in England and Wales or Scotland under the Companies Act 1985 (or one of the earlier Companies Acts which it replaced) applies to be registered as proprietor of a registered estate or registered charge, it must lodge evidence of the extent of its powers to hold and sell, mortgage, lease and otherwise deal with land and, in the case of a charge, to lend money on mortgage. The evidence must consist of the charter, statute, rules, memorandum and articles of association or other documents constituting the corporation. The registrar may require further evidence (Land Registration Rules 2003 ("LRR 2003") rule 183(1) and (2)).

If the corporation is a registered social landlord within the meaning of the Housing Act 1996, the application must contain or be accompanied by a certificate to that effect (LRR 2003 rule 183(3)).

If the corporation is an unregistered housing association within the meaning of the Housing Associations Act 1985 and the application relates to grant-aided land as defined in Schedule 1 to that Act, the application must contain or be accompanied by a certificate to that effect (LRR 2003 rule 183(4)).

Companies Registered under the Companies Acts

Where an application is made to register a company registered in England and Wales or Scotland under the Companies Act 1985 (or one of the earlier Companies Acts which it replaced) as proprietor of land or a charge, it is not necessary to lodge its memorandum and articles of association. The company's registered number must, however, be stated on the application form (LRR 2003 rule 181(1)), and will appear in the entry of the company as proprietor. The same applies where a company is applying for a caution against first registration.

If the company is a registered social landlord within the meaning of the Housing Act 1996, the application must contain or be accompanied by a certificate to that effect (LRR 2003 rule 181(2)).

If the company is an unregistered housing association within the meaning of the Housing Associations Act 1985 and the application relates to grant-aided land as defined in Schedule 1 to that Act, the application must contain or be accompanied by a certificate to that effect (LRR 2003 rule 181(3)).

Registration of Charge Created by a Company

Where an application is made to register a charge created by a company, the applicant must produce to the registrar a certificate issued under the Companies Act 1985 section 401 that the charge has been registered under section 395 of that Act (LRR 2003 rule 111(1)). If the company is registered in Scotland, the certificate required is a certificate issued under section 418 of the Act that the charge has been registered under section 410 of that Act. If the company is registered in Northern Ireland the certificate required is a certificate issued under the Companies (N.I.) Order 1986 article 409 that the charge has been registered under article 403 of that Order.

If the applicant does not produce the appropriate certificate, the registrar is required to enter a note in the register that the charge is subject to the provisions of the Companies Act 1985 section 395 (or section 410 of that Act for a Scottish company or article 403 of the Companies (N.I.) Order 1986 for a Northern Ireland company) (LRR 2003 rule 111(2)). Those provisions provide that where the prescribed particulars of the charge are not delivered to the Registrar of Companies within the prescribed period, the charge is void against the liquidator or administrator of the company and any creditor of the company.

Execution of Deeds by Companies

Where a deed is to be executed by a company registered under the Companies Acts, or an unregistered company, using its common seal, the form of execution set out in Schedule 9 to LRR 2003 is:

The common seal of (*name of company*)
was affixed in the presence of:
....
               Signature of director   [company seal of company]
....
               Signature of secretary

This form of execution is also suitable for a company incorporated outside Great Britain which has a common seal, with such adaptations as may be necessary.

Where a deed is to be executed by a company registered under the Companies Acts, or an unregistered company, without using a common seal, the form of execution set out in Schedule 9 to LRR 2003 is:

Signed as a deed by (*name of company*)   *Signature*
                                                                         Director
acting by [a director and its secretary]   *Signatures*
[two directors]   [Secretary] [Director]

Where the deed is to be executed on behalf of a company incorporated outside Great Britain without using a common seal, the form of execution set out in Schedule 9 to LRR 2003 is:

Signed as a deed on behalf of (*name of company*), a company incorporated in (*territory*), by (*full name(s) of person(s) signing*), being [a] person[s] who, in accordance with the laws of that territory, [is] [are] acting under the authority of the company

Signature(s)

Authorised signatory/ies

Compulsory Purchase

Where a public body is acquiring land under compulsory purchase powers it may still be able to come to an agreement with the proprietor and take a transfer in the usual way. If the owner of the land cannot be found, or will not co-operate, the compulsory purchase may be effected by way of deed poll or general vesting declaration.

Deed Poll
Where an owner refuses to accept the compensation, or does not show a good title, or refuses to convey or release the land, the acquiring authority may execute a deed poll to vest the land in itself (Compulsory Purchase Act 1965 section 9). The acquiring authority pays the compensation into court for the benefit of the owners.

The deed poll must contain a description of the land in respect of which the payment into court was made, and declare the circumstances under which, and the names of the parties to whose credit, the payment into court was made (Compulsory Purchase Act 1965 section 9(3)).

The effect of the deed poll is to vest absolutely in the acquiring authority all the estate and interest in the land of the parties for whose use the compensation was paid into court (Compulsory Purchase Act 1965 section 9(4)).

Where, in the case of a registered title, the recitals in the deed poll show that that the statutory procedures have been followed correctly, this will be sufficient evidence for the purpose of rule 161 of the Land Registration Rules 2003 ("LRR 2003"). The deed poll is a registrable disposition under the Land Registration Act 2002 ("LRA 2002") section 27. The acquiring authority should deliver to the registry:
 (a) an application in form AP1;
 (b) the deed poll;
 (c) form DI giving the information as to overriding interests required by LRR 2003 rule 57, including any documentary evidence of the interest; and
 (d) the fee payable. A fee calculator for all types of application is on the

Land Registry's website at www.landregistry.gov.uk/fees.
A person applying to register a disposition of a registered estate must provide information to the registrar in form DI about any of the overriding interests (other than local land charges or public rights) set out in Schedule 3 to LRA 2002 that affect the estate to which the application relates and are within the actual knowledge of the applicant. For details see *Overriding Interests*, page 223. The applicant must produce to the registrar any documentary evidence of the interest which is in his possession or under his control (LRR 2003 rule 57). The registrar may enter a notice in the register in respect of any such interest.

The applicant is not required, however, to provide information about interests that, under LRA 2002 section 33 or 90(4), cannot be protected by notice. Such interests are:
  (a) interests under a trust of land or under a Settled Land Act 1925 settlement;
  (b) a leasehold estate in land granted for three years or less from the date of the grant and which is not required to be registered;
  (c) a restrictive covenant between lessor and lessee, so far as relating to the demised premises;
  (d) an interest which is capable of being registered under the Commons Registration Act 1965;
  (e) an interest in any coal or coal mine, or the rights attached to any such interest, or the rights of any person under the Coal Industry Act 1994 section 38, 49 or 51; and
  (f) leases created for public-private partnerships relating to transport in London, within the meaning given by the Greater London Authority Act 1999 section 218.

The applicant is also not required to provide information about a leasehold estate in land which falls within paragraph 1 of Schedule 3 to LRA 2002 but, at the time of the application, has one year or less to run.

In the case of unregistered land, the execution of a deed poll attracts compulsory registration. The acquiring authority should deliver to the registry:
  (a) an application in form FR1;
  (b) sufficient details, by plan or otherwise, so that the land can be clearly identified on the Ordnance Survey map;
  (c) all deeds and documents relating to the title that are in the control of the applicant;
  (d) a list in duplicate in form DL of all the documents delivered;
  (e) form DI giving the information as to overriding interests required by LRR 2003 rule 28; and
  (f) the fee payable. A fee calculator for all types of application is on the Land Registry's website at www.landregistry.gov.uk/fees.

A person applying for first registration must provide information to the registrar in form DI about any of the overriding interests (other than local land charges or public rights) set out in Schedule 1 to LRA 2002 that affect the estate to which the application relates and are within the actual knowledge of the applicant, but are not apparent from the deeds and documents accompanying the application (LRR 2003 rule 28). For details see *Overriding Interests*, page 223. The registrar may enter a notice in the register in respect of any such interest.

The applicant is not required, however, to provide information about interests that, under LRA 2002 section 33 or 90(4), cannot be protected by notice. Such interests are:
- (a) interests under a trust of land or under a Settled Land Act 1925 settlement;
- (b) a leasehold estate in land granted for three years or less from the date of the grant and which is not required to be registered;
- (c) a restrictive covenant between lessor and lessee, so far as relating to the demised premises;
- (d) an interest which is capable of being registered under the Commons Registration Act 1965;
- (e) an interest in any coal or coal mine, or the rights attached to any such interest, or the rights of any person under the Coal Industry Act 1994 section 38, 49 or 51; and
- (f) leases created for public-private partnerships relating to transport in London, within the meaning given by the Greater London Authority Act 1999 section 218.

The applicant is also not required to provide information about a leasehold estate in land which falls within paragraph 1 of Schedule 1 to LRA 2002 but, at the time of the application, has one year or less to run.

General Vesting Declaration

When authorised to acquire land under a compulsory purchase order, an acquiring authority can vest the land in itself by way of a general vesting declaration (Compulsory Purchase (Vesting Declarations) Act 1981 section 1). The acquiring authority must follow the relevant provisions laid down in that Act and in the Compulsory Purchase of Land (Vesting Declarations) Regulations 1990. Where the vesting would result in the severance of an owner's property, he may serve notice of objection to the severance (Compulsory Purchase (Vesting Declarations) Act 1981 section 12).

In the case of a registered title the acquiring authority is not able to apply for an official search with priority using form OS1 or OS2 but may reserve a period of priority by an outline application; see *Outline Applications*, page 222.

In making its application for registration the acquiring authority should deliver to the registry:
- (a) an application in form AP1;

(b) a certified copy of the general vesting declaration (showing the stamp duty impressed on the original) in the form prescribed in Form 1 in the Schedule to the Compulsory Purchase of Land (Vesting Declarations) Regulations 1990, and including a plan if only part of the land in the title is affected;
(c) a certificate by the authority's chief executive officer that the service of notice required by the Compulsory Purchase (Vesting Declarations) Act 1981 section 6 was completed on a specified date;
(d) (where appropriate) confirmation by the chief executive officer that no notice of objection to severance has been served;
(e) form DI giving the information as to overriding interests required by LRR 2003 rule 57, including any documentary evidence of the interest; and
(f) the fee payable. A fee calculator for all types of application is on the Land Registry's website at www.landregistry.gov.uk/fees.

A person applying to register a disposition of a registered estate must provide information to the registrar in form DI about any of the overriding interests (other than local land charges or public rights) set out in Schedule 3 to LRA 2002 that affect the estate to which the application relates and are within the actual knowledge of the applicant. For details see *Overriding Interests*, page 223. The applicant must produce to the registrar any documentary evidence of the interest which is in his possession or under his control (LRR 2003 rule 57). The registrar may enter a notice in the register in respect of any such interest.

The applicant is not required, however, to provide information about interests that, under LRA 2002 section 33 or 90(4), cannot be protected by notice. Such interests are:
(a) interests under a trust of land or under a Settled Land Act 1925 settlement;
(b) a leasehold estate in land granted for three years or less from the date of the grant and which is not required to be registered;
(c) a restrictive covenant between lessor and lessee, so far as relating to the demised premises;
(d) an interest which is capable of being registered under the Commons Registration Act 1965;
(e) an interest in any coal or coal mine, or the rights attached to any such interest, or the rights of any person under the Coal Industry Act 1994 section 38, 49 or 51; and
(f) leases created for public-private partnerships relating to transport in London, within the meaning given by the Greater London Authority Act 1999 section 218.

The applicant is also not required to provide information about a leasehold estate in land which falls within paragraph 1 of Schedule 3 to LRA 2002 but, at the time of the application, has one year or less to run.

In the case of unregistered land, the execution of a general vesting declaration does not attract compulsory registration.

Constructive, Implied and Resulting Trusts

In *Gissing v Gissing* [1971] AC 886, [1970] 3 WLR 255, [1970] 2 All ER 780 (HL), Lord Diplock said:
> "A resulting, implied or constructive trust ... is created by a transaction between the trustee and the *cestui que trust* in connection with the acquisition by the trustee of a legal estate in land, whenever the trustee has so conducted himself that it would be inequitable to allow him to deny to the *cestui que trust* a beneficial interest in the land acquired. And he will be held so to have conducted himself if by his words or conduct he has induced the *cestui que trust* to act to his own detriment in the reasonable belief that by so acting he was acquiring a beneficial interest in the land."

Any implied, resulting or constructive trust which consists of or includes land is a trust of land (Trusts of Land and Appointment of Trustees Act 1996 section 1). The creation of resulting, implied or constructive trusts is not required to be in writing (Law of Property Act 1925 section 53(2) and Law of Property (Miscellaneous Provisions) Act 1989 section 2(5)). The registrar is not, however, affected with notice of a trust (Land Registration Act 2002 ("LRA 2002") section 78).

Where a transferee takes the land expressly subject to a claim or interest which may be void for want of registration, it may be argued that he takes subject to a constructive trust. In *Lloyd v Dugdale* [2001] EWCA Civ 1754, [2001] All ER (D) 306 (Nov), [2002] 2 P&CR 13 (CA), Sir Christopher Slade summarised the principles to be extracted from *Ashburn Anstalt v Arnold* [1989] Ch 1, [1988] 2 WLR 706, [1988] 2 All ER 147 (CA); *Binions v Evans* [1972] Ch 359, [1972] 2 WLR 729, [1972] 2 All ER 70 (CA); *Lyus v Prowsa Developments Ltd* [1982] 1 WLR 1044, [1982] 2 All ER 953; *IDC Group Ltd v Clark* (1993) 65 P & CR 179, [1992] 49 EG 103 (CA); and *Melbury Road Properties 1995 Ltd v Kreidi* [1999] 3 EGLR 108, [1999] 43 EG 157. Those principles are:

(1) Even where the vendor of land has stipulated that the sale shall be subject to stated possible incumbrances or prior interests, there is no general rule that the court will impose a constructive trust on the purchaser to give effect to them.

(2) The court will not impose a constructive trust in such circumstances unless it is satisfied that the conscience of the estate owner is affected so that it would be inequitable to allow him to deny the claimant an interest in the property.

(3) In deciding whether or not the conscience of the new estate owner is

affected in such circumstances, the crucially important question is whether he has undertaken a new obligation, not otherwise existing, to give effect to the relevant incumbrance or prior interest. If, but only if, he has undertaken such a new obligation will a constructive trust be imposed.
(4) A contractual licence is not to be treated as creating a proprietary interest in land so as to bind third parties who acquire the land with notice of it, on this account alone.
(5) Proof that the purchase price paid by a transferee has been reduced on the footing that he would give effect to the relevant incumbrance or prior interest may provide some indication that the transferee has undertaken a new obligation to give effect to it. However, since in relation to title to land certainty is of prime importance, it is not desirable that constructive trusts of land should be imposed in reliance on inferences from "slender materials".

No notice may be entered in the register in respect of any interest under a trust of land (LRA 2002 section 33(a)). Where a constructive, implied or resulting trust has arisen, it may be protected by a restriction. A restriction does not confer any priority; it simply prevents an entry being made in the register if it is not permitted under the wording of the restriction.

An applicant for a restriction should deliver to the registry:
(a) an application in form RX1;
(b) the fee payable. A fee calculator for all types of application is on the Land Registry's website at www.landregistry.gov.uk/fees.

The appropriate restriction is usually Form A, which is:

"No disposition by a sole proprietor of the registered estate (except a trust corporation) under which capital money arises is to be registered unless authorised by an order of the court."

Payment of the capital money on a sale, lease or mortgage of the legal estate to two or more trustees or a trust corporation overreaches the beneficial interests under a trust of land (Law of Property Act 1925 section 27 as amended by the Trusts of Land and Appointment of Trustees Act 1996). This applies equally to a constructive, implied or resulting trust.

Contracts for Sale (including Sub-sale)

A contract for sale of registered land may be protected by the entry in the register of an agreed notice, a unilateral notice and/or by a restriction. A notice does not necessarily mean that the contract is valid but does mean that the priority of the contract will be protected on any registered disposition (Land Registration Act 2002 ("LRA 2002") sections 32, 29 and 30). A restriction does not confer any priority; it simply prevents an entry being made in the register if it is not permitted under the wording of the restriction.

It has been common for practitioners not to protect a contract where completion is expected to follow within a short period of time. It is probable that, when electronic conveyancing comes into being, the entry of an agreed notice of the contract will be a normal step in the process.

LRA 2002 section 72(6)(a) provides that rules may make provision for priority periods in connection with the noting in the register of a contract for the making of a registrable disposition of a registered estate or charge. At October 2003 no such rules have been made.

Agreed Notice
An applicant should deliver to the registry:
   (a) an application in form AN1;
   (b) the contract or a certified copy of it;
   (c) the consent of the registered proprietor of the land where this is not contained in form AN1; and
   (d) the fee payable. A fee calculator for all types of application is on the Land Registry's website at www.landregistry.gov.uk/fees.

Where the contract is in respect of a sub-sale, the earlier contract or a certified copy of it should be included with the application. This is not necessary if there is already a notice of the earlier contract in the register.

The entry made in the register will give details of the interest protected.

Where the registered proprietor does not consent to the entry in the register of an agreed notice, the original agreement signed by the registered proprietor may be sufficient to satisfy the registrar as to the validity of the applicant's claim for the purposes of LRA 2002 section 34(3)(c). In any event an application for entry of a unilateral notice may still be made. A unilateral notice may be preferred where the applicant does not wish the terms of the contract to be open to public scrutiny.

Unilateral Notice
An applicant should deliver to the registry:
   (a) an application in form UN1;
   (b) a plan of the affected land (where the contract affects part only of the land in the registered title); and
   (c) the fee payable. A fee calculator for all types of application is on the Land Registry's website at www.landregistry.gov.uk/fees.

Form UN1 should be completed on the following lines to show the interest of the applicant:
   "purchaser under a contract for sale dated ... made between [*registered proprietor*] and [*purchaser*]."

In the case of a sub-sale both contracts should be shown:
   "purchaser under a contract for sale dated ... made between [*purchaser*]

and [*sub-purchaser*], [*purchaser*] being the purchaser under a contract for sale dated ... made between [*registered proprietor*] and [*purchaser*]."
The wording must establish the link between the registered proprietor and the person who is to be shown as the beneficiary of the notice.

The unilateral notice will give brief details of the interest protected and identify the beneficiary of that notice.

Restriction

As a result of LRA 2002 section 42(2) no restriction may be entered for the purpose of protecting the priority of an interest which is, or could be, the subject of a notice. This does not necessarily prevent a restriction being entered in addition to the notice of the contract. Although the notice will protect the priority of the contract, a restriction may be used to ensure that any conditions in relation to another disposition by the registered proprietor are complied with. The consent of the registered proprietor to the entry of the restriction is required.

An applicant should deliver to the registry:
(a) an application in form RX1;
(b) the consent of the registered proprietor of the land (unless this is given in panel 15 of form RX1 or the applicant's conveyancer certifies that he holds such consent. The certificate may be given in panel 11 of form RX1); and
(c) the fee payable. A fee calculator for all types of application is on the Land Registry's website at www.landregistry.gov.uk/fees.

A possible form of restriction based on Form N in Schedule 4 to LRR 2003 is:

"No disposition of the registered estate by the proprietor of the registered estate is to be registered without a written consent signed by [*purchaser*] of [*address*] or his conveyancer."

A restriction in this form does not require the approval of the registrar under LRA 2002 section 43(3).

Copyhold

Any copyhold land then remaining in existence was enfranchised on 1 January 1926 (Law of Property Act 1922 section 128). Such enfranchisement did not affect any rights of the lord or tenant in any mines and minerals or ancillary rights, or any rights of the lord in respect of fairs, markets or sporting rights (Law of Property Act 1922 12th Schedule). The Copyhold Act 1852 section 48 and the Copyhold Act 1894 section 23 excepted similar rights in respect of enfranchisements made under those

Acts.

Any unregistered manorial rights override first registration or a registered disposition (Land Registration Act 2002 ("LRA 2002") sections 11, 12, 29 and 30). Such rights will cease to have overriding status at the end of ten years from 13 October 2003 (LRA 2002 section 117). Within that period, therefore, such rights should be protected by an application for a caution against first registration where the land is unregistered, or by the entry of a notice where the land is registered. No fee may be charged for the application (LRA 2002 section 117(2)).

Where on first registration the title deduced reveals that the rights of the lord have been preserved under the Law of Property Act 1922 or the earlier Copyhold Acts, a notice to that effect is entered in the property register. The absence of such a notice is not, however, conclusive that the land was not formerly copyhold.

From time to time applications are made to the registry to have the notice cancelled on the grounds that section 128 and the Twelfth Schedule to the Law of Property Act 1922 have been repealed by the Statute Law (Repeals) Act 1969. Such applications are misconceived since the repeal of an enactment does not, unless the contrary intention appears, affect any right, privilege, obligation or liability acquired, accrued or incurred under that enactment (Interpretation Act 1978 section 16). No contrary intention appears in the Statute Law (Repeals) Act 1969.

Caution Against First Registration

A person applying for a caution against first registration should deliver to the registry:

(a) an application in form CT1; and
(b) a plan allowing the extent of the land to which the caution relates to be identified clearly on the Ordnance Survey map, unless this can be clearly identified from the description in panel 2 on form CT1.

Either one of the cautioners, or someone authorised by the cautioners, must make the statutory declaration in panel 9 of form CT1, or the cautioner's conveyancer must complete the certificate in panel 10. In either case no documents should be exhibited.

The interest stated in the form will appear in the property register of the individual caution register, together with a description of the legal estate to which the caution relates. The description of the legal estate will refer to a caution plan based on the Ordnance Survey map.

An example of the certificate in panel 10 would be:

"I certify that the Cautioner is interested in the property described in panel 2 as being entitled to a manorial right affecting that property being [*set out nature of the manorial right*]."

Agreed Notice

An applicant should deliver to the registry:
  (a) an application in form AN1;
  (b) a statement of the nature of the manorial right or (if available) a copy of any document under which the right arises; and
  (c) the consent of the registered proprietor of the land where this is not contained in form AN1.

The entry made in the register will give details of the manorial right protected.

Where the registered proprietor does not consent to the entry in the register of an agreed notice, an application for entry of a unilateral notice may still be made.

Unilateral Notice

An applicant should deliver to the registry:
  (a) an application in form UN1; and
  (b) a plan of the affected land (where the manorial right affects only part of the land in the registered title).

Form UN1 should be completed on the following lines to show the interest of the applicant:

"person having the benefit of a manorial right being [*set out nature of the manorial right*]."

The unilateral notice will give brief details of the manorial right protected and identify the beneficiary of that notice.

Correction of Mistakes in an Application or Accompanying Document

Where an application or an accompanying document contains a mistake, the registrar may, if he thinks fit, make an alteration to correct the mistake. In the case of a mistake of a clerical or like nature, the alteration has effect in all circumstances as if made by the applicant or other interested party or parties. In the case of any other mistake, the alteration has effect as if made by the applicant or other interested party or parties only if the applicant and any other interested party has requested, or consented to, the alteration (Land Registration Rules 2003 rule 130).

If an applicant discovers such a mistake during the course of an application, he should draw it to the attention of the registrar and ask the registrar to correct the mistake.

Costs

Costs Payable by the Registrar
If the register is altered under the Land Registration Act 2002 ("LRA 2002") Schedule 4 in a case not involving rectification, the registrar may pay such amount as he thinks fit in respect of any costs or expenses reasonably incurred by a person in connection with the alteration which have been incurred with the consent of the registrar. Even where the registrar has not consented to the incurring of costs or expenses, he may still make a payment if it appears to him that the costs or expenses had to be incurred urgently and it was not reasonably practicable to apply for his consent. He may also still make a payment if he has subsequently approved the incurring of the costs or expenses. See *Alteration of the Register*, page 26.

Where a person is entitled to be indemnified by the registrar under LRA 2002 Schedule 8, an indemnity under that schedule is payable in respect of loss consisting of costs or expenses incurred by the claimant in relation to the matter only if such costs or expenses are reasonably incurred by the claimant with the consent of the registrar. The requirement for consent does not, however, apply where the costs or expenses must be incurred by the claimant urgently and it is not reasonably practicable to apply for the registrar's consent. If the registrar approves the incurring of costs or expenses after they have been incurred, they are treated as having been incurred with his consent. See *Indemnity*, page 161, as to when a person is entitled to be indemnified by the registrar.

Interest is payable on indemnity for costs or expenses at the applicable rate set for court judgment debts for the period from the date when the claimant pays them to the date of payment (Land Registration Rules 2003 ("LRR 2003") rule 195). In calculating the exact period in respect of which interest is payable, the date when the claimant pays the costs or expenses is excluded, but the date of payment by the registrar is included.

If no indemnity is payable to a claimant under LRA 2002 Schedule 8, the registrar may pay such amount as he thinks fit in respect of any costs or expenses reasonably incurred by the claimant in connection with the claim which have been incurred with the consent of the registrar. Even where the registrar has not consented to the incurring of costs or expenses, he may still make such a payment if it appears to him that the costs or expenses had to be incurred urgently and it was not reasonably practicable to apply for his consent. He may also still make a payment if he has subsequently approved the incurring of the costs or expenses.

In all these cases the consent of the registrar to the incurring of costs or expenses does not mean that he will necessarily pay all, or indeed any, of those costs or expenses.

Where a claim to indemnity for costs under LRA 2002 Schedule 8 cannot be resolved by agreement with the registrar, a person may apply to the High Court or a county court for the determination of any question as to whether he is entitled to such indemnity or as to the amount of the indemnity. The requirement that the registrar consents to the incurring of costs or expenses does not apply to the costs of such an application to the court or of any legal proceedings arising out of such an application.

Costs Payable by a Third Party
Any person who has incurred costs in relation to proceedings before the registrar may request the registrar to make an order requiring a party to those proceedings to pay the whole or part of those costs (LRR 2003 rule 202). The registrar may make such an order only where those costs were occasioned by the unreasonable conduct of the party in question in relation to the proceedings.

This relates to proceedings before the registrar, not to proceedings before the adjudicator.

The request for the payment of costs must be made by delivering to the registrar a written statement by 12 noon on the twentieth business day after the completion of the proceedings to which the request relates. A business day is a day when the Land Registry is open to the public, that is every day except Saturdays, Sundays, Christmas Day, Good Friday or any other day either specified or declared by proclamation under the Banking and Financial Dealings Act 1971 section 1 or appointed by the Lord Chancellor.

The statement must identify the party against whom the order is sought and include an address where notice may be served on that party; state in full the grounds for the request; give an address to which communications may be sent; and be signed by the person making the request or his conveyancer.

The registrar must give notice of the request to the party against whom the order is sought at the address stated and also at any address for service for him stated in a registered title that relates to the proceedings. The notice gives the recipient a period ending at 12 noon on the twentieth business day after the issue of the notice, or such other period as the registrar thinks appropriate, to deliver a written response to the registrar by the method and to the address stated in the notice.

The response must state whether or not the recipient opposes the request; if he does, he must state in full the grounds for that opposition and give an address to which communications may be sent. The response must be signed by the recipient or his conveyancer.

The registrar must determine the matter on the basis of the written request and any response submitted to him; all the circumstances including the conduct of the parties; and the result of any enquiries he considers it necessary to make. He may make an order requiring the party against whom it is made to pay to the requesting party the whole, or such part as the registrar thinks fit, of the costs incurred in the proceedings by the person who made the request. The order may specify the sum to be paid or require the costs to be assessed by the court (if not otherwise agreed), and specify the basis of the assessment to be used by the court.

The registrar must send all parties his written reasons for any such order he makes. Such an order is enforceable as an order of the court (LRA 2002 section 76(4)). A person aggrieved by the order may appeal to a county court, which may make any order which appears appropriate (LRA 2002 section 76(5)).

Credit Unions

A society registered under the Industrial and Provident Societies Act 1965 as a credit union in accordance with the Credit Unions Act 1979 is a body corporate with perpetual succession and a common seal (Industrial and Provident Societies Act 1965 section 3). The name of a credit union includes the words "credit union" or, provided its registered office is in Wales, "undeb credyd".

A credit union may hold, purchase or take on lease in its own name any land for the purpose of conducting its business thereon but for no other purpose; it may sell, exchange, mortgage or lease any such land, and erect, alter or pull down buildings on it (Credit Unions Act 1979 section 12). It can also hold an interest in land as a mortgagee.

In view of the limitations on holding land in the Credit Unions Act 1979 section 12, where an application is made to register a credit union as proprietor of land, the application should be supported by a statement of the purposes for which the land has been acquired. The statement is usually made by the secretary of the credit union or the conveyancer acting for it.

Death of Applicant for Registration

If an applicant dies before an application to the registrar has been completed, the application may be continued by his personal representative (Land Registration Rules 2003 rule 18). The personal representative should lodge a copy of the probate or letters of administration to show that he is the person to whom the applicant's interest has devolved by operation of law and thus entitled to continue the application.

Where the deceased applicant was applying to be registered as proprietor, the personal representative should consider whether to be registered as proprietor himself or whether to deal with the registered estate or registered charge without being registered as proprietor. See *Personal representatives*, page 231.

Debentures

A debenture usually contains one or more charges by way of security by a company. If the debenture does not in fact charge land it cannot be protected at the Land Registry. The charge may be a legal charge, a fixed equitable charge or a floating charge; see *Legal Charges*, page 184; *Equitable Charges*, page 126; and *Floating Charges*, page 140.

Registration of a charge in a debenture at the Land Registry does not remove the need for it to be registered under the Companies Act 1985. Although the Land Registration Act 2002 section 121 allows the Lord Chancellor to make rules about the transmission, by the Land Registry to the Registrar of Companies, of applications for registration of charges under the Companies Act 1985, no such rules have yet been made. The application to the Companies Registry must therefore be made separately.

When making an application for the registration of a charge created by a company registered under the Companies Acts, a limited liability partnership incorporated under the Limited Liability Partnerships Act 2000, or a Northern Ireland company, the applicant must produce to the Land Registry:

(a) a certificate issued under the Companies Act 1985 section 401 that the charge has been registered under section 395 of that Act; or

(b) (where the company is registered in Scotland) a certificate issued under the Companies Act 1985 section 418 that the charge has been registered under section 410 of that Act; or

(c) (where the company is registered in Northern Ireland under the former Northern Ireland Companies Acts or under the Companies (N.I.) Order 1986) a certificate issued under article 409 of the 1986 Order that the charge has been registered under article 403 of that Order.

If the applicant does not produce the relevant certificate with the application for registration of the charge, the registrar must enter a note in the register that the charge is subject to the provisions of the Companies Act 1985 section 395 or section 410, or article 403 of the Companies (N.I.) Order 1986 (as appropriate). Those provisions provide that where the prescribed particulars of the charge are not delivered to the Registrar of Companies within the prescribed period, the charge is void against the liquidator or administrator of the company and any creditor of the company.

The registrar is required to enter such a note only where a legal charge is being registered, not when notice of a charge is being entered in the register.

Deeds of Arrangement

A deed of arrangement may be entered into between a debtor and some, or all, of his creditors, to satisfy their claims partially and so avoid the commencement of bankruptcy proceedings. No notice of a deed of arrangement may be entered in the register (Land Registration Act 2002 ("LRA 2002") section 87(2)).

Usually a deed of arrangement contains a declaration of trust in favour of the trustee of the deed in respect of any registered land of which the debtor is registered proprietor. This may be coupled with an irrevocable power of attorney allowing the trustee to transfer the registered land.

A deed of arrangement is treated as an interest affecting an estate or charge for the purposes of LRA 2002 (LRA 2002 section 87(1)). It cannot, however, be an overriding interest belonging to a person in actual occupation for the purposes of paragraph 2 of Schedule 1 or Schedule 3 to LRA 2002 (LRA 2002 section 87(3)).

The trustee of a deed of arrangement may be treated as a person having a right or claim in relation to a registered estate or charge for the purposes of LRA 2002 section 42(1)(c) if he is applying for a restriction in Form L or Form N (Land Registration Rules 2003 ("LRR 2003") rule 93(t)). The registrar must give notice of such an application to the proprietor of the registered estate or charge concerned (LRA 2002 section 42(3)).

A restriction does not confer any priority; it simply prevents an entry being made in the register if it is not permitted under the wording of the restriction.

Restriction

The trustee should deliver to the registry:
  (a) an application in form RX1; and
  (b) the fee payable. A fee calculator for all types of application is on the Land Registry's website at www.landregistry.gov.uk/fees.

Panel 13 of RX1 should be completed on the following lines:
  "The interest is that specified in rule 93(t) of the Land Registration Rules 2003, the applicant being the trustee under a Deed of Arrangement dated ... made between [*parties*] under the provisions of the Deeds of Arrangement Act 1914."

Panel 10 should be completed as to the appropriate restriction.

Form L is:

"No disposition [*or specify details*] of the registered estate [(other than a charge)] by the proprietor of the registered estate [or by the proprietor of any registered charge] is to be registered without a certificate signed by [*name*] of [*address*] (*or* [his conveyancer] [*or specify appropriate details, for example* signed on behalf of [*name*] of [*address*] by its secretary or conveyancer]) that the provisions of [*specify clause, paragraph or other*

particulars] of [*specify details*] have been complied with."
Form N is:
"No disposition [*or specify details*] of the registered estate [other than a charge] by the proprietor of the registered estate [or by the proprietor of any registered charge] is to be registered without a written consent signed by [*name*] of [*address*] (or [his conveyancer] [*or specify appropriate details, for example* signed on behalf of [*name*] of [*address*] by its secretary or conveyancer])."

Demesne Land

Demesne land held by the Crown is not land held for an estate in fee simple and therefore was not capable of registration under the Land Registration Act 1925. The Land Registration Act 2002 ("LRA 2002") section 79 provides that Her Majesty may grant an estate in fee simple out of demesne land to Herself. Such a grant must be followed by an application for first registration or the grant is to be regarded as not having been made (LRA 2002 section 79(2)).

The period in which the application for first registration must be made is two months beginning with the date of the grant. If, on the application of Her Majesty, the registrar is satisfied that there is a good reason for doing so, he may by order extend the period for registration. If the registrar makes an order extending the period for registration where LRA 2002 section 79(2) has already applied, that application of section 79(2) is treated as not having occurred (LRA 2002 section 79(5)).

Applications for first registration should be made using Form FR1 with such modifications as are appropriate (Land Registration Rules 2003 ("LRR 2003") rule 23(2)). Grants of legal estates in land by the Queen out of demesne land to other parties are normally subject to compulsory registration. See *First registration*, page 133.

None of the requirements with respect to formalities or enrolment contained in any enactment relating to the Duchy of Lancaster or the Duchy of Cornwall now apply to dispositions by a registered proprietor (LRA 2002 section 84). For example, the enrolment provisions in the Duchy of Cornwall Management Act 1863 section 30 no longer applies to dispositions of registered land.

Cautions Against First Registration

For the period of ten years from 13 October 2003, the Queen may lodge a caution against first registration of demesne land as if she held the demesne land for an unregistered estate in fee simple absolute in possession (LRA 2002 section 81 and Schedule 12 paragraph 15(1)). The application must be made using application form CT1 and contain sufficient details, by plan or otherwise, so that the extent of the demesne land to which the caution relates can be identified clearly on the Ordnance Survey map.

Any such caution lodged under LRA 2002 section 15, as applied by section 81 of that Act, will cease to have effect at the end of the period of ten years from 13 October 2003, except in relation to applications for first registration made before the end of that period.

Where the land to which a caution against first registration relates is demesne land, either the Queen or the owner of a legal estate affecting the demesne land may apply for the cancellation of the caution. Where the Queen is applying for cancellation, the application must be made using application form CCT with such modifications as are appropriate.

In other respects cautions against first registration of demesne land operate in the same way as other cautions against first registrations, See *Cautions Against First Registration*, page 59.

Disputes

In general anyone may object to an application to the registrar (Land Registration Act 2002 ("LRA 2002") section 73(1)). In the case of an application for the cancellation of a caution against first registration under LRA 2002 section 18, only the person who lodged the caution in question, or the person for the time being shown as cautioner in the cautioner's register, may object (LRA 2002 section 73(2) and Land Registration Rules 2003 ("LRR 2003") rule 52). In the case of an application for the cancellation of a unilateral notice under LRA 2002 section 36, only the person shown in the register as the beneficiary of the notice in question, or a person entitled to be registered as the beneficiary of that notice, may object (LRA 2002 section 73(3) and LRR 2003 rule 86(7)).

The objector must object to an application by delivering to the registrar a written statement signed by the objector or his conveyancer (LRR 2003 rule 19). The statement must state that the objector objects to the application, state the grounds for the objection and give the full name of the objector and an address to which communications may be sent.

Where an objection is made the registrar gives notice of it to the applicant and may not determine the application until the objection has been disposed of. If, however, the registrar is satisfied that the objection is groundless, he need not give notice of it to the applicant and may determine the application (LRA 2002 section 73(5) and (6)).

If it is not possible to dispose of an objection by agreement, the registrar must refer the matter to the Adjudicator to Her Majesty's Land Registry (LRA 2002 section 73(7)). The registrar prepares a case summary which is sent to the adjudicator when the case is formally referred to him (Land Registration (Referral to the Adjudicator to HM Land Registry) Rules 2003 rule 5). The case summary gives the adjudicator brief details of the case and sufficient information to allow him to make an initial decision as to whether he will hear the case himself.

The adjudicator may, instead of deciding a matter himself, direct a party to the dispute to commence proceedings in court, within a specified period, for the purpose of obtaining the court's decision on the matter (LRA 2002 section 110(1)). A person aggrieved by a decision of the adjudicator may appeal to the High Court (LRA 2002 section 111). A requirement of the adjudicator is enforceable as an order of the court (LRA 2002 section 112).

The case summary prepared by the registrar contains details of the parties and their representatives and details of the application. It is accompanied by copies of any documents referred to. Before sending the case summary to the adjudicator, the registrar must send a copy of it and a list of the accompanying documents to the parties, who may comment on anything in it. The registrar may amend the summary in the light of any comments, but is not required to do so. The case summary does not form part of the pleadings in the proceedings before the adjudicator and does not set out the parties' detailed arguments or deal with their evidence.

Where, in determining a dispute relating to an application under LRA 2002 Schedule 6 paragraph 1 for the registration of a person who has been in adverse possession of registered land, the adjudicator determines that it would be unconscionable because of an equity by estoppel for the registered proprietor to seek to dispossess the applicant, but that the circumstances are not such that the applicant ought to be registered as proprietor, the adjudicator must determine how the equity due to the applicant is to be satisfied. He may for that purpose make any order that the High Court could make in the exercise of its equitable jurisdiction (LRA 2002 section 110(4)).

If, on an appeal to the High Court relating to an application under LRA 2002 Schedule 6 paragraph 1 for the registration of a person who has been in adverse possession of registered land, the court determines that it would be unconscionable because of an equity by estoppel for the registered proprietor to seek to dispossess the applicant, but that the circumstances are not such that the applicant ought to be registered as proprietor, the court must determine how the equity due to the applicant is to be satisfied (LRA 2002 section 111(3)).

The adjudicator may also, on application, make any order which the High Court could make for the rectification or setting aside of a document which:
(a) effects a registrable disposition of a registered estate or registered charge;
(b) effects a disposition in respect of a registered estate or registered charge which may be the subject of a notice in the register;

(c) is a contract to make a disposition falling within (a) or (b) above; or
(d) effects a transfer of an interest which may be the subject of a notice in the register.

The general law about the effect of an order of the High Court for the rectification or setting aside of a document applies to any such order of the adjudicator (LRA 2002 section 108).

Division of Registered Titles

The registrar may open an individual register for part of the registered estate in a registered title and retain the existing register for the remainder. On first registration he may open an individual register for each separate area of land of the proprietor's registered estate as he designates.

The division of a registered title may be as the result of an application by the proprietor of the registered estate and of any registered charge over it, or because the registrar considers it desirable for the keeping of the register of title, or on the registration of a charge of part of the registered title. An application by the proprietor which is not a charge of part should be made in Form AP1. It should be accompanied by a plan identifying the division sought. For the position where the application is for a charge of part, see *Legal Charges*, page 184.

Where the proprietor has not made an application but division is effected because the registrar considers it desirable for the keeping of the register of title, the registrar must notify the proprietor of the registered estate and any registered charge, unless they have agreed to the division. In these circumstances the registrar may make a new edition of any individual register or make entries on any individual register to reflect the division (Land Registration Rules 2003 ("LRR 2003") rule 3(5)).

LRR 2003 rule 70 applies on division where a registered estate in land includes any mines or minerals but there is no note on the register that they are included, and it is appropriate, when describing any of the registered estates created on division, to do so by reference to the land where the mines or minerals are or may be situated. In such circumstances the registrar may make an entry in the property register to the effect that such description is an entry made under LRR 2003 rule 5(a) and is not a note that the registered estate includes the mines or minerals for the purposes of extending the payment of indemnity to such mines or minerals. LRR rule 5(a) provides that the property register must contain a description of the registered estate.

Embankments or Sea or River Walls

A non-statutory right in respect of an embankment or sea or river wall is an unregistered interest which overrides first registration and also overrides registered dispositions (Land Registration Act 2002 ("LRA 2002") sections 11, 12, 29 and 30, Schedule 1 paragraph 13 and Schedule 3 paragraph 13). After the period of ten years beginning on 13 October 2003, the automatic protection as an overriding interest will cease (LRA 2002 section 117(1)). The liability will have arisen by custom, tenure, prescription, grant, or a covenant supported by a rentcharge.

The person having the benefit of the right should protect it on the register before the expiry of the ten year period. If the burdened land is unregistered he should apply for a caution against first registration. If the burdened land is registered he should apply for the entry in the register of a notice. In either case, provided the application is made within the ten year period, no fee is payable.

Caution Against First Registration
A person applying for a caution against first registration should deliver to the registry:
  (a) an application in form CT1;
  (b) a plan allowing the extent of the land to which the caution relates to be identified clearly on the Ordnance Survey map, unless this can be clearly identified from the description in panel 2 on form CT1.
Panel 9 or 10 of form CT1 should be completed on the following lines to show the interest of the applicant:
"the person entitled to enforce a liability [to repair] [to contribute towards the cost of repair] of [*specify the embankment or wall in question*] arising by reason of [*summarise the basis on which the interest arises*] and payable by [*name of registered proprietor*]."
For the effect of the caution against first registration see *Cautions Against First Registration*, page 59.

Agreed Notice
An applicant should deliver to the registry:
  (a) an application in form AN1;
  (b) documentary evidence of the creation or existence of the non-statutory right in respect of an embankment or sea or river wall;
  (c) the consent of the registered proprietor of the land where this is not contained in form AN1.
The entry made in the register will give details of the interest protected.

Where the registered proprietor does not consent to the entry in the register of an agreed notice, an application for entry of a unilateral notice may still be made.

Unilateral Notice
An applicant should deliver to the registry:
   (a) an application in form UN1; and
   (b) a plan of the affected land (where the non-statutory right in respect of an embankment or sea or river wall affects only part of the land in the registered title).

Form UN1 should be completed on the following lines to show the interest of the applicant:
   "the person entitled to enforce a liability [to repair] [to contribute towards the cost of repair] of [*specify the embankment or wall in question*] arising by reason of [*summarise the basis on which the interest arises*] and payable by [*name of registered proprietor*]."

The unilateral notice will give brief details of the interest protected and identify the beneficiary of that notice.

Enlargement of Long Leases

A lease originally created for a term of not less than 300 years of which at least 200 years remain unexpired may, if it meets the requirements in the Law of Property Act 1925 ("LPA 1925") section 153, be enlarged into a fee simple. The requirements in section 153 are:
   (a) there must not be any trust or right of redemption affecting the term in favour of the owner of the reversionary estate;
   (b) there must not be any rent payable other than a peppercorn or other rent having no monetary value; or a rent having been payable, not being a peppercorn rent or other rent having no monetary value, the rent has been released or become barred by lapse of time, or has in any other way ceased to be payable; and
   (c) there must not be any right of re-entry affecting the leasehold estate or any superior leasehold estate out of which it was created.

Enlargement cannot be effected where the lease sought to be enlarged is a sublease and the headlease is itself incapable of enlargement. A yearly rent not exceeding £1 that has not been collected or paid for twenty years or more is deemed to have ceased to be payable (LPA 1925 section 153(4)).

Where the conditions for enlargement are not met, it may still be possible to acquire the freehold under the Leasehold Reform Act 1967; see *Re 51 Bennington Road, Aston* [1993] The Times 21 July and *Leasehold Enfranchisement*, page 167.

Freehold Title Unregistered
Where the freehold title is unregistered, an applicant should deliver to the registry:

(a) an application in form FR1;
(b) sufficient details, by plan or otherwise, so that the land can be clearly identified on the Ordnance Survey map;
(c) the deed of enlargement and a certified copy;
(d) the lease or a certified copy or examined abstract of it;
(e) (where the leasehold title is unregistered) all deeds and documents relating to the leasehold title that are in the control of the applicant;
(f) a statutory declaration of non-payment of the rent over a period of twenty years where it is necessary to show that a rent not exceeding £1 is deemed to have ceased to be payable;
(g) a list in duplicate in form DL of all the documents delivered;
(h) form DI giving the information as to overriding interests required by the Land Registration Rules 2003 ("LRR 2003") rule 28; and
(i) the fee payable. A fee calculator for all types of application is on the Land Registry's website at www.landregistry.gov.uk/fees.

If the leasehold title is already registered, it will be closed.

Rule 28 of LRR 2003 provides that a person applying for first registration must provide information to the registrar in form DI about any of the overriding interests (other than local land charges or public rights) set out in Schedule 1 to the Land Registration Act 2002 ("LRA 2002") that affect the estate to which the application relates and are within the actual knowledge of the applicant. For details see *Overriding Interests*, page 223. The registrar may enter a notice in the register in respect of any such interest.

The applicant is not required, however, to provide information about interests that, under LRA 2002 section 33 or 90(4), cannot be protected by notice. Such interests are:
(a) interests under a trust of land or under a Settled Land Act 1925 settlement;
(b) a leasehold estate in land granted for three years or less from the date of the grant and which is not required to be registered;
(c) a restrictive covenant between lessor and lessee, so far as relating to the demised premises;
(d) an interest which is capable of being registered under the Commons Registration Act 1965;
(e) an interest in any coal or coal mine, or the rights attached to any such interest, or the rights of any person under the Coal Industry Act 1994 section 38, 49 or 51; and
(f) leases created for public-private partnerships relating to transport in London, within the meaning given by the Greater London Authority Act 1999 section 218.

The applicant is also not required to provide information about a leasehold estate in land which falls within paragraph 1 of Schedule 1 to LRA 2002 but, at the time of the application, has one year or less to run.

An entry is made in the property register of the freehold title to show that the fee simple has been acquired by enlargement and is therefore subject to the matters set out in LPA 1925 section 153(8). Any charges affecting the leasehold title are reflected in the charges register of the freehold title.

Where the applicant is unable to produce full details of the lease so that it is not certain that the conditions for enlargement have been met, the registrar may still grant an absolute freehold title on the basis of the available evidence. In that case the entry in the property register of the freehold title, in addition to referring to the matters set out in LPA 1925 section 153(8), makes clear that the registered title is subject to all estates rights and interests vested in any other person or persons if and so far as the enlargement was ineffective.

Freehold Title Registered
Where the freehold title is registered, a person who has executed a deed of enlargement may apply for alteration of the register. The applicant should deliver to the registry:
- (a) an application in form AP1;
- (b) the deed of enlargement (and certified copy if the original deed is to be returned);
- (c) the lease or a certified copy or examined abstract of it;
- (d) (where the leasehold title is unregistered) all deeds and documents relating to the leasehold title that are in the control of the applicant;
- (e) a statutory declaration of non-payment of the rent over a period of twenty years where it is necessary to show that a rent not exceeding £1 is deemed to have ceased to be payable; and
- (f) the fee payable. A fee calculator for all types of application is on the Land Registry's website at www.landregistry.gov.uk/fees.

The registrar must give notice of the proposed alteration to any person who would be affected by it, unless he is satisfied that such notice is unnecessary (LRR 2003 rule 128).

If the leasehold title is already registered, it is closed.

An entry is made in the property register of the freehold title to show that the fee simple has been acquired by enlargement and is therefore subject to the matters set out in LPA 1925 section 153(8). Any charges affecting the leasehold title are reflected in the charges register of the freehold title.

Equitable Charges

A person who has obtained an equitable charge against the legal estate in registered land may apply for the entry in the register of a notice in respect of the equitable charge. The equitable chargee is not able to apply for an

Equitable Charges

official search with priority using form OS1 or OS2 but may reserve a period of priority by an outline application. See *Outline Applications*, page 222.

Where an equitable charge is in respect only of a beneficial interest in registered land held under a trust of land, a notice cannot be entered in the register (Land Registration Act 1925 ("LRA 2002") section 33). In that case it is possible to apply for the entry of a restriction.

An application for a notice may be for an agreed notice or a unilateral notice. In the case of an application for an agreed notice, the registrar may approve the application without the consent of the proprietor where he is satisfied of the validity of the applicant's claim. Normally the production of the equitable charge enables the registrar to be so satisfied. A unilateral notice may be preferred where the applicant does not wish the terms of the charge to be open to public scrutiny.

Agreed Notice of the Equitable Charge
An applicant should deliver to the registry:
   (a) an application in form AN1;
   (b) the equitable charge or a certified copy of it; and
   (c) the fee payable. A fee calculator for all types of application is on the Land Registry's website at www.landregistry.gov.uk/fees.
The entry made in the register will give details of the interest protected.

When the equitable charge has been discharged, an application to cancel the agreed notice should be made using application form CN1 and lodging the form of receipt or other evidence of the discharge.

Unilateral Notice of the Equitable Charge
An applicant should deliver to the registry:
   (a) an application in form UN1; and
   (b) the fee payable. A fee calculator for all types of application is on the Land Registry's website at www.landregistry.gov.uk/fees.
Form UN1 should be completed on the following lines to show the interest of the applicant:
   "equitable chargee under [*specify the document creating the equitable charge*] dated ... made between [*registered proprietor*] and [*beneficiary of the unilateral notice*]."
The unilateral notice will give brief details of the interest protected and identify the beneficiary of that notice.

When the equitable charge has been discharged, an application to cancel the unilateral notice should be made by the beneficiary of the notice, using application form UN2. If the beneficiary fails to do so, the registered proprietor of the land may apply for the cancellation of the unilateral notice using application form UN4.

Restriction where the Equitable Charge is over a Beneficial Interest

If there is no restriction in Form A on the register, a person having the benefit of an equitable charge over a beneficial interest under a trust of land has a sufficient interest for the purposes of LRA 2002 section 43(1)(c) to apply for a restriction in Form A to ensure that a survivor of the joint proprietors (unless a trust corporation) will not be able to give a valid receipt for capital money (LRR 2003 rule 93(a)). Form A is:

"No disposition by a sole proprietor of the registered estate (except a trust corporation) under which capital money arises is to be registered unless authorised by an order of the court."

The person having the benefit of an equitable charge over a beneficial interest under a trust of land may consider applying for a restriction on the following lines to ensure that he receives notice of a disposition:

"No disposition of the registered estate is to be registered without a certificate signed by the applicant for registration or his conveyancer that written notice of the disposition was given to [*name of equitable chargee*] at [*address for service*], being the person with the benefit of an equitable charge on the beneficial interest of [*name of chargor*] dated … made between [*parties*]."

This restriction does not of itself prevent a disposition, provided it is complied with. This is because the interest of the person having the benefit of the equitable charge will be overreached where the requirements of Form A have been met (Law of Property Act 1925 section 27).

The registrar must give notice of an application for a restriction to the proprietor of the registered estate concerned (LRA 2002 section 45).

A restriction does not confer any priority; it simply prevents an entry being made in the register if it is not permitted under the wording of the restriction.

If applying for a restriction in Form A, the person having the benefit of an equitable charge over a beneficial interest under a trust of land should deliver to the registry an application in form RX1. No fee is payable where the application is in respect of a restriction in Form A only.

Panel 13 of RX1 should be completed on the following lines:

"The interest is that specified in rule 93(a) of the Land Registration Rules 2003, the applicant having the benefit of a charge over a beneficial interest in the registered estate."

Panel 10 should be completed as to the restriction in Form A set out above.

If applying for a restriction on the lines set out above, the person having the benefit of an equitable charge over a beneficial interest under a trust of land should deliver to the registry:

(a) an application in form RX1; and
(b) the fee payable. A fee calculator for all types of application is on the Land Registry's website at www.landregistry.gov.uk/fees.

Panel 13 of RX1 should be completed on the following lines:

"The interest is that of a person with the benefit of an equitable charge over a beneficial interest in the registered estate held under a trust of land."

Panel 10 should be completed on the lines set out above.

When the equitable charge has been discharged, an application to withdraw this restriction should be made using application form RX4. The equitable chargee named in the restriction should sign panel 13 of form RX4.

Priority of Equitable Charges

There are no specific provisions in LRA 2002 dealing with the priority of competing equitable charges. In the light of the basic rule as to priorities set out in LRA 2002 section 28, therefore, the priority of such charges accords with the dates when they were created, the first in time having priority.

Orders under Law of Property Act 1925 Section 90

Where an order for sale is made by the court in reference to an equitable mortgage on land, the court may, in favour of a purchaser, make a vesting order conveying the land; or may appoint a person to convey the land or create and vest in the mortgagee a legal term of years absolute to enable him to carry out the sale (Law of Property Act 1925 section 90).

If the court has made a vesting order transferring registered land, this must be completed by registration (LRA 2002 section 27). The applicant should deliver to the registry:

(a) an application in form AP1;
(b) the court order or a sealed copy of that order; and
(c) the fee payable. A fee calculator for all types of application is on the Land Registry's website at www.landregistry.gov.uk/fees.

If the court has made an order appointing a person to convey the land, that order, or a sealed copy of it, should be lodged in support of the application to register a transfer executed by that person.

Where the court has made an order vesting in the equitable mortgagee a legal term of years absolute to enable him to carry out a sale, the mortgagee should apply for an agreed notice in respect of that term. The registrar may approve an application for an agreed notice without the consent of the proprietor where he is satisfied of the validity of the applicant's claim (LRA 2002 section 34(3)(c)). Normally the production of the court order enables the registrar to be so satisfied. The mortgagee should deliver to the registry:

(a) an application in form AN1;
(b) the court order or a sealed copy of that order; and
(c) the fee payable. A fee calculator for all types of application is on the Land Registry's website at www.landregistry.gov.uk/fees.

Equitable Easements

Before the coming into force of the Land Registration Act 2002 on 13 October 2003, equitable easements that were openly exercised and enjoyed as appurtenant to the dominant tenement could take effect as overriding interests on the registered servient title under the Land Registration Rules 1925 rule 258 (*Celsteel Ltd v Alton House Holdings Ltd* [1985] 1 WLR 204, [1985] 2 All ER 562, reversed in part on another point – [1986] 1 WLR 512, [1986] 1 All ER 608 (CA)). Any such equitable easement which was an overriding interest in relation to a registered estate immediately before 13 October 2003 is treated as an unregistered interest which overrides registered dispositions within Schedule 3 paragraph 3, Land Registration Act 2002 ("LRA 2002") (LRA 2002 Schedule 12 paragraph 9).

All other equitable easements are not overriding interests under Schedule 1 or Schedule 3 to LRA 2002 and must be protected by way of notice in the register. The express grant or reservation of a legal easement out of registered land must be completed by registration (LRA 2002 section 27(2)(d)) and until then it takes effect as an equitable easement. On registration it becomes a legal easement and a notice of it is entered in the register of the servient land (LRA 2002 Schedule 2 paragraph 7).

Equitable easements which are not capable of taking effect as legal easements (for example easements for life or easements created by a document which is not a deed) should be protected by agreed notice or, where an agreed notice is not possible, by a unilateral notice.

Agreed Notice
An applicant should deliver to the registry:
  (a) an application in form AN1;
  (b) the document creating the equitable easement or a certified copy of it; and
  (c) the fee payable. A fee calculator for all types of application is on the Land Registry's website at www.landregistry.gov.uk/fees.
The entry made in the register will give details of the interest protected.

Unilateral Notice
An applicant should deliver to the registry:
  (a) an application in form UN1; and
  (b) the fee payable. A fee calculator for all types of application is on the Land Registry's website at www.landregistry.gov.uk/fees.
Form UN1 should be completed on the following lines to show the interest of the applicant:
  "having the benefit of an equitable right of [*specify the easement*] created by a [*name of document*] dated ... made between [*parties*]."
The unilateral notice will give brief details of the interest protected and

identify the beneficiary of that notice.

Estate Right or Interest

When a vendor has doubts as to his title to a piece of land, he may convey or transfer it for such estate, right or interest (if any) as he may have in it. A conveyance containing such a description would not be a good root of title to such land, since a good root must show nothing to cast doubt on the title of the disposing parties.

Where the land conveyed or transferred for estate right or interest is unregistered, any application for first registration of it should be supported by sufficient evidence to show title to that land. This is often by way of statutory declarations. Even though the title is open to objection, it may still be registered with absolute freehold, absolute leasehold, or good leasehold title if the registrar is of the opinion that the defect will not cause the holding under the title to be disturbed (Land Registration Act 2002 ("LRA 2002") sections 9(3) and 10(4)).

A vendor may convey or transfer his estate right or interest in the land where he is in adverse possession of the land but has been so for less than the appropriate period under the Limitation Act 1980. LRA 2002 section 3(2) provides that a person may apply for first registration if the legal estate is vested in him or he is entitled to require the legal estate to be vested in him. Accordingly, where the applicant for first registration has not been in adverse possession for the requisite period under the Limitation Act 1980, no class of title can be granted.

European Economic Interest Groupings

A European Economic Interest Grouping ("EEIG") is formed of two or more legal bodies or natural persons, which have their central administrations or carry on their principal activities in different member states of the European Union. An EEIG registered in Great Britain is a body corporate (European Economic Interest Grouping Regulations 1989 regulation 3). Only the manager (or, where there are two or more, each of the managers) may represent the EEIG in respect of dealings with third parties (Council Regulation (EEC) No 2137/85 article 20). Where the manager is not a natural person it must designate one or more natural persons to represent it (European Economic Interest Grouping Regulations 1989 regulation 5). Accordingly execution of a deed by an EEIG should be on the following

lines:
"Signed as a deed by [*name of natural person*] the [sole] [joint] [representative of the] manager(s) of [*name of EEIG*] in the presence of ...."

An application to register an EEIG as the proprietor of registered land or of a registered charge should be supported by the usual documentation, accompanied by the result of a recent search in the Companies Registry against the EEIG and evidence of appointment of the manager or the natural person designated as representative.

In view of the nature of an EEIG and the restrictions on its powers contained in Council Regulation (EEC) No 2137/85 and the European Economic Interest Grouping Regulations 1989, a restriction on the following lines is required:
"No disposition of the [registered estate] [registered charge dated ...] by the proprietor of [the registered estate] [that registered charge] is to be registered without a certificate signed by the conveyancer to [*name of EEIG*] that the manager or managers or its representative who has or have executed the deed, has or have been duly appointed and has or have the power to bind the proprietor; that the proprietor is not in receivership or administrative receivership and has not been wound up or dissolved and generally that the provisions of Council Regulation (EEC) No 2137/85 and the European Economic Interest Grouping Regulations 1989 (SI 1989/638) have been complied with."

Where the EEIG does not have an indefinite duration, a restriction on the following lines is also required:
"No disposition by the proprietor of the [registered estate] [registered charge dated ...] completed on or after [*date when duration of EEIG ceases*] is to be registered unless its conveyancer has certified that the duration of the proprietor has been extended and that it remained a body corporate on the date of such disposition."

In the light of article 25 of Council Regulation (EEC) No 2137/85, all deeds entered into by an EEIG must indicate legibly:

(a) the name of the grouping preceded or followed either by the words "European Economic Interest Grouping" or by the initials "EEIG", unless those words or initials already occur in the name;
(b) the location of the registry in which the grouping is registered, together with the grouping's entry at that registry; and
(c) the grouping's official address.

The European Economic Interest Grouping Regulations 1989 regulation 19(1) provides that Part III of the Insolvency Act 1986 applies to EEIGs, and their establishments, registered under those Regulations, as if they were companies registered under the Companies Act 1985. The matters set out under *Administrative Receivers*, page 6, *Liquidators*, page 197, and *Receivers*, page 249, apply. At the end of three months from the date of receipt by the registrar of companies of a notice of the conclusion of the liquidation of an EEIG, the EEIG is dissolved (European Economic Interest Grouping Regulations 1989 regulation 8(2)).

Exclusive Use

Sometimes deeds grant an exclusive use of a piece of land or of a building or part of it. For example, in *Reilly v Booth* (1890) 44 Ch D 12 (CA), exclusive use of a gateway was granted, and in *McClymont v Primecourt Property Management Ltd* [2000] All ER (D) 1871, exclusive user of a garden. In *Reilly v Booth* Lopes LJ said, in a passage cited by Lord Ashbourne in *Metropolitan Railway Company v Fowler* [1893] AC 416 (HL):

> "The exclusive or unrestricted use of a piece of land, I take it, beyond all question passes the property or ownership in that land, and there is no easement known to law which gives exclusive and unrestricted use of a piece of land. It is not an easement in such a case, it is property that passes."

When ownership has passed in this way, the land or building over which the exclusive user has been granted is included in the registered title, with an entry in the property register to show that as to this land it is only the exclusive use which is included in the title.

First Registration

When First Registration is Possible

An application for first registration may be made in respect of an unregistered estate in land, a rentcharge, franchise, or *profit a prendre* in gross (Land Registration Act 2002 ("LRA 2002") section 3(1)). It is no longer possible to apply for first registration of an unregistered manor. If the application is in respect of a leasehold estate in land, the lease must either be for a discontinuous period or for a term of which more than seven years are unexpired. In calculating the duration of the lease for this purpose, a person holding in the same right both a lease in possession and a lease to take effect in possession on, or within a month of, the end of the lease in possession, may, to the extent they relate to the same land, treat them as one continuous term.

The applicant may apply to be registered as proprietor of the legal estate on first registration if the estate is vested in him or he is entitled to require the estate to be vested in him. For example, a person entitled solely and absolutely under a trust of land may apply. A person who has contracted to buy an unregistered legal estate, however, cannot apply to be registered as proprietor before completion of the contract (LRA 2002 section 3(6)). A person with a leasehold estate vested in him as mortgagee may not apply in respect of that leasehold estate while there is a subsisting right of redemption (LRA 2002 section 3(5)).

No application for first registration of a leasehold estate under a "PPP lease" can be made (LRA 2002 section 90(1)). A "PPP lease" is one within the meaning given by the Greater London Authority Act 1999 section 218, which makes provision about leases created for public-private partnerships relating to transport in London.

Compulsory First Registration
It is compulsory to apply for first registration of any freehold estate in land, or leasehold estate in land with more than seven years left to run, on the occurrence of any of the following:
- (a) a transfer, conveyance or assignment for valuable or other consideration (if the estate transferred has a negative value, it is regarded as transferred for valuable or other consideration (LRA 2002 section 4(6));
- (b) a transfer, conveyance or assignment by way of gift;
- (c) a transfer, conveyance or assignment in pursuance of an order of any court;
- (d) an assent (including a vesting assent);
- (e) a transfer, conveyance or assignment where the Housing Act 1985 section 171A applies (disposal by a landlord leading to a person's ceasing to be a secure tenant; the preserved right to buy applies);
- (f) a first legal mortgage protected by the deposit of the title deeds; and
- (g) a grant by the Queen out of demesne land of an estate in fee simple absolute in possession, other than a grant to Herself.

It is compulsory to apply for first registration on the grant of any of the following leases out of an unregistered estate in land:
- (a) a lease for more than seven years from the date of the grant for valuable or other consideration (if the estate granted has a negative value, it is regarded as granted for valuable or other consideration (LRA 2002 section 4(6));
- (b) a lease for more than seven years from the date of the grant by way of gift;
- (c) a lease for more than seven years from the date of the grant in pursuance of an order of any court;
- (d) a lease for any length of term, which takes effect in possession more than three months from the date of the grant (in the case of a sublease it is compulsory to register only if the lease out of which it is granted has, at the date of that grant, more than seven years to run);
- (e) a lease for any length of term in pursuance of Part 5 of the Housing

Act 1985 (the right to buy);
  (f) a lease where the Housing Act 1985 section 171A applies (disposal by a landlord leading to a person's ceasing to be a secure tenant; the preserved right to buy applies); and
  (g) a lease by the Queen out of demesne land for more than seven years.

It is *not* compulsory to apply for first registration in respect of any of the following:
  (a) an assignment of a mortgage term;
  (b) an assignment or surrender of a lease to the owner of the immediate reversion where the term is to merge in that reversion;
  (c) a mortgage by demise which is not a first legal mortgage protected by the deposit of the title deeds;
  (d) any transaction relating to a rentcharge;
  (e) any transaction relating to a franchise;
  (f) any transaction relating to a *profit a prendre* in gross;
  (g) a transfer or grant creating a trust where the settlor retains the whole of the beneficial interest;
  (h) a transfer or grant uniting the bare legal title and the beneficial interest in property held under a trust under which the settlor retained the whole of the beneficial interest;
  (i) any transaction relating solely to mines and minerals held apart from the surface;
  (j) a transfer, conveyance or assignment giving effect to the appointment of new trustees;
  (k) an express or implied vesting declaration in a deed of appointment of a new trustee;
  (l) a transfer by operation of law (for example, the vesting of a deceased's estate in his personal representatives); and
  (m) a general vesting declaration under the Compulsory Purchase (Vesting Declarations) Act 1981.

Duty to Apply for First Registration

Where compulsory first registration applies, the estate owner, or his successor in title, must apply for first registration within two months. Where the event triggering compulsory first registration is a mortgage, it is the mortgagor, not the mortgagee, who is required to apply. In such circumstances, however, the mortgagee may make an application for first registration in the name of the mortgagor, whether or not the mortgagor consents (Land Registration Rules 2003 ("LRR 2003") rule 21). Where the mortgage is not a first legal mortgage protected by the deposit of the title deeds, the mortgagee may not apply for first registration without the consent of the mortgagor.

Any interested party may apply to the registrar for an order extending the period of two months in which the application for first registration must be made. Such application may be made by way of letter setting out the reasons why the order should be made. No fee is payable. If the registrar is satisfied there is good reason for doing so, he may by order provide that the period for registration ends on such later date as he may specify in the order (LRA 2002 section 6(5)).

Where it is compulsory to apply for first registration but an application has not been made within two months, or by any later date stated in an order of the registrar, the transfer, grant or creation of a legal estate becomes void as regards the transfer, grant or creation of the legal estate (LRA 2002 section 7(1)). In the case of a transfer, the title to the legal estate reverts to the transferor who holds it on a bare trust for the transferee. In the case of a lease or first mortgage the grant or creation has effect as a contract made for valuable consideration to grant or create the legal estate concerned.

If the registrar makes an order extending the period for registration where LRA 2002 section 7(1) has already applied, that application of section 7(1) is treated as not having occurred (LRA 2002 section 7(3)). The possibility of reverter arising under section 7(1) is disregarded for the purposes of determining whether a fee simple is a fee simple absolute.

If the legal estate is retransferred, regranted or recreated because of a failure to comply with the requirement for first registration, the transferee, grantee or mortgagor is liable to the other party for all the proper costs of and incidental to the retransfer, regrant or recreation of the legal estate. That person is also liable to indemnify the other party in respect of any other liability reasonably incurred by him because of the failure to comply with the requirement of registration (LRA 2002 section 8).

Application for First Registration
An applicant should deliver to the registry:
- (a) an application in form FR1;
- (b) sufficient details, by plan or otherwise, so that the land can be clearly identified on the Ordnance Survey map;
- (c) in the case of a leasehold estate, the lease, if in the control of the applicant, and a certified copy;
- (d) all deeds and documents relating to the title that are in the control of the applicant;
- (e) a list in duplicate in form DL of all the documents delivered;
- (f) form DI giving the information as to overriding interests required by the Land Registration Rules 2003 rule 28; and
- (g) the fee payable. A fee calculator for all types of application is on the Land Registry's website at www.landregistry.gov.uk/fees.

On an application to register a rentcharge, franchise or *profit a prendre* in gross, the land to be identified under (b) above is the land affected by that estate.

For the position where the application is for first registration of an estate in mines and minerals held apart from the surface, see *Mines and Minerals*, page 207.

Unless all the land above and below the surface is included in the application for first registration, the applicant must supply a plan of the surface on, under or over which the land to be registered lies, and sufficient information to define the vertical and horizontal extents of the land (LRR 2003 rule 26). This requirement does not apply where only mines and minerals are excluded from the application.

Rule 28 of LRR 2003 provides that a person applying for first registration must provide information to the registrar in form DI about any of the overriding interests (other than local land charges or public rights) set out in Schedule 1 to LRA 2002 that affect the estate to which the application relates and are within the actual knowledge of the applicant, but are not apparent from deeds and documents accompanying the application. For details see *Overriding Interests*, page 223. The registrar may enter a notice in the register in respect of any such interest.

The applicant is not required, however, to provide information about interests that, under LRA 2002 section 33 or 90(4), cannot be protected by notice. Such interests are:

(a) interests under a trust of land or under a Settled Land Act 1925 settlement;
(b) a leasehold estate in land granted for three years or less from the date of the grant and which is not required to be registered;
(c) a restrictive covenant between lessor and lessee, so far as relating to the demised premises;
(d) an interest which is capable of being registered under the Commons Registration Act 1965;
(e) an interest in any coal or coal mine, or the rights attached to any such interest, or the rights of any person under the Coal Industry Act 1994 section 38, 49 or 51; and
(f) leases created for public-private partnerships relating to transport in London, within the meaning given by the Greater London Authority Act 1999 section 218.

The applicant is also not required to provide information about a leasehold estate in land which falls within paragraph 1 of Schedule 1 to LRA 2002 but, at the time of the application, has one year or less to run.

Where the applicant for first registration is unable to produce a full documentary title, the application must be supported by evidence to satisfy the registrar that the applicant is entitled, or required, to apply for first registration and, where appropriate, to account for the absence of documentary evidence of title. This means that the evidence must show that the applicant has the legal estate vested in him or that he is entitled to require the legal estate to be vested in him. In practice the evidence is usually in the form of statutory declarations exhibiting any appropriate supporting documents.

The Land Registry assumes that the applicant requests the return of all documents relating to the title except any statutory declaration, subsisting lease, subsisting charge or the latest document of title (for example the conveyance to the applicant). Those documents will be returned if the applicant lodges a certified copy with the application for first registration.

Examination of Title

In examining the title shown by the documents accompanying an application for first registration, the registrar may have regard to any examination by a conveyancer prior to the application and to the nature of the property (LRR 2003 rule 29). The registrar may make searches and enquiries and give notices to other persons, direct that searches and enquiries be made by the applicant and advertise the application (LRR 2003 rule 30).

A person may be registered with absolute title if the registrar is of the opinion that the person's title to the estate is such as a willing buyer could properly be advised by a competent professional adviser to accept. The registrar may disregard the fact that the title appears to him to be open to objection if he is of the opinion that the defect will not cause the holding under the title to be disturbed (LRA 2002 section 9(2) and (3)).

For the classes of title which may be granted as a result of the examination of title and the effect of first registration with a particular class of title, see *Classes of Title*, page 86.

The benefit of an appurtenant right may be entered in the register on first registration if, on examining the title, the registrar is satisfied that the right subsists as a legal estate and benefits the registered estate. Where the existence of the appurtenant right is not apparent on the face of the title deeds, a written application may accompany form FR1 providing details of the right and evidence of its existence. This application should be listed in panel 4 of Form FR1. If the registrar is satisfied that the right subsists as a legal estate and benefits the registered estate, he may enter it in the register.

On first registration the registrar, whenever practicable, enters in the proprietorship register the price paid or value declared. That entry will remain until there is a change of proprietor or some other change in the register of title which the registrar considers would render the entry misleading (LRR 2003 rule 8(2)).

The registrar enters a notice in the register of the burden of any interest which appears from his examination of title to affect the registered title (LRR 2003 rule 35). This does not apply to interests that, under section 33 or 90(4) of LRA 2002, cannot be protected by notice. Such interests are:

(a) interests under a trust of land or under a Settled Land Act 1925 settlement;

(b) a leasehold estate in land granted for three years or less from the date of the grant and which is not required to be registered;

First Registration

   (c) a restrictive covenant between lessor and lessee, so far as relating to the demised premises;
   (d) an interest which is capable of being registered under the Commons Registration Act 1965;
   (e) an interest in any coal or coal mine, or the rights attached to any such interest, or the rights of any person under the Coal Industry Act 1994 section 38, 49 or 51; and
   (f) leases created for public-private partnerships relating to transport in London, within the meaning given by the Greater London Authority Act 1999 section 218.

Rule 35 also does not apply to public rights and local land charges. Nor does it apply to an interest which appears to the registrar to be of a trivial or obvious character, or the entry of a notice which would be likely to cause confusion or inconvenience.

   If it appears to the registrar on first registration that an agreement prevents the acquisition of rights of light or air for the benefit of the registered estate, he may make an entry in the property register of that estate (LRR 2003 rule 36).

   In defined circumstances, before completing an application for registration with absolute title of a leasehold title, the registrar must serve notice of the application on that proprietor. Those circumstances are where:
   (a) the lease was granted out of an unregistered legal estate, or the reversion was registered but the grant of the lease was not required to be completed by registration;
   (b) at the time of the application the immediate reversion to the lease is registered;
   (c) the lease is not noted in the register of that reversionary title; and
   (d) it is not apparent from the application that the proprietor of that reversionary title consents to the registration.

On completing registration of the leasehold estate the registrar must enter notice of the lease in the register of that reversionary title (LRR 2003 rule 37).

   Where a first legal mortgage is the event that triggers compulsory first registration, the registrar must enter the mortgagee as the proprietor of that charge if he is satisfied of that person's entitlement (LRR 2003 rule 22). As regards any other legal mortgage which is either a charge on the legal estate that is being registered or a charge on such a charge, the registrar must enter the mortgagee as the proprietor of that charge if he is satisfied of that person's entitlement (LRR 2003 rule 34).

   If, while a person is required to apply for first registration of a legal estate, there is a dealing with that estate, LRA 2002 applies to that dealing as if the dealing had taken place after the date of first registration. Where the dealing is delivered for registration with the application for first registration, it has effect from the time of making that application (LRR 2003 rule 38).

Floating Charges

Where, on first registration of land held by a company, it appears to the registrar from his examination of the title that it is subject to a floating charge, he will enter a notice of it in the charges register (Land Registration Rules 2003 ("LRR 2003") rule 35). If the debenture creating the floating charge contains a proviso which prohibits the creation of any other charges ranking in priority to or *pari passu* with the floating charge, a note of that proviso is included in the notice of the floating charge. The entry of a notice in respect of a floating charge in the charges register does not remove the need for it to be registered under the Companies Act 1985.

When a floating charge relating to registered land is created, the chargee is not able to apply for an official search with priority using form OS1 or OS2, but may reserve a period of priority by an outline application. See *Outline Applications*, page 222.

A floating charge relating to registered land should be protected by an application for an agreed notice. An applicant should deliver to the registry:
 (a) an application in form AN1;
 (b) the debenture creating the floating charge or a certified copy of it; and
 (c) the fee payable. A fee calculator for all types of application is on the Land Registry's website at www.landregistry.gov.uk/fees.

The entry made in the register will give details of the interest protected.

Where a purchaser from the chargor company is seeking to have the notice of the floating charge cancelled, he should deliver application form CN1 to the registry at the same time as his application to register the transfer. The application for cancellation should be supported by a letter signed by the company's secretary or solicitor to the effect that no event has occurred which would crystallise the charge.

If a floating charge crystallises, an application should be made for a notice in respect of the variation of the existing notice. This will show that the charge has become a fixed charge (LRR 2003 rule 84(4)). An applicant should deliver to the registry:
 (a) an application in form AN1;
 (b) evidence of the crystallisation; and
 (c) the fee payable. A fee calculator for all types of application is on the Land Registry's website at www.landregistry.gov.uk/fees.

A unilateral notice may be preferred where the applicant does not wish the terms of the charge to be open to public scrutiny. The applicant should deliver to the registry:
 (a) an application in form UN1; and
 (b) the fee payable. A fee calculator for all types of application is on the Land Registry's website at www.landregistry.gov.uk/fees.

Form UN1 should be completed on the following lines to show the interest of the applicant:

"having the benefit of a floating charge created by a [*specify the document creating the floating charge*] dated ... made between [*registered proprietor*] and [*beneficiary of the unilateral notice*]."

The unilateral notice will give brief details of the interest protected and identify the beneficiary of that notice.

Flying Freeholds

When an application for first registration is made, unless all the land above and below the surface is included in the application for first registration, the applicant must provide a plan of the surface on, under or over which the land to be registered lies, and sufficient information to define the vertical or horizontal extents of the land (Land Registration Rules 2003 rule 26(1)). This does not apply where it is only mines and minerals that are excluded from the application.

Where the application for first registration shows that the land being registered is affected by a flying freehold, an appropriate entry is made in the property register. An example of such an entry is:

"NOTE: As to the part tinted blue on the title plan only the rooms over the passageway which form part of 15 Front Street are included in the title."

Rule 251 of the Land Registration Rules 1925 provided that, where a title was registered under the Land Registration Act 1925, the registration of a person as proprietor of land vested in him all appurtenances appertaining or reputed to appertain to the land or any part of it, or, at the time of registration, demised, occupied, or enjoyed with the land, or reputed or known as part or parcel of or appurtenant to the land or any part of it. Rule 251 also provided that this included the appropriate rights and interests which, had there been a conveyance of the land, would have passed under the Law of Property Act 1925 section 62. The Land Registration Act 2002 sections 11(3) and 12(3) provides that the registered freehold or leasehold estate is vested in the proprietor together with all interests subsisting for the benefit of the estate. The result of these provisions is that if, for example, there is a room projecting over an adjoining owner's land or a cellar projecting under that land, this is usually included in the occupier's registered title even though it falls outside the red edging on the title plan, no details of the flying freehold having been supplied to the registry at the time of registration.

Where a flying freehold has not been reflected by an entry in the property register, an application may be made for an alteration to the register. The applicant should deliver to the registry:

(a) an application in form AP1;
(b) a statement of the alteration being applied for;

(c) all relevant evidence held by the applicant which is pertinent to the application to alter the register; and

(d) the fee payable. A fee calculator for all types of application is on the Land Registry's website at www.landregistry.gov.uk/fees.

Foreshore

The foreshore is the shore and bed of the sea and of any tidal water, below the line of the medium high tide between the spring and neap tides. There is a presumption that the Crown owns the foreshore, although extensive tracts of the foreshore are in fact owned by other parties.

In the light of this presumption, where it appears to the registrar that any of the land in an application for first registration comprises foreshore, he must serve notice of the application on the Crown Estate Commissioners (Land Registration Rules 2003 ("LRR 2003") rule 31). He must also serve notice on the Chancellor of the Duchy of Lancaster in the case of land in the county palatine of Lancaster and on the Port of London Authority in the case of land within its jurisdiction. In the case of land in the counties of Devon and Cornwall and the Isles of Scilly, the registrar must also serve notice on such person as the Duke of Cornwall, or the possessor for the time being of the Duchy of Cornwall, appoints. Where the land is within the jurisdiction of the Port of London Authority, the registrar must also serve notice of the application on such person as the Duke of Cornwall, or the possessor for the time being of the Duchy of Cornwall, appoints.

The notice must allow a period ending at 12 noon on the twentieth business day after the date of issue of the notice in which to object to the application. A business day is a day when the Land Registry is open to the public, that is every day except Saturdays, Sundays, Christmas Day, Good Friday or any other day either specified or declared by proclamation under the Banking and Financial Dealings Act 1971 section 1 or appointed by the Lord Chancellor.

Such a notice need not be served where, if it was served, it would be served on the applicant for first registration (LRR 2003 rule 31(3)).

Where the registered land consists of foreshore belonging to the Queen in right of the Crown or the Duchy of Lancaster or to the Duchy of Cornwall, the period of adverse possession required before an application may be made is sixty years rather than ten years (Land Registration Act 2002 Schedule 6 paragraph 13). For these purposes land is treated as foreshore if it has been foreshore at any time in the ten years before the application by the squatter for registration.

Franchises

A franchise is "an incorporeal hereditament which has been authoritatively defined as a royal privilege or branch of the royal prerogative subsisting in the hands of a subject, by grant from the King" (*Spook Erection Ltd v Secretary of State for the Environment* [1989] QB 300, [1988] 3 WLR 291, [1988] 2 All ER 667 (CA)). Franchises of forest, free chase, park or free warren were abolished by the Wild Creatures and Forest Laws Act 1971 section 1(1).

Franchises were not capable of registration under the Land Registration Act 1925 but may now be the subject of voluntary registration (Land Registration Act 2002 ("LRA 2002") section 3). It is not, however, compulsory to apply for first registration of the title to a franchise.

Unregistered franchises which affect a registered title are overriding interests and are therefore protected even though no entry in respect of them appears on the register (LRA 2002 Schedule 1 paragraph 10 and Schedule 3 paragraph 10). Such franchises will cease to be overriding interests at the end of ten years from 13 October 2003 (LRA 2002 section 117(1)). Accordingly, if they affect unregistered land, an application to lodge a caution against first registration should be made before the end of the period. If they affect registered land, an application for the entry in the register of a notice should be made before the end of the period. In practice this is likely to be a unilateral notice.

Caution Against First Registration
An applicant should deliver to the registry:
(a) an application in form CT1; and
(b) a plan (or other sufficient details) to allow the land to which the caution relates to be identified clearly on the Ordnance Survey map.

No fee is payable for applications lodged during the ten year period beginning on 13 October 2003 (LRA 2002 section 117(2)).

Form CT1 should be completed on the following lines to show the interest of the applicant:

"owner of the following franchise affecting the land: [*set out details of the franchise including details of the grant under which it arose*]."

The caution does not in itself have any effect on the validity or priority of the franchise, but the cautioner will have the opportunity to object to the application for first registration unless notice of the franchise is entered in the register (LRA 2002 section 16).

Unilateral Notice
An applicant should deliver to the registry:
(a) an application in form UN1; and
(b) a plan of the affected land (where the franchise affects only part of the

land in the registered title).

No fee is payable for applications lodged during the ten year period beginning on 13 October 2003 (LRA 2002 section 117(2)).

Form UN1 should be completed on the following lines to show the interest of the applicant:

"owner of the following franchise affecting the land: [*set out details of the franchise including details of the grant under which it arose*]."

The unilateral notice will give brief details of the interest protected and identify the beneficiary of that notice.

First Registration of Franchise

An applicant should deliver to the registry:
  (a) an application in form FR1;
  (b) sufficient details, by plan or otherwise, so that the area of land to which the franchise relates can be clearly identified on the Ordnance Survey map;
  (c) all deeds and documents relating to the title that are in the control of the applicant;
  (d) a list in duplicate in form DL of all the documents delivered;
  (e) form DI giving the information as to overriding interests required by the Land Registration Rules 2003 ("LRR 2003") rule 28; and
  (f) the fee payable. A fee calculator for all types of application is on the Land Registry's website at www.landregistry.gov.uk/fees.

The LRR 2003 differentiate between an "affecting franchise" and a "relating franchise". An affecting franchise is one which relates to a defined area of land and is an adverse right affecting, or capable of affecting, the title to an estate or charge. A relating franchise is one which is not an affecting franchise.

On first registration of an affecting franchise, a title plan based on the Ordnance Survey map is created and referred to in the description of the registered estate in the property register. The area identified on the title plan is indexed on the index map and will then be revealed on the result of an official search of the index map in respect of the land affected, made under LRR 2003 rule 145. An application for an official search of the index map is made in form SIM.

On first registration of a relating franchise, no title plan is created. The franchise is indexed in the index of relating franchises and manors. This is an index of verbal descriptions of registered franchises which are relating franchises, pending applications for first registration of such franchises, and registered manors. It also includes cautions against first registration where the subject of the caution is a relating franchise. and pending applications for such cautions. The index contains the relevant title numbers, arranged by administrative area. Registered relating franchises are not revealed on an official search of the index map, but are revealed on the result of an official search of the index of relating franchises and manors. An application for an official search of the index of relating franchises and manors is made in form SIF.

Leases of Registered Franchises
Where there is a grant out of a registered franchise of a lease, an application must be made to register the lease (LRA 2002 section 27(2)(c)). If the lease is for a term of more than seven years from the date of the grant, the application is completed by the entry in the register of:
   (a) the grantee (or his successor in title) as proprietor of the lease; and
   (b) a notice in respect of the lease.
If the lease is for a term not exceeding seven years from the date of the grant, the application is completed only by the entry of a notice in respect of the lease (LRA 2002 Schedule 2 paragraphs 4 and 5).

Any lease, however short, out of a registered franchise is required to be registered.

An applicant should deliver to the registry:
   (a) an application in form AP1;
   (b) the lease and a certified copy; and
   (c) the fee payable. A fee calculator for all types of application is on the Land Registry's website at www.landregistry.gov.uk/fees.

Fraud

The entry of a person in the register as the proprietor of a legal estate vests the legal estate in him even where it would not otherwise have vested in him (Land Registration Act 2002 ("LRA 2002") section 58). Accordingly if, for example, a person is registered as proprietor as the result of a forged or fraudulent transfer, the legal estate is still vested in him. This is the case whether the transfer is void or merely voidable.

Although the legal estate has so vested, this does not prevent an application being made for alteration of the register under Schedule 4 to LRA 2002; see *Alteration of the Register*, page 26 and *Rectification*, page 253. An alteration of the register is a rectification if it involves the correction of a mistake and prejudicially affects the title of a registered proprietor.

Where an alteration which would be a rectification affects the title of the proprietor of a registered estate in land, no order may be made by the court or the registrar without that proprietor's consent in relation to land in his possession, unless he has by fraud or lack of proper care caused or substantially contributed to the mistake, or it would be unjust for any other reason for the alteration not to be made. For example, where a husband and wife were the registered proprietors of land and the husband forged the wife's signature on a transfer into his sole name, on registration of the transfer the legal estate would vest in him alone. Because of his fraud, an order for alteration to the register to show the husband and wife as registered proprietors would normally be made, even though the husband has remained in possession. If an innocent purchaser from the husband was registered as proprietor before the forgery came to light, an order for an alteration would not usually be made to affect that proprietor if he is in possession.

Where the register is rectified as a result of fraud or forgery, the question arises whether a person who has suffered loss by reason of the rectification is entitled to be indemnified by the registrar. For these purposes, paragraph 1(2)(b) of Schedule 8 to LRA 2002 provides that the proprietor of a registered estate or charge claiming in good faith under a forged disposition is, where the register is rectified, to be regarded as having suffered loss by reason of such rectification as if the disposition had not been forged. No indemnity is payable by the registrar, however, for any loss suffered wholly or partly as a result of the claimant's own fraud, or wholly as a result of his own lack of proper care. Where any loss is suffered by a claimant partly as a result of his own lack of proper care, any indemnity payable to him is to be reduced to such extent as is fair having regard to his share in the responsibility for the loss. For these purposes, any fraud or lack of proper care on the part of a person from whom the claimant derives title (otherwise than under a disposition for valuable consideration which is registered or protected by an entry in the register) is to be treated as if it were fraud or lack of care on the part of the claimant (LRA 2002 Schedule 8 paragraph 5). See *Indemnity*, page 161.

A registered proprietor may have reason to believe that he is at risk from fraud or forgery. In such circumstances he may apply for a restriction on the following lines:

"No disposition of the registered estate by the proprietor of the registered estate is to be registered."; or

"No disposition of the registered estate by the proprietor of the registered estate is to be registered without a written consent signed by [*name of his conveyancer*] of [*address*]."

The registered proprietor should deliver to the registry:
   (a) an application in form RX1; and
   (b) the fee payable. A fee calculator for all types of application is on the Land Registry's website at www.landregistry.gov.uk/fees.

Panel 10 should be completed as to the appropriate restriction.

Where an inhibition was entered in the register prior to 13 October 2003, LRA 2002 applies to it as that Act applies to restrictions entered under that Act (LRA 2002 Schedule 12 paragraph 2(2)).

Freezing Orders

Where a person has applied to the court for a freezing order affecting registered land, or has the benefit of a freezing order or an undertaking given in place of a freezing order, he may apply for a restriction in Form AA, BB, CC, or DD, as appropriate (Land Registration Rules 2003 ("LRR 2003") rule 93(h) and (i)). This applies equally where the International Criminal Court applies for a restriction in Form AA, BB, CC, or DD in respect of a freezing order, or applies for a freezing order, under Schedule 6 to the International Criminal Court Act 2001 (LRR 2003 rule 93(r)).

The Land Registration Act 2002 ("LRA 2002") applies in relation to freezing orders under the International Criminal Court Act 2001, as it applies in relation to orders affecting land made by the court for the purpose of enforcing judgments or recognisances, except that no notice may be entered in the register of title in respect of such orders. In the light of the decision in *Stockler v Fourways Estates Limited* [1984] 1 WLR 25, [1983] 3 All ER 501, an application for a notice is likewise not appropriate in respect of other freezing orders.

An application to the court for a freezing order affecting registered land is a pending land action and may be protected by a notice or restriction. In practice, an application for an agreed notice will be the usual course of action.

The applicant for a restriction or agreed notice or unilateral notice is not able to apply for an official search with priority using form OS1 or OS2 but may reserve a period of priority by an outline application. See *Outline Applications*, page 222.

Under the Land Registration Act 1925, freezing orders were usually protected by inhibitions. The LRA 2002 applies to any inhibitions entered under the 1925 Act as it applies to restrictions under the 2002 Act (LRA 2002 Schedule 12 paragraph 2(2)).

Notice in Respect of a Pending Action
An applicant for an agreed notice should deliver to the registry:
  (a) an application in form AN1;
  (b) the application to the court for the freezing order; and
  (c) the fee payable. A fee calculator for all types of application is on the Land Registry's website at www.landregistry.gov.uk/fees.

This is likely to be sufficient to satisfy the registrar of the validity of the applicant's claim in accordance with LRA 2002 section 34(3)(c). Where the applicant wishes to apply for a unilateral notice he should deliver to the registry:
  (a) an application in form UN1; and
  (b) the fee payable. A fee calculator for all types of application is on the Land Registry's website at www.landregistry.gov.uk/fees.

Form UN1 should be completed on the following lines to show the interest of the applicant:

"applicant in an application for a freezing order in the ... Court [*set out full court reference and parties*]."

Restriction

The applicant should deliver to the registry:
   (a) an application in form RX1; and
   (b) the fee payable. A fee calculator for all types of application is on the Land Registry's website at www.landregistry.gov.uk/fees.

Panel 13 of RX1 should be completed on the following lines:

"The interest is that specified in rule 93 [(h) of the Land Registration Rules 2003, the applicant being a person with the benefit of a freezing order or an undertaking given in place of a freezing order (*as appropriate*)] [(i) of the Land Registration Rules 2003, the applicant being a person who has applied for a freezing order] [(r) of the Land Registration Rules 2003, the application being in respect of a freezing order or application for a freezing order (*as appropriate*) under Schedule 6 to the International Criminal Court Act 2001]."

Panel 10 should be completed as to the appropriate restriction. Form AA is:

"Under an order of the (*name*) Court made on (*date*) (*action no*) no disposition by the proprietor of the registered estate is to be registered except under a further order of the Court."

Form BB is:

"Under an order of the (*name*) Court made on (*date*) (*action no*) no disposition by the proprietor of the charge is to be registered except under a further order of the Court."

Form CC is:

"Pursuant to an application made on (*date*) to the (*name*) Court for a freezing order to be made under (*statutory provision*) no disposition by the proprietor of the registered estate is to be registered except with the consent of (*the person applying*) or under a further order of the Court."

Form DD is:

"Pursuant to an application made on (*date*) to the (*name*) Court for a freezing order to be made under (*statutory provision*) no disposition by the proprietor of the charge is to be registered except with the consent of (*the person applying*) or under a further order of the Court."

Friendly Societies

Friendly societies which are registered under the Friendly Societies Act 1992 are incorporated, while those still registered under the Friendly Societies Act

1974 are unincorporated. If a friendly society is a charity, it is an exempt charity. See *Charities*, page 69.

Friendly Societies Registered under the Friendly Societies Act 1974

A friendly society registered under the 1974 Act may acquire land if this is permitted by its rules. The transfer should be to all the trustees. There is no limit to the number of trustees of a friendly society who can be registered as proprietors. The names of the trustees in the proprietorship register may be followed by an appropriate description such as: "the trustees of the Old Sarum Friendly Society".

The business address of the society should be given as an address for service.

If the survivor of the trustees will not be able to give a valid receipt for capital money, a restriction in Form A is required on the register. Form A is:

"No disposition by a sole proprietor of the registered estate (except a trust corporation) under which capital money arises is to be registered unless authorised by an order of the court."

A disposition by a friendly society should be executed by the current trustees of the society. If these are not also the existing registered proprietors, the society's solicitor or secretary should certify that they are the present trustees. A person dealing with the trustees is not required to enquire as to their authority to dispose of or deal with land (Friendly Societies Act 1974 section 53(1) as substituted by the Friendly Societies Act 1992).

Where an unincorporated friendly society which is a registered proprietor has become incorporated under the Friendly Societies Act 1992, an application should be made for an alteration to bring the register up to date. The friendly society should deliver to the registry:

(a) an application in form AP1;
(b) the original or a certified copy of the certificate of incorporation; and
(c) the fee payable. A fee calculator for all types of application is on the Land Registry's website at www.landregistry.gov.uk/fees.

Friendly Societies Registered under the Friendly Societies Act 1992

All friendly societies registered under the Friendly Societies Act 1992 are incorporated societies and have power to acquire, hold, charge and dispose of land. The last word of the name of an incorporated friendly society is "Limited" or "Cyfyngedig". In the case of an incorporated friendly society which is a collecting society the last three words of the name are "Collecting Society Limited" or "Cymdeithas Casglu Cyfyngedig".

Where a friendly society registered under the Friendly Societies Act 1992 is registered as proprietor of registered land or of a registered charge, no restriction is usually required to be entered in the register.

Gifts

To pass a legal estate, a gift of land must be made by a deed.

Unregistered Land
When the title to land is unregistered, an application for first registration must be made after a deed of gift has transferred a legal freehold estate in the land or a legal leasehold estate in the land for a term which, at the time of the gift, has more than seven years to run (Land Registration Act 2002 ("LRA 2002") section 4). The requirement to apply for first registration does not apply to mines and minerals held apart from the surface.

The person taking under the gift must apply for first registration within two months of the gift. He may apply to the registrar for an order that the period for registration ends on a later date, which date will be specified in the order, if made. The registrar will make such an order if he is satisfied that there is good reason for doing so (LRA 2002 section 6(5)).

If the requirement of registration is not complied with following the gift, the legal estate reverts to the donor who holds it on a bare trust for the donee (LRA 2002 section 7). Where an order is made under LRA 2002 section 6(5), this reverter of the legal estate is treated as not having occurred.

If there has to be a further deed because of the failure to apply for first registration following the original deed of gift, the donee will be liable for the proper costs of the donor in respect of the new deed (LRA 2002 section 8).

A person applying for first registration must provide information to the registrar in form DI about any of the overriding interests (other than local land charges or public rights) set out in Schedule 1 to LRA 2002 that affect the estate to which the application relates and are within the actual knowledge of the applicant, but are not apparent from the deeds and documents accompanying the application (Land Registration Rules 2003 ("LRR 2003") rule 28). For details see *Overriding Interests*, page 223. The registrar may enter a notice in the register in respect of any such interest.

The applicant is not required, however, to provide information about interests that, under section 33 or 90(4) of LRA 2002, cannot be protected by notice. Such interests are:
    (a) interests under a trust of land or under a Settled Land Act 1925 settlement;
    (b) a leasehold estate in land granted for three years or less from the date of the grant and which is not required to be registered;
    (c) a restrictive covenant between lessor and lessee, so far as relating to the demised premises;
    (d) an interest which is capable of being registered under the Commons Registration Act 1965;
    (e) an interest in any coal or coal mine, or the rights attached to any such

interest, or the rights of any person under the Coal Industry Act 1994 section 38, 49 or 51; and
(f) leases created for public-private partnerships relating to transport in London, within the meaning given by the Greater London Authority Act 1999 section 218.

The applicant is also not required to provide information about a leasehold estate in land which falls within paragraph 1 of Schedule 1 to LRA 2002 but, at the time of the application, has one year or less to run.

A donee applying for first registration should deliver to the registry:
(a) an application in form FR1;
(b) sufficient details, by plan or otherwise, so that the land can be clearly identified on the Ordnance Survey map;
(c) all deeds and documents relating to the title that are in the control of the applicant;
(d) a list in duplicate in form DL of all the documents delivered;
(e) form DI giving the information as to overriding interests required by LRR 2003 rule 28; and
(f) the fee payable. A fee calculator for all types of application is on the Land Registry's website at www.landregistry.gov.uk/fees.

In the case of a leasehold estate, the lease, if in the possession or control of the applicant, and a certified copy must also be lodged.

In examining the title the registrar may have regard to any examination by a conveyancer prior to the application and to the nature of the property. He may make searches and enquiries and give notice to other persons, direct that searches and enquiries be made by the applicant, and advertise the application (LRR 2003 rule 30).

The applicant may be registered with absolute title if the registrar is of the opinion that the applicant's title is such as a willing buyer could properly be advised by a competent professional adviser to accept. In the case of a leasehold title this suffices for a good leasehold title; for an absolute title the registrar must in addition approve the lessor's title to grant the lease. In considering the applicant's title, the registrar may disregard the fact that the title appears to him to be open to objection if he is of the opinion that the defect will not cause the holding under the title to be disturbed.

It was previously the practice of the Land Registry to make an entry on the register referring to the Insolvency Act 1986 when first registration was triggered by a gift. That practice was discontinued in 2000.

Registered Land

A transfer by way of gift of registered land must be made in form TR1 (for the whole of the land in a registered title); TR3 (for a registered charge); TR4 (for a portfolio of charges); TR5 (for a portfolio of whole titles); TP1 (for part of the land in a registered title); or TP3 (for a portfolio of titles). Until the transfer of the registered estate or registered charge is completed by registration, it does not operate at law (LRA 2002 section 27(1)).

The donee is not able to apply for an official search with priority using form OS1 or OS2 but may reserve a period of priority by an outline application. See *Outline Applications*, page 222.

A person applying to register a disposition of a registered estate must provide information to the registrar in form DI about any of the overriding interests (other than local land charges or public rights) set out in Schedule 3 to LRA 2002 that affect the estate to which the application relates and are within the actual knowledge of the applicant. For details see *Overriding Interests*, page 223. The applicant must produce to the registrar any documentary evidence of the interest that is under his control (LRR 2003 rule 57). The registrar may enter a notice in the register in respect of any such interest.

The applicant is not required, however, to provide information about interests that, under section 33 or 90(4) of LRA 2002, cannot be protected by notice. Such interests are:

(a) interests under a trust of land or under a Settled Land Act 1925 settlement;

(b) a leasehold estate in land granted for three years or less from the date of the grant and which is not required to be registered;

(c) a restrictive covenant between lessor and lessee, so far as relating to the demised premises;

(d) an interest which is capable of being registered under the Commons Registration Act 1965;

(e) an interest in any coal or coal mine, or the rights attached to any such interest, or the rights of any person under the Coal Industry Act 1994 section 38, 49 or 51; and

(f) leases created for public-private partnerships relating to transport in London, within the meaning given by the Greater London Authority Act 1999 section 218.

The applicant is also not required to provide information about a leasehold estate in land which falls within paragraph 1 of Schedule 3 to LRA 2002 but, at the time of the application, has one year or less to run.

A donee applying to register a transfer of registered land should deliver to the registry:

(a) an application in form AP1;

(b) form TR1, TR3, TR4, TR5, TP1, or TP3 (as appropriate);

(c) information as to overriding interests required by LRR 2003 rule 57, including any documentary evidence of the interest; and

(d) the fee payable. A fee calculator for all types of application is on the Land Registry's website at www.landregistry.gov.uk/fees.

The priority of any interest affecting the registered estate is not affected by a gift of registered land, whether or not the interest or the gift is registered (LRA 2002 section 28).

Where a donee is seeking indemnity following rectification of the register, any fraud or lack of proper care by the donor is treated as fraud or lack of proper care by the donee for the purposes of paragraph 5 of Schedule 8 to LRA 2002; see *Indemnity*, page 161.

For the position where an order of the court under the Insolvency Act 1986 section 339, 340, 343 or 423 requires the register to be altered following the bankruptcy of the donor, see *Voidable Transactions*, page 43.

Historical Information

It is possible to apply for an historical edition of a registered title where this is held by the registrar in electronic form. The application should be made in Form HC1 and should specify the date of the edition in question and indicate whether it is the last edition on that date, or all editions on that date, which are required. An application which does not specify such a date may be rejected. For the fee payable see the Land Registry's website at www.landregistry.gov.uk/fees.

Where the registrar is keeping in electronic form an edition of the registered title as it existed at the date specified in the application, he must issue a copy of it. If only part of the edition requested is kept by the registrar in electronic form, he must issue a copy of that part.

In most conveyancing transactions it is not necessary to consider historical editions of the registered title, but they may be relevant where, for example, consideration is being given to whether certain registered titles were at some point in common ownership, so as to extinguish easements or restrictive covenants by unity of seisin. Another example is where consideration is being given to whether a former owner is liable on implied covenants for title, the benefit of which runs with the registered estate under the Law of Property (Miscellaneous Provisions) Act 1994 section 7.

Housing Action Trusts

Housing action trusts are established by the Secretary of State with a view to renovating areas of run down housing. They have powers to acquire land. While a housing action trust can dispose of land with the consent of the Secretary of State, it may not dispose of a house which is for the time being subject to a secure tenancy or an introductory tenancy, except to a registered social landlord or to a local housing authority or other local authority (Housing Act 1988 section 79(2)). This does not, however, prevent a disposal of a house under the right to buy provisions in Part 5 of the Housing Act 1985.

In the light of these limitations on disposals, when registering a housing action trust as the proprietor of a registered estate, the registrar enters a restriction in accordance with the power contained in the Land Registration Act 2002 section 42(1)(a). The restriction is on the following lines:

"No disposition by the proprietor of the registered estate is to be registered without the consent of the Secretary of State unless either:
- (a) it is a disposition of a house or flat under Part 5 of the Housing Act 1985 (Right to Buy); or
- (b) it is a disposition to one or more individuals and the disposition certifies that it consists of a single house or flat or there is a certificate to that effect signed by the Solicitor or Chief Executive of the registered proprietor; or
- (c) the disposition certifies that no part of the land consists of a house or a flat or there is a certificate to that effect signed by the Solicitor or Chief Executive of the registered proprietor; or
- (d) it is a charge."

An application to register a disposition by a housing action trust should include the necessary evidence to meet the requirements of this restriction.

Where a housing action trust disposes of a house which is subject to a secure tenancy or an introductory tenancy to a registered social landlord, the transfer or conveyance must contain a statement that the requirement of the Housing Act 1988 section 81 as to consent applies to a subsequent disposal of the house by the registered social landlord. The Housing Act 1988 section 81 requires that in these circumstances the registered social landlord will not dispose of the house without the consent of the Secretary of State, unless the disposal is to a person having the right to buy under Part 5 of the Housing Act 1985 or having the right to acquire under Part I of the Housing Act 1996. Where the registered social landlord has mortgaged the house, this requirement for consent also applies to a disposal in exercise of the power of sale.

Where a transfer or conveyance contains the statement required by the Housing Act 1988 section 81 and the registered social landlord is being registered as proprietor, the registrar enters a restriction in Form X (Housing Act 1988 section 81(10)). Form X is:

"No disposition by the proprietor of the registered estate or in exercise of the power of sale or leasing in any registered charge (except an exempt disposal as defined by section 81(8) of the Housing Act 1988) is to be registered without the consent of the Secretary of State to that disposition under the provisions of section 81 of that Act."

Exempt disposals as defined by the Housing Act 1988 section 81(8) are:
- (a) the disposal of a dwelling-house to a person having the right to buy it under Part 5 of the Housing Act 1988 (whether the disposal is in fact

made under that Part or otherwise);
(b) the disposal of a dwelling-house to a person having the right to acquire it under Part I of the Housing Act 1996 (whether or not the disposal is in fact made under provisions having effect by virtue of the Housing Act 1996 section 17);
(c) a compulsory disposal within the meaning of Part 5 of the Housing Act 1985;
(d) the disposal of an easement or rentcharge;
(e) the disposal of an interest by way of security for a loan;
(f) the grant of a secure tenancy or what would be a secure tenancy but for any of paragraphs 2 to 12 of Schedule 1 to the Housing Act 1985;
(g) the grant of an assured tenancy or an assured agricultural occupancy, within the meaning of Part I of the Housing Act 1988, or what would be such a tenancy or occupancy but for any of paragraphs 4 to 8 of Schedule 1 to that Act; and
(h) the transfer of an interest held on trust for any person where the disposal is made in connection with the appointment of a new trustee or in connection with the discharge of any trustee.

Housing Associations

The law relating to housing associations is largely contained in the Housing Associations Act 1985 in respect of unregistered housing associations and in the Housing Act 1996 in respect of registered housing associations. The Housing Associations Act 1985 section 1 defines a housing association as a society, body of trustees or company:
(a) which is established for the purpose of, or amongst whose objects or powers are included those of, providing, constructing, improving or managing, or facilitating or encouraging the construction or improvement of, housing accommodation, and
(b) which does not trade for profit or whose constitution or rules prohibit the issue of capital with interest or dividend exceeding such rate as may be prescribed by the Treasury, whether with or without differentiation as between share and loan capital.

Registration of Unregistered Housing Association as Proprietor of Land
Where an unregistered housing association acquires land, it may be grant-aided land. Grant-aided land is defined in Housing Associations Act 1985 Schedule 1 as land:
(a) in respect of which a payment by way of annual grant or subsidy under the statutory provisions referred to in paragraph 2 of that

Schedule falls or fell to be made in respect of a period ending after 24 January 1974; or

(b) on which is, or has been, secured a loan made under the statutory provisions referred to in paragraph 3 of that Schedule, in respect of which a repayment (by way of principal or interest or both) falls or fell to be made after 24 January 1974.

A disposition of grant-aided land by an unregistered housing association requires the consent of the Housing Corporation, if the land is in England, or of the National Assembly for Wales, if the land is in Wales.

An application to register an unregistered housing association as proprietor of a registered estate in respect of grant-aided land must contain, or be accompanied by, a certificate to that effect (Land Registration Rules 2003 ("LRR 2003") rules 181(3), 182(3) and 183(4)). Where such a certificate is given, a restriction to the following effect is entered in the proprietorship register in the case of land in England:

"No disposition by the proprietor of the registered estate is to be registered without the consent of the Housing Corporation when such consent is required under the provisions of section 9 of the Housing Associations Act 1985."

In the case of grant-aided land in Wales the restriction is to the following effect:

"No disposition by the proprietor of the registered estate is to be registered without the consent of the National Assembly for Wales when such consent is required under the provisions of section 9 of the Housing Associations Act 1985."

Where the housing association is a charity, the appropriate statement required by the Charities Act 1993 section 37(5) and LRR 2003 rule 179 should be made in the transfer to the charity. See *Charities*, page 69.

Where the housing association is a company registered in England and Wales or Scotland, the company's registered number must be stated in the application (LRR 2003 rule 181(1)). This information is usually given in the transfer or, in the case of a conveyance, in panel 9 of form FR1.

Where a corporation or body of trustees holding on charitable or public trusts applies to be registered as proprietor, the application must be accompanied by the document creating the trust (LRR 2003 rule 182(1)). Where a corporation aggregate, to which rules 181 and 182 do not apply, applies to be registered as proprietor, the application must be accompanied by evidence of the extent of its powers to hold and sell, mortgage, lease and otherwise deal with land and, in the case of a charge, to lend money on mortgage. That evidence must include the charter, statute, rules, memorandum and articles of association or other documents constituting the corporation, together with such further evidence as the registrar may require (LRR 2003 rule 183(1) and (2)). In practice, arrangements are often made by housing associations with the head office of the Land Registry so that this material does not need to be lodged with every application.

Dispositions of Registered Titles by Unregistered Housing Associations
Applications to register dispositions by unregistered housing associations should meet the requirements of any restriction on the register. Where such restriction refers to the consent of the Housing Corporation, or the National Assembly for Wales, under the Housing Associations Act 1985 section 9, evidence of that consent need not be lodged for the following:
   (a) transfers and leases under the right to buy and right to acquire schemes;
   (b) shared ownership leases;
   (c) sales in accordance with a compulsory purchase order;
   (d) enfranchisement under the Leasehold Reform Act 1967 or the Leasehold Reform, Housing and Urban Development Act 1993;
   (e) a mortgage not affecting houses or flats; and
   (f) the grant or release of an easement.

Registered Housing Associations
Housing associations registered under the Housing Act 1996 are registered social landlords; see *Registered Social Landlords*, page 254.

Implied Covenants

A registrable disposition may be expressed to be made either with full title guarantee or with limited title guarantee or, in the case of an instrument in the Welsh language, *gyda gwarant teitl llawn* or *gyda gwarant teitl cyfyngedig* (Land Registration Rules 2003 ("LRR 2003") rule 67(1)). The effect of using these expressions is to imply covenants by the person making the disposition, as set out in Part I of the Law of Property (Miscellaneous Provisions) Act 1994. In either case, the implied covenantor in a registrable disposition is not liable under such implied covenants for anything which, at the time of the disposition, was entered in the register in relation to the interest in question.

A disposition "with full title guarantee" or "*gyda gwarant teitl llawn*" implies the following covenants:
   (a) that the person making the disposition has the right (with the concurrence of any other person conveying the property) to dispose of the property as he purports to;
   (b) that the person making the disposition will at his own cost do all that he reasonably can to give the person to whom he disposes of the property the title he purports to give;
   (c) that the person making the disposition is disposing of the property free

from all charges and incumbrances (whether monetary or not) and all other rights exercisable by third parties, other than any charges, incumbrances or rights which that person does not and could not reasonably be expected to know about;

(d) (where the disposition is of leasehold land) that the lease is subsisting at the time of the disposition and there is no subsisting breach of a condition or tenant's obligation, and nothing which at that time would render the lease liable to forfeiture;

(e) (where the disposition is a mortgage of property subject to a rentcharge) that the mortgagor will fully and promptly observe and perform all the obligations under the instrument creating the rentcharge that are for the time being enforceable with respect to the property by the owner of the rentcharge in his capacity as such; and

(f) (where the disposition is a mortgage of leasehold land) that the mortgagor will fully and promptly observe and perform all the obligations under the lease subject to the mortgage that are for the time being imposed on him in his capacity as tenant under the lease.

A disposition "with limited title guarantee" or "*gyda gwarant teitl cyfyngedig*" implies the covenants set out at (a), (b), (d), (e) and (f) above, and the following covenant:

(g) that the person making the disposition has not since the last disposition for value:

(i) charged or incumbered the property by means of any charge or incumbrance which subsists at the time when the disposition is made, or granted third party rights in relation to the property which so subsist, or

(ii) suffered the property to be so charged or incumbered or subjected to any such rights,

and that he is not aware that anyone else has done so since the last disposition for value.

The operation of any covenant implied in an instrument by virtue of Part I of the Law of Property (Miscellaneous Provisions) Act 1994 may be limited or extended by a provision of that instrument (Law of Property (Miscellaneous Provisions) Act 1994 section 8(1)). Where a document effecting a registrable disposition contains such a provision, that document must include a statement referring to the section of that Act in which the covenant is set out. That statement must be in one of the following forms (LRR 2003 rule 68):

(a) The covenant set out in section ... of the Law of Property (Miscellaneous Provisions) Act 1994 shall [not] extend to ... ; or

(b) The [transferor] [lessor] shall not be liable under any of the covenants set out in section ... of the Law of Property (Miscellaneous Provisions) Act 1994.

Where a registrable disposition of leasehold land limits or extends the implied covenant set out at (d) above, a reference to the covenant may be made in the register (LRR 2003 rule 67(6)). No other reference to any covenant implied by Part I of the Law of Property (Miscellaneous Provisions) Act 1994 will be made on the register in any other circumstances. No reference will be made to any covenant implied by the Law of Property Act 1925 section 76 as applied by the Law of Property (Miscellaneous Provisions) Act 1994 section 11(1)).

Transfers of pre-1996 Leases
Unless the contrary intention is expressed, the following covenants are implied in a transfer of a registered leasehold estate which is not a new tenancy for the purposes of the Landlord and Tenant (Covenants) Act 1995 section 1 (Land Registration Act 2002 Schedule 12 paragraph 20):

(a) (in the case of a transfer of the whole of the land comprised in the registered lease) the transferee covenants with the transferor that during the residue of the term granted by the registered lease the transferee and the persons deriving title under him will:

(i) pay the rent reserved by the lease,

(ii) comply with the covenants and conditions contained in the lease, and

(iii) keep the transferor and the persons deriving title under him indemnified against all actions, expenses and claims on account of any failure to comply with clauses (i) and (ii);

(b) (in the case of a transfer of part of the land comprised in the registered lease) the transferee covenants with the transferor that during the residue of the term granted by the registered lease the transferee and the persons deriving title under him will:

(i) where the rent reserved by the lease is apportioned, pay the rent apportioned to the part transferred,

(ii) comply with the covenants and conditions contained in the lease so far as affecting the part transferred, and

(iii) keep the transferor and the person deriving title under him indemnified against all actions, expenses and claims on account of any failure to comply with clauses (i) and (ii);

(c) (in the case of a transfer of part of the land comprised in the registered lease where the transferor continues to hold land under that lease) the transferor covenants with the transferee that during the residue of the term granted by the registered lease the transferor and the persons deriving title under him will:

(i) where the rent reserved by the lease is apportioned, pay the rent apportioned to the part retained,

(ii) comply with the covenants and conditions contained in the lease so far as affecting the part retained, and

(iii) keep the transferee and the persons deriving title under him indemnified against all actions, expenses and claims on account of any failure to comply with clauses (i) and (ii).

Where a transfer of such a registered leasehold estate modifies or negatives any of the covenants implied under paragraphs (a) and (b), an entry is made in the register that the covenants have been so modified or negatived (LRR 2003 rule 66).

Transfer of a Registered Estate Subject to a Rentcharge

In addition to the covenants implied under Part I of the Law of Property (Miscellaneous Provisions) Act 1994, where a registered estate is transferred subject to a rentcharge, the covenants referred to in the Law of Property Act 1925 section 77 (as modified by LRR 2003 rule 69) are also implied.

In a transfer for valuable consideration of the whole of the land affected by a rentcharge, there is implied a covenant by the transferee with the transferor that the transferee or the persons deriving title under him will at all times, from the date of the transfer or other date therein stated:

(a) duly pay the rentcharge and observe and perform all the covenants, agreements and conditions contained in the deed or other document creating the rentcharge, and thenceforth on the part of the owner of the land to be observed and performed; and

(b) save harmless and keep indemnified the transferor and his estate and effects from and against all proceedings, costs, claims and expenses on account of any omission to pay the rentcharge or any part thereof, or any breach of the said covenants, agreements and conditions.

Where a rentcharge has been apportioned in respect of any land, with the consent of the owner of the rentcharge, these covenants are implied in the transfer in the like manner as if the apportioned rentcharge were the rentcharge referred to and the document creating the rentcharge related solely to that land.

In a transfer for valuable consideration of part of the land affected by a rentcharge, subject to a part of that rentcharge which has been or is by that transfer apportioned (but in either case without the consent of the owner of the rentcharge) in respect of the land transferred, there is implied a covenant by the transferee with the transferor that the transferee or the persons deriving title under him will at all times, from the date of the transfer or other date therein stated:

(a) pay the apportioned rent and observe and perform all the covenants (other than the covenant to pay the entire rent) and conditions contained in the deed or other document creating the rentcharge, so far as the same relate to the land conveyed; and

(b) save harmless and keep indemnified the transferor and his respective estate and effects from and against all proceedings, costs, claims and expenses on account of any omission to pay the said apportioned rent, or any breach of any of the said covenants and conditions, so far as the same relate as aforesaid.

Implied Covenants

On a transfer of a registered estate subject to a rentcharge any covenant implied by the Law of Property Act 1925 section 77(1)(A) or (B) may be modified or negatived by adding suitable words to the transfer (LRR 2003 rule 69(4)).

Indemnity

A person is entitled to be indemnified by the registrar if he suffers loss by reason of:
  (a) rectification of the register;
  (b) a mistake the correction of which would involve rectification of the register;
  (c) a mistake in an official search;
  (d) a mistake in an official copy;
  (e) a mistake in a document kept by the registrar which is not an original and is referred to in the register;
  (f) the loss or destruction of a document lodged at the registry for inspection or safe custody;
  (g) a mistake in the cautions register; or
  (h) failure by the registrar to perform his duty under the Land Registration Act 2002 ("LRA 2002") section 50 to give notice of the creation of a statutory charge.

Rectification for these purposes means an alteration of the register which involves the correction of a mistake and prejudicially affects the title of a registered proprietor. References to a mistake in something include anything mistakenly omitted from it as well as anything mistakenly included in it (LRA 2002 Schedule 8 paragraph 11).

A person who suffers loss by reason of the upgrade of a title under LRA 2002 section 62 is treated for the purposes of an indemnity claim as having suffered loss by reason of rectification of the register.

Where the register is rectified following a forgery, the proprietor of a registered estate or charge claiming in good faith under the forged disposition is treated for the purposes of an indemnity claim as having suffered loss by reason of such rectification as if the disposition had not been forged.

No indemnity, however, is paid in the following cases:
  (a) on account of any mines or minerals or the existence of any right to work or get mines or minerals, unless it is noted in the register that the registered title includes the mines and minerals;
  (b) on account of any loss suffered by a claimant wholly or partly as a result of his own fraud; or
  (c) on account of any loss suffered by the claimant wholly as a result of

his own lack of proper care.

Where any loss is suffered by a claimant partly as a result of his own lack of proper care, any indemnity payable to him is reduced to such extent as is fair having regard to his share in the responsibility for the loss (LRA 2002 Schedule 8 paragraph 5(2)).

When deciding whether there has been any fraud or lack of care on the part of the claimant, any fraud or lack of care on the part of a person from whom he derives title is treated as if it were the claimant's fraud or lack of care. This does not apply, however, where the claimant derives title from such a person under a disposition for valuable consideration which is registered or protected by an entry in the register.

Where the indemnity is payable in respect of an estate, interest or charge, the value of such estate, interest or charge is regarded, in a case where there is rectification, as not exceeding its value immediately before the rectification (but as if there were to be no rectification). Where correcting a mistake would involve rectification of the register but there is to be no rectification, the value of such estate, interest or charge is regarded as its value at the time when the mistake which caused the loss was made (LRA 2002 Schedule 8 paragraph 6).

For the position where indemnity is being sought in respect of costs, see *Costs*, page 114.

Where a claim to indemnity under LRA 2002 Schedule 8 cannot be resolved by agreement with the registrar, a person may apply to the High Court or a county court for the determination of any question as to whether he is entitled to such indemnity or as to the amount of the indemnity. The requirement that the registrar consents to the incurring of costs or expenses does not apply to the costs of such an application to the court or of any legal proceedings arising out of such an application.

Interest is payable on the amount of any indemnity paid at the applicable rate set for court judgment debts (Land Registration Rules 2003 rule 195). Where there has been rectification, it is payable for the period from the date of rectification to the date of payment, but excluding any period or periods where the registrar or the court is satisfied that the claimant has not taken reasonable steps to pursue with due diligence the claim for indemnity or, where relevant, the application for rectification. Where there has not been rectification, interest is payable for the period from the date the loss is suffered by reason of the relevant mistake, loss, destruction or failure to the date of payment, but excluding any period or periods where the registrar or the court is satisfied that the claimant has not taken reasonable steps to pursue with due diligence the claim for indemnity or, where relevant, the application for rectification.

In calculating the exact period in respect of which interest is payable, the date of payment is included but the date of the rectification, or the date the loss is suffered, is excluded.

For the purposes of the Limitation Act 1980, a liability to pay an indemnity under LRA 2003 Schedule 8 is a simple contract debt and the cause of action arises at the time when the claimant knows, or but for his own default might have known, of the existence of his claim.

When an indemnity is paid, including interest on an indemnity, the registrar is entitled to recover the amount paid from any person who caused or substantially contributed to the loss by his fraud. The registrar is also, for the purpose of recovering that amount, entitled to enforce the following rights of action:
  (a) any right of action (of whatever nature and however arising) which the claimant would have been entitled to enforce had the indemnity not been paid; and
  (b) where the register has been rectified, any right of action (of whatever nature and however arising) which the person in whose favour the register has been rectified would have been entitled to enforce had it not been rectified.

This is without prejudice to any other rights the registrar may have (LRR 2003 Schedule 8 paragraph 10). For example, the registrar may be able to recover indemnity by enforcing an implied covenant for title given by the person who purported to transfer the estate to the claimant.

Indemnity Covenants

Where the proprietor of a registered estate has given an indemnity covenant, the registrar may make an entry in respect of it in the proprietorship register (Land Registration Rules 2003 ("LRR 2003") rule 65). This applies whether the indemnity covenant is given in respect of a restrictive covenant or other matter that affects the registered estate or in respect of a positive covenant that relates to that estate.

If the existence of the indemnity covenant is apparent from the register in some other way, the registrar need not make an entry. This might arise where the indemnity covenant is included amongst restrictive covenants and is set out with them in the charges register. Where the registrar does make an entry, it normally refers to the deed that contains the indemnity covenant.

There is no need to make a specific application for an entry in respect of an indemnity covenant when this is included in a deed lodged as part of an application in respect of a registrable disposition. The entry will be made by the registrar if he considers it appropriate.

Where an entry has been made in respect of an indemnity covenant, the registrar must remove it from the register if it appears to him that the covenant does not bind the current proprietor of the registered estate (LRR 2003 rule 65(3)).

Industrial and Provident Societies

An industrial and provident society registered under the Industrial and Provident Societies Act 1965 is a corporate body. Unless its registered rules direct otherwise, an industrial and provident society may hold, purchase or take on lease in its own name any land and may sell, exchange, mortgage or lease any such land (Industrial and Provident Societies Act 1965 section 30). A purchaser, assignee, mortgagee or tenant is not bound to inquire as to the authority for any such dealing with the land by the society (Industrial and Provident Societies Act 1965 section 30(1)(a)). As a result a restriction does not need to be entered in the proprietorship register merely because the proprietor is an industrial and provident society.

On an application to register an industrial and provident society as proprietor a copy of the rules should be lodged (Land Registration Rules 2003 rule 183(1)). In practice, arrangements are often made by industrial and provident societies with the head office of the Land Registry so that the rules do not need to be lodged with every application. For the position where the society is also a charity, unregistered housing association, or registered social landlord, see, respectively *Charities*, page 69; *Housing Associations*, page 155; and *Registered Social Landlords*, page 254.

Unlike a company registered under the Companies Acts or a limited liability partnership incorporated under the Limited Liability Partnerships Act 2000, there is no requirement for the registration number of an industrial and provident society to be entered in the proprietorship register. If it is desired that this registration number be entered immediately after the name of the industrial and provident society, this should be specifically requested in the application.

Inhibitions

An inhibition is an entry which was made in the register under the Land Registration Act 1925 section 57 preventing the registration or entry of any dealing with registered land or with a registered charge. No new inhibitions can be entered in the register after the coming into force of the Land Registration Act 2002 ("LRA 2002") on 13 October 2003.

LRA 2002 applies to any existing inhibition as it applies to restrictions entered under that Act (LRA 2002 Schedule 12 paragraph 2(2)).

Cancellation of an Inhibition
An application to cancel an inhibition must be made in Form RX3 and be accompanied by such evidence as will satisfy the registrar that the inhibition

is no longer required. Where the inhibition was entered pursuant to an order of the court, normally, it is cancelled only pursuant to an order for its cancellation obtained from the court. If the inhibition was entered in pursuance of an order of the court under the Criminal Justice Act 1988, the Drug Trafficking Act 1994 or the Terrorism Act 2000, the written release by any prosecutor (as defined in those Acts) suffices in place of a court order.

Modification of an Inhibition
The registrar may make an order disapplying an inhibition in relation to a specified disposition or class of dispositions (LRA 2002 section 41(2)). An application for such an order must be made in Form RX2. The application must give details of the order sought (including details of the disposition or the kind of dispositions in question), explain why the applicant has a sufficient interest in the inhibition, and state why the applicant considers that the registrar should make the order.

A note of the terms of any order made by the registrar under LRA 2002 section 41(2) is entered in the register.

Internal Waters

The Land Registration Act 2002 applies to land covered by internal waters of the United Kingdom which are within England and Wales (Land Registration Act 2002 section 130). "England" means the area consisting of the counties established by the Local Government Act 1972 section 1, Greater London and the Isles of Scilly, while "Wales" means the combined area of the counties which were created by the Local Government Act 1972 section 20 (as originally enacted) (Interpretation Act 1978 Schedule 1).

A coastal county or other administrative area normally extends up to the low water mark on its seaward side. In the case of estuaries the county boundary is at the seaward limit of the estuary shown by the Ordnance Survey.

It is possible for the Lord Chancellor to extend by order the application of the Land Registration Act 2002 to other land covered by internal waters of the United Kingdom which is adjacent to England and Wales. No such order has, at October 2003, been made.

Joint Proprietors

Where joint proprietors are registered as proprietors of a registered estate, they hold the legal estate as joint tenants on a trust of land, whether or not they also hold the equitable interest as joint tenants (Law of Property Act 1925 sections 34 and 36). The registrar is not affected by notice of such a trust (Land Registration Act 2002 section 78). No more than four joint proprietors can be entered in the proprietorship register at any one time, unless the land is vested in trustees for charitable, ecclesiastical, or public purposes (Trustee Act 1925 section 34).

If the registrar enters two or more registered proprietors of a registered estate, he must enter a Form A restriction where the survivor of them will not be able to give a valid receipt for capital money. The prescribed forms of transfer of registered land (TR1, TR2, TR5, TP1, TP2 and TP3) all contain a panel headed "Declaration of trust" containing the alternatives:

(a) The Transferees are to hold the Property on trust for themselves as joint tenants.
(b) The Transferees are to hold the Property on trust for themselves as tenants in common in equal shares.
(c) The Transferees are to hold the Property *(complete as necessary)*.

Unless the transferees declare that they are holding the property on trust for themselves as joint tenants, the registrar will enter the restriction in Form A, which is:

"No disposition by a sole proprietor of the registered estate (except a trust corporation) under which capital money arises is to be registered unless authorised by an order of the court."

See also *Beneficial Interests of Joint Proprietors of Land*, page 49.

Where a joint proprietor of a registered estate or a registered charge dies, an application may be made for alteration of the register by the removal of the deceased joint proprietor. The application may conveniently be made in application form AP1 and must be accompanied by evidence of the death (Land Registration Rules 2003 ("LRR 2003") rule 164). It is not essential to use form AP1 (LRR 2003 rule 13(2)).

Where a registered charge has two or more proprietors, a valid receipt for the money secured by it may be given by:

(a) the registered proprietors;
(b) the survivors or survivor of the registered proprietors; or
(c) the personal representative of the last survivor of the registered proprietors.

Land Registry Act 1862

The Land Registry Act 1862 was the first Act under which the title to land was registered. It did not require dispositions of land to be registered and it was not essential for a land certificate to be issued. The Land Registry Act 1862 is now repealed (Land Registration Act 2002 section 122). Even before that repeal, the Land Transfer Act 1875 section 125 and subsequently the Land Registration Act 1925 section 137(1) provided that no application for the registration of an estate under the 1862 Act was to be entertained.

Any land which is registered under the 1862 Act should now be registered under the Land Registration Act 2003 by an application for first registration in the usual way. See *First Registration*, page 133. If a land certificate issued under the 1862 Act is available, it should be lodged with the application for first registration.

If a person requires a copy of any information included in a record of title made under the Land Registry Act 1862, he should apply to the registrar by way of a letter setting out what is required.

Leasehold Enfranchisement

The Leasehold Reform Act 1967 confers upon qualifying tenants the right to acquire the freehold or an extended lease. Such right may also be exercised by the personal representatives of a tenant who held the right at his death, so long as the tenancy is vested in them (Commonhold and Leasehold Reform Act 2002 section 142). The personal representatives may not give notice of their desire to have the freehold or an extended lease later than two years after the grant of probate or letters of administration. For extended leases under that Act or under the Leasehold Reform, Housing and Urban Development Act 1993 see *Leases*, page 169. For collective enfranchisement under the Leasehold Reform, Housing and Urban Development Act 1993 see *Collective Enfranchisement*, page 91.

Enfranchisement under the Leasehold Reform Act 1967 may be possible in circumstances where the details of the lease and of the lessor are not fully known but where nevertheless enlargement of the lease under the Law of Property Act 1925 section 153 is precluded; see *Re 51 Bennington Road, Aston* [1993] The Times 21 July.

Notice under Leasehold Reform Act 1967

Any right of a tenant or his personal representatives arising from a notice served on the landlord under the Leasehold Reform Act 1967 is not capable of being an overriding interest within the Land Registration Act 2002 ("LRA

2002") Schedule 1 or Schedule 3 (Leasehold Reform Act 1967 section 5(5)). It may be the subject of a notice as if it were an estate contract. Where the registered proprietor of the freehold estate is prepared to consent to the entry of a notice on his title, application may be made for the entry of an agreed notice. Where the registered proprietor does not consent, an application for entry of a unilateral notice may still be made.

Agreed Notice
An applicant should deliver to the registry:
   (a) an application in form AN1;
   (b) a certified copy of the notice under the Leasehold Reform Act 1967;
   (c) the consent of the registered proprietor of the land where this is not contained in form AN1; and
   (d) the fee payable. A fee calculator for all types of application is on the Land Registry's website at www.landregistry.gov.uk/fees.
The entry made in the register will give details of the interest protected.

Unilateral Notice
An applicant should deliver to the registry:
   (a) an application in form UN1;
   (b) a plan of the affected land (where the notice under the Leasehold Reform Act 1967 affects only part of the land in the registered title); and
   (c) the fee payable. A fee calculator for all types of application is on the Land Registry's website at www.landregistry.gov.uk/fees.
Form UN1 should be completed on the following lines to show the interest of the applicant:
   "intending purchaser, notice of enfranchisement under the Leasehold Reform Act 1967 having been given on [*date*] to [*name and address of the landlord*]."
Where the applicant has taken an assignment from the tenant of the benefit of the rights under notice in accordance with the Leasehold Reform Act 1967 section 5(2), form UN1 should be completed on the following lines to show the interest of the applicant:
   "assignee of rights under the Leasehold Reform Act 1967 by virtue of an assignment dated ... made between [*former tenant*] and [*applicant*], the rights having arisen on [*date*] by the service of notice of enfranchisement on [*name and address of the landlord*]."
The unilateral notice will give brief details of the interest protected and identify the beneficiary of that notice.

Registration of Transfer of the Freehold
The application for the registration of the transfer of the freehold reversion should be made in the usual way; see *First Registration*, page 133 or *Transfers*, page 298, as appropriate. The application should show, either by a

statement in the transfer or on the application form, that the transfer is made under the Leasehold Reform Act 1967. Certain special considerations also apply; they are dealt with below.

Discharge of Registered Charges on the Freehold Title
Any registered charges may be discharged or released using form DS1 or DS3, as appropriate, in the usual way. In addition, the Leasehold Reform Act 1967 section 13 enables the tenant to pay money into court to satisfy the claims of a chargee on the reversionary title. The applicable procedure is set out in the Civil Procedure Rules 1998 Practice Direction 56 paragraph 13.

Rentcharges
In certain circumstances a rentcharge affecting the property may be discharged by payment of money into court. The procedure is set out in the Civil Procedure Rules 1998 Practice Direction 56 paragraph 13.

Rights and Burdens under the Leasehold Reform Act 1967 section 10
Where the fact that the transfer is made pursuant to the Leasehold Reform Act 1967 has been indicated to the registry, appropriate entries are made in the register as to the rights passing under section 10(2) of that Act, unless the effect of that section is expressly negatived in the text of the transfer. Where new easements or restrictive covenants are imposed in the transfer under section 10(3) and (4) of the 1967 Act, appropriate entries are made in the register.

Leases

See *First Registration*, page 133, for leases granted out of unregistered land, and *Classes of Title*, page 86 for details of the various classes of leasehold title.

An owner of a registered estate has power to grant a lease or underlease (as appropriate) for any term of years absolute of less duration than his own registered estate, subject to any entry in the register to the contrary.

Where the registered estate is an estate in land, the following grants of terms of years absolute are required to be completed by registration (Land Registration Act 2002 ("LRA 2002") section 27(2)):
(a) for a term of more than seven years from the date of the grant;
(b) to take effect in possession after the end of the period of three months beginning with the date of the grant;
(c) under which the right to possession is discontinuous;
(d) in pursuance of the right to buy under Part 5 of the Housing Act 1985; or
(e) in circumstances where the Housing Act 1985 section 171A applies

(disposal by a landlord which leads to a person's no longer being a secure tenant; preserved right to buy).

Where the registered estate is a franchise or manor, the grant of any lease must be completed by registration.

Where there is a grant out of an estate in land of a term of years absolute which is required to be completed by registration, the grantee, or his successor in title, must be entered in the register as the proprietor of the lease and a notice in respect of the lease must be entered in the register of the reversionary title. In the case of a grant out of a registered franchise or manor of a lease for a term of more than seven years from the date of the grant, the grantee, or his successor in title, must be entered in the register as the proprietor of the lease and a notice in respect of the lease must be entered in the register of the reversionary title. In the case of a grant out of a registered franchise or manor of a lease for a term not exceeding seven years from the date of the grant, a notice in respect of the lease must be entered in the register of the reversionary title.

Leases of Land not Exceeding Seven Years

A leasehold estate in land granted for a term not exceeding seven years from the date of the grant usually cannot be registered or, if for three years or less, noted on the register. It is an interest which overrides first registration and registered dispositions (LRA 2002 Schedule 1 paragraph 1 and Schedule 3 paragraph 1). The following leases not exceeding seven years are registrable dispositions and do not take effect as overriding interests:

(a) a grant of a term of years absolute to take effect in possession after the end of the period of three months beginning with the date of the grant;

(b) a grant of a term of years absolute under which the right to possession is discontinuous;

(c) a grant of a term of years absolute in pursuance of the right to buy under Part 5 of the Housing Act 1985; or

(d) a grant of a term of years absolute in circumstances where the Housing Act 1985 section 171A applies (disposal by a landlord which leads to a person's no longer being a secure tenant; preserved right to buy).

Prior to the coming into force of LRA 2002, leases granted for a term not exceeding twenty-one years were overriding interests under the Land Registration Act 1925. A lease which was an overriding interest under the Land Registration Act 1925 immediately before 13 October 2003 continues to be an unregistered interest overriding both first registration and registered dispositions (LRA 2002 Schedule 12 paragraph 12).

Even where a lease not exceeding seven years is an overriding interest, if the lease contains an option to renew or to purchase the reversion, such option is not an interest which overrides registered dispositions and must be protected by a notice on the lessor's registered title. See *Options*, page 220.

A notice may be entered in respect of a lease exceeding three years even

when that lease is not required to be registered. In practice the application will be for an agreed notice. An applicant should deliver to the registry:
 (a) an application in form AN1;
 (b) the lease or a certified copy of it;
 (c) the consent of the registered proprietor of the land where this is not contained in form AN1; and
 (d) the fee payable. A fee calculator for all types of application is on the Land Registry's website at www.landregistry.gov.uk/fees.
The entry made in the register will give details of the interest protected.

Leases which are Registrable Dispositions
A person applying to register a lease granted out of a registered estate must provide information to the registrar in form DI about any of the overriding interests (other than local land charges or public rights) set out in Schedule 3 to LRA 2002 that affect the estate to which the application relates and are within the actual knowledge of the applicant. For details see *Overriding Interests*, page 223. The applicant must produce to the registrar any documentary evidence of the interest that is under his control (Land Registration Rules 2003 (LRR 2003") LRR 2003 rule 57). The registrar may enter a notice in the register in respect of any such interest.

The applicant is not required, however, to provide information about interests that, under section 33 or 90(4) of LRA 2002, cannot be protected by notice. Such interests are:
 (a) interests under a trust of land or under a Settled Land Act 1925 settlement;
 (b) a leasehold estate in land granted for three years or less from the date of the grant and which is not required to be registered;
 (c) a restrictive covenant between lessor and lessee, so far as relating to the demised premises;
 (d) an interest which is capable of being registered under the Commons Registration Act 1965;
 (e) an interest in any coal or coal mine, or the rights attached to any such interest, or the rights of any person under the Coal Industry Act 1994 section 38, 49 or 51; and
 (f) leases created for public-private partnerships relating to transport in London, within the meaning given by the Greater London Authority Act 1999 section 218.
The applicant is also not required to provide information about a leasehold estate in land which falls within paragraph 1 of Schedule 3 to LRA 2002 but, at the time of the application, has one year or less to run.

An applicant should deliver to the registry:
 (a) an application in form AP1;
 (b) the lease;
 (c) a certified copy lease (if the original lease is to be returned);

(d) any consent required under a restriction on the lessor's title;
(e) any consent by a chargee on the lessor's title;
(f) form DI giving the information as to overriding interests required by LRR 2003 rule 57, including any documentary evidence of the interest; and
(g) the fee payable. A fee calculator for all types of application is on the Land Registry's website at www.landregistry.gov.uk/fees.

On registration of the lease, it is allotted its own title number. Notice of the registered lease is entered on the lessor's registered title without any need for a separate application or further fee.

If the lease contains a provision that prohibits or restricts dispositions of the leasehold estate, an entry is made in the property register stating that all estates, rights, interests, powers and remedies arising on or by reason of a disposition made in breach of that prohibition or restriction are excepted from the effect of registration (LRR 2003 rule 6(2)).

The effect of this entry is that it is the responsibility of a purchaser of the leasehold title to ensure that any necessary consent has been obtained from the lessor. The registrar makes no enquiry as to whether such consent has been given.

Where a right of re-entry is contained in a lease, the registrar need not make any entry regarding such right in the registered title of the reversionary estate (LRR 2003 rule 77).

Variation of a Lease

In construing a deed of variation of a lease, a court gives effect to the intention of the parties, unless it is compelled, by the nature of the changes made, to hold that the effect of the deed is to bring about a surrender and regrant by operation of law. This occurs only where the variation affects the legal estate and either increases the extent of the premises demised or the term for which they are held (*Friends' Provident Life Office v British Railways Board* [1996] 1 All ER 336 (CA)).

An application to register the variation of a registered lease must be accompanied by the instrument effecting the variation and evidence to satisfy the registrar that the variation has effect at law (LRR 2003 rule 78). An applicant should deliver to the registry:
(a) an application in form AP1;
(b) the deed of variation;
(c) a certified copy deed (if the original is to be returned);
(d) the fee payable. A fee calculator for all types of application is on the Land Registry's website at www.landregistry.gov.uk/fees.

Where the variation has been made by an order pursuant to the Landlord and Tenant Act 1987 section 35, that order should be lodged in place of the deed of variation.

Where an application is to be made for a notice of any variation of a lease effected by or under the Landlord and Tenant Act 1987 section 38 (including any variation as modified by an order under section 39(4) of that Act), it must be for an agreed notice using application form AN1.

Acquisition of an Extended Lease under the Leasehold Reform Act 1967
Any right of a tenant or his personal representatives arising from a notice served on the landlord under the Leasehold Reform Act 1967 is not capable of being an overriding interest within LRA 2002 Schedule 1 or 3 (Leasehold Reform Act 1967 section 5(5)). It may be the subject of a notice as if it were an estate contract. Where the registered proprietor of the freehold estate is prepared to consent to the entry of a notice on his title, application may be made for the entry of an agreed notice. Where the registered proprietor does not consent, an application for entry of a unilateral notice may still be made.

Agreed Notice
An applicant should deliver to the registry:
  (a) an application in form AN1;
  (b) a certified copy of the notice under the Leasehold Reform Act 1967;
  (c) the consent of the registered proprietor of the land where this is not contained in form AN1; and
  (d) the fee payable. A fee calculator for all types of application is on the Land Registry's website at www.landregistry.gov.uk/fees.
The entry made in the register will give details of the interest protected.

Unilateral Notice
An applicant should deliver to the registry:
  (a) an application in form UN1;
  (b) a plan of the affected land (where the notice under the Leasehold Reform Act 1967 affects only part of the land in the registered title); and
  (c) the fee payable. A fee calculator for all types of application is on the Land Registry's website at www.landregistry.gov.uk/fees.
Form UN1 should be completed on the following lines to show the interest of the applicant:
  "tenant having on [*date*] given notice under the Leasehold Reform Act 1967 to [*name and address of the landlord*] in respect of the grant of an extended lease."
Where the applicant has taken an assignment from the tenant of the benefit of the rights under notice in accordance with the Leasehold Reform Act 1967 section 5(2), form UN1 should be completed on the following lines to show the interest of the applicant:
  "assignee of rights under the Leasehold Reform Act 1967 by virtue of an assignment dated ... made between [*former tenant*] and [*applicant*], the rights having arisen on [*date*] by the service of notice on [*name and address of the landlord*] in respect of the grant of an extended lease."

The unilateral notice will give brief details of the interest protected and identify the beneficiary of that notice.

Registration of Extended Lease

The application for registration of the extended lease should be made in the usual way, see *Leases which are Registrable Dispositions*, page 171. The application should show, either by a statement in the lease or on the application form, that the lease is made under the Leasehold Reform Act 1967.

Unless the extended lease falls within the exceptions to the Leasehold Reform Act 1967 section 14, any prior mortgagee's consent to the extended lease is implied. A mortgagee's consent to the extended lease does not generally need to be lodged with the application.

Where the existing lease is registered, an application should also be made to close that registered title and cancel the notice in respect of that lease on the lessor's registered title; see *Determination of Registered Leases*, page 181.

For the position where the existing lease is not registered but is noted on the lessor's registered title, see *Cancellation of a Noted Lease*, page 183.

Acquisition of a Lease under the Leasehold Reform, Housing and Urban Development Act 1993

The Leasehold Reform, Housing and Urban Development Act 1993 ("LRHUDA 1993") confers upon a qualifying tenant of a flat an individual right to acquire from the landlord a new lease in substitution for an existing lease. Such right may also be exercised by the personal representatives of a tenant who held the right at his death, so long as the tenancy is vested in them (Commonhold and Leasehold Reform Act 2002 section 132). The personal representatives may not give notice of their desire to acquire the new lease later than two years after the grant of probate or letters of administration. The new lease is at a peppercorn rent for a term expiring ninety years after the term date of the existing lease (LRHUDA 1993 section 56). A premium, calculated under the LRHUDA 1993 Schedule 13, is payable. A lease granted under these provisions must contain a statement in the following form (LRR 2003 rule 196(2)):

"This lease is granted under section 56 of the Leasehold Reform, Housing and Urban Development Act 1993."

Notice to Acquire New Lease

The notice served by a qualifying tenant under LRHUDA 1993 section 42 claiming to exercise the right to acquire a new lease of the flat is not capable of being an overriding interest within LRA 2002 Schedule 1 paragraph 2 or Schedule 3 paragraph 2 (LRHUDA 1993 section 97(1)). It may be the subject of a notice as if it were an estate contract. Where the registered proprietor of the freehold estate is prepared to consent to the entry of a notice on his title, application may be made for the entry of an agreed notice. Where the registered proprietor does not consent, an application for entry of a unilateral notice may still be made.

Agreed Notice: An applicant should deliver to the registry:
  (a) an application in form AN1;
  (b) a certified copy of the notice under LRHUDA 1993 section 42;
  (c) the consent of the registered proprietor of the land where this is not contained in form AN1; and
  (d) the fee payable. A fee calculator for all types of application is on the Land Registry's website at www.landregistry.gov.uk/fees.

The entry made in the register will give details of the interest protected.

Unilateral Notice: An applicant should deliver to the registry:
  (a) an application in form UN1;
  (b) a plan of the affected land (where the notice under LRHUDA 1993 section 42 affects only part of the land in the registered title); and
  (c) the fee payable. A fee calculator for all types of application is on the Land Registry's website at www.landregistry.gov.uk/fees.

Form UN1 should be completed on the following lines to show the interest of the applicant:

"qualifying tenant having given notice under section 42 of the Leasehold Reform, Housing and Urban Development Act 1993 on [*date*] to [*name and address of the landlord*] [and to [*name and address of any third party in the tenant's existing lease*]]."

The unilateral notice will give brief details of the interest protected and identify the beneficiary of that notice.

Application for Vesting Order

If the qualifying tenant wishes to make a claim to exercise the right to acquire a new lease of his flat but the landlord cannot be found or his identity cannot be ascertained, the court may make a vesting order (LRHUDA 1993 section 50(1)). An application for such a vesting order is treated as a pending land action (LRHUDA 1993 section 97(2)(b)) and cannot therefore be an overriding interest within LRA 2002 Schedule 1 paragraph 2 or Schedule 3 paragraph 2 (LRA 2002 section 87(3)). Such an application may be protected by a notice, a restriction, or both.

Notice: The applicants for an agreed notice should deliver to the registry:
  (a) an application in form AN1;
  (b) the application to the court for the vesting order; and
  (c) the fee payable. A fee calculator for all types of application is on the Land Registry's website at www.landregistry.gov.uk/fees.

This is likely to be sufficient to satisfy the registrar as to the validity of the applicants' claim in accordance with LRA 2002 section 34(3)(c). Where the applicants wish to apply for a unilateral notice they should deliver to the

registry:
- (a) an application in form UN1;
- (b) a plan of the affected land (where the vesting order is sought in respect of only part of the land in the registered title); and
- (c) the fee payable. A fee calculator for all types of application is on the Land Registry's website at www.landreg.gov.uk/fees.

Form UN1 should be completed on the following lines to show the interest of the applicant:

"qualifying tenants in an application under section 50(1) of the Leasehold Reform, Housing and Urban Development Act 1993 in the [... County Court] [... Division of the High Court of Justice] [*state full court reference and parties*]."

The unilateral notice will give brief details of the interest protected and identify the beneficiaries of that notice.

Restriction: The applicants for a vesting order under the LRHUDA 1993 section 50(1) may be treated as having a right or claim in relation to a registered estate or charge for the purposes of LRA 2002 section 42(1)(c) if they are applying for a restriction in Form N (LRR 2003 rule 93(q)). The registrar must give notice of the application for a restriction to the proprietor of the registered estate or charge concerned (LRA 2002 section 42(3)).

A restriction does not confer any priority; it simply prevents an entry being made in the register if it is not permitted under the wording of the restriction.

The applicants should deliver to the registry:
- (a) an application in form RX1; and
- (b) the fee payable. A fee calculator for all types of application is on the Land Registry's website at www.landregistry.gov.uk/fees.

Panel 10 should be completed as to the appropriate restriction. Form N is:

"No disposition [*or specify details*] of the registered estate [(other than a charge)] by the proprietor of the registered estate [or by the proprietor of any registered charge] is to be registered without a written consent signed by [*name*] of [*address*] (or [his conveyancer] [*or specify appropriate details, for example* signed on behalf of [*name*] of [*address*] by its secretary or conveyancer])."

Vesting Order

Where the court makes a vesting order under LRHUDA 1993 section 50(1), LRA 2002 applies in relation to that order as it applies in relation to an order affecting land which is made by the court for the purpose of enforcing a judgment or recognisance (LRHUDA 1993 section 97(2)(a)). Such a vesting order cannot be an overriding interest within LRA 2002 Schedule 1 paragraph 2 or Schedule 3 paragraph 2 (LRA 2002 section 87(3)), but it may be protected by a notice, a restriction, or both.

Notice: The applicant for an agreed notice should deliver to the registry:
  (a) an application in form AN1;
  (b) the vesting order or a certified copy of it; and
  (c) the fee payable. A fee calculator for all types of application is on the Land Registry's website at www.landregistry.gov.uk/fees.

The entry made in the register will give details of the interest protected.
  The applicant for a unilateral notice should deliver to the registry:
  (a) an application in form UN1;
  (b) a plan of the affected land (where the vesting order is sought in respect of only part of the land in the registered title); and
  (c) the fee payable. A fee calculator for all types of application is on the Land Registry's website at www.landregistry.gov.uk/fees.

Form UN1 should be completed on the following lines to show the interest of the applicant:
  "tenant having the benefit of an order under section 50(1) of the Leasehold Reform, Housing and Urban Development Act 1993 made by the [… County Court] [… Division of the High Court of Justice] [*state full court reference and parties*]."

The unilateral notice will give brief details of the interest protected and identify the beneficiaries of that notice.

Restriction: A person who has obtained a vesting order under the LRHUDA 1993 section 50(1) may be treated as having a right or claim in relation to a registered estate or charge for the purposes of LRA 2002 section 42(1)(c) if he is applying for a restriction in form L or Form N (LRR 2003 rule 93(p)). The registrar must give notice of the application for a restriction to the proprietor of the registered estate or charge concerned (LRA 2002 section 42(3)).

A restriction does not confer any priority; it simply prevents an entry being made in the register if it is not permitted under the wording of the restriction.

  The applicants should deliver to the registry:
  (a) an application in form RX1; and
  (b) the fee payable. A fee calculator for all types of application is on the Land Registry's website at www.landregistry.gov.uk/fees.

Panel 10 should be completed as to the appropriate restriction. Form L is:
  "No disposition [*or specify details*] of the registered estate [(other than a charge)] by the proprietor of the registered estate [or by the proprietor of any registered charge] is to be registered without a certificate signed by [*name*] of [*address*] (*or* [his conveyancer] [*or specify appropriate details, for example* signed on behalf of [*name*] of [*address*] by its secretary or conveyancer]) that the provisions of [*specify clause, paragraph or other particulars*] of [*specify details*] have been complied with."

Form N is:

"No disposition [*or specify details*] of the registered estate [(other than a charge)] by the proprietor of the registered estate [or by the proprietor of any registered charge] is to be registered without a written consent signed by [*name*] of [*address*] (or [his conveyancer] [*or specify appropriate details, for example* signed on behalf of [*name*] of [*address*] by its secretary or conveyancer])."

Once a new lease has been granted to the tenant it must be registered. Unless the existing lease falls within the limited exception in LHRUDA 1993 section 58(2), the new lease is binding on the persons interested in any mortgage on the landlord's title, even where the grant of such a lease is otherwise unauthorised (LRHUDA 1993 section 58(1)). It is therefore usually unnecessary to include consents of mortgagees with the application to register the new lease.

If the tenant's existing lease is unregistered and is subject to a mortgage entitling the mortgagee to possession of the documents of title relating to the existing lease, then, within one month of the registration of the new lease, it must be delivered to that mortgagee by the tenant (LRHUDA 1993 section 58(5)). Failure to do this has the same effect as the breach of an obligation under the existing mortgage (LRHUDA 1993 section 58(6)).

Restrictive Covenants in Leases

On registration of a person as proprietor of a leasehold estate, that estate is vested in him, together with all interests subsisting for the benefit of the estate, but subject to implied and express covenants, obligations and liabilities incident to that estate. It is not possible, however, to enter notice in the register in respect of restrictive covenants between lessor and lessee, so far as relating to the demised premises (LRA 2002 section 33(c)). Where a restrictive covenant between a lessor and lessee does not relate to the demised premises, an application should be made for a notice to be entered on the affected title. This might arise where the lessor is covenanting in respect of a neighbouring property which he owns, as in *Oceanic Village Ltd v United Attractions Ltd* [2000] Ch 234, [2000] 2 WLR 476, [2000] 1 All ER 975, or where a tenant covenants not to open a competing business within a certain radius of the demised premises.

Agreed Notice

An applicant should deliver to the registry:
    (a) an application in form AN1;
    (b) the document containing the restrictive covenant or a certified copy of it;
    (c) the consent of the registered proprietor of the land where this is not contained in form AN1; and
    (d) the fee payable. A fee calculator for all types of application is on the Land Registry's website at www.landregistry.gov.uk/fees.

The entry made in the register will give details of the interest protected.

Where the registered proprietor does not consent to the entry in the register of an agreed notice, an application for entry of a unilateral notice may still be made.

Unilateral Notice
An applicant should deliver to the registry:
(a) an application in form UN1;
(b) a plan of the affected land (where the contract affects only part of the land in the registered title); and
(c) the fee payable. A fee calculator for all types of application is on the Land Registry's website at www.landregistry.gov.uk/fees.

Form UN1 should be completed on the following lines to show the interest of the applicant:

"having the benefit of a restrictive covenant contained in a [Lease] [Deed] dated ... made between [*names of parties*] which, although between lessor and lessee, does not relate to the demised premises."

The unilateral notice will give brief details of the interest protected and identify the beneficiaries of that notice.

Apportionment of Rent
A transfer of a registered leasehold estate in land containing a legal apportionment of, or exoneration from, the rent reserved by the lease must include the statement prescribed by LRR 2003 rule 60(1). Where the lessor does not consent to the apportionment it will take effect in equity only. The statement must be in the additional provisions panel of the transfer and may contain any necessary alterations and additions. The statement is:

"Liability for the payment of [*if applicable* the previously apportioned rent of (*amount*) being part of] the rent reserved by the registered lease is apportioned between the Transferor and the Transferee as follows:
- (*amount*) shall be payable out of the Property and the balance shall be payable out of the land remaining in title number (*title number of retained land*) or
- the whole of that rent shall be payable out of the Property and none of it shall be payable out of the land remaining in title number (*title number of retained land*) or
- the whole of that rent shall be payable out of the land remaining in title number (*title number of retained land*) and none of it shall be payable out of the Property."

Where in a transfer of part of a registered leasehold estate which is held under an old tenancy that part is, without the consent of the lessor, expressed to be exonerated from, or charged with, the entire rent, the covenants in LRA 2002 Schedule 12 paragraph 20(3) or (4), if implied, are modified (LRR 2003 rule 60(2) and (3)). An old tenancy is a tenancy which is not a new tenancy for the purposes of the Landlord and Tenant (Covenants) Act 1995 section 1. See also *Implied Covenants*, page 157, on when such covenants are implied.

The covenants in paragraph 20(3) as modified are:

"The transferee covenants with the transferor that during the residue of the term granted by the registered lease the transferee and the persons deriving title under him will:
(i) pay the entire rent,
(ii) comply with the covenants and conditions contained in the lease so far as affecting the part transferred but extended to a covenant to pay the entire rent, and
(iii) keep the transferor and the person deriving title under him indemnified against all actions, expenses and claims on account of any failure to comply with clauses (i) and (ii)."

The covenants in paragraph 20(4) as modified are:

"The transferor covenants with the transferee that during the residue of the term granted by the registered lease the transferor and the persons deriving title under him will:
(i) pay the entire rent,
(ii) comply with the covenants and conditions contained in the lease so far as affecting the part retained but extended to a covenant to pay the entire rent, and
(iii) keep the transferee and the persons deriving title under him indemnified against all actions, expenses and claims on account of any failure to comply with clauses (i) and (ii)."

Extensions of Leases (Other than under the Leasehold Reform Act 1967 or LRHUDA 1993)

A variation of a lease which affects the legal estate and either increases the extent of the premises demised or the term for which they are held, takes effect in law as a surrender of the existing lease and the grant of a new lease (*Friends' Provident Life Office v British Railways Board* [1996] 1 All ER 336 (CA)). In addition to an application to register the new lease, where the existing lease is registered, an application should also be made to close that registered title and cancel the notice in respect of that lease on the lessor's registered title; see *Determination of Registered Leases*, page 181. For the position where the existing lease is not registered but is noted on the lessor's registered title, see *Cancellation of a Noted Lease*, page 183. For details of applications to register the new lease where it is granted out of unregistered land, see *First Registration*, page 133. For details of applications to register the new lease where it is out of registered land, see *Leases which are Registrable Dispositions*, page 171.

In some cases the new lease is made expressly subject to the old lease. if so, the old lease is not surrendered and the existing leasehold title remains subsisting. In these circumstances the proprietor of any charge affecting the existing lease may have an interest in the new lease. Accordingly, when making an application to register such a new lease, it is also necessary to lodge any charges affecting the old lease or list them in panel 10 of form FR1 or panel 11 of form AP1. Where appropriate, an entry on the following lines will be made in the charges register of the registered title of the new lease:

"The land is subject to such rights as may be subsisting in favour of the persons interested in a charge dated ... made between ... of the lease dated ... referred to in the Schedule of leases hereto."

Determination of Registered Leases

The evidence required in support of an application following the determination of a registered lease depends on the manner in which the leasehold estate has determined.

Merger

Even where a leasehold estate and its immediate reversionary title have become vested in the same person in the same capacity, it is a matter of intention as to whether or not the leasehold estate is to be determined on merger. The applicant should therefore always make it clear on the application form that merger is intended.

An applicant should deliver to the registry:
(a) an application in form AP1;
(b) a transfer in form TR1 or other appropriate deed vesting the reversionary estate in the applicant;
(c) the original lease; and
(d) the fee payable. A fee calculator for all types of application is on the Land Registry's website at www.landregistry.gov.uk/fees.

Surrender

An applicant should deliver to the registry:
(a) an application in form AP1;
(b) a transfer in form TR1 effecting the surrender or a statutory declaration setting out the facts which constitute the surrender by operation of law and exhibiting any supporting documents;
(c) the original lease (if available);
(d) (if the reversionary estate is unregistered) an examined abstract of the reversionary title and the counterpart lease; and
(e) the fee payable. A fee calculator for all types of application is on the Land Registry's website at www.landregistry.gov.uk/fees.

Disclaimer

For disclaimer by a trustee in bankruptcy, see *Bankruptcy,* page 34. For disclaimer by a liquidator, see *Liquidators,* page 197.

Effluxion of Time
When the term of a lease has expired the registered title is not closed unless an application is made. An applicant should deliver to the registry:
  (a) an application in form AP1;
  (b) the original lease;
  (c) evidence that the Landlord and Tenant Act 1954 does not apply to the lease or that the lease has determined in accordance with particular provisions of that Act; and
  (d) the fee payable. A fee calculator for all types of application is on the Land Registry's website at www.landregistry.gov.uk/fees.

Forfeiture
Where there has been peaceable re-entry following non-payment of rent or other breach of covenant, an applicant should deliver to the registry:
  (a) an application in form AP1;
  (b) the original lease and any underleases;
  (c) the consent of any registered chargees;
  (d) a statutory declaration setting out the facts as to the re-entry on a specified date;
  (e) (if the reversionary estate is unregistered) an examined abstract of the reversionary title and the counterpart lease; and
  (f) the fee payable. A fee calculator for all types of application is on the Land Registry's website at www.landregistry.gov.uk/fees.
Where the forfeiture is based on a court order, an applicant should deliver to the registry:
  (a) an application in form AP1;
  (b) the original lease and any underleases;
  (c) the consent of any registered chargees;
  (d) the claim form indicating the reason for the forfeiture;
  (e) a certified copy of the court order;
  (f) the sheriff's return or a statutory declaration setting out the facts as to the re-entry on a specified date;
  (g) (if the reversionary estate is unregistered) an examined abstract of the reversionary title and the counterpart lease; and
  (h) the fee payable. A fee calculator for all types of application is on the Land Registry's website at www.landregistry.gov.uk/fees.

Notice
Where a lease allows for determination by notice and it has been so determined, an applicant should deliver to the registry:
  (a) an application in form AP1;
  (b) the original lease;
  (c) a statutory declaration exhibiting a copy of the notice served and setting out the method and date of service (a copy of the notice receipted by the lessor or lessee to whom it was sent suffices in place

of a statutory declaration);
(d) (if the reversionary estate is unregistered) an examined abstract of the reversionary title and the counterpart lease; and
(e) the fee payable. A fee calculator for all types of application is on the Land Registry's website at www.landregistry.gov.uk/fees.

Cancellation of a Noted Lease
Where a registered lease is determined, the notice of that lease on the lessor's registered title is cancelled at the same time as the leasehold title. A registered superior title may, however, be subject to an unregistered lease. In that case a notice of the lease appears on the superior title. On determination of the unregistered lease an application should be made for that notice to be cancelled. An applicant should deliver to the registry:
(a) an application in form CN1 (completing panel 10 when appropriate);
(b) the original lease;
(c) the leasehold deeds and documents to show that the title to the lease has vested in the applicant (including a current land charges search; any entries should be accounted for) or other evidence of the determination of the lease;
(d) the counterparts of any subsisting underleases;
(e) the fee payable. A fee calculator for all types of application is on the Land Registry's website at www.landregistry.gov.uk/fees.

Right to Determine a Registered Lease
Where it appears to the registrar that a right to determine a registered estate is exercisable, he may enter the fact in the property register of the affected title (LRA 2002 section 64 and LRR 2003 rule 125(1)). Where a right to determine a registered leasehold estate has arisen, an applicant may apply for such an entry by delivering to the registry:
(a) an application in form AP1;
(b) evidence to satisfy the registrar that the applicant has the right to determine the registered leasehold estate and that the right is exercisable; and
(c) the fee payable. A fee calculator for all types of application is on the Land Registry's website at www.landregistry.gov.uk/fees.

Before making an entry the registrar must give notice of the application to the proprietor of the registered estate in question and the proprietor of any registered charge on that estate.

When such an entry has been made, an application to cancel it must be supported by evidence to satisfy the registrar that the right to determine the leasehold estate is not exercisable. The application for cancellation may be made by:
(a) the person entitled to determine the registered estate;
(b) the proprietor of the registered estate to which the entry relates;

(c) a person entitled to be registered as proprietor of that estate; or
(d) any other person whom the registrar is satisfied has an interest in the removal of the entry.

Legal Charges

A registered proprietor of a registered estate has power to create a charge expressed to be by way of legal mortgage and to charge the estate at law with the payment of money. A legal charge of a registered estate may be made in form CH1. It is no longer possible to charge a registered estate by a mortgage by demise or sub-demise (Land Registration Act 2002 ("LRA 2002") section 23). The grant of a legal charge must be completed by registration; until then the charge takes effect in equity only (LRA 2002 section 27). Registration of a charge is effected when the chargee or his successor in title is entered in the register as the proprietor of the charge. On completion of registration, the charge has effect as a charge by deed by way of legal mortgage (LRA 2002 section 51).

For the position where a charge drawn as a legal charge cannot be registered, see *Equitable Charges*, page 126. An example of when a legal charge cannot be registered is where a consent is required under a restriction but that consent is not forthcoming.

An applicant to register a legal charge should deliver to the registry:
(a) an application in form AP1;
(b) the charge;
(c) a certified copy charge (if the original charge is to be returned); and
(d) the fee payable. A fee calculator for all types of application is on the Land Registry's website at www.landregistry.gov.uk/fees.

Where an application is made to register a charge created by a company, the applicant must produce to the registrar a certificate issued under the Companies Act 1985 section 401 that the charge has been registered under section 395 of that Act (Land Registration Rules 2003 ("LRR 2003") rule 111(1)). If the company is registered in Scotland, the certificate required is a certificate issued under section 418 of the 1985 Act that the charge has been registered under section 410 of that Act. If the company is registered in Northern Ireland the certificate required is a certificate issued under the Companies (N.I.) Order 1986 article 409 that the charge has been registered under article 403 of that Order.

If the applicant does not produce the appropriate certificate, the registrar is required to enter a note in the register that the charge is subject to the provisions of the Companies Act 1985 section 395 (or section 410 of that Act for a Scottish company or article 403 of the Companies (N.I.) Order 1986 for a Northern Ireland company) (LRR 2003 rule 111(2)). Those provisions provide that where the prescribed particulars of the charge are not delivered to the Registrar of Companies within the prescribed period, the charge is void against the liquidator or administrator of the company and any creditor of the company.

If the chargee requires the entry of a restriction preventing registration of a disposition by the registered proprietor of the registered estate without the consent of the chargee, the application must be made in form RX1. Alternatively, if a standard form of restriction is sought, the application may be in panel 7 of form CH1 or in a charge approved for the purposes of LRR 2003 rule 92. An approved charge for these purposes is one the form of which (including the application for the restriction) has first been approved by the registrar. A possible form of restriction is Form P, which is:

"No disposition [*or specify details*] of the registered estate [(other than a charge)] by the proprietor of the registered estate is to be registered without a written consent signed by the proprietor for the time being of the charge dated ... in favour of [*chargee*] referred to in the charges register [(or his conveyancer *or specify appropriate details*)] or, if appropriate, signed on such proprietor's behalf by [its secretary or conveyancer *or specify appropriate details*]."

Further Advances

The proprietor of a registered charge may make further advances on the security of the charge ranking in priority to a subsequent charge if he has not received from the subsequent chargee notice of the creation of the subsequent charge (LRA 2002 section 49(1)). Such notice is treated to have been received:

Method of delivery	*Time of receipt*
Post to an address in the UK	The second working day after posting
Leaving it at a postal address	The working day after it was left
Post to an address outside the UK	The seventh working day after posting
Document exchange	On the second working day after it was left at the sender's document exchange
Fax	The working day after transmission
Electronic transmission to an electronic address entered in the register as an address for service or e-mail or other electronic means of delivery	The second working day after transmission

A working day for these purposes is any day from Monday to Friday (inclusive) which is not Christmas Day, Good Friday or any other day either specified or declared by proclamation under the Banking and Financial

Dealings Act 1971 section 1 or appointed by the Lord Chancellor. A notice posted or transmitted after 1700 hours on a working day or posted or transmitted on a day which is not a working day is to be treated as having been posted or transmitted on the next working day.

The proprietor of a registered charge may also make further advances on the security of the charge ranking in priority to a subsequent charge if the advance is made pursuant to an obligation and, at the time of the creation of the subsequent charge, the obligation was entered in the register (LRA 2002 section 49(3)). Where the proprietor of a registered charge, or a person applying to be so registered, is under an obligation to make further advances on the security of that charge, he may apply for the obligation to be entered in the register. The application must be in form CH2 unless it is contained in panel 7 of form CH1 or in a charge the form of which has been approved by the registrar (LRR 2003 rule 108).

The proprietor of a registered charge may also make further advances on the security of the charge ranking in priority to a subsequent charge if the parties to the prior charge have agreed a maximum amount for which the charge is security and, at the time of the creation of the subsequent charge, the agreement was entered in the register (LRA 2002 section 49(4)). Where the parties have agreed such a maximum amount, the proprietor of a registered charge, or a person applying to be registered as proprietor, may apply for such agreement to be entered in the register. The application must be made in form CH3.

Other than as set out above, tacking in relation to a charge over registered land is possible only with the agreement of the subsequent chargee (LRA 2002 section 49(6)).

Priorities

Subject to any entry in the register to the contrary, registered charges on the same registered estate, or on the same registered charge, are taken to rank as between themselves in the order shown in the register (LRA 2002 section 48(1) and LRR 2003 rule 101).

Where a deed or other document alters the priority between registered charges, an application should be made for an entry in the register to reflect that altered priority. Such a deed is often referred to as a deed of postponement. The application must be made by or with the consent of the proprietor, or a person entitled to be registered as the proprietor, of any registered charge whose priority is adversely affected by the alteration (LRR 2003 rule 102). Such consent is not required from a person who has executed the deed or document which alters the priority.

The applicant should deliver to the registry:
(a) an application in form AP1;
(b) the deed or document altering the priority of the registered charges;
(c) a certified copy deed or document (if the original is to be returned);

Legal Charges

    (d) any consent required (or a conveyancer's certificate confirming that he holds any necessary consents); and
    (e) the fee payable. A fee calculator for all types of application is on the Land Registry's website at www.landregistry.gov.uk/fees.

Consolidation
A chargee who has a right of consolidation in relation to a registered charge may apply for an entry in respect of that right to be made in the register in which the charge is registered. The chargee should deliver to the registry:
    (a) an application in form AP1 (or FR1 if part of an application for first registration);
    (b) form CC;
    (c) certified copies of any unregistered charges that are consolidated; and
    (d) the fee payable. A fee calculator for all types of application is on the Land Registry's website at www.landregistry.gov.uk/fees.

Deeds of Variation
An application to register a deed or other document varying the terms of a registered charge must be made by, or with the consent of, the proprietor of the registered charge and the proprietor of the estate charged. It must be accompanied by the consent of the proprietor, or a person entitled to be registered as proprietor, of any registered charge of equal or inferior priority that is prejudicially affected by the variation (LRR 2003 rule 113). Such consent is not required from any person who has executed the deed of variation.
    The applicant should deliver to the registry:
    (a) an application in form AP1;
    (b) the deed of variation of the registered charge;
    (c) a certified copy deed (if the original is to be returned);
    (d) any consent required (or a conveyancer's certificate confirming that he holds any necessary consents); and
    (e) the fee payable. A fee calculator for all types of application is on the Land Registry's website at www.landregistry.gov.uk/fees.
A note of the variation is made in the register if the registrar is satisfied that the proprietor of any other registered charge of equal or inferior priority to that of the varied charge who is prejudicially affected by the variation is bound by it. If the registrar is not so satisfied, he may make an entry to the effect that a deed which is expressed to vary the terms of the registered charge has been entered into.

Remedies
Unless there are entries in the register to the contrary, the proprietor of a registered charge is taken to have the powers of disposition conferred by law on the owner of a legal mortgage (LRA 2002 section 52(1)). This has effect

only for the purpose of preventing the title of a disponee being questioned and does not affect the lawfulness of a disposition.

LRA 2002 section 96(2) provides that no period of limitation under the Limitation Act 1980 section 16 shall run against any person in relation to a registered estate in land or rentcharge. Accordingly, even where a mortgagee is in possession, the mortgagor does not lose his right to redeem.

A mortgagee is required by the Family Law Act 1996 section 56 to serve notice on a spouse who is not a party to the action and who has the benefit of a matrimonial homes right notice or a matrimonial homes right caution, of an action for enforcement of the mortgagee's security. The mortgagee may apply in form MH3 for an official search certificate of the result of search for this purpose, which will reveal whether a matrimonial home rights notice or matrimonial home rights caution is entered in the register, and whether there is a pending application for the entry of a matrimonial home rights notice. A matrimonial home rights notice is a notice registered under the Family Law Act 1996 section 31(10)(a), section 32, Schedule 4 paragraph 4(3)(a) or 4(3)(b), or the Matrimonial Homes Act 1983 section 2(8) or section 5(3)(b), or the Matrimonial Homes Act 1967 section 2(7) or section 5(3)(b). A matrimonial home rights caution is a caution registered under the Matrimonial Homes Act 1967 before 14 February 1983.

Power of Sale

A transfer of a registered estate by a proprietor of a registered charge under the power of sale must be in form TR2 or TP2. For registration of a transfer see *Transfers*, page 298.

A sale by the chargee is subject to any matters which appear on the register and have priority over the charge under which the power of sale is being exercised. It overreaches any caution registered in the proprietorship register, other than a matrimonial home rights caution registered prior to the charge and not subsequently postponed to the charge. Overriding interests in existence at the time of registration of the charge are not overreached by a transfer under the power of sale.

Where the chargee has a surplus arising from the sale after discharging prior charges, the expenses of the sale and his own charge, he holds it on trust to pay it to the person entitled to the mortgaged property (Law of Property Act 1925 section 105). LRA 2002 section 54 provides that for the purposes of the Law of Property Act 1925 section 105, a person is taken to have notice of anything in the register immediately before the disposition on sale. As a result the chargee should inspect the register to ascertain whether there is any subsequent chargee to whom he should pay the balance of the proceeds of sale.

Foreclosure

Where a person has obtained an order for foreclosure absolute, he should deliver to the registry:

Legal Charges

(a) an application in form AP1;
(b) the foreclosure order absolute or an office copy of it (or a conveyancer's certificate confirming that he holds such order or office copy); and
(c) the fee payable. A fee calculator for all types of application is on the Land Registry's website at www.landregistry.gov.uk/fees.

On completion of the application, the registration of the charge in respect of which the order was made, and any entry in respect of an interest over which that charge has priority, are cancelled. The applicant is entered as proprietor of the registered estate.

Discharge of Registered Charge

A discharge of a registered charge should be in form DS1 and a release of part of the registered estate from a registered charge should be in form DS3. Forms DS1 and DS3 must be executed as deeds or authenticated in such other manner as the registrar may approve. The registrar is entitled to accept and act upon any other proof of satisfaction of a charge that he may regard as sufficient (LRR 2003 rule 114).

Where a charge is registered in the name of two or more proprietors, a valid receipt for the money secured by it may be given by:
(a) the registered proprietors;
(b) the survivors or survivor of the registered proprietors; or
(c) the personal representative of the last survivor of the registered proprietors.

A person applying to register the discharge or release of a registered charge should deliver to the registry:
(a) an application in form AP1 or DS2 (for use with DS1 only);
(b) form DS1 or DS3; and
(c) any evidence necessary to show that the correct person has executed form DS1 or DS3.

Sub-charges

A proprietor of a registered charge has power to charge at law with the payment of money indebtedness secured by the registered charge. A sub-charge of a registered charge may not be created in any other way (LRA 2002 section 23(2)(b) and (3)). The grant of a sub-charge of a registered charge must be completed by registration, the sub-chargee or his successor in title being entered in the register as proprietor of the sub-charge (LRA 2002 section 27(3)(b) and Schedule 2 paragraph 11).

The registered proprietor of a sub-charge has the same powers as the sub-chargor in relation to the property subject to the principal charge or any intermediate charge.

An applicant to register a sub-charge should deliver to the registry:
(a) an application in form AP1;

(b) the sub-charge;
(c) a certified copy sub-charge (if the original sub-charge is to be returned); and
(d) the fee payable. A fee calculator for all types of application is on the Land Registry's website at www.landregistry.gov.uk/fees.

Transfer of Charge

A transfer of a registered charge must be completed by registration, the transferee, or his successor in title, being entered in the register as proprietor of the charge (LRA section 27(3)(a) and Schedule 2 paragraph 10). The transfer must be in form TR3, TR4 or AS2, as appropriate.

An applicant to register a transfer of a registered charge should deliver to the registry:
(a) an application in form AP1;
(b) a transfer in form TR3, TR4 or AS2; and
(c) the fee payable. A fee calculator for all types of application is on the Land Registry's website at www.landregistry.gov.uk/fees.

Legal Easements

Legal Easements Arising Prior to First Registration

On first registration the estate is vested in the registered proprietor together with all interests subsisting for the benefit of the estate (Land Registration Act 2002 ("LRA 2002") sections 11(3) and 12(3)). This includes the benefit of any subsisting legal easements. If, at the time of first registration, the registrar is satisfied that a right subsists as a legal estate and benefits the registered estate, he may enter the benefit of that appurtenant right in the register. This will be as the result of the registrar's examination of the title or his consideration of a written application providing details of the right and evidence of its existence. Where the easement arose by prescription or is an implied easement, evidence of it is usually by way of statutory declarations. If the registrar is not satisfied that the right subsists as a legal interest benefiting the registered estate, he may enter details of the right claimed in the property register with such qualification as he considers appropriate (Land Registration Rules 2003 ("LRR 2003") rule 33).

On first registration the estate is vested in the registered proprietor subject to any easements which are the subject of an entry in the register in relation to the estate, and/or, in the case of a leasehold title, which are incident to the leasehold estate (LRA 2002 sections 11(4)(a) and 12(4)(a) and (b)). The registrar must enter a notice in the register of the burden of any easement which appears from his examination to affect the registered estate, except any which appear to him to be of a trivial or obvious character, or the entry of a notice in respect of which would be likely to cause confusion or inconvenience (LRR 2003 rule 35). Even where no entry is made as to a subjective legal easement on first registration, it is an overriding interest within LRA 2002 Schedule 1 paragraph 3.

A person applying for first registration must provide information to the registrar in form DI about any legal easements which are within his actual knowledge and affect the estate to which the application relates. The registrar may enter a notice in the register in respect of any such legal easement (LRR 2003 rule 28).

Legal Easements Arising After First Registration

The express grant or reservation of a legal easement over registered land must be completed by registration. This does not apply to a grant as a result of the operation of the Law of Property Act 1925 section 62. Registration is completed by the entry of a notice of the easement in the register and, if the dominant tenement is registered, an entry in the property register of that title (LRA 2002 section 27(2)(d) and (7) and Schedule 2 paragraph 7). Until completed by registration, such an easement is only equitable.

The benefit of a legal easement can be entered in the register only as appurtenant to a registered estate; it cannot be registered independently (LRA 2002 section 59(1)).

On registration of a transfer or charge of part of a registered title, entries are made in the new title created and the retained or uncharged title in respect of any easements granted or reserved in the transfer or charge. In the case of a charge of part such entries are made only if the registrar decides that the charged part is to be comprised in a registered title separate from the uncharged part.

An applicant for an entry of the benefit of an appurtenant easement contained in a deed of grant should deliver to the registry:

(a) an application in form AP1;
(b) the deed of grant;
(c) a certified copy (if the original deed is to be returned);
(d) (if the right is granted over unregistered land) an abstract or epitome showing the grantor's title to the unregistered estate; and
(e) the fee payable. A fee calculator for all types of application is on the Land Registry's website at www.landregistry.gov.uk/fees.

Where the right is granted over unregistered land and the registrar is not satisfied that the right claimed subsists as a legal estate appurtenant to the applicant's registered estate, he may enter details of the right claimed in the property register with such qualification as he considers appropriate.

Where illegal user has prevented the acquisition of a vehicular right of way by prescription (*Hanning v Top Deck Travel Group Ltd* (1994) 68 P & CR 14 (CA) and *Brandwood v Bakewell Management Limited* [2003] EWCA Civ 23, [2003] All ER (D) 302 (Jan) (CA)), an easement may be obtained (if the land is in England) under the Countryside and Rights of Way Act 2000 section 68 and the Vehicular Access Across Common and Other Land (England) Regulations 2002. Where the application is based on an easement arising under those Regulations, in place of the deed of grant, the applicant should lodge copies of the notices and information served under the Regulations and the receipt for the compensation paid.

Even where the user of a road or track has been illegal under the Road Traffic Acts, a prescriptive right under the doctrine of lost modern grant may have been established by twenty years' user prior to 1930. This was the case in *Hayling v Harper* [2003] All ER (D) 41 (Apr) (CA) where Carnwath LJ indicated that the matter of use had to be looked at broadly. A cottage had been built in the late nineteenth century, and there was no evidence of the method of access until 1946, but clear evidence after that date that a track had been used for vehicular access. There was no evidence that anything different had, or might have, happened before 1946, and accordingly a right of way was established by virtue of the doctrine of lost modern grant.

An applicant for the entry of the benefit of an implied or prescriptive appurtenant easement should deliver to the registry:

(a) an application in form AP1;
(b) evidence, usually statutory declarations, to satisfy the registrar that the easement subsists as a legal estate appurtenant to the applicant's registered estate; and
(c) the fee payable. A fee calculator for all types of application is on the Land Registry's website at www.landregistry.gov.uk/fees.

Where the registrar is not satisfied that the right claimed subsists as a legal estate appurtenant to the applicant's registered estate, he may enter details of the right claimed in the property register with such qualification as he considers appropriate.

An applicant whose dominant tenement is unregistered and who is applying for the entry of a notice in respect of an easement affecting a registered title, should deliver to the registry:

(a) an application in form AP1;
(b) the deed of grant;
(c) a certified copy (if the original deed is to be returned);
(d) (if an implied or prescriptive easement) evidence, usually statutory declarations, of the existence of the easement;
(e) the fee payable. A fee calculator for all types of application is on the Land Registry's website at www.landregistry.gov.uk/fees.

Where it appears to the registrar that a registered estate is subject to a legal easement, he may enter a notice in the register in respect of that easement (LRA 2002 section 37). In that case the registrar must give notice to the registered proprietor and to any person who appears to him to be entitled to the interest protected by the notice or whom the registrar otherwise considers appropriate (LRR 2003 rule 89). If the registered proprietor applies for the entry of the notice, or consents to an application for such an entry, the registrar is not obliged to give notice to him. The registrar is also not obliged to give notice under rule 89 to any person who has applied for, or consented to, the entry of the notice, nor is he so obliged if that person's name and address for service are not set out in the registered title in question.

Unregistered Legal Easements which Override Registered Dispositions
Although all legal easements override first registration, the position is not the same for registered dispositions. In the light of LRA 2002 Schedule 3 paragraph 3, a legal easement overrides a registered disposition only if:
  (a) at the time of the disposition it is within the actual knowledge of the person to whom the disposition is made; or
  (b) at the time of the disposition it would have been obvious on a reasonably careful inspection of the land over which the easement is exercisable; or
  (c) the person entitled to the easement proves that it has been exercised in the period of one year ending with the day of the disposition.

But any easement which was an overriding interest immediately before 13 October 2003, but which would not fall within LRA 2002 Schedule 3 paragraph 3 if created on or after 13 October 2003, continues to be an overriding interest (LRA 2002 Schedule 12 paragraph 9). For a period of three years beginning on 13 October 2003 any unregistered legal easement overrides a registered disposition (LRA 2002 Schedule 12 paragraph 10). An unregistered easement over registered land arising on or after 13 October 2003 is a legal easement only if it is an implied or prescriptive easement.

A person applying to register a registrable disposition of a registered estate must provide information to the registrar in form DI about any legal easements falling within Schedule 3 paragraph 3 which are within his actual knowledge and affect the estate to which the application relates. The applicant must produce to the registrar any documentary evidence of the existence of any such legal easements as is under his control. The registrar may enter a notice in the register in respect of any such legal easement (LRR 2003 rule 57).

Licences

Bare licences and contractual licences are not, without more, interests in land binding on a purchaser, even if he has notice (*Ashburn Anstalt v Arnold* [1989] Ch 1, [1988] 2 WLR 706, [1988] 2 All ER 147 (CA)). For the position where, on the facts of a particular case, a constructive trust or an equity by estoppel has arisen, see *Constructive, Implied and Resulting Trusts*, page 108, and *Proprietary Estoppel*, page 248.

Whether a licence coupled with an interest (that is a licence collateral to a proprietary interest) is an overriding interest depends on the status of that interest. For example, where a person has a licence to enter on land in the exercise of a legal *profit a prendre*, the legal *profit* is capable of being an overriding interest under the Land Registration Act 2002 ("LRA 2002") Schedule 1 paragraph 3 or Schedule 3 paragraph 3 and the licence has the same status. If the *profit* is only equitable then neither it nor the licence has overriding status and should be protected by entry of a notice. The entry of a notice in respect of the *profit* in practice protects the licence as well, since this is irrevocable while the interest subsists. For the protection of a *profit a prendre* see *Profits a Prendre*, page 242.

For the purposes of LRA 2002, land in the possession of a licensee is treated as being in the possession of the licensor (LRA 2002 section 131). This applies, for example, when establishing that the proprietor is in possession for the purposes of upgrading a possessory title under LRA 2002 section 62(5), or when establishing whether the proprietor is in possession for the purposes of LRA 2002 Schedule 4 paragraphs 3(2) or 6(2) where alteration of the register is sought.

Limited Liability Partnerships

A limited liability partnership incorporated under the Limited Liability Partnerships Act 2000 has full powers to deal with land. It is a body corporate with legal personality separate from that of its members. The name of such a limited liability partnership must end with one of the following expressions or abbreviations: "limited liability partnership", "partneriaeth atebolrwydd cyfyngedig", "llp", "LLP", "pac", or "PAC".

Where a limited liability partnership incorporated under the Limited Liability Partnerships Act 2000 applies to be registered as proprietor of a registered estate or a registered charge, the application must state the limited liability partnership's registered number (Land Registration Rules 2003 ("LRR 2003") rule 181(4)). In practice the registered number is usually stated in panel 6 of the Transfer in form TR1 or in panel 9 of application form FR1. The registered number commences "OC" for limited liability partnerships registered in England and Wales or "SO" for limited liability partnerships registered in Scotland. The registered number is included in the entry of the limited liability partnership as proprietor in the proprietorship register or charges register.

Registration of Charge Created by a Limited Liability Partnership
Where an application is made to register a charge created by a limited liability partnership incorporated under the Limited Liability Partnerships

Act 2000, the applicant must produce to the registrar a certificate issued under the Companies Act 1985 section 401 that the charge has been registered under section 395 of that Act (LRR 2003 rule 111(1)). If the limited liability partnership is registered in Scotland, the certificate required is a certificate issued under section 418 of the 1985 Act that the charge has been registered under section 410 of that Act.

If the applicant does not produce the appropriate certificate, the registrar is required to enter a note in the register that the charge is subject to the provisions of the Companies Act 1985 section 395 (or section 410 for a Scottish limited liability partnership) (LRR 2003 rule 111(2)). Those sections provide that where the prescribed particulars of the charge are not delivered to the Registrar of Companies within the prescribed period, the charge is void against the liquidator or administrator of the limited liability partnership and any creditor of the limited liability partnership.

Execution of Deeds by Limited Liability Partnerships

Where a deed is to be executed by a limited liability partnership incorporated under the Limited Liability Partnerships Act 2000, without using a common seal, the form of execution set out in Schedule 9 to LRR 2003 is:

Signed as a deed by (*name of limited liability partnership*) acting by two members	*Signature*	Member
	Signature	Member

Where a deed is to be executed by a limited liability partnership incorporated under the Limited Liability Partnerships Act 2000, using its common seal, the following form of execution may be used:

The common seal of (*name of limited liability partnership*)
was affixed in the presence of:
....   [common seal of limited
          Signature of member   liability partnership]
....
          Signature of member

Limited Owner's Charge

A limited owner's charge arises where a tenant for life or statutory owner of settled land discharges inheritance tax or any other liabilities to which special priority is given by statute. The charge may be overreached by a disposition under the Settled Land Act 1925 section 72(3) or the Law of Property Act 1925 section 2(2) and (3).

No notice may be entered on the register in respect of a limited owner's charge (Land Registration Act 2002 ("LRA 2002") section 33). The protection for the limited owner's charge is the restriction in Form G, H or I, as appropriate, entered in the case of settled land to ensure capital money is paid to at least two trustees or a trust corporation. If there is no such restriction entered in the proprietorship register, the person having the benefit of the limited owner's charge is entitled to apply for the appropriate restriction (Land Registration Rules 2003 Schedule 7 paragraph 3(2)).

The registrar must give notice of an application for a restriction to the proprietor of the registered estate or charge concerned (LRA 2002 section 45).

A restriction does not confer any priority; it simply prevents an entry being made in the register if it is not permitted under the wording of the restriction.

If applying for a restriction in Form G, H or I, the person having the benefit of a limited owner's charge should deliver to the registry:

(a) an application in form RX1; and
(b) the fee payable. A fee calculator for all types of application is on the Land Registry's website at www.landregistry.gov.uk/fees.

Panel 13 of RX1 should be completed on the following lines:

"The applicant's interest is an interest in settled land as specified in Schedule 7 paragraph 3(2) of the Land Registration Rules 2003."

Panel 10 should be completed as to Form G, H or I, as appropriate.

Form G is applicable where the tenant for life is the registered proprietor of the settled land and there are trustees of the settlement. Form G is:

"No disposition is to be registered unless authorised by the Settled Land Act 1925, or by any extension of those statutory powers in the settlement, and no disposition under which capital money arises is to be registered unless the money is paid to [*name*] of [*address*] and [*name*] of [*address*], (the trustees of the settlement, who may be a sole trust corporation or, if individuals, must number at least two but not more than four) or into court."

Form H is applicable where the statutory owners are the trustees of the settlement and registered proprietors of the settled land. Form H is:

"No disposition is to be registered unless authorised by the Settled Land Act 1925, or by any extension of those statutory powers in the settlement, and, except where the sole proprietor is a trust corporation, no disposition under which capital money arises is to be registered unless the money is paid to at least two proprietors."

Form I is applicable where the tenant for life is the registered proprietor of the settled land and there are no trustees of the settlement. Form I is:

"No disposition under which capital money arises, or which is not authorised by the Settled Land Act 1925 or by any extension of those statutory powers in the settlement, is to be registered."

Limited Partnerships

A limited partnership created under the Limited Partnership Act 1907 is not a separate legal entity. It does not have the corporate status of a limited liability partnership incorporated under the Limited Liability Partnerships Act 2000, for which see *Limited Liability Partnerships*, page 194.

A transfer to a limited partnership must be to the names of the individual partners, not to the partnership name. If there are more than four partners the transfer should be to four of them to hold the legal estate on trust for the partnership. No reference to the partnership is made on the register. Since the beneficial interests are held under a tenancy in common, the following restriction in Form A is entered in the proprietorship register in accordance with the Land Registration Act 2002 section 44(1):

"No disposition by a sole proprietor of the registered estate (except a trust corporation) under which capital money arises is to be registered unless authorised by an order of the court."

The partners may also, if they wish, apply in the additional provisions panel of the transfer or in application form RX1 for a restriction in Form Q, which is:

"No disposition [*or specify details*] of the registered estate by the proprietor of the registered estate is to be registered after the death of [*name of the current proprietor(s) whose personal representative's consent will be required*] without the written consent of the personal representatives of the deceased."

Although no reference to the limited partnership is made on the register, the proprietors may specifically apply to have any trading name entered in the proprietorship register. This will appear after the last address for service in the entry of the proprietors, in the form "trading as [*trading name*]".

Liquidators

Where a company is the registered proprietor of a registered estate or registered charge, its liquidator may apply for an entry to be made as to his appointment. In practice a liquidator rarely makes such an application but instead provides evidence of his appointment to a purchaser, which the purchaser lodges with his application for registration of the transfer to him.

Entry of Notice of Liquidator's Appointment
The liquidator should deliver to the registry:
    (a) an application in form AP1;
    (b) evidence of appointment (see *Evidence of Appointment*, below); and

(c) the fee payable. A fee calculator for all types of application is on the Land Registry's website at www.landregistry.gov.uk/fees.

Evidence of Appointment

The evidence required varies depending on the type of liquidation. The same evidence is required whether for entry of a notice of the liquidator's appointment or for the registration of a transfer by him.

Creditors' Voluntary Winding-up
The following documents are required:
  (a) a copy of the resolution passed at the company's meeting that the company be wound up and appointing a liquidator; and
  (b) either a copy of a resolution passed at the creditor's meeting appointing a liquidator or a certificate by the liquidator appointed at the company's meeting (or his conveyancer) that the meeting of the creditors was duly held at which either the appointment of the liquidator by the company's meeting was confirmed or no resolution nominating a liquidator was passed.

Members' Voluntary Winding-up
The following documents are required:
  (a) a copy of the resolution appointing the liquidator; and
  (b) a certificate by the liquidator or his conveyancer that a statutory declaration of solvency complying with the requirements of the Insolvency Act 1986 section 89 has been filed with the registrar of companies.

Winding-up by the Court
The following documents are required:
  (a) a copy of the order of the court appointing the liquidator; or
  (b) the appointment of the liquidator by the Secretary of State; or
  (c) a copy of the winding-up order of the court and either a copy of the resolution passed at the creditors' meeting appointing a liquidator, or a certificate by the liquidator (appointed at the contributories' meeting) that the meeting of the creditors was duly held at which either the appointment of the liquidator by the contributories' meeting was confirmed or no resolution nominating a liquidator was passed.

Disclaimer by Liquidator

A liquidator may disclaim any onerous property comprised in the insolvent estate and is entitled to do so even if he has taken possession of the property or attempted to sell it (Insolvency Act 1986 section 178). In the case of land it is normally a leasehold estate which is disclaimed. The disclaimer is not effective unless a copy of it has been served on any underlessee or mortgagee claiming under the company or any other person who claims an interest in the property or is under any liability in respect of the property.

Any person claiming an interest in the disclaimed property may apply to the court for a vesting order vesting the property in him or in a trustee on his behalf (Insolvency Act 1986 section 181). A person who is under a liability in respect of a disclaimed property, which liability will not be discharged by the disclaimer, may also apply for a vesting order.

If no vesting order is made, a lease which has been disclaimed vests in the lessor and so will determine. If no vesting order is made, a freehold which has been disclaimed vests in the Crown by escheat.

Where a liquidator has disclaimed a registered lease, an applicant should deliver to the registry:

(a) an application in form AP1 showing the application as "Disclaimer of lease"; if the lease is noted on a superior title the application should also be made in respect of that title so that the notice of the lease may be cancelled;
(b) the lease;
(c) evidence of the appointment of the liquidator (see *Evidence of Appointment,* above) unless there is already an entry in the register of the liquidator's appointment;
(d) a certificate signed by the liquidator that all notices required to be served under the Insolvency Act 1986 have been served and that he is not aware of any application to the court for a vesting order under the Insolvency Act 1986 section 181;
(e) an office copy of the notice of disclaimer; and
(f) the fee payable. A fee calculator for all types of application is on the Land Registry's website at www.landregistry.gov.uk/fees.

Where the disclaimed lease has not been registered but has been noted against a registered title, an applicant should deliver to the registry:

(a) an application in form CN1, panel 9 being completed by entering details of the lease and placing an "X" against "disclaimer";
(b) the lease;
(c) the deeds and documents relating to the leasehold title;
(d) a certificate signed by the liquidator that all notices required to be served under the Insolvency Act 1986 have been served and that he is not aware of any application to the court for a vesting order under the Insolvency Act 1986 section 181;
(e) an office copy of the notice of disclaimer;
(f) evidence of the appointment of the liquidator (see *Evidence of Appointment* above); and
(g) the fee payable. A fee calculator for all types of application is on the Land Registry's website at www.landregistry.gov.uk/fees.

Where the property has been disclaimed and an order has been made by the court vesting the property in some other person, an applicant should deliver to the registry:

(a) an application in form AP1;
(b) an office copy of the court order; and
(c) the fee payable. A fee calculator for all types of application is on the Land Registry's website at www.landregistry.gov.uk/fees.

Local Land Charges

A local land charge is an unregistered interest which overrides first registration and also overrides registrable dispositions (Land Registration Act 2002 ("LRA 2002") Schedule 1 paragraph 6 and Schedule 3 paragraph 6). This includes a local land charge the status of which as an overriding interest under the Land Registration Act 1925 was preserved by the Local Land Charges Act 1975 section 19(3) (LRA 2002 Schedule 12 paragraph 13). A person applying for first registration is not required to provide information to the registrar about local land charges (Land Registration Rules 2003 ("LRR 2003") rule 28(2)(d)); neither is a person applying to register a registrable disposition of a registered estate (LRR 2003 rule 57(2)(c)).

Although a local land charge is an overriding interest, it may be protected by notice or restriction. If it is protected by notice it ceases to be an overriding interest, and does not revert to being an overriding interest if the notice is cancelled incorrectly (LRA 2002 sections 29(3) and 30(3)). In practice, however, a local land charge is usually registered in the local land charges registers and is not entered at the Land Registry.

Some local land charges create monetary charges. A charge over registered land which is a local land charge may be realised only if the charge is registered (LRA 2002 section 55). An application to register the title to such a charge must be supported by evidence of the charge (LRR 2003 rule 104). Such evidence may be the declaration in writing creating the charge, where that is required by legislation, or a sealed resolution of the local authority which recites the facts giving rise to the charge and resolves that application is made for its registration.

When applying for substantive registration of a monetary local land charge, the applicant authority should deliver to the registry:
(a) an application in form AP1;
(b) documentary evidence of the charge;
(c) a certified copy of that evidence (if the original evidence is to be returned); and
(d) the fee payable. A fee calculator for all types of application is on the Land Registry's website at www.landregistry.gov.uk/fees.

If the statutory charge has effect to postpone a charge which is already entered on the register or is the basis for an entry in the register, the applicant authority must also deliver form SC with the application (LRR 2003 rule 105(1)). Where the applicant satisfies the registrar that the statutory charge has the priority specified in form SC, an entry is made in the charges register showing that priority. If the applicant does not so satisfy the registrar but the registrar considers that the applicant has an arguable case, an entry may be made in the charges register that the applicant claims the priority in question. In either case the registrar gives notice to the registered proprietor of any existing registered charge and any person who appears to the registrar to be entitled to a charge protected by a notice. In the case of a charge protected by a notice, the registrar is obliged to serve notice only if the chargee's name and address for service appear in the register of the title in question.

Lost Deeds

Where the deeds have been lost, an application for first registration must be supported by evidence to satisfy the registrar that the applicant holds the legal estate sought to be registered and to account for the loss of the deeds (Land Registration Rules 2003 rule 27). The evidence usually consists of statutory declarations exhibiting any appropriate supporting documents and setting out the facts. The evidence required in each case naturally depends on the particular facts but it will need both to show that the applicant holds the legal estate and to account for the loss of the deeds.

Evidence that the applicant holds the legal estate falls into two categories, evidence by way of reconstruction of the title and (in the light of the possibility of fraud) evidence of identity of the applicant. Copies or drafts of lost deeds may often be obtained from the solicitors who acted at the time. If the estate is mortgaged evidence of the mortgage should be included. If there is no charge on the property, the declaration should confirm that at the time of the loss the owner had not created any charge on the land and had not deposited the deeds by way of security.

The declarations should establish that the applicant has been in actual occupation of the land or (if such be the case) in receipt of the rents from it, without any adverse claim. Where rent has been received, full details of the lease should be provided.

Where the property is leasehold, copies of the deeds may be available from the lessor, who should also be able to confirm who has paid the rent. The lessor may also have details as to licences to assign, where this is a requirement of the lease.

Where the land falls within the areas covered by any of the former deeds registries, copies of deeds or of memorials of deeds may be available from the appropriate archive service. Memorials did not, though, normally show whether the land was subject to restrictive covenants.

The evidence of identity required varies depending on the circumstances. For example, the Land Registry does not usually require evidence of identity where the application is lodged by a conveyancer in whose custody the deeds have been lost. For full details of the registry's requirements on identity, see the Practice Guide available at www.landregistry.gov.uk.

The evidence of the loss of the deeds should establish, where possible, who held the deeds and where they were held at the time of their loss, how they were lost and what has been done to try and recover them. It should also establish, where appropriate, that the deeds were held for safe custody without any lien or other charge, and not by way of security for a debt.

Manors

A manor is an incorporeal hereditament. It is no longer possible to register the title to a manor (Land Registration Act 2002 ("LRA 2002") section 3). Manors which have already been registered under the Land Registration Act 1925 remain on the register but the proprietor of a registered manor may apply for the title to the manor to be removed from the register (LRA 2002 section 119).

The registered title to a manor has no filed plan. Registrations of manors are listed in the index of franchises and manors which can be searched in respect of any particular administrative area using Form SIF. The result of such a search does not, however, reveal any caution against first registration of a manor which may have been in existence on 13 October 2003. To ascertain whether there is such a caution, a search of the index map using Form SIM is required.

Deregistration of Manor

An application by the registered proprietor for the title to a manor to be removed from the register comprises the following documents:
    (a) form AP1 showing the nature of application as "deregistration of manor"; and
    (b) the land certificate.

No fee is payable for the removal of a manor from the register.

Manorial Rights

A manorial right is an overriding interest under Schedules 1 and 3 to LRA 2002. Manorial rights are not defined in LRA 2002 but were defined in the Land Registration Act 1925 as having the same meaning as in Part V of the Law of Property Act 1922. They include:
    (a) any right of the lord or tenant in or to any mines, minerals, limestone,

lime, clay, stone, gravel, pits, or quarries, and any associated rights of search, winning, working and carrying away;
(b) the rights, franchises, royalties, or privileges of the lord in respect of any fairs, markets, rights of chase or warren, piscaries, or other rights of hunting, shooting, fishing, fowling, or otherwise taking game, fish or fowl; and
(c) any liability subsisting on 1 January 1926 for the construction, maintenance, cleansing, or repair of any dykes, ditches, canals, sea or river walls, piles, bridges, levels, ways and other works required for the protection or general benefit of any land within a manor or for abating nuisances therein.

Manorial incidents will cease to be overriding interests at the end of ten years from 13 October 2003 (LRA 2002 section 117(1)). Accordingly, if they affect unregistered land, an application to lodge a caution against first registration should be made before the end of the period. If they affect registered land, an application for the entry in the register of a notice should be made before the end of the period. In practice this is likely to be a unilateral notice.

Caution Against First Registration
An applicant should deliver to the registry:
 (a) an application in form CT1; and
 (b) a plan (or other sufficient details) to allow the land to which the caution relates to be identified clearly on the Ordnance Survey map.

No fee is payable for applications lodged during the ten year period beginning on 13 October 2003 (LRA 2002 section 117(2)).

Form CT1 should be completed on the following lines to show the interest of the applicant:

"owner of the following manorial incidents affecting the land: [*set out details of the manorial incidents including details of any deed etc under which they arose*]."

The caution does not in itself have any effect on the validity or priority of the manorial incidents, but the cautioner will have the opportunity to object to the application for first registration unless notice of the manorial interests is entered in the register (LRA 2002 section 16).

Unilateral Notice
An applicant should deliver to the registry:
 (a) an application in form UN1; and
 (b) a plan of the affected land (where the manorial incidents affect only part of the land in the registered title).

No fee is payable for applications lodged during the ten year period beginning on 13 October 2003 (LRA 2002 section 117(2)).

Form UN1 should be completed on the following lines to show the

interest of the applicant:
> "owner of the following manorial incidents affecting the land: [*set out details of the manorial incidents including details of any deed etc under which they arose*]."

The unilateral notice will give brief details of the interest protected and identify the beneficiaries of that notice.

Leases of Registered Manors

Where there is a grant out of a registered manor of a lease, an application must be made to register the lease (LRA 2002 section 27(2)(c)). If the lease is for a term of more than seven years from the date of the grant, the application is completed by the entry in the register of:

(a) the grantee (or his successor in title) as proprietor of the lease; and

(b) a notice in respect of the lease.

If the lease is for a term not exceeding seven years from the date of the grant, the application is completed only by the entry of a notice in respect of the lease (LRA 2002 Schedule 2 paragraphs 4 and 5).

Any lease, however short, out of a registered manor is required to be registered. If this is not desired, consideration should be given to deregistering the manor.

An applicant should deliver to the registry:

(a) an application in form AP1;

(b) the lease; and

(c) the fee payable. A fee calculator for all types of application is on the Land Registry's website at www.landregistry.gov.uk/fees.

Matrimonial Home Occupation Rights

The right of a spouse to occupy the matrimonial home conferred by the Family Law Act 1996 ("FLA 1996") is not capable of falling within the Land Registration Act 2002 ("LRA 2002") Schedule 1 paragraph 2 or Schedule 3 paragraph 2, which deal with the overriding status of interests of persons in actual occupation (FLA 1996 section 31(10) as substituted by LRA 2002 Schedule 11 paragraph 34(2)).

An application may be made under FLA 1996 section 31(10)(a) or Schedule 4 paragraph 4(3)(b) for the entry of an agreed notice in the register. It is not possible to apply for a unilateral notice (Land Registration Rules 2003 rule 80). The application must be made in application form MH1. A spouse's rights of occupation may subsist in respect only of one property at a time; any previous registration must be revealed on application form MH1 and will be cancelled. Where the application is made after the court has made an order under FLA 1996 section 33(5), an office copy of that order must be lodged with form MH1. Alternatively a conveyancer may certify in panel 10 of form MH1 that he holds such an office copy.

Notice of the application is sent to the registered proprietor.

Where the court has made an order under FLA 1996 section 33(5), an application to renew the registration of a matrimonial home rights notice under FLA 1996 Schedule 4 paragraph 4(3)(a) should be made in application form MH2. An office copy of the order made under FLA 1996 section 33(5) must be lodged with form MH2. Alternatively a conveyancer may certify in panel 8 of form MH2 that he holds such an office copy.

For bankruptcy and matrimonial home occupation rights, see *Bankruptcy and the Matrimonial Home*, page 44.

Cancellation of Notice

An application to cancel a matrimonial home rights notice may be made using form AP1 or Land Registry form MH4. The evidence in support consists of:

(a) the death certificate of one of the spouses; or

(b) an official copy of the decree or order of the court terminating the marriage; or

(c) an official copy of the court's order terminating the rights of occupation; or

(d) a release in writing signed by the spouse who has the rights.

Where the court has made an order under FLA 1996 section 33(5) which is referred to in the register, evidence must also be lodged to show that such order has ceased to have effect.

Mental Health Act 1983 Patients

Where a receiver appointed by the Court of Protection has transferred land on behalf of a patient, the application to register the transfer should be accompanied by an office copy of the sealed order or direction of the court authorising the disposition, or by a certified copy of such office copy. The same applies where a receiver has not been appointed but the Court of Protection has issued an order or direction authorising a named person to sell the property in question.

Where the receiver acquires a registered estate in the name of the patient, the patient is usually registered as proprietor without any entry in the register referring to the Mental Health Act 1983. Where, however, the receiver is to be registered as proprietor, a restriction on the following lines is entered in the register:

"No disposition of the registered estate by the proprietor of the registered estate is to be registered unless made pursuant to an order of the Court under the Mental Health Act 1983."

The order or direction authorising the acquisition, or an office copy or certified copy of it, should always accompany the application for registration.

No one who has been in adverse possession of a registered estate may apply to be registered as proprietor of that estate during any period in which the existing registered proprietor is unable because of mental disability to make decisions about issues of the kind to which such an application would give rise, or unable to communicate such decisions because of mental disability or physical impairment. Where it appears to the registrar that this applies, he may include a note to that effect in the register. For these purposes "mental disability" means a disability or disorder of the mind or brain, whether permanent or temporary, which results in an impairment or disturbance of mental functioning (Land Registration Act 2002 Schedule 6 paragraph 8(2), (3) and (4)). Where it is desired that the registrar make such a note in the register, application should be made using application form AP1, supported by appropriate evidence of the mental disability or physical impairment.

Mere Equities

A mere equity is an equitable right which falls short of being an equitable interest. The courts have not laid down what distinguishes an equitable interest from a mere equity but the latter seems usually to involve a claim to discretionary relief in equity which relates to property. Examples are the right to rectify a deed for mutual mistake, a right to set aside a transfer for fraud or undue influence, and a right to seek relief from forfeiture of a lease after peaceable re-entry.

The Land Registration Act 2002 section 116 declares, for the avoidance of doubt, that, in relation to registered land, a mere equity has effect from the time the equity arises as an interest capable of binding successors in title, subject to the rules about the effect of dispositions on priority. For the rules about the effect of dispositions on priority, see *Priorities*, page 239.

The purchaser of a later equitable interest in the registered title does not therefore take free from the mere equity, even though he has no notice of it. This is different from the position with unregistered land where the purchaser would take free in this case (*Phillips v Phillips* (1861) 4 De GF & J 208).

To protect the priority of a mere equity against a registrable disposition made for valuable consideration, it may be appropriate to make an application for a unilateral notice. For example, in the case of a right to have a deed rectified for mutual mistake, an applicant should deliver to the

registry:
- (a) an application in form UN1;
- (b) a plan of the affected land (where the deed to be rectified affects only part of the land in the registered title); and
- (c) the fee payable. A fee calculator for all types of application is on the Land Registry's website at www.landregistry.gov.uk/fees.

Form UN1 should be completed on the following lines to show the interest of the applicant:

"having the right to have a [Transfer] [Deed] dated ... made between ... rectified for mutual mistake."

The unilateral notice will give brief details of the interest protected and identify the beneficiaries of that notice.

Mines and Minerals

First Registration

It is not compulsory to register mines and minerals held apart from the surface. Where an application for first registration of mines and minerals is made, investigation of title often needs to go beyond the normal fifteen year root. Evidence, typically by way of statutory declarations, of the working of the mines and minerals assists in showing a good title. If the land was formerly copyhold, evidence to show the effect of enfranchisement on the mines and minerals should be lodged. Mines and minerals were often retained by the lord on enfranchisement. In many areas mines and minerals were reserved to the Crown on the original grant of the land; where appropriate, a disclaimer of ownership by the Crown might be lodged. If the land was subject to inclosure, the Inclosure Act and Award should be considered since these often deal with the ownership of mines and minerals.

An applicant for first registration of mines and minerals should deliver to the registry:
- (a) an application in form FR1;
- (b) a plan of the surface under which the mines and minerals lie;
- (c) any other sufficient details, by plan or otherwise, so that the mines and minerals can be clearly identified;
- (d) full details of rights incidental to the working of the mines and minerals;
- (e) in the case of a leasehold estate, the lease, if in the control of the applicant, and a certified copy;
- (f) all deeds and documents relating to the title that are in the control of the applicant;
- (g) a list in duplicate in form DL of all the documents delivered;
- (h) form DI giving the information as to overriding interests required by

the Land Registration Rules 2003 ("LRR 2003") rule 28; and
(i) the fee payable. A fee calculator for all types of application is on the Land Registry's website at www.landregistry.gov.uk/fees.

Where the evidence lodged is not sufficient to allow an absolute title to be granted, a qualified title may be considered. The qualification will be on the following lines:

"The inclusion of the mines and minerals in this title does not affect or prejudice the enforcement of any estate right or interest therein existing before [*the date of first registration*]."

Where the registrar is satisfied, on first registration of an estate comprising or including the land beneath the surface, that the mines and minerals are included in or excluded from the applicant's title, he makes an appropriate note in the register (LRR 2003 rule 32).

Registered Land

In the light of the Land Registration Act 2002 ("LRA 2002") sections 11(3) and 12(3) and the definition of land in section 132(1), mines and minerals are included in a registered title of land where there is no entry on the register that they are excluded.

If a registered estate includes mines or minerals but there is no note in the register to that effect, the registered proprietor of that estate may apply for a note to be entered that the registered estate includes the mines or minerals or specified mines or minerals (LRR 2003 rule 71). The applicant should deliver to the registry:

(a) an application in form AP1;
(b) evidence to satisfy the registrar that the mines or minerals were vested in the applicant for first registration of the registered estate at the time of first registration and were so vested in the same capacity as the remainder of the estate in land then sought to be vested; this evidence is similar to that outlined above in respect of first registrations; and
(c) the fee payable. A fee calculator for all types of application is on the Land Registry's website at www.landregistry.gov.uk/fees.

LRR 2003 rule 70 applies where a registered estate in land includes any mines or minerals but there is no note on the register that they are included, and it is appropriate when describing the registered estate to do so by reference to the land where the mines or minerals are or may be situated. This arises, for example, on a transfer or charge of part of the land or on amalgamation or sub-division of the registered title. In such circumstances the registrar may make an entry in the property register to the effect that such description is an entry made under LRR 2003 rule 5(a) and is not a note that the registered estate includes the mines or minerals for the purposes of extending the payment of indemnity to such mines or minerals. LRR rule 5(a) provides that the property register must contain a description of the registered estate.

Overriding Interests

For interests in any coal or coal mine see *Coal*, page 90. No notice may be entered in the register in respect of any such rights (LRA 2002 section 33(e)).

In the case of land which was registered before 1898, unregistered rights to mines and minerals and incidental rights created before 1898 override both first registration and registered dispositions.

In the case of land which was registered between 1898 and 1925 inclusive, unregistered rights to mines and minerals and incidental rights created before the date of registration of the title override both first registration and registered dispositions.

Indemnity

No indemnity under LRA 2002 Schedule 8 is payable on account of any mines or minerals or the existence of any right to work or get mines or minerals, unless it is noted in the register that the title of the registered estate concerned includes the mines and minerals (LRA 2002 Schedule 8 paragraph 2). Although mines and minerals are taken as included in a registered title if there is no entry excluding them in the register, this does not of itself found an indemnity claim. There must be a note that they are included in the title.

Notices

A notice is an entry in the register in respect of the burden of an interest affecting a registered estate or a registered charge. The entry of a notice does not necessarily mean that the interest is valid, but it does mean that the priority of the interest, if valid, is protected for the purposes of the Land Registration Act 2002 ("LRA 2002") sections 29 and 30 (LRA 2002 section 32). For details of this priority protection, see *Priorities*, page 239.

No notice may be entered in the register in respect of any of the following interests (LRA 2002 sections 33 and 90(4)):

(a) an interest under a trust of land;
(b) an interest under a settlement under the Settled Land Act 1925;
(c) a leasehold estate in land which is granted for a term of three years or less from the date of the grant and which is not required to be registered;
(d) a restrictive covenant made between a lessor and lessee, so far as relating to the demised premises;
(e) an interest which is capable of being registered under the Commons Registration Act 1965;
(f) an interest in any coal or coal mine, the rights attached to any such

interest and the rights of any person under the Coal Industry Act 1994 section 38, 49 or 51; and

(g) leases created for public-private partnerships relating to transport in London, within the meaning given by the Greater London Authority Act 1999 section 218.

A notice may be entered by the registrar, for example as a result of his examination of title on first registration, or where he finds that the title is affected by an unregistered interest which overrides first registration and which is capable of being noted. In the latter example, the registrar must give notice to the registered proprietor and to any person who appears to him to be entitled to the interest protected by the notice or whom he otherwise considers appropriate (Land Registration Rules 2003 ("LRR 2003") rule 89). The registrar need not give notice to a registered proprietor who applies for the entry of the notice or consents to the application for the notice. Nor need the registrar give notice to any other person if that person has applied for, or consented to, the notice, or whose name and address for service do not appear on the register of the title in question.

Where a registrable disposition requires completion of registration by the entry of a notice, the registrar must enter such a notice in the register (LRA 2002 section 38). This includes, for example, the entry of a notice of a lease on the lessor's title on the registration of a lease, or the entry of a notice on the grantor's title on the express grant of a legal easement.

A person claiming to be entitled to the benefit of an interest affecting a registered estate or registered charge may apply for the entry of either an agreed notice or a unilateral notice. The right to apply for the entry of a notice must not be exercised without reasonable cause (LRA 2002 section 77(1)). This duty to act reasonably is owed to any person who suffers damage in consequence of its breach (LRA 2002 section 77(2)).

Agreed Notice

The registrar may approve the entry of an agreed notice only if:
(a) the applicant is the registered proprietor of the estate or charge in question;
(b) the applicant is a person entitled to be registered as proprietor of the estate or charge in question;
(c) the registered proprietor of the estate or charge in question, or the person entitled to be registered as such, consents to the entry of the notice; or
(d) the registrar is satisfied as to the validity of the claim
(LRA 2002 section 34).

In respect of the following notices an applicant cannot apply for a unilateral notice, but must apply for an agreed notice (LRR 2003 rule 80):
(a) a matrimonial home rights notice;
(b) an inheritance tax notice;

(c) a notice in respect of an order under the Access to Neighbouring Land Act 1992;
(d) a notice of any variation of a lease effected by or under an order under the Landlord and Tenant Act 1987 section 38, including any variation as modified by an order under section 39(4) of that Act;
(e) a notice in respect of a public right; or
(f) a notice in respect of a customary right.

An applicant for an agreed notice should deliver to the registry:
(a) an application in form AN1;
(b) the order or document giving rise to the interest claimed. If there is no such order or document, other details of the interest claimed;
(c) where applicable, the consent of the proprietor or the person entitled to be registered as proprietor;
(d) where applicable, evidence that the person in question is entitled to be registered as proprietor;
(e) where applicable, evidence to satisfy the registrar as to the validity of the applicant's claim; and
(f) the fee payable. A fee calculator for all types of application is on the Land Registry's website at www.landregistry.gov.uk/fees.

Where the application is for a matrimonial home rights notice or its renewal the appropriate application form is form MH1 or MH2; see *Matrimonial Home Occupation Rights*, page 204.

The entry of the notice will give details of the interest protected and, in the case of a notice of a variation of an interest protected by a notice, details of the variation.

Cancellation of a Notice Other than a Unilateral Notice or a Matrimonial Home Rights Notice

An applicant for the cancellation of a notice other than a unilateral notice or a matrimonial home rights notice should deliver to the registry:
(a) an application in form CN1;
(b) evidence to show that the interest has determined; and
(c) the fee payable. A fee calculator for all types of application is on the Land Registry's website at www.landregistry.gov.uk/fees.

Where the registrar is satisfied that the interest protected by the notice has come to an end, he cancels the notice or makes an entry in the register that the interest in question has come to an end. If the interest in question has come to an end in part only, an appropriate entry is made in the register to reflect this.

Unilateral Notice

A unilateral notice may be entered without the consent of the registered proprietor and without the registrar's being satisfied of the validity of the applicant's claim. Where the registrar enters a unilateral notice, he gives notice of the entry to the registered proprietor of the registered estate or registered charge affected.

A person must not exercise the right to apply for the entry of a notice without reasonable cause (LRA 2002 section 77(1)). That statutory duty is owed to any person who suffers damage in consequence of its breach (LRA 2002 section 77(2)). A person in breach of such duty is therefore liable in damages to a person who suffers loss in consequence.

An applicant for a unilateral notice should deliver to the registry:
(a) an application in form UN1;
(b) a plan of the affected land (where the interest to be protected affects only part of the land in the registered title); and
(c) the fee payable. A fee calculator for all types of application is on the Land Registry's website at www.landregistry.gov.uk/fees.

The statutory declaration in panel 11 of form UN1 or the conveyancer's certificate in panel 12 must set out the nature of the applicant's interest.

The first part of a unilateral notice entered on the register identifies that it is a unilateral notice and gives brief details of the interest protected. The second part identifies the beneficiary of the notice. A person entitled to the benefit of an interest protected by a unilateral notice may apply to be entered in the register in place of, or in addition to, the registered beneficiary. An applicant to be registered as beneficiary of an existing unilateral notice should deliver to the registry:
(a) an application in form UN3;
(b) evidence of the applicant's title to the interest protected by the unilateral notice, for example a transfer of the interest to the applicant; and
(c) the fee payable. A fee calculator for all types of application is on the Land Registry's website at www.landregistry.gov.uk/fees.

Before entering the applicant in the register, the registrar serves notice on the registered beneficiary of the unilateral notice, but need not do so if the registered beneficiary signs form UN3 or otherwise consents to the application, or if the applicant is the registered beneficiary's personal representative and evidence of his title to act accompanies the application.

Removal of a Unilateral Notice

The registered beneficiary of a unilateral notice may apply in application form UN2 for the removal of the notice from the register. No fee is payable. The application may also be made by the personal representative or trustee in bankruptcy of the registered beneficiary, in which event evidence of his appointment must accompany the application.

Cancellation of a Unilateral Notice

The registered proprietor, or a person entitled to be registered as proprietor, of the registered estate or registered charge to which the unilateral notice relates, may apply for the cancellation of that notice (LRA 2002 section 36). The application must be made in application form UN4. No fee is payable. Where the application is by a person entitled to be registered, it must be accompanied by evidence of his entitlement, or his conveyancer must complete the certificate in panel 11 of form UN4.

The registrar gives the registered beneficiary notice of the action and informs him that if he does not exercise his right to object within the relevant period, the registrar must cancel the unilateral notice. The relevant period is the period ending at 12 noon on the fifteenth business day after the date of issue of the notice or such longer period as the registrar may allow following a request by the beneficiary. The beneficiary must set out in such a request why a longer period should be allowed, and must make the request before the expiry of the period ending at 12 noon on the fifteenth business day after the date of issue of the notice. The registrar may, if he considers it appropriate, seek the views of the person who applied for cancellation. If, after considering such views and all other relevant matters, he is satisfied that a longer period should be allowed, he may allow such period as he thinks appropriate, whether or not the period is the same as any period requested by the beneficiary. The longer period may never exceed a period ending at 12 noon on the thirtieth business day after the issue of the notice (LRR 2003 rule 86). A business day is a day when the Land Registry is open to the public, that is every day except Saturdays, Sundays, Christmas Day, Good Friday or any other day either specified or declared by proclamation under the Banking and Financial Dealings Act 1971 section 1 or appointed by the Lord Chancellor.

A person entitled to be registered as the beneficiary of the unilateral notice may object to an application for cancellation of that notice (LRR 2003 rule 86(7)).

Where the registered beneficiary or person entitled to be registered as beneficiary wishes to object to the cancellation of the unilateral notice, he must within the relevant period deliver to the registrar a written statement signed by the objector or his conveyancer (LRR 2003 rule 19). The statement must state that the objector objects to the cancellation of the unilateral notice, state the grounds for the objection and give the full name of the objector and an address to which communications may be sent.

Where an objection is made the registrar gives notice of it to the applicant for cancellation of the unilateral notice and may not cancel the unilateral notice until the objection has been disposed of. If, however, the registrar is satisfied that the objection is groundless, he need not give notice to the applicant and may cancel the unilateral notice (LRA 2002 section 73).

If it is not possible to dispose of an objection by agreement, the registrar must refer the matter to the Adjudicator to Her Majesty's Land Registrar. The adjudicator may, instead of deciding a matter himself, direct a party to the matter to commence proceedings, within a specified period, in the court for the purpose of obtaining the court's decision on the matter (LRA 2002 section 110(1)). A person aggrieved by a decision of the adjudicator may appeal to the High Court (LRA 2002 section 111). See *Disputes*, page 120.

Notices of Deposit

A notice of deposit or notice of intended deposit was entered on the register in respect of a lien created under the Land Registration Act 1925 section 66. It has not been possible to make such an entry since the coming into force of the Land Registration Rules 1995 on 3 April 1995. In the light of the decision in *United Bank of Kuwait v Sahib* [1997] Ch 107, [1996] 3 WLR 372, [1996] 3 All ER 215 (CA), it appears that it was not possible to create an equitable charge by deposit of a land certificate or charge certificate after the coming into force of the Law of Property (Miscellaneous Provisions) Act 1989 section 2 on 27 September 1989.

Where a notice of deposit, or a notice of intended deposit, of a land certificate or of a charge certificate has been entered in the register before 3 April 1995, it operates as a caution under the Land Registration Act 1925 section 54, and the Land Registration Rules 2003 rules 216 to 219 apply accordingly. This is so even if the registrar has destroyed the land certificate or charge certificate in accordance with the power contained in the Land Registration Act 2002 (Transitional Provisions) Order 2003 article 22(5) (article 25 of the Order).

Any entry of a notice of deposit or notice of intended deposit subsisting on the register therefore continues to take effect as a caution against dealings; see *Cautions Against Dealings*, page 56.

Official Copies

An official copy of the register, or of any document kept by the registrar which is referred to in the register or which relates to an application, is admissible in evidence to the same extent as the original (Land Registration Act 2002 ("LRA 2002") section 67(1)). If there is a mistake in the official copy, a person who relies on that copy is not liable for loss suffered by another person by reason of the mistake. A person is entitled to be indemnified by the registrar if he suffers loss by reason of a mistake in an official copy.

Official copies are often of documents kept by the registry which are not originals. As between the parties to a disposition relating to a registered title, the copy document kept by the registry is to be taken to be correct and to contain all the material parts of the original document (LRA 2002 section 120). No party to such disposition is to be affected by any provision of the original document not contained in the copy kept by the registry, nor can any party require production of the original document.

An application may be made using form OC1 for:
(a) an official copy of an individual register;
(b) an official copy of any title plan referred to in an individual register;
(c) an official copy of an individual caution register and any caution plan referred to in it; and
(d) a certificate of inspection of any title plan.

A separate application must be made for each registered title or caution against first registration.

A certificate of inspection of a title plan reveals whether the land in question is in the relevant title and whether it is affected by any colour or other reference shown on the title plan.

An application may be made using form OC2 for an official copy of any document referred to in the register of title and kept by the registry, and any other document relating to an application that is kept by the registry. This does not extend to:
(a) any exempt information document;
(b) any edited information document which has been replaced by another edited information document under the Land Registration Rules 2003 ("LRR 2003") rule 136(6);
(c) any form EX1A (reasons for exemption in support of an application to designate a document as an exempt information document);
(d) any form CIT (application in connection with court proceedings, insolvency and tax liability);
(e) any form to which form CIT has been attached (for example form OC1, OC2 or SIM);
(f) any document or copy of any document prepared by the registry in connection with an application in a form to which form CIT has been attached; and
(g) (during the period of two years beginning with 13 October 2003) any transitional period document.

Exempt Information Documents

A person may apply for the registrar to designate a document an exempt information document if he claims that the document contains prejudicial information (LRR 2003 rule 136). The document must be one referred to in the register of title, or one that relates to an application to the registry, the original or a copy of which is kept by the registrar. Such application may accompany the application that will lead to the document's being kept by the registry. Prejudicial information in this context means:

(a) information that relates to an individual who is the applicant and, if disclosed to other persons (whether to the public generally or specific persons) would, or would be likely to, cause substantial unwarranted damage or substantial unwarranted distress to the applicant or another; or
(b) information that if disclosed to other persons (whether to the public generally or specific persons) would, or would be likely to, prejudice the commercial interests of the applicant.

The application to designate a document an exempt information document must be made in form EX1 and EX1A. Form EX1A states the reasons for exemption. In addition to the document in question the applicant must deliver to the registry a copy which excludes the prejudicial information and which is certified as being a true copy of the document from which the prejudicial information has been excluded.

Provided the registrar is satisfied that the applicant's claim is not groundless, he must designate the document an exempt information document; if, however, he considers that so designating it could prejudice the keeping of the register, he may cancel the application. Where a document is designated an exempt information document, the edited copy is known as the edited information document and it is this which is supplied in response to a request for an official copy.

Where a document has been designated an exempt information document, it is possible to make another application so that further information is excluded from the edited information document and a new edited information document is prepared (LRR 2003 rule 136(6)).

It is possible for a person to apply for an official copy of an exempt information document using application form EX2 and stating why he considers that an official copy of the edited information document is not sufficient for his purposes. The applicant also has to state on form EX2 why he considers that none of the information omitted from the edited information document is prejudicial information. If he accepts that some or all of the information is prejudicial information, he is required to give details and state why he considers that the public interest in providing an official copy of the exempt information document outweighs the public interest in not doing so.

The registrar gives notice of any such application to the person who applied for the document to be designated an exempt information document, unless he is satisfied that such notice is unnecessary or impracticable.

The registrar will supply an official copy of the exempt information document if he decides that none of the information excluded from the edited information document is prejudicial information. He does so also if he decides that, although some or all of the information excluded is prejudicial information, the public interest in providing an official copy of the exempt information document to the applicant outweighs the public interest in not doing so (LRR 2003 rule 137).

A person who applied for a document to be designated an exempt information document may apply in form EX3 to have the designation removed.

Transitional Period Documents

During the period of two years commencing on 13 October 2003, a person may obtain a copy of a transitional period document only at the registrar's discretion (LRR 2003 rule 139). A transitional period document is:
  (a) a lease or charge or a copy lease or copy charge kept by the registrar since before 13 October 2003, where an entry referring to the lease or charge was made in the register of title before that date; or
  (b) any other document kept by the registrar which is not referred to in the register of title but relates to an application to the registrar and was received by the registrar before 13 October 2003.

Once a document has been designated an exempt information document, it ceases to be a transitional period document for this purpose.

Official Searches

An application may be made for an official search with priority or an official search without priority.

Official Search with Priority

An official search with priority may be made only by a purchaser of the title in question. The search may be in respect of the individual register of a registered title or of a pending application for first registration (Land Registration Rules 2003 ("LRR 2003") rule 147). A "purchaser" for this purpose is a person who has entered into, or intends to enter into, a registrable disposition of a registered estate or registered charge for valuable consideration. "Valuable consideration" does not include marriage consideration or a nominal consideration in money (Land Registration Act 2002 section 132(1)).

The application may be made in form OS1 for a search of the whole of the land in a registered title or application for first registration, and form OS2 for a search of part. Where the application for search is in form OS2, any accompanying plan must be delivered in duplicate.

The result of search reveals details of any adverse entries made in the individual register since the end of the day specified in the application as the "search from" date. It also reveals any pending application or pending official search affecting the registered title entered on the day list. The date and time at which the priority period expires are stated.

The priority period provided by the official search is the period beginning at the time when the application for the official search is entered on the day list and ending at midnight marking the end of the thirtieth business day thereafter. A business day is any day except Saturday, Sunday, Christmas Day, Good Friday or any other day either specified or declared by proclamation under the Banking and Financial Dealings Act 1971 section 1 or appointed by the Lord Chancellor. See *Priorities*, page 239, for the position where two or more official search certificates with priority relating to the same registrable estate or charge or to the same registered land have been issued.

The priority period resulting from an official search in respect of a registrable disposition is also conferred on any prior registrable disposition affecting the same registered land on which that application is dependent (LRR 2003 rule 151). For example, in the common situation where a person is purchasing registered land and is entering into a legal charge at the same time, a search by the intending chargee confers the same priority period on the intending transferee. The same applies where the search relates to a pending first registration.

Where an application is lodged, or deemed to be lodged, at the same time as the priority period of a search expires, the application is taken as being made within that priority period (LRR 2003 rule 154).

A person who has made an application for an official search with priority may withdraw that official search (LRR 2003 rule 150). Where an entry has already been made in the register in respect of a disposition protected by the search, the search cannot be withdrawn. On withdrawal the priority period ceases to have effect.

Official Searches Without Priority

Any person may apply for an official search without priority using application form OS3 (LRR 2003 rule 155). If an accompanying plan is required, it must be delivered in duplicate.

Similar information is supplied with the result of an official search without priority as with the result of an official search with priority, but no priority period is given.

Where an intending applicant is not a purchaser, so that only an official search without priority may be made, the possibility of reserving a period by means of an outline application should be considered. See *Outline Applications*, page 222.

Official Searches of the Index

The registrar keeps an index map, an index of relating franchises and manors and an index of proprietors' names.

Searches of the Index Map
The index map is a large scale map from which it is possible to ascertain, in relation to a parcel of land, whether there is:
  (a) a pending application for first registration (other than of title to a relating franchise);
  (b) a pending application for a caution against first registration (other than where the subject of the caution is a relating franchise);
  (c) a registered estate in land;
  (d) a registered rentcharge;
  (e) a registered *profit a prendre* in gross;
  (f) a registered affecting franchise; or
  (g) a caution against first registration (other than where the subject of the caution is a relating franchise).
If there is such a registered estate or caution, the index map provides the title number.
    An affecting franchise is a franchise which relates to a defined area of land and is an adverse right affecting, or capable of affecting, the title to an estate or charge. A relating franchise is a franchise which is not an affecting franchise.
    An application for an official search of the index map is made using application form SIM. A plan may be unnecessary if the land can be identified by postal description. If, however, the registrar so requires, an applicant must provide a copy of an extract from the Ordnance Survey map on the largest scale published showing the land to which the application relates (Land Registration Rules 2003 ("LRR 2003") rule 145). For the fee payable see the fee calculator on the Land Registry's website at www.landregistry.gov.uk/fees.
    It should be remembered that the index map is an index. If the result of a search of the index map reveals an affecting title number, the applicant should obtain office copies of the register and title plan of that title.

Searches of the Index of Relating Franchises and Manors
The index of relating franchises and manors is an index of verbal descriptions of:
  (a) pending applications for first registrations of title to relating franchises;
  (b) pending applications for cautions against first registration where the subject of the caution is a relating franchise;
  (c) registered franchises which are relating franchises;

(d) registered manors; and

(e) cautions against first registration where the subject of the caution is a relating franchise.

If there are any such registered estates and cautions, the index provides the title numbers arranged by administrative area.

An application for an official search of the index of relating franchises and manors is made using application form SIF. For the fee payable see the fee calculator on the Land Registry's website at www.landregistry.gov.uk/fees.

In form SIF the applicant specifies whether he is searching in respect of manors or relating franchises or both, and specifies the administrative areas in respect of which he is searching.

Searches of the Index of Proprietors' Names

The index of proprietors' names shows for each individual register the name of the proprietor of the registered estate and the proprietor of any registered charge together with the title number (LRR 2003 rule 11). A person may apply for a search to be made in the index in respect of either his own name or the name of some other person in whose property he can satisfy the registrar that he is interested generally. For example he may be interested as personal representative or trustee in bankruptcy.

An application for a search in the index of proprietors' names is made using form PN1. Only one name can be searched on each form; where there is a former name or alternative name a separate form PN1 should be used for each. For the fee payable see the fee calculator on the Land Registry's website at www.landregistry.gov.uk/fees.

Options

An option to purchase, or to renew a lease of, registered land may be protected by the entry in the register of an agreed notice, a unilateral notice and/or by a restriction. A notice does not necessarily mean that the option is valid but does mean that the priority of the option will be protected on any registered disposition (Land Registration Act 2002 ("LRA 2002") sections 32, 29 and 30). A restriction does not confer any priority; it simply prevents an entry being made in the register if it is not permitted under the wording of the restriction. The protection given to the option may also extend to the subsequent estate contract when the option is exercised (*Armstrong & Holmes Ltd v Holmes* [1993] 1 WLR 1482, [1994] 1 All ER 826).

Where the option is contained in a lease which is an overriding interest, the option should be protected by entry on the register even where no entry may be made as to the lease itself (because the lease is for a term not exceeding three years and is not otherwise registrable). This applies even if the interest to be granted under the option is another lease which will be an overriding interest.

Agreed Notice
An applicant should deliver to the registry:
  (a) an application in form AN1;
  (b) the original document granting the option or a certified copy of it;
  (c) the consent of the registered proprietor of the land where this is not contained in form AN1; and
  (d) the fee payable. A fee calculator for all types of application is on the Land Registry's website at www.landregistry.gov.uk/fees.
The entry made in the register will give details of the interest protected.

Where the registered proprietor does not consent to the entry on the register of an agreed notice, the original document granting the option signed by the registered proprietor may be sufficient to satisfy the registrar as to the validity of the applicant's claim for the purposes of LRA 2002 section 34(3)(c). In any event an application for entry of a unilateral notice may still be made. A unilateral notice may be preferred where the applicant does not wish the terms of the contract to be open to public scrutiny.

Unilateral Notice
An applicant should deliver to the registry:
  (a) an application in form UN1;
  (b) a plan of the affected land (where the option affects only part of the land in the registered title); and
  (c) the fee payable. A fee calculator for all types of application is on the Land Registry's website at www.landregistry.gov.uk/fees.
Form UN1 should be completed on the following lines to show the interest of the applicant:
"having the benefit of an option [to purchase] [to renew a lease] contained in a [*name of document*] dated ... made between ... ."
The unilateral notice will give brief details of the interest protected and identify the beneficiary of that notice.

Restriction
As a result of LRA 2002 section 42(2) no restriction may be entered for the purpose of protecting the priority of an interest which is, or could be, the subject of a notice. This does not necessarily prevent the entry of a restriction in addition to the notice of the option. Although the notice will protect the priority of the option, a restriction may be used to ensure that any conditions in relation to another disposition by the registered proprietor are complied with. The consent of the registered proprietor to the entry of the restriction is required.

An applicant should deliver to the registry:
(a) an application in form RX1;
(b) full details of the required restriction;
(c) the consent of the registered proprietor of the land (unless this is given in panel 15 of form RX1 or the applicant's conveyancer certifies that he holds such consent. The certificate may be given in panel 11 of form RX1); and
(d) the fee payable. A fee calculator for all types of application is on the Land Registry's website at www.landregistry.gov.uk/fees.

A possible form of restriction based on Form N in Schedule 4 to LRR 2003 is:

"No disposition of the registered estate by the proprietor of the registered estate is to be registered without a written consent signed by [*person having benefit of right of pre-emption*] of [*address*] or his conveyancer."

A restriction in this form would not require the approval of the registrar under LRA 2002 section 43(3).

Outline Applications

An outline application is a means of reserving a priority period for certain applications which cannot be protected by an official search with priority. The period reserved by the outline application is a period expiring at 12 noon on the fourth business day following the day that the outline application is made. A business day is a day when the Land Registry is open to the public, that is every day except Saturdays, Sundays, Christmas Day, Good Friday or any other day either specified or declared by proclamation under the Banking and Financial Dealings Act 1971 section 1 or appointed by the Lord Chancellor.

If, during that reserved period, the applicant delivers to the correct office of the registry the relevant application form bearing the official reference number of the outline application, together with the appropriate documentation and the prescribed fee, the application is dealt with in accordance with the date and time at which the outline application was received (Land Registration Rules 2003 ("LRR 2003") rule 54).

The right, interest or matter which is the subject of an outline application must exist at the time the outline application is made. For example, it is not possible to make an outline application in respect of a contract for sale which is to be protected by an agreed notice, before the contracts have been exchanged.

An outline application cannot be made in respect of any application which can be protected by an official search with priority; see *Official Searches*, page 217. Nor is it possible to use an outline application in respect of an application for first registration, an application for a caution against first registration or in respect of the cautions register, or any application dealing with part only of the land in a registered title.

The outline application must either be made orally at the appropriate Land Registry office, by telephone to a Land Registry Telephone Services centre, or electronically by a method approved by the registrar, such as Land Registry Direct. In each case the applicant must provide the following particulars:

(a) the title number(s) affected;
(b) if there is only one proprietor or applicant for first registration and that person is an individual, his surname, otherwise the proprietor's or such applicant's full name or the full name of one of the proprietors or such applicants, as appropriate;
(c) the nature of the application;
(d) the name of the applicant; and
(e) the name and address of the person or firm lodging the application.

The applicant is notified of the official reference number and this must be entered in the outline application panel of the relevant panel on the appropriate application form.

The existence of an outline application will be revealed on an official search.

Where the application with the supporting documentation is not delivered to the registry until after the period reserved by the outline application has expired, that application is treated as a fresh application and receives priority from the time when it is taken to be made in accordance with LRR 2003 rule 15.

Examples of applications which may be protected by an outline application are notices, restrictions, assents, and transfers not for value, providing the application deals with the whole of the land in a registered title, whether or not also dealing with the whole of the land in any other registered title.

Overriding Interests

The Land Registration Act 2002 ("LRA 2002") draws a distinction between unregistered interests which override first registration (which are set out in Schedule 1 and section 90) and unregistered dispositions which override registered dispositions (which are set out in Schedule 3 and section 90). Although many of the interests are the same in both schedules, there are important differences.

Unregistered Interests which Override First Registration

On first registration, the registered estate is vested in the proprietor subject to any of the following interests which affect the estate at that time and which are not the subject of an entry in the register of that estate (LRA 2002 sections 11 and 12):

Leasehold Estates in Land

A lease of land granted for a term not exceeding seven years from the date of the grant overrides first registration, unless such lease is one required to be registered under LRA 2002 section 4(1)(d), (e) or (f). A grant out of an unregistered freehold estate, or leasehold estate with more than seven years to run, which is to take effect in possession after the end of the period of three months beginning with the date of the grant, is required to be registered under LRA 2002 section 4(1)(d). A grant of a lease out of an unregistered legal estate in land pursuant to the Housing Act 1985 Part 5 (the right to buy) is required to be registered under LRA 2002 section 4(1)(e). A grant of a lease out of an unregistered legal estate in land in circumstances where the Housing Act 1985 section 171A applies (disposal by landlord which leads to a person's no longer being a secure tenant; the preserved right to buy) is required to be registered under LRA 2002 section 4(1)(f).

A lease granted for a term not exceeding twenty-one years was an overriding interest under the Land Registration Act 1925 section 70(1)(k). Any such overriding interest subsisting in relation to a registered estate on 13 October 2003 continues to have overriding effect (LRA 2002 Schedule 12 paragraph 12).

Interests of Persons in Actual Occupation

An interest belonging to a person in actual occupation, so far as relating to land of which he is in actual occupation, except for an interest under a settlement under the Settled Land Act 1925, overrides first registration. Such an overriding interest extends only to land in the registered title which is actually occupied by the person having the interest. This reverses the effect of *Ferrishurst Ltd v Wallcite Ltd* [1999] Ch 355, [1999] 2 WLR 667, [1999] 1 All ER 977 (CA).

The interest protected is not confined to a right of occupation, for example an option to purchase in favour of the person in actual occupation may be an overriding interest.

Easements and Profits a Prendre

A legal easement or *profit a prendre* overrides first registration.

Customary Rights

A customary right overrides first registration. Customary rights are rights enjoyed by members of a local community or a defined class of such community members. They are usually ancient in their origin.

Public Rights

A public right overrides first registration. Public rights are rights which are exercisable by any member of the public, such as a public right of way over a highway (*Overseas Investment Services Ltd v Simcobuild Construction Ltd* (1995) 70 P & CR 322, [1996] 1 EGLR 49 (CA)). The vesting of the fee simple of a highway in the highway authority may be a public right for this purpose (*Secretary of State for the Environment, Transport and the Regions v Baylis (Gloucester) Ltd* [2000] All ER(D) 563, (2000) 80 P & CR 324).

Local Land Charges

See *Local Land Charges*, page 200.

Mines and Minerals

See *Coal*, page 90, and *Mines and Minerals*, page 207.

Franchise

See *Franchises*, page 143.

Manorial Rights

See *Manors*, page 202.

Crown Rents

A right to rent which was reserved to the Crown on the granting of any freehold estate (whether or not the right is still vested in the Crown) overrides first registration. In practice such Crown rents occur most commonly on conveyances of foreshore by the Board of Trade.

Such Crown rents will cease to be overriding interests at the end of ten years from 13 October 2003 (LRA 2002 section 117(1)). An application for the entry in the register of a notice should be made before the end of the period. In practice this is likely to be a unilateral notice. An applicant should deliver to the registry:

(a) an application in form UN1; and
(b) a plan of the affected land (where the Crown rent affects only part of the land in the registered title).

No fee is payable for applications lodged during the ten year period beginning on 13 October 2003 (LRA 2002 section 117(2)).

Form UN1 should be completed on the following lines to show the interest of the applicant:

"owner of the following Crown rent affecting the land: [*set out details of the Crown rent including details of the grant under which it arose*]."

The unilateral notice will give brief details of the interest protected and identify who are the beneficiaries of that notice.

Non-statutory Rights in Respect of an Embankment or Sea or River Wall

See *Embankments or Sea or River Walls*, page 123.

Rights to Payment in Lieu of Tithe
A right to payment in lieu of tithe overrides first registration. In practice these are only likely to be corn rents where the liability to pay arises by an Act other than a Tithe Act and is in commutation of tithes.

Such rights will cease to be overriding interests at the end of ten years from 13 October 2003 (LRA 2002 section 117(1)). An application for the entry in the register of a notice should be made before the end of the period. In practice this is likely to be a unilateral notice. An applicant should deliver to the registry:

(a) an application in form UN1; and
(b) a plan of the affected land (where the right to payment in lieu of tithe affects only part of the land in the registered title).

No fee is payable for applications lodged during the ten year period beginning on 13 October 2003 (LRA 2002 section 117(2)).

Form UN1 should be completed on the following lines to show the interest of the applicant:

"owner of the following right to payment in lieu of tithe affecting the land: [*set out details of the corn rent including details of the Act under which it arose*]."

The unilateral notice will give brief details of the interest protected and identify the beneficiaries of that notice.

PPP Leases Relating to Transport in London
See *PPP Leases Relating to Transport in London*, page 238.

Rights Acquired under the Limitation Act 1980
For the period of three years beginning on 13 October 2003, a right acquired under the Limitation Act 1980 before 13 October 2003 overrides first registration (LRA 2002 Schedule 12 paragraph 7). This applies even if the squatter is no longer in actual occupation.

Unregistered Interests which Override Registered Dispositions
A registrable disposition for valuable consideration of a registered estate or registered charge is subject to any interest falling within LRA 2002 Schedule 3 which affects the estate at the time of the disposition and which is not the subject of an entry in the register of that estate (LRA 2002 sections 29 and 30). Any interest which has been the subject of a notice in the register at any time on or after 13 October 2003 is not treated as falling within LRA 2002 Schedule 3 for these purposes.

The unregistered interests which override registered dispositions are mainly the same as those described above as overriding first registration. The differences are:

Leasehold Estates in Land
A lease the grant of which constitutes a registrable disposition does not

override another registrable disposition.

Interests of Persons in Actual Occupation

In addition to the exception of interests under settlements referred to above, the following interests of a person in actual occupation are not included in LRA 2002 Schedule 3:

(a) an interest of a person of whom enquiry was made before the disposition and who failed to disclose the right when he could reasonably have been expected to do so;

(b) an interest which belongs to a person whose occupation would not have been obvious on a reasonably careful inspection of the land at the time of the disposition and of which the person to whom the disposition is made does not have actual knowledge at that time; and

(c) a leasehold estate in land granted to take effect in possession after the end of the period of three months beginning with the date of the grant and which has not taken effect in possession at the time of the disposition.

Under the Land Registration Act 1925 section 70(1)(g) an interest could be an overriding interest by virtue of a person's receipt of rents and profits. Such an interest subsisting on 13 October 2003 will continue to override registered dispositions provided the receipt of rents and profits continues (LRA 2002 Schedule 12 paragraph 8). Such an interest does not override if enquiry was made of the person having the benefit of it before the disposition and that person failed to disclose the right when he could reasonably have been expected to do so.

Easements and Profits a Prendre

Although all legal easements and *profits a prendre* override first registration, the position is not the same for registered dispositions. In the light of LRA 2002 Schedule 3 paragraph 3, a legal easement or *profit a prendre* overrides a registered disposition only if:

(a) at the time of the disposition it is within the actual knowledge of the person to whom the disposition is made; or

(b) at the time of the disposition it would have been obvious on a reasonably careful inspection of the land over which the easement or profit is exercisable; or

(c) the person entitled to the easement or *profit* proves that it has been exercised in the period of one year ending with the day of the disposition; or

(d) in the case of a *profit a prendre*, it is registered under the Commons Registration Act 1965.

Any easement or *profit a prendre*, however, which was an overriding interest immediately before 13 October 2003, but which would not fall within LRA 2002 Schedule 3 paragraph 3 if created on or after 13 October 2003, continues to be an overriding interest (LRA 2002 Schedule 12 paragraph 9). This includes equitable easements that were openly exercised and enjoyed as appurtenant to the dominant tenement which took effect as overriding interests on the registered servient title under the Land Registration Rules 1925 rule 258.

For a period of three years beginning on 13 October 2003 any unregistered legal easement or *profit a prendre* will override a registered disposition (LRA 2002 Schedule 12 paragraph 10). Any unregistered easement or *profit a prendre* over registered land arising on or after 13 October 2003, will be a legal easement or profit only if it is an implied or prescriptive easement or profit.

Rights Acquired under the Limitation Act 1980
LRA 2002 Schedule 12 paragraph 7 does not apply on a registered disposition. Instead, for the period of three years beginning with 13 October 2003 there is included in LRA 2002 Schedule 3 a right under paragraph 18(1) of Schedule 12 (LRA 2002 Schedule 12 paragraph 11).

LRA 2002 Schedule 12 paragraph 18(1) provides that where a registered estate in land is held in trust for a person by virtue of the Land Registration Act 1925 section 75(1) immediately before 13 October 2003, he is entitled to be registered as the proprietor of the estate. The position under the Land Registration Act 1925 was that where a registered proprietor's title had been extinguished by adverse possession, it was open to the squatter to apply for the closure of the registered proprietor's title which was deemed, in the meantime, to be held on trust for the squatter by the registered proprietor (Land Registration Act 1925 section 75(1)).

Overseas Insolvency Proceedings

A liquidator for the purposes of Council Regulation (EC) No 1346/2000 is any person or body whose function is to administer or liquidate assets of which a debtor has been divested or to supervise the administration of his affairs. Such a liquidator may apply for a note to be entered in the register of a judgment opening insolvency proceedings that falls within article 3(1) of that Council Regulation.

The application should be made in form AP1 and be accompanied by evidence of the judgment, for example an official copy of the judgment with a certified translation of it.

Partnerships

A partnership is not a corporate body. For limited liability partnerships incorporated under the Limited Liability Partnerships Act 2000, see *Limited Liability Partnerships*, page 194, and for limited partnerships see *Limited Partnerships*, page 197.

A transfer to a partnership must be to the names of the individual partners, not to the partnership name. If there are more than four partners the transfer should be to four of them to hold the legal estate on trust for the partnership. No reference to the partnership is made on the register. Since the beneficial interests are held under a tenancy in common, the following restriction in Form A is entered in the proprietorship register in accordance with the Land Registration Act 2002 section 44(1):

> "No disposition by a sole proprietor of the registered estate (except a trust corporation) under which capital money arises is to be registered unless authorised by an order of the court."

The partners may also, if they wish, apply in the additional provisions panel of the transfer, or in application form RX1, for a restriction in Form Q, which is:

> "No disposition [*or specify details*] of the registered estate by the proprietor of the registered estate is to be registered after the death of [*name of the current proprietor(s) whose personal representatives' consent will be required*] without the written consent of the personal representatives of the deceased."

Although no reference to the partnership is made on the register, the proprietors may specifically apply to have any trading name entered in the proprietorship register. This will appear after the last address for service in the entry of the proprietors, in the form "trading as [*trading name*]".

Pending Land Actions

For the position where a pending land action relates to an application for a property adjustment order in matrimonial proceedings, see *Property Adjustment Orders*, page 246. For a pending land action relating to an application for an access to neighbouring land order, see *Access to Neighbouring Land Orders*, page 1. On a pending land action relating to an application under the Leasehold Reform, Housing and Urban Development Act 1993, see *Collective Enfranchisement*, page 91 and *Leases*, page 169.

A pending land action is treated as an interest affecting an estate or charge for the purposes of the Land Registration Act 2002 ("LRA 2002") (LRA 2002 section 87(1)). It cannot, however, be an overriding interest belonging to a person in actual occupation for the purposes of paragraph 2 of Schedule 1 or 3 to LRA 2002 (LRA 2002 section 87(3)).

A pending land action may be protected by the entry on the register of a notice or a restriction or both of these. The application may be made by the person taking the action or proceedings, or his assignee or chargee (Land Registration Rules 2003 ("LRR 2003") rule 172). A restriction does not confer any priority; it simply prevents an entry being made in the register if it is not permitted under the wording of the restriction.

In practice, an application for an agreed notice will be the usual course of action. An applicant should deliver to the registry:
  (a) an application in form AN1;
  (b) the sealed claim form and notice of issue; and
  (c) the fee payable. A fee calculator for all types of application is on the Land Registry's website at www.landregistry.gov.uk/fees.

This is likely to be sufficient to satisfy the registrar of the validity of the applicant's claim in accordance with LRA 2002 section 34(3)(c). The entry made in the register will give details of the interest protected.

Where the applicant wishes to apply for a unilateral notice he should deliver to the registry:
  (a) an application in form UN1;
  (b) a plan of the affected land (where the pending action affects only part of the land in the registered title); and
  (c) the fee payable. A fee calculator for all types of application is on the Land Registry's website at www.landregistry.gov.uk/fees.

Form UN1 should be completed on the following lines to show the interest of the applicant:

"applicant in an action in the [… Division of the High Court] [… County Court] [*set out full court reference and parties*] for [*state nature of the action*]."

The unilateral notice will give brief details of the interest protected and identify the beneficiary of that notice.

If a restriction is sought, the applicant should deliver to the registry:
  (a) an application in form RX1; and
  (b) the fee payable. A fee calculator for all types of application is on the Land Registry's website at www.landregistry.gov.uk/fees.

The form of restriction sought depends on the nature of the pending land action. One possibility based on Form N in Schedule 4 to LRR 2003 is:

"No disposition of the registered estate by the proprietor of the registered estate is to be registered without a written consent signed by [*applicant*] of [*address*] or his conveyancer."

A restriction in this form would not require the approval of the registrar under LRA 2002 section 43(3). The registrar must give notice of such an application to the proprietor of the registered estate or charge concerned (LRA 2002 section 42(3)).

Personal Representatives

On the death of a sole proprietor, or of the survivor of joint proprietors, of a registered estate or registered charge, the personal representative of such proprietor may apply to become registered as proprietor of that estate or charge. The personal representative should deliver to the registry:
   (a) an application in form AP1;
   (b) (i) the original grant of probate or letters of administration, or a certified copy or office copy of it; or
   (ii) a court order appointing the applicant personal representative, or a certified copy or office copy of it; or
   (iii) (where a conveyancer is acting for the applicant) a certificate given by the conveyancer that he holds the original or an office copy of such grant of probate, letters of administration or court order; and
   (c) the fee payable. A fee calculator for all types of application is on the Land Registry's website at www.landregistry.gov.uk/fees.

Where the personal representative is seeking to become registered jointly with another personal representative who is already registered as proprietor, the registrar will serve notice on that existing proprietor (Land Registration Rules 2003 ("LRR 2003") rule 163(5)).

Where the personal representative is seeking to become registered in place of another personal representative who is already registered as proprietor, the application must also be accompanied by evidence to show that the appointment of the personal representative whom the applicant is replacing has been terminated (LRR 2003 rule 163(3)).

Where the personal representative is registered as proprietor, the following is added after the personal representative's name: "[executor] [executrix] [administrator] [administratrix] of [*name*] deceased".

Where the land was settled before the death of the sole or last surviving joint proprietor and not by his Will and the settlement continues after his death, an application to register the special personal representatives must be accompanied by the grant limited to the settled land. In that case the following is added after the personal representative's name: "special [executor] [executrix] [administrator] [administratrix] of [*name*] deceased".

For assents by personal representatives see *Assents*, page 30.

An application to register a transfer by a personal representative, who is not already registered as proprietor, must be accompanied by the grant of probate or letters of administration or a certified copy or office copy of it. The registrar is not under a duty to investigate the reasons a transfer of registered land by a personal representative of a deceased sole proprietor or last surviving joint proprietor is made. Nor is he required to consider the contents of the Will and, provided the terms of any restriction on the register are complied with, he must assume, whether or not he knows of the terms of the Will, that the personal representative is acting correctly and within his powers (LRR 2003 rule 162).

Where the personal representatives hold the registered estate on a trust of land created by the deceased's Will, or on a trust of land arising under the laws of intestacy which is subsequently varied, and their powers have been limited by the Trusts of Land and Appointment of Trustees Act 1996 ("TLATA 1996") section 8, they must apply for a restriction in Form C (LRR 2003 rule 94(3)). If an application is not made, any person who has an interest in the due administration of the estate may apply for a restriction in Form C (LRR 2003 rule 93(d)). The applicant should deliver to the registry:

(a) an application in form RX1; and
(b) the fee payable. A fee calculator for all types of application is on the Land Registry's website at www.landregistry.gov.uk/fees.

Panel 13 of RX1 should be completed on the following lines:

"The interest is that specified in rule 93(d) of the Land Registration Rules 2003, the applicant being a person interested in the due administration of the estate of [*name*] deceased."

Panel 10 should be completed as to the restriction in Form C. Form C is:

"No disposition by [*name*], the [executor] [administrator] of [*name*] deceased, other than a transfer as personal representative, is to be registered unless he makes a statutory declaration, or his conveyancer gives a certificate, that the disposition is in accordance with the terms [of the will of the deceased *or* the law relating to intestacy as varied by a deed dated *specify details of deed or specify appropriate details*] or [some variation *or* further variation] thereof referred to in the declaration or certificate, or is necessary for the purposes of administration."

Where a trust of land imposes limitations on the powers of the trustees under TLATA 1996 section 8, for example a requirement to obtain a consent before sale, and the legal estate is vested in the personal representatives of a sole or last surviving trustee, the personal representatives must apply for a restriction in Form B (LRR 2003 rule 94(4) and (7)). This does not apply if the land is held on charitable, ecclesiastical or public trusts. If such an application is not made, any person who has an interest under the trust of land where the powers of the trustees are limited under TLATA 1996 section 8 may apply for the restriction in Form B. The applicant should deliver to the registry:

(a) an application in form RX1; and
(b) the fee payable. A fee calculator for all types of application is on the Land Registry's website at www.landregistry.gov.uk/fees.

Where the applicant is a person who has an interest under a trust of land, panel 13 of RX1 should be completed on the following lines:

"The interest is that specified in rule 93(c) of the Land Registration Rules 2003, the applicant being a person who has an interest in the registered estate held under a trust of land where the powers of the trustees are limited by section 8 of the Trusts of Land and Appointment of Trustees

Act 1996."

Panel 10 should be completed as to the restriction in Form B. Form B is:

"No disposition [*or specify details*] by the proprietors of the registered estate is to be registered unless they make a statutory declaration, or their conveyancer gives a certificate, that the disposition [*or specify details*] is in accordance with [*specify the disposition creating the trust*] or some variation thereof referred to in the declaration or certificate."

Plans

Land Registry title plans are produced using the Ordnance Survey's large scale digital map data. Although this data is supplied in a single consistent format, it is surveyed and digitised at different scales. It is not possible to achieve perfect accuracy in drawing features on a plan. The Ordnance Survey publishes expected confidence levels in the accuracy of their maps in terms of relative and absolute accuracy. For example, on a map originally surveyed at 1:1250 scale, if two points on the ground are 60.0m apart, there is a 68% likelihood that the equivalent distance on the map is between 59.6m and 60.4m, a 95% likelihood that the equivalent distance on the map is between 59.2m and 60.8m, and a 99% likelihood that the equivalent distance on the map is between 59.0m and 61.0m. Further information and examples appear on the Ordnance Survey's website at www.ordnancesurvey.gov.uk.

This means that measurements scaled from title plans do not necessarily match measurements taken on the ground. The scale of the Ordnance Survey map also dictates how physical features are shown on a title plan. Where, for example, a hedge and a wall run close together on the ground, it may be that they are shown on the plan by a single firm black line because the gap between the two features cannot be shown at the scale in question. Even where only one physical feature is represented by a firm black line on the Ordnance Survey map it may be a wide hedge or a narrow fence. Again a small projection in a boundary might be shown on a plan surveyed at 1:1250 scale where a plan surveyed at 1:2500 scale would show a straight line. Even if the latter plan is enlarged to 1:1250 scale, it will still not show the projection.

In *Alan Wibberley Building Ltd v Insley* [1999] 1 WLR 894, [1999] 2 All ER 897 (HL), Lord Hope of Craighead said:

"The use of maps or plans such as those published by the Ordnance Survey is now widespread and has obvious advantages. Ordnance Survey maps are prepared to a high standard of accuracy and are frequently and appropriately used to fix boundaries by reference, for example, to Ordnance Survey field numbers. But like all maps they are subject to limitations. The most obvious are those imposed by scale. No map can reproduce to anything like the same scale of detail every feature which is found on the ground. Furthermore the Ordnance Survey does not fix private boundaries. The purpose of the survey is topographical, not taxative. Even the most detailed Ordnance Survey map may not show every feature on the ground which can be used to identify the extent of the owner's land. In the present case the Ordnance Survey map shows the hedge, but it does not show the ditch. So there is no reason in principle in this case for preferring the line on the map to other evidence which may be relevant to identify the boundary."

Plans for use in transfers of part or other deeds relating to an application to the registry should be prepared bearing in mind the following guidelines. The plan should:

(a) be drawn to scale and show that scale;
(b) bear a north point;
(c) be at 1:1250 or 1:500 scale for urban properties or 1:2500 for rural properties;
(d) not be reduced in scale by copying;
(e) not be marked or referred to as for identification purposes only;
(f) not contain a disclaimer under the Property Misdescriptions Act 1991;
(g) show sufficient detail to be identified on the Ordnance Survey map;
(h) show buildings and other features in their correct or intended positions;
(i) show clearly the land in question, for example by edging, colouring or hatching;
(j) have edgings of a thickness that do not obscure any other detail;
(k) identify different floor levels (where appropriate);
(l) show intricate boundaries with a larger scale or inset plan;
(m) show measurements in metric units, to two decimal places;
(n) show undefined boundaries accurately and, where necessary, by reference to measurements; and
(o) show measurements that correspond as far as possible to scaled measurements.

Positive Covenants

Where the proprietor, or any previous proprietor, of a registered estate has given a positive covenant relating to that estate, the registrar may make an entry in respect of it in the proprietorship register (Land Registration Rules 2003 ("LRR 2003") rule 64).

If the existence of the positive covenant is apparent from the register in some other way, the registrar need not make an entry. This might be so where the positive covenant is included amongst restrictive covenants and is set out with them in the charges register. Where the registrar does make an entry, it normally refers to the deed that contains the positive covenant.

There is no need to make a specific application for an entry in respect of a positive covenant when this is included in a deed lodged as part of an application in respect of a registrable disposition. The entry will be made by the registrar if he considers it appropriate.

Where an entry has been made in respect of a positive covenant, the registrar must remove it from the register if it appears to him that the covenant does not bind the current proprietor of the registered estate (LRR 2003 rule 64(3)).

The burden of positive covenants does not run with freehold land (*Rhone v Stephens* [1994] 2 AC 310, [1994] 2 WLR 429, [1994] 2 All ER 65 (HL)). Positive covenants may be made enforceable against successors in title of the covenantor by creating an estate rentcharge for a nominal amount. For the protection of estate rentcharges see *Rentcharges*, page 255.

Positive covenants are sometimes protected by ensuring that a subsequent purchaser enters into a new deed of covenant with the person having the benefit of the original covenant. This arrangement may involve a positive covenant that this be done and be supported by an application for a restriction. The applicant for such restriction should deliver to the registry:

(a) an application in form RX1;
(b) full details of the required restriction;
(c) the consent of the registered proprietor of the land, where this consent is not contained in form RX1; and
(d) the fee payable. A fee calculator for all types of application is on the Land Registry's website at www.landregistry.gov.uk/fees.

Possible forms of restriction are Form L or Form M. Form L is:

"No disposition [*or specify details*] of the registered estate [(other than a charge)] by the proprietor of the registered estate [or by the proprietor of any registered charge] is to be registered without a certificate [signed by [*name*] of [*address*] (or [his conveyancer] *or specify details*)] [signed on behalf of [*name*] of [*address*] by [its secretary or conveyancer *or specify appropriate details*]] that the provisions of [*specify clause, paragraph or other particulars*] of [*specify details*] have been complied with."

Form M is:

"No disposition [*or specify details*] of the registered estate [(other than a charge)] by the proprietor of the registered estate [or by the proprietor of any registered charge] is to be registered without a certificate signed by the proprietor for the time being of the estate registered under title number [*title number*] [(or his conveyancer *or specify appropriate details*)] or, if appropriate, signed on such proprietor's behalf by [its secretary or conveyancer *or specify appropriate details*], that the provisions of [*specify clause, paragraph or other particulars*] of [*specify details*] have been complied with."

Powers of Attorney

It is not possible to note the appointment of an attorney by a registered proprietor in an individual register.

Where any document which has been executed by an attorney is delivered to the registry, there must also be produced:
  (a) the power of attorney; or
  (b) a certified copy which meets the requirements laid down in the Powers of Attorney Act 1971 section 3; or
  (c) an office copy of an enduring power of attorney registered with the Court of Protection under the Enduring Powers of Attorney Act 1985; or
  (d) a certificate by a conveyancer in Form 1.

Form 1 is:
  Date of power of attorney ...
  Donor of power of attorney ...
  Donee of power of attorney ...
  I/We ... of ... certify that
  - the power of attorney ("the power") is in existence [and is made under (*state statutory provisions under which the power is made if applicable*)],
  - the power is dated ...,
  - I am/we are satisfied that the power is validly executed as a deed and authorises the attorney to execute the document on behalf of the donor of that power, and
  - I/we hold [the instrument creating the power] *or* [a copy of the power by means of which its contents may be proved under section 3 of the Powers of Attorney Act 1971] *or* [a document which under section 4 of the Evidence and Powers of Attorney Act 1940 or section 7(3) of the Enduring Powers of Attorney 1985 is sufficient evidence of the contents of the power].

  Signature of conveyancer .... Date ......

Evidence of Non-revocation

Where a transaction between the donee of the power of attorney and a person dealing with him is completed more than twelve months from the date of the power, the registrar may require evidence of non-revocation of the power to be produced (Land Registration Rules 2003 ("LRR 2003") rule 62). The evidence may be a statutory declaration by the person who dealt with the attorney or a certificate given by that person's conveyancer in Form 2. Form 2 is:
  Date of power of attorney ...
  Donor of power of attorney ...
  I/We ... of ... do solemnly and sincerely [declare] [certify] that at the time

of completion of the ... to me/us/my client I/we/my client had no knowledge–
- of a revocation of the power, or
- of the death or bankruptcy of the donor or, if the donor is a corporate body, its winding up or dissolution, or
- of any incapacity of the donor where the power is not a valid enduring power, or

Where the power is in the form prescribed for an enduring power–
- that the power was not in fact a valid enduring power, or
- of an order or direction of the Court of Protection which revoked the power, or
- of the bankruptcy of the attorney, or

Where the power was given under section 9 of the Trusts of Land and Appointment of Trustees Act 1996–
- of an appointment of another trustee of the land in question, or
- of any other event which would have the effect of revoking the power, or
- of any lack of good faith on the part of the person(s) who dealt with the attorney, or
- that the attorney was not a person to whom the functions of the trustees could be delegated under section 9 of the Trusts of Land and Appointment of Trustees Act 1996, or

Where the power is expressed to be by way of security–
- that the power was not in fact given by way of security, or
- of any revocation of the power with the consent of the attorney, or
- of any other event which would have had the effect of revoking the power.

Where a certificate is given–
Signature of conveyancer .... Date ......; or

Where a Statutory Declaration is made–
And I/we make this solemn declaration conscientiously believing the same to be true and by virtue of the provisions of the Statutory Declarations Act 1835.

Signature of Declarant(s) .... Date ......

DECLARED at ... before me, a person entitled to administer oaths.
Name ...
Address ...
Qualification ...
Signature ...

Evidence in Support of Power Delegating Trustees' Functions to a Beneficiary

Where a document executed by an attorney, to whom functions have been delegated under the Trusts of Land and Appointment of Trustees Act 1996 section 9, is delivered to the registrar, he may require evidence that the person who dealt with the attorney did so in good faith and had no knowledge at the time of the completion of the transaction that the attorney was not a person to whom the functions of the trustees in relation to the land in question could be delegated under section 9 (LRR 2003 rule 63).

The evidence may be a statutory declaration by the person who dealt with the attorney or a certificate given by that person's conveyancer in Form 3 or, where evidence of non-revocation is also required, in Form 2. Form 3 is:

Date of power of attorney ...
Donor of power of attorney ...
I/We ... of ... do solemnly and sincerely [declare] [certify] that at the time of completion of the ... to me/us/my client I/we/my client had no knowledge–
- of any lack of good faith on the part of the person(s) who dealt with the attorney, or
- that the attorney was not a person to whom the functions of the trustees could be delegated under section 9 of the Trusts of Land and appointment of Trustees Act 1996.

Where a certificate is given–
Signature of conveyancer .... Date ......; or
Where a Statutory Declaration is made–
And I/we make this solemn declaration conscientiously believing the same to be true and by virtue of the provisions of the Statutory Declarations Act 1835.
Signature of Declarant(s) .... Date ......
DECLARED at ... before me, a person entitled to administer oaths.
Name ...
Address ...
Qualification ...
Signature ...

PPP Leases Relating to Transport in London

Public-private partnership ("PPP") leases for the purposes of this section are leases created for public-private partnerships relating to transport in London within the meaning given by the Greater London Authority Act 1999 section 218. No application for voluntary registration of such a lease may be made, neither does the requirement of registration apply on the grant or transfer of a leasehold estate in land under a PPP lease (Land Registration Act 2002 ("LRA 2002") section 90(1) and (2)).

The grant of a term of years absolute under a PPP lease is not required to be completed by registration. The express grant of an interest falling within the Law of Property Act 1925 section 1(2), for example a legal easement, where the interest is created for the benefit of a leasehold estate in land under a PPP lease is not required to be completed by registration (LRA 2002 section 90(3)).

No notice may be entered in the register in respect of an interest under a PPP lease (LRA 2002 section 90(4)).

A PPP lease is an unregistered interest which overrides first registration and also an unregistered interest which overrides registered dispositions (LRA 2002 section 90(5)). An applicant is not, however, required to provide any information about a PPP lease under the duty contained in the Land Registration Rules 2003 rules 28 and 57.

Priorities

For the relative priority between registered charges, see *Legal Charges*, page 184.

The basic rule is that the priority of an interest affecting a registered estate or charge is not affected by a disposition of the estate or charge (Land Registration Act 2002 ("LRA 2002") section 28). It makes no difference for the purposes of LRA 2002 section 28 whether the interest or disposition is registered. In effect, therefore, the rule is that the first in time by date of creation prevails. This basic rule is, however, subject to modification in the common event of a disposition for value of a registered estate or a registered charge, and in the less common event of an Inland Revenue charge.

Registered Dispositions of Estates for Valuable Consideration
"Valuable consideration" for this purpose does not include marriage consideration or a nominal consideration in money.

Completion by registration of a registrable disposition for valuable consideration of a registered estate has the effect of postponing to the interest under the disposition any interest affecting the estate immediately before the disposition whose priority is not protected at the time of registration (LRA 2002 section 29). The priority of an interest is protected for these purposes if it is a registered charge or the subject of a notice in the register, or it is an overriding interest within LRA 2002 Schedule 3, or it appears from the register to be excepted from the effect of registration. Additionally, in the case of a disposition of a leasehold estate, the priority of an interest is also protected if the burden of the interest is incident to the estate.

For overriding interests within LRA 2002 Schedule 3, see *Overriding Interests*, page 223. Any interest which has been the subject of a notice in the register at any time on or after 13 October 2003 is not treated as an overriding interest for these purposes.

Where the grant of a leasehold estate in land out of a registered estate does not involve a registrable disposition, LRA 2002 section 29 has effect as if the grant involved such a disposition and the disposition were registered at the time of the grant (LRA 2002 section 29(4)).

The following example illustrates the working of LRA 2002 sections 28 and 29:

- A is registered proprietor of a freehold estate in land.
- On 5 January 2004, A grants B a restrictive covenant affecting the whole of the estate. B does not apply for a notice to be registered.
- On 5 February 2004, A grants C an estate contract affecting the whole of the estate and notice of the estate contract is entered on the register on 10 February 2004.
- On 5 March 2004 A transfers part of the land in the title by way of gift to D and D is registered as proprietor of the new title so created on 10 March 2004.
- On 5 April 2004 A transfers the remainder of the land in the original title on sale to E and E is registered as proprietor on 9 April 2002.

Considering the relative priorities on 12 April 2002, B's interest has priority to C's interest. D's registered estate is subject to the interests of both B and C. E's registered estate is subject only to the interest of C, which was protected by notice at the relevant time.

Registered Dispositions of Charges for Valuable Consideration

"Valuable consideration" for this purpose does not include marriage consideration or a nominal consideration in money.

Completion by registration of a registrable disposition for valuable consideration of a registered charge has the effect of postponing to the interest under the disposition any interest affecting the charge immediately before the disposition whose priority is not protected at the time of registration (LRA 2002 section 30). The priority of an interest is protected for these purposes if it is a registered charge or the subject of a notice in the register, or it is an overriding interest within LRA 2002 Schedule 3, or it appears from the register to be excepted from the effect of registration. Additionally, in the case of a disposition of a charge which relates to a leasehold estate, the priority of an interest is also protected if the burden of the interest is incident to the estate.

For overriding interests within LRA 2002 Schedule 3, see *Overriding Interests*, page 223. Any interest which has been the subject of a notice in the register at any time on or after 13 October 2003 is not treated as an overriding interest for these purposes.

Inland Revenue Charges

The effect of a disposition of a registered estate or registered charge on a charge under the Inheritance Tax Act 1984 section 237 is determined, not in accordance with LRA 2002 sections 29 and 30 as described above, but in accordance with the Inheritance Act 1984 sections 237(6) and 238 (LRA 2002 section 31). This has the effect that a purchaser in good faith for money or money's worth takes free from the Inland Revenue charge in the absence of registration.

Priority of Applications

Where an application for an entry in the register is protected, any entry made in the register during the priority period relating to the application is postponed to any entry made in pursuance of it (LRA 2002 section 72(2)). An application for an entry is protected for these purposes if it is one to which a priority period relates and it is made before the end of that period. LRA 2002 section 72(2) does not apply, however, if the earlier entry was itself made in pursuance of a protected application and its priority period ranks ahead of the later application.

If it appears to the registrar that LRA 2002 section 72(2) might apply to an entry, he may defer dealing with the application for such entry.

Where a court makes an order under LRA 2002 section 46(3) that an entry is to have overriding priority, this prevails over an application for another entry.

A purchaser may obtain a priority period for his application by applying for an official search with priority using application form OS1 or OS2, as appropriate. See *Official Searches*, page 217. The priority period is the period beginning at the time when the application for the official search is entered on the day list and ending at midnight marking the end of the thirtieth business day thereafter. A business day is any day except Saturday, Sunday, Christmas Day, Good Friday or any other day either specified or declared by proclamation under the Banking and Financial Dealings Act 1971 section 1 or appointed by the Lord Chancellor.

Where two or more official search certificates with priority relating to the same registrable estate or charge or to the same registered land have been issued and are in operation, the certificates take effect, in respect to the priority conferred, in the order the applications for search were entered on the day list, unless the applicants agree otherwise. Where one transaction is dependent upon another, the registrar must assume, unless the contrary appears, that the applicants have agreed that their applications for search have priority so as to give effect to the sequence of the documents effecting the transactions (Land Registration Rules 2003 ("LRR 2003") rule 153).

Where two or more applications relating to the same registered title are made at the same time by the same applicant, they rank in such order as he may specify. Where the applications are not made by the same applicant, they rank in such order as the applicants specify that they have agreed. If the applicants have not specified the agreed order of priority, the registrar notifies them and requests them to agree within a specified time. Should the applicants not agree within this period, the registrar proposes the order of priority and serves notice of his proposal on the applicants. If any applicant objects to this proposal there is a dispute between the applicants. See *Disputes*, page 120 for how such a dispute may be resolved. Where one transaction is dependent upon another, the registrar must assume, unless the contrary appears, that the applicants have specified that the applications are to have priority so as to give effect to the sequence of the documents effecting the transactions (LRR 2003 rule 55).

Profits a Prendre

Profits a prendre were not capable of registration under the Land Registration Act 1925 but a *profit a prendre* in gross may now be the subject of voluntary registration (Land Registration Act 2002 ("LRA 2002") section 3). It is not, however, compulsory to apply for first registration of the title to a *profit a prendre* in gross. It is not possible to register a profit which is appurtenant to land separately from that land (LRA 2002 section 59(1)).

Legal Profits Arising Prior to First Registration
On first registration the estate is vested in the registered proprietor together with all interests subsisting for the benefit of the estate (LRA 2002 sections 11(3) and 12(3)). This includes the benefit of any subsisting appurtenant legal profits. If, at the time of first registration, the registrar is satisfied that a right subsists as a legal estate and benefits the registered estate, he may enter the benefit of that appurtenant right in the register. This will be as the result of the registrar's examination of the title or his consideration of a written application providing details of the right and evidence of its existence. Where the profit has arisen by prescription, this evidence is usually by way of statutory declarations. If the registrar is not satisfied that the right subsists as a legal interest benefiting the registered estate, he may enter details of the right claimed in the property register with such qualification as he considers appropriate (Land Registration Rules 2003 ("LRR 2003") rule 33).

On first registration the estate is vested in the registered proprietor subject to any profits which are the subject of an entry in the register in relation to the estate, and/or, in the case of a leasehold title, which are incident to the leasehold estate (LRA 2002 sections 11(4)(a) and 12(4)(a) and (b)). The registrar must enter a notice in the register of the burden of any profit which appears from his examination to affect the registered estate, except any which appear to him to be of a trivial or obvious character, or the entry of a notice in respect of which would be likely to cause confusion or inconvenience (LRR 2003 rule 35). No notice may be entered in the register in respect of a profit which is a right of common capable of being registered under the Commons Registration Act 1965 (LRA 2002 section 33(d)). Even where no entry is made as to a subjective legal profit on first registration, it is an overriding interest within LRA 2002 Schedule 1 paragraph 3.

A person applying for first registration must provide information to the registrar in form DI about any legal profits which are within his actual knowledge and affect the estate to which the application relates, other than any which are capable of being registered under the Commons Registration Act 1965. The registrar may enter a notice in the register in respect of any such legal profit (LRR 2003 rule 28).

Legal Profits Arising After First Registration

The express grant or reservation of a legal profit (other than one capable of being registered under the Commons Registration Act 1965) over registered land must be completed by registration. This does not apply to a grant as a result of the operation of the Law of Property Act 1925 section 62. Registration in the case of an appurtenant legal profit is completed by the entry of a notice of the profit in the register and, if the dominant tenement is registered, an entry in the property register of that title (LRA 2002 section 27(2)(d) and (7) and Schedule 2 paragraph 7). Until completed by registration, such a profit is only equitable. In the case of a legal profit in gross the grantee must be registered as proprietor of the profit and a notice in respect of the profit must be entered in the register (LRA 2002 Schedule 2 paragraph 6).

On registration of a transfer or charge of part of a registered title, entries are made, in the new title created and the retained or uncharged title, in respect of any appurtenant legal profits granted or reserved in the transfer or charge. An entry in respect of a profit in gross is made in the servient title. In the case of a charge of part such entries are made only if the registrar decides that the charged part is to be comprised in a separate registered title from the uncharged part.

An applicant for an entry of the benefit of an appurtenant legal profit contained in a deed of grant should deliver to the registry:
 (a) an application in form AP1;
 (b) the deed of grant;
 (c) a certified copy (if the original deed is to be returned);
 (d) (if the right is granted over unregistered land) an abstract or epitome showing the grantor's title to the unregistered estate; and
 (e) the fee payable. A fee calculator for all types of application is on the Land Registry's website at www.landregistry.gov.uk/fees.

Where the right is granted over unregistered land and the registrar is not satisfied that the right claimed subsists as a legal estate appurtenant to the applicant's registered estate, he may enter details of the right claimed in the property register with such qualification as he considers appropriate.

An applicant for an entry of the benefit of an implied or prescriptive appurtenant profit should deliver to the registry:
 (a) an application in form AP1;
 (b) evidence, usually statutory declarations, to satisfy the registrar that the profit subsists as a legal estate appurtenant to the applicant's registered estate; and
 (c) the fee payable. A fee calculator for all types of application is on the Land Registry's website at www.landregistry.gov.uk/fees.

Where the registrar is not satisfied that the right claimed subsists as a legal estate appurtenant to the applicant's registered estate, he may enter details of the right claimed in the property register with such qualification as he considers appropriate.

An applicant whose dominant tenement is unregistered and who is applying for the entry of a notice in respect of a profit affecting a registered title, should deliver to the registry:
 (a) an application in form AP1;
 (b) the deed of grant;
 (c) a certified copy (if the original deed is to be returned);
 (d) (if an implied or prescriptive profit) evidence, usually statutory declarations, of the existence of the profit;
 (e) the fee payable. A fee calculator for all types of application is on the Land Registry's website at www.landregistry.gov.uk/fees.

Where it appears to the registrar that a registered estate is subject to a legal profit (other than one capable of being registered under the Commons Registration Act 1965), he may enter a notice in the register in respect of that profit (LRA 2002 section 37). In that case the registrar must give notice to the registered proprietor and to any person who appears to him to be entitled to the interest protected by the notice or whom the registrar otherwise considers appropriate (LRR 2003 rule 89). If the registered proprietor applies for the entry of the notice, or consents to an application for such an entry, the registrar is not obliged to give notice to him. Nor is the registrar obliged to give notice under LRR 2003 rule 89 to any person who has applied for, or consented to, the entry of the notice, or if that person's name and address for service are not set out in the registered title in question.

Unregistered Legal Profits which Override Registered Dispositions

Although all legal profits override first registration, the position is not the same for registered dispositions. In the light of LRA 2002 Schedule 3 paragraph 3, a legal profit overrides a registered disposition only if:
 (a) at the time of the disposition it is within the actual knowledge of the person to whom the disposition is made; or

(b) at the time of the disposition it would have been obvious on a reasonably careful inspection of the land over which the profit is exercisable; or

(c) the person entitled to the profit proves that it has been exercised in the period of one year ending with the day of the disposition; or

(d) it is registered under the Commons Registration Act 1965.

Any profit, however, which was an overriding interest immediately before 13 October 2003, but which would not fall within LRA 2002 Schedule 3 paragraph 3 if created on or after 13 October 2003, continues to be an overriding interest (LRA 2002 Schedule 12 paragraph 9). For a period of three years beginning on 13 October 2003 any unregistered legal profit will override a registered disposition (LRA 2002 Schedule 12 paragraph 10). An unregistered profit over registered land arising on or after 13 October 2003 is a legal profit only if it is an implied or prescriptive profit.

A person applying to register a registrable disposition of a registered estate must provide information to the registrar in form DI about any legal profits (other than those capable of being registered under the Commons Registration Act 1965) falling within Schedule 3 paragraph 3 which are within his actual knowledge and affect the estate to which the application relates. The applicant must produce to the registrar any documentary evidence of the existence of any such legal profits as is under his control. The registrar may enter a notice in the register in respect of any such legal profit (LRR 2003 rule 57).

First Registration of Profit a Prendre in Gross

An applicant should deliver to the registry:
(a) an application in form FR1;
(b) sufficient details, by plan or otherwise, so that the area of land which is affected by the profit can be clearly identified on the Ordnance Survey map;
(c) all deeds and documents relating to the title that are in the control of the applicant;
(d) a list in duplicate in form DL of all the documents delivered; and
(e) the fee payable. A fee calculator for all types of application is on the Land Registry's website at www.landregistry.gov.uk/fees.

Registration of Profit a Prendre in Gross Created over Registered Land

An applicant should deliver to the registry:
(a) an application in form AP1;
(b) the deed creating the profit;
(c) any consent required under a restriction on the grantor's title;
(d) any consent by a chargee on the grantor's title; and
(e) the fee payable. A fee calculator for all types of application is on the Land Registry's website at www.landregistry.gov.uk/fees.

On registration of the profit, it is allotted its own title number. Notice of the registered profit is entered on the grantor's registered title without any need for a separate application or further fee.

Property Adjustment Orders

An application for a property adjustment order under the Matrimonial Causes Act 1983 section 24 is treated as an interest affecting an estate or charge for the purposes of the Land Registration Act 2002 ("LRA 2002") (LRA 2002 section 87(1)). It cannot, however, be an overriding interest belonging to a person in actual occupation for the purposes of paragraph 2 of Schedule 1 or 3 to LRA 2002 (LRA 2002 section 87(3)).

An application for a property adjustment order may be protected by the entry on the register of a notice or a restriction or both of these. A restriction does not confer any priority; it simply prevents an entry being made in the register if it is not permitted under the wording of the restriction.

The application for the entry of a notice or restriction should be delivered to the registry immediately after the application for the property adjustment order has been filed in the court (*Whittingham v Whittingham* [1979] Fam 19, [1978] 2 WLR 936, [1978] 3 All ER 805 (CA)). It is immaterial that the application in the petition or answer does not particularise a property (*Perez-Adamson v Perez Rivas* [1987] Fam 89, [1987] 2 WLR 500, [1987] 3 All ER 20 (CA)). The court's powers under the Matrimonial Causes Act 1973 section 37 to review a disposition have been held to include power to review a disposition that would otherwise have defeated a prospective claim which was unprotected in the register (*Kemmis v Kemmis* [1988] 1 WLR 1307 (CA)).

In practice, an application for an agreed notice will be the usual course of action. An applicant should deliver to the registry:

(a) an application in form AN1;

(b) a copy of the petition or answer claiming relief; and

(c) the fee payable. A fee calculator for all types of application is on the Land Registry's website at www.landregistry.gov.uk/fees.

This is likely to be sufficient to satisfy the registrar of the validity of the applicant's claim in accordance with LRA 2002 section 34(3)(c). The entry made in the register will give details of the interest protected.

Where the applicant wishes to apply for a unilateral notice he should deliver to the registry:

(a) an application in form UN1;

(b) a plan of the affected land (where the application for a property adjustment order affects only part of the land in the registered title); and

(c) the fee payable. A fee calculator for all types of application is on the Land Registry's website at www.landregistry.gov.uk/fees.

Form UN1 should be completed on the following lines to show the interest of the applicant:

"petitioner for a property adjustment order under the Matrimonial Causes Act 1973 in the [... Division of the High Court] [... County Court] [*set out full court reference and parties*]."

The unilateral notice will give brief details of the interest protected and identify the beneficiary of that notice.

If a restriction is sought, the applicant should deliver to the registry:
(a) an application in form RX1; and
(b) the fee payable. A fee calculator for all types of application is on the Land Registry's website at www.landregistry.gov.uk/fees.

A possible form of restriction based on Form N in Schedule 4 to LRR 2003 is:

"No disposition of the registered estate by the proprietor of the registered estate is to be registered without a written consent signed by [*applicant*] of [*address*] or his conveyancer."

A restriction in this form would not require the approval of the registrar under LRA 2002 section 43(3). The registrar must give notice of such an application to the proprietor of the registered estate concerned (LRA 2002 section 42(3)).

Where the petitioner and respondent already hold the property as beneficial joint tenants, consideration should be given to severing the equitable joint tenancy. See *Severance of a Beneficial Joint Tenancy*, page 286.

The procedure for protecting a property adjustment order depends on the form of the order made. Where it has the effect of creating a trust of land, an application should be made for a restriction in Form A where this is not already entered in the proprietorship register. Form A is:

"No disposition by a sole proprietor of the registered estate (except a trust corporation) under which capital money arises is to be registered unless authorised by an order of the court."

The applicant should deliver to the registry an application in form RX1. No fee is payable where the application is in respect of a restriction in Form A only.

Where the applicant is a person who has an interest under a trust of land, panel 13 of RX1 should be completed on the following lines:

"The interest is that specified in rule 93(a) of the Land Registration Rules 2003, the applicant being a person who has an interest in the registered estate held under a trust of land."

The order of the court may provide for the immediate sale of the property and the distribution of the proceeds of sale. Such an order does not require to be the subject of an entry in the register.

Where the order provides that one party should enter into a charge in favour of the other, the protection of such charge depends on whether it is a registrable charge or an equitable charge. See *Legal Charges*, page 184 and *Equitable Charges*, page 126.

Proprietary Estoppel

Where the owner of land creates an expectation in another person that that person will receive some right or interest over the land and that person acts to his detriment as a result of that expectation, an equity arises in favour of that person by estoppel. If the owner refuses to grant the right or interest in question, an application for relief may be made to the court. The court has discretion as to the form of relief it grants; see for example *Crabb v Arun District Council* [1976] Ch 179, [1975] 3 WLR 487, [1975] 3 All ER 865 (CA); *Taylor Fashions v Liverpool Victoria Friendly Society* [1981] QB 133, [1981] 2 WLR 576, [1981] 1 All ER 897; and *Gillett v Holt* [2001] Ch 210, [2000] 3 WLR 315, [2000] 2 All ER 289 (CA).

There has been doubt as to the nature of the interest after the proprietary estoppel has arisen but before the court has made its decision. The Land Registration Act 2002 ("LRA 2002") section 116 declares for the avoidance of doubt that, in relation to registered land, an equity by estoppel has effect from the time the equity arises as an interest capable of binding successors in title, subject to the rules about the effect of dispositions on priority. For the rules about the effect of dispositions on priority, see *Priorities*, page 239.

Between the time the equity by estoppel arises and the time the court gives effect to it, the interest may be protected by a unilateral notice. If the person claiming the equity is in actual possession of the land over which the equity is claimed, it may be protected as an overriding interest under LRA 2002 Schedule 3 paragraph 2. An applicant for a unilateral notice should deliver to the registry:

(a) an application in form UN1;
(b) a plan of the affected land (where the equity claimed affects only part of the land in the registered title); and
(c) the fee payable. A fee calculator for all types of application is on the Land Registry's website at www.landregistry.gov.uk/fees.

Form UN1 should be completed on the following lines to show the interest of the applicant:

"having an equity arising by proprietary estoppel as a result of [*set out facts which give rise to the proprietary estoppel*]."

The unilateral notice will give brief details of the interest protected and identify the beneficiary of that notice.

Receivers

This section deals with receivers appointed under the Law of Property Act 1925 section 109. For administrative receivers, see *Administrative Receivers*, page 6; and for receivers appointed under the Mental Health Act 1983, see *Mental Health Act 1983 Patients*, page 205. For receivers appointed by court order, see *Receivers Appointed by Order of the Court*, page 251.

The appointment of a receiver is not capable of being noted on the register of any title of which the company is registered proprietor.

Address for Service
The receiver should ensure that the company's address for service shown in the register is such as will allow notices to be received. If an additional address for service (up to three are permitted) or an amended address for service is required the receiver should deliver to the registry:
  (a) an application in form AP1;
  (b) a certified copy of the appointment of the receiver; and
  (c) a certified copy of the debenture or charge under which the receiver is appointed (if not already noted or registered).
No fee is payable.

Restriction
A receiver may wish to apply for a restriction in respect of a registered title owned by the company. A restriction does not confer any priority; it simply prevents an entry being made in the register if it is not permitted under the wording of the restriction.

The receiver should deliver to the registry:
  (a) an application in form RX1;
  (b) full details of the required restriction;
  (c) a statement signed by the receiver or his conveyancer that the applicant is the receiver of the registered proprietor company; and
  (d) the fee payable. A fee calculator for all types of application is on the Land Registry's website at www.landregistry.gov.uk/fees.
A possible form of restriction based on Form N in Schedule 4 to the Land Registration Rules 2003 ("LRR 2003") is:
"No disposition of the registered estate by the proprietor of the registered estate is to be registered without a written consent signed by [*receiver*] of [*address*] or his conveyancer."
A restriction in this form would not require the approval of the registrar under Land Registration Act 2002 ("LRA 2002") section 43(3).

Sale by Receiver
A receiver's powers of dealing with the legal estate under the Law of Property Act 1925 section 109 are limited, but are frequently extended under

the terms of the mortgage or debenture. Under the terms of most mortgages or debentures, the receiver acts as agent of the mortgagor, and so a transferee will require a release in respect of the mortgage or debenture under which the receiver was appointed. The appointment of a receiver causes any floating charge to crystallise.

Where the mortgagor becomes bankrupt or goes into liquidation, the receiver can continue to act but ceases to be an agent of the mortgagor. Any power of attorney given to the receiver by the mortgagor ceases once a bankruptcy or winding-up commences, although the receiver may have contractual rights under the mortgage or debenture to dispose of the property of the mortgagor, and these rights survive the bankruptcy or winding-up (*Barrows v Chief Land Registrar* The Times 20 October 1977). Where the receiver is disposing under such contractual rights, the following form of execution may be used:

Signed as a deed by [*company*]
by its receiver [*name of receiver*]
pursuant to powers granted to him   [*name of company*]
by clause ... of a [*name of deed*]   by its receiver [*name of*
dated ... in favour of ... in the   *receiver*]
presence of:
(*Signature name and address of witness*)

Where the winding-up of a company has commenced, the court has power to set aside a floating charge under the Insolvency Act 1986 section 245. The court also has powers to set aside transactions at an undervalue and to vary or revoke extortionate credit transactions (Insolvency Act 1986 sections 238, 339, 244 and 343). These powers may invalidate the mortgage or debenture under which the receiver has been appointed. Where the mortgagor is a company, the transferee should ensure that the debenture has been registered at the Companies Registry under the Companies Act 1985 section 395. Where the transferee is aware that the liquidator is seeking to have the debenture avoided, he should disclose this when applying to register the transfer by the receiver.

A person applying to register a disposition of a registered estate must provide information to the registrar in form DI about any of the overriding interests (other than local land charges or public rights) set out in Schedule 3 to LRA 2002 that affect the estate to which the application relates and are within the actual knowledge of the applicant. For details see *Overriding Interests*, page 223. The applicant must produce to the registrar any documentary evidence of the interest that is under his control (LRR 2003 rule 57). The registrar may enter a notice in the register in respect of any such interest.

The applicant is not required, however, to provide information about interests that, under section 33 or 90(4) of LRA 2002, cannot be protected by notice. Such interests are:

(a) interests under a trust of land or under a Settled Land Act 1925 settlement;
(b) a leasehold estate in land granted for three years or less from the date of the grant and which is not required to be registered;
(c) a restrictive covenant between lessor and lessee, so far as relating to the demised premises;
(d) an interest which is capable of being registered under the Commons Registration Act 1965;
(e) an interest in any coal or coal mine, or the rights attached to any such interest, or the rights of any person under the Coal Industry Act 1994 section 38, 49 or 51; and
(f) leases created for public-private partnerships relating to transport in London, within the meaning given by the Greater London Authority Act 1999 section 218.

The applicant is also not required to provide information about a leasehold estate in land which falls within paragraph 1 of Schedule 3 to LRA 2002 but, at the time of the application, has one year or less to run.

A transferee of a registered title from a receiver should deliver to the registry:
(a) an application in form AP1;
(b) the transfer;
(c) a certified copy of the receiver's appointment;
(d) a certified copy of the debenture under which the receiver was appointed (unless this is already noted on the register of the title being sold);
(e) releases in respect of any charges appearing on the title;
(f) details of any challenge to the validity of the debenture by a liquidator of the company;
(g) form DI giving the information as to overriding interests required by LRR 2003 rule 57, including any documentary evidence of the interest; and
(h) the fee payable. A fee calculator for all types of application is on the Land Registry's website at www.landregistry.gov.uk/fees.

Receivers Appointed by Order of the Court

For administrative receivers see *Administrative Receivers*, page 6 and for receivers appointed under the Mental Health Act 1983 see *Mental Health Act 1983 Patients*, page 205.

No notice of an order appointing a receiver may be entered in the register (Land Registration Act 2002 ("LRA 2002") section 87(2)).

An order appointing a receiver is treated as an interest affecting an estate or charge for the purposes of LRA 2002 (LRA 2002 section 87(1)). It cannot, however, be an overriding interest belonging to a person in actual occupation for the purposes of paragraph 2 of Schedule 1 or 3 to LRA 2002 (LRA 2002 section 87(3)).

The receiver may be treated as a person having a right or claim in relation to a registered estate or charge for the purposes of LRA 2002 section 42(1)(c) if he is applying for a restriction in Form L or Form N (Land Registration Rules 2003 ("LRR 2003") rule 93(s)). The registrar must give notice of such an application to the proprietor of the registered estate or charge concerned (LRA 2002 section 42(3)).

In the light of the decision in *Clayhope Properties Ltd v Evans and Jennings* [1986] 1 WLR 1223, [1986] 2 All ER 795 (CA), it would seem that this applies to any receivership of land created by order of the court and is not limited to receiverships which could bind a purchaser.

A restriction does not confer any priority; it simply prevents an entry being made in the register if it is not permitted under the wording of the restriction.

Restriction
The receiver should deliver to the registry:
  (a) an application in form RX1; and
  (b) the fee payable. A fee calculator for all types of application is on the Land Registry's website at www.landregistry.gov.uk/fees.
Panel 13 of RX1 should be completed on the following lines:
  "The interest is that specified in rule 93(s) of the Land Registration Rules 2003, the applicant being the receiver appointed by ... Court on [*date*]."
Panel 10 should be completed as to the appropriate restriction. Form L is:
  "No disposition [*or specify details*] of the registered estate [(other than a charge)] by the proprietor of the registered estate [or by the proprietor of any registered charge] is to be registered without a certificate signed by [*name*] of [*address*] (*or* [his conveyancer] [*or specify appropriate details, for example* signed on behalf of [*name*] of [*address*] by its secretary or conveyancer]) that the provisions of [*specify clause, paragraph or other particulars*] of [*specify details*] have been complied with."
Form N is:
  "No disposition [*or specify details*] of the registered estate [other than a charge] by the proprietor of the registered estate [or by the proprietor of any registered charge] is to be registered without a written consent signed by [*name*] of [*address*] (or [his conveyancer] [*or specify appropriate details, for example* signed on behalf of [*name*] of [*address*] by its secretary or conveyancer])."

Rectification

Rectification is an alteration of the register which comprises the correction of a mistake and which prejudicially affects the title of a registered proprietor (Land Registration Act 2002 ("LRA 2002") Schedule 4 paragraph 1). For alterations which do not amount to rectification, see *Alteration of the Register*, page 26. Where there is rectification, indemnity may be payable; see *Indemnity*, page 161.

Where rectification of a registered estate in land by court order is sought and the proprietor of that estate is in possession of the land, the court will make such an order only if:
 (a) the proprietor consents to it; or
 (b) he has caused or substantially contributed to the mistake by fraud or lack of proper care; or
 (c) it would be for any other reason unjust for the alteration not to be made.

A proprietor is in possession of the land if it is physically in his possession or in that of a person who is entitled to be registered as the proprietor. Land in the possession of a tenant is treated as in the possession of the landlord, and similarly in the cases of mortgagee and mortgagor, licensee and licensor, and beneficiary and trustee (LRA 2002 section 131).

Where rectification of a registered estate in land by court order is sought and the proprietor of that estate is not in possession of the land, the court will make such an order if it has power to do so, unless there are exceptional circumstances which justify its not doing so (LRA 2002 Schedule 4 paragraph 3(3)).

The court order for alteration of the register must state the title number of the title affected and the alteration that is to be made. It must also direct the registrar to make the alteration.

An applicant should deliver to the registry:
 (a) an application in form AP1;
 (b) the court order for alteration of the register or a sealed copy of that court order; and
 (c) the fee (if any) payable. A fee calculator for all types of application is on the Land Registry's website at www.landregistry.gov.uk/fees.

Where application is made direct to the registrar for an alteration which amounts to rectification, the same principles as to the protection of a proprietor in possession apply. Equally, where the proprietor is not in possession and the registrar has power to make the alteration, the application must be approved, unless there are exceptional circumstances which justify not making the alteration.

The registrar may make such enquiries as he thinks fit and must give notice of the proposed alteration to any person who would be affected by it, unless he is satisfied that such notice is unnecessary (Land Registration

Rules 2003 rule 128). Rule 128 does not, however, apply to alteration of the register in the specific circumstances covered by any other rule.

An applicant for an alteration of the register otherwise than pursuant to a court order should deliver to the registry:
   (a) an application in form AP1;
   (b) a statement of the alteration being applied for;
   (c) all relevant evidence held by the applicant which is pertinent to the application to alter the register; and
   (d) the fee (if any) payable. A fee calculator for all types of application is on the Land Registry's website at www.landregistry.gov.uk/fees.

Where the application leads to an objection, LRA 2002 section 73 applies; see *Disputes*, page 120.

Registered Social Landlords

A registered social landlord within the meaning of the Housing Act 1996 is a body contained in the register kept under section 1 of that Act. Such a body may be a registered charity which is a housing association, or a registered industrial and provident society or a registered company either of which must satisfy the conditions in the Housing Act 1996 section 2(2). Those conditions are that the body is non-profit-making and is established for the purpose of, or has among its objects or powers, the provision, construction, improvement or management of houses for letting, houses for occupation by members of the body, or hostels.

Where a registered social landlord is applying to be registered as proprietor of a registered estate or registered charge, the application must contain or be accompanied by a certificate that the applicant is a registered social landlord within the meaning of the Housing Act 1996 (Land Registration Rules 2003 ("LRR 2003") rules 181(2), 182(2) or 183(3)). This is in addition to any requirements arising from the fact that the applicant is a charity, an industrial and provident society or a company, for which see *Charities*, page 69; *Industrial and Provident Societies*, page 164; or *Companies*, page 102.

A registered social landlord has power under the Housing Act 1996 section 8, but not otherwise, to dispose of land. That power is subject to the consent of the Housing Corporation or the National Assembly for Wales (Housing Act 1996 section 9). Where a registered social landlord is registered as proprietor of land a restriction on the following lines is entered:

"No disposition by the proprietor of the land is to be registered without the consent of [the Housing Corporation] [the National Assembly for Wales] when such consent is required under the provisions of section 9 of the

Housing Act 1996."

In certain circumstances set out in the Housing Act 1996 section 10, consent is not required. These include disposals to tenants under the right to buy or right to acquire.

Where a house is sold by a registered social landlord at a discount, the transfer contains a covenant to repay a proportion of the discount if the purchaser disposes of the house within three years. This takes effect as a charge and an entry in respect of it is entered in the charges register of the purchaser's title.

Where the disposal is of a house in a National Park, an area of outstanding natural beauty or an area designated as a rural area, the transfer or conveyance may contain a covenant limiting the freedom of the purchaser to dispose of the property. In such case a restriction in Form Y is entered automatically in the proprietorship register (Land Registration Act 2002 section 44(2) and LRR 2003 rule 95(2)(h)). Form Y is:

"No transfer or lease by the proprietor of the registered estate or by the proprietor of any registered charge is to be registered unless a certificate by [*specify relevant registered social landlord*] is given that the transfer or lease is made in accordance with section 13 of the Housing Act 1996."

Rentcharges

After 21 August 1977 the only new rentcharges which may be created are those falling within the Rentcharges Act 1977 section 2. In practice the only new rentcharges likely to be created are estate rentcharges. An estate rentcharge is defined by the Rentcharges Act 1977 section 2(4) and (5) in the following terms:

(4) For the purposes of this section "estate rentcharge" means (subject to subsection (5) below) a rentcharge created for the purpose –

(a) of making covenants to be performed by the owner of the land affected by the rentcharge enforceable by the rent owner against the owner for the time being of the land; or

(b) of meeting, or contributing towards, the cost of the performance by the rent owner of covenants for the provision of services, the carrying out of maintenance or repairs, the effecting of insurance or the making of any payment by him for the benefit of the land affected by the rentcharge or for the benefit of that and other land.

(5) A rentcharge of more than a nominal amount shall not be treated as an estate rentcharge for the purposes of this section unless it represents a payment for the performance by the rent owner of any such covenant as is mentioned in subsection (4)(b) above which is reasonable in relation to that covenant.

Rentcharges Created out of Unregistered Land

On first registration of land the estate is vested in the registered proprietor subject to any rentcharges which are the subject of an entry in the register in relation to the estate. The registrar must enter a notice in the register of the burden of any rentcharge which appears from his examination to affect the registered estate (Land Registration Rules 2003 ("LRR 2003") rule 35).

It is not compulsory to register the title to a rentcharge created out of unregistered land, but it is possible to make a voluntary application to register a legal rentcharge which is either perpetual, or is held for a term of years of which more than seven years are unexpired at the date of the application for first registration of the rentcharge (Land Registration Act 2002 ("LRA 2002") section 3). An applicant should deliver to the registry:

(a) an application in form FR1;
(b) sufficient details, by plan or otherwise, so that the area of land which is affected by the rentcharge can be clearly identified on the Ordnance Survey map;
(c) all deeds and documents relating to the title that are in the control of the applicant;
(d) a list in duplicate in form DL of all the documents delivered; and
(e) the fee payable. A fee calculator for all types of application is on the Land Registry's website at www.landregistry.gov.uk/fees.

Registration of Rentcharge Created over Registered Land

The express grant or reservation of a legal rentcharge over registered land, other than one created for a term of years not exceeding seven years from the date of creation, must be completed by registration. For registration to be completed, the rent owner must be registered as proprietor of the rentcharge and a notice in respect of the rentcharge must be entered in the register of the title to the land (LRA 2002 Schedule 2 paragraph 6). Until completed by registration the rentcharge takes effect in equity only.

An applicant should deliver to the registry:
(a) an application in form AP1;
(b) the deed creating the rentcharge;
(c) any consent required under a restriction on the grantor's title;
(d) any consent by a chargee on the grantor's title; and
(e) the fee payable. A fee calculator for all types of application is on the Land Registry's website at www.landregistry.gov.uk/fees.

On registration of the rentcharge, it is allotted its own title number. Notice of the registered rentcharge is entered on the grantor's registered title without any need for a separate application or further fee.

Adverse Possession of Registered Rentcharges

The registration of an adverse possessor of a registered rentcharge is dealt with in LRR 2003 Schedule 8. This provides for a procedure similar to that in respect of adverse possession of registered land in LRA 2002 Schedule 6. Accordingly a person may apply to be registered as proprietor of the registered rentcharge if he has been in adverse possession of the registered rentcharge for ten years ending on the date of the application. The registered rentcharge need not have been registered throughout this period.

When such an application is made, the registrar gives notice of it to the proprietor of the registered rentcharge and the proprietor of any registered charge. That person may require the application to be dealt with under LRR 2003 Schedule 8 paragraph 5. If he does not do so the applicant is registered as the new proprietor of the rentcharge. The period allowed for reply under the notice is the period ending at 12 noon on the sixty-fifth business day after the date of issue of the notice. A business day is a day when the Land Registry is open to the public, that is every day except Saturdays, Sundays, Christmas Day, Good Friday or any other day either specified or declared by proclamation under the Banking and Financial Dealings Act 1971 section 1 or appointed by the Lord Chancellor.

If a person given notice of an application requires that it is dealt with under LRR 2003 Schedule 8 paragraph 5, he must give notice to the registrar in Form NAP, a copy of which accompanies any notice of application based on adverse possession. When notice in Form NAP has been given to the registrar, the applicant is entitled to be registered as the new proprietor only if either of the conditions in paragraph 5 is met.

The first condition is that:
(a) it would be unconscionable because of an equity by estoppel for the registered proprietor to seek to assert his title to the registered rentcharge against the applicant, and
(b) the circumstances are such that the applicant ought to be registered as the proprietor.

The second condition is that the applicant is for some other reason entitled to be registered as the proprietor of the registered rentcharge.

Where the applicant cannot bring himself within either condition his application is rejected. He may then make a further application to be registered as proprietor of the registered rentcharge if he is in adverse possession of that rentcharge from the date of the application until the last day of the period of two years beginning with the date of its rejection. On that further application the applicant will be registered as the new proprietor of the registered rentcharge.

There are restrictions on making applications, similar to those relating to applications based on adverse possession of land; see *Adverse Possession*, page 8 and LRR 2003 Schedule 8.

Where a person is entitled to be registered as proprietor of a registered rentcharge under LRA 2002 Schedule 6 as a result of non-payment of the rentcharge, the registered rentcharge is cancelled. This does not apply if, were that person to be registered as proprietor of that rentcharge, he would be subject to a registered charge or registered lease or other interest protected in the register (LRR 2003 rule 192).

Where as a result of an application under LRA 2002 Schedule 6, a person is registered as proprietor of a registered rentcharge or that registered title is closed or the registered rentcharge is cancelled (the title comprising also other rentcharges), no previous registered proprietor of the rentcharge may recover any rent due under the rentcharge from a person who has been in adverse possession of the rentcharge (LRR 2003 rule 193). This applies whether the adverse possession arose as a result of non-payment of the rent or by receipt of the rent from the person liable to pay it.

Application under LRA 2002 Schedule 6 Paragraph 1 for Registration by Person in Adverse Possession of Registered Rentcharge

Where an applicant has not previously had an application under LRA 2002 Schedule 6 paragraph 1 rejected, he should deliver to the registry:

(a) an application in form ADV1;
(b) a statutory declaration made by the applicant not more than one month before the application, together with any necessary supporting statutory declarations, to provide evidence of adverse possession of the rentcharge against which the application is made for a period of not less than ten years ending on the date of application;
(c) any additional evidence which the applicant considers necessary to support the claim; and
(d) the fee payable. A fee calculator for all types of application is on the Land Registry's website at www.landregistry.gov.uk/fees.

The statutory declaration by the applicant must also contain:

(i) confirmation that LRA 2002 Schedule 6 paragraph 1(2) as amended by LRR 2003 Schedule 8 does not apply. Paragraph 1(2) provides that a person may not make an application under Schedule 6 paragraph 1 if he is a defendant in proceedings by the registered proprietor of the rentcharge for recovery of the rent or to enter into possession of the land out of which the rentcharge issues, or if judgment in such proceedings has been given against him in the last two years. It also provides that he may not make such an application if the registered proprietor of the rentcharge of which he was in adverse possession has entered into possession of the land out of which the rentcharge issues.

(ii) confirmation that to the best of his knowledge the restriction on applications in LRA 2002 Schedule 6 paragraph 8 does not apply. Paragraph 8 provides that no one who has been in adverse possession of a registered rentcharge may apply to be registered as proprietor of that rentcharge during, or before the end of twelve months after the end of, any period in which the existing registered proprietor is for the purposes of the Limitation (Enemies and War Prisoners) Act 1945 an

enemy or detained in enemy territory. It also provides that no one who has been in adverse possession of a registered rentcharge may apply to be registered as proprietor of that rentcharge during any period in which the existing registered proprietor is unable because of mental disability to make decisions about issues of the kind to which such an application would give rise, or unable to communicate such decisions because of mental disability or physical impairment;
  (iii) confirmation that to the best of his knowledge the rentcharge is not, and has not been during any of the period of alleged adverse possession, subject to a trust (other than one where the interest of each of the beneficiaries is an interest in possession);
  (iv) confirmation that the proprietor of the registered rentcharge has not re-entered the land out of which the rentcharge issues; and
  (v) if, should a person given notice of the application require that it be dealt with under LRA 2002 Schedule 6 paragraph 5 as amended by LRR 2003 Schedule 8, it is intended to rely on one or both of the conditions set out in that paragraph, the facts supporting such reliance.

The applicant must also supply such additional evidence as the registrar directs after the application has been considered (LRR 2003 rule 17).

Application under LRA 2002 Schedule 6 Paragraph 6 for Registration by Person in Adverse Possession of Registered Rentcharge

Where an applicant has had an application under LRA 2002 Schedule 6 paragraph 1 rejected, he may be able to make a further application under LRA 2002 Schedule 6 paragraph 6 if he has been in adverse possession for a further two years from the date of rejection. The applicant should deliver to the registry:
  (a) an application in form ADV1;
  (b) a statutory declaration made by the applicant not more than one month before the application, together with any necessary supporting statutory declarations, to provide evidence of adverse possession of the rentcharge against which the application is made for a period of not less than two years beginning with the date of rejection of the original application and ending on the date of application;
  (c) any additional evidence which the applicant considers necessary to support the claim; and
  (d) the fee payable. A fee calculator for all types of application is on the Land Registry's website at www.landregistry.gov.uk/fees.

The statutory declaration by the applicant must also contain:
  (i) full details of the previous rejected application;
  (ii) confirmation that to the best of his knowledge the restriction on applications in LRA 2002 Schedule 6 paragraph 8 does not apply. Paragraph 8 provides that no one who has been in adverse possession

of a registered rentcharge may apply to be registered as proprietor of that rentcharge during, or before the end of twelve months after the end of, any period in which the existing registered proprietor is for the purposes of the Limitation (Enemies and War Prisoners) Act 1945 an enemy or detained in enemy territory. It also provides that no one who has been in adverse possession of a registered rentcharge may apply to be registered as proprietor of that rentcharge during any period in which the existing registered proprietor is unable because of mental disability to make decisions about issues of the kind to which such an application would give rise, or unable to communicate such decisions because of mental disability or physical impairment;

(iii) confirmation that to the best of his knowledge the rentcharge is not, and has not been during any of the period of alleged adverse possession, subject to a trust (other than one where the interest of each of the beneficiaries is an interest in possession);

(iv) confirmation that the proprietor of the registered rentcharge has not re-entered the land out of which the rentcharge issues; and

(v) confirmation that LRA 2002 Schedule 6 paragraph 6(2) as amended by LRR 2003 Schedule 8 does not apply. Paragraph 6(2) provides that a person may not make an application under Schedule 6 paragraph 6 if he is a defendant in proceedings by the registered proprietor of the rentcharge for recovery of the rent or to enter into possession of the land out of which the rentcharge issues, or if judgment in such proceedings has been given against him in the last two years. It also provides that he may not make such an application if the registered proprietor of the rentcharge of which he was in adverse possession has entered into possession of the land out of which the rentcharge issues.

The applicant must also supply such additional evidence as the registrar directs after the application has been considered (LRR 2003 rule 17).

Restraint Orders

An application for a restraint order under the Proceeds of Crime Act 2002 section 41 or the Terrorism Act 2000 Schedule 4 paragraph 5(1) or (2) is treated as a pending land application. The same applies to an application for an interim receiving order under the Proceeds of Crime Act 2002 section 246. An application for either of these orders may be protected by the entry on the register of a notice or a restriction or both of these. A restriction does not confer any priority; it simply prevents an entry being made in the register if it is not permitted under the wording of the restriction.

In practice, an application for an agreed notice will be the usual course

of action. An applicant should deliver to the registry:
  (a) an application in form AN1;
  (b) the application to the court for the order; and
  (c) the fee payable. A fee calculator for all types of application is on the Land Registry's website at www.landregistry.gov.uk/fees.

This is likely to be sufficient to satisfy the registrar of the validity of the applicant's claim in accordance with the Land Registration Act 2002 ("LRA 2002") section 34(3)(c). The entry made in the register will give details of the interest protected.

Where the applicant wishes to apply for a unilateral notice he should deliver to the registry:
  (a) an application in form UN1;
  (b) a plan of the affected land (where the application for the restraint order affects only part of the land in the registered title); and
  (c) the fee payable. A fee calculator for all types of application is on the Land Registry's website at www.landregistry.gov.uk/fees.

Form UN1 should be completed on the following lines to show the interest of the applicant:

"applicant in an application for [a restraint order] [an interim receiving order] to be made under [*state statutory provision*]."

The unilateral notice will give brief details of the interest protected and identify the beneficiary of that notice.

If a restriction is sought, the applicant should deliver to the registry:
  (a) an application in form RX1; and
  (b) the fee payable. A fee calculator for all types of application is on the Land Registry's website at www.landregistry.gov.uk/fees.

The restriction will be in Form GG or Form HH and the applicant is regarded as having sufficient interest to apply for the restriction (Land Registration Rules 2003 ("LRR 2003") rule 93(m) and (v)). The registrar must give notice of such an application to the proprietor of the registered estate or charge concerned (LRA 2002 section 42(3)). Form GG is:

"Pursuant to an application for [a restraint order] [an interim receiving order] to be made under [*state statutory provision*] and under any order made as a result of that application, no disposition by the proprietor of the registered estate is to be registered without the consent of [*name of prosecutor or other person applying*] or under a further order of the Court."

Form HH is:

"Pursuant to an application for [a restraint order] [an interim receiving order] to be made under [*state statutory provision*] and under any order made as a result of that application, no disposition by the proprietor of the registered charge dated (*date*) (referred to above) is to be registered without the consent of [*name of prosecutor or other person applying*] or under a further order of the Court."

Where a person has obtained a restraint order or interim receiving order it is not possible to protect that order by a notice but that person is regarded as having sufficient interest to apply for a restriction in Form EE or FF (LRR 2003 rule 93(l) and (u)). The registrar must give notice of an application for such a restriction to the proprietor of the registered estate or charge concerned (LRA 2002 section 42(3)).

The applicant for such a restriction should deliver to the registry:
(a) an application in form RX1; and
(b) the fee payable. A fee calculator for all types of application is on the Land Registry's website at www.landregistry.gov.uk/fees.

Form EE is:

"Under [a restraint order] [an interim receiving order] made under [*state statutory provision*] on [*date*] [*claim no*] no disposition by the proprietor of the registered estate is to be registered without the consent of [*name of the prosecutor or other person who applied for the order*] or under a further order of the Court."

Form FF is:

"Under [a restraint order] [an interim receiving order] made under [*state statutory provision*] on [*date*] [*claim no*] no disposition by the proprietor of the registered charge dated (*date*) (referred to above) is to be registered without the consent of [*name of the prosecutor or other person who applied for the order*] or under a further order of the Court."

Restrictions

A restriction is an entry in the register regulating the circumstances in which a disposition of a registered estate or charge may be the subject of an entry in the register. It may prohibit the making of an entry in respect of any disposition, or of certain kinds of disposition, indefinitely or for a specified period or until the occurrence of a specified event. For example, a restriction may prohibit the registration of a disposition of a registered estate without the written consent of a named person.

Where a restriction is entered in the register, no entry may be made in respect of a disposition to which the restriction applies unless it is in accordance with the restriction or the registrar makes an order. The registrar may by order disapply or modify a restriction in respect of a particular disposition or class of dispositions (Land Registration Act 2002 ("LRA 2002") section 41).

The registrar may enter a restriction if it appears to him that it is necessary or desirable to do so for the purpose of:
(a) preventing invalidity or unlawfulness in relation to dispositions of a registered estate or charge;

(b) securing that interests which are capable of being overreached on a disposition of a registered estate or charge are overreached; or

(c) protecting a right or claim in relation to a registered estate or charge.

The registrar may enter such restriction without an application having been made. If he does so, he gives notice of the entry to the registered proprietor (LRA 2002 section 42(3)).

No restriction may be entered, however, for the purpose of protecting the priority of an interest which is, or could be, the subject of a notice (LRA 2002 section 42(2)). This does not necessarily prevent the entry of a restriction in addition to a notice. Although the notice will protect the priority of the interest, a restriction may be used to ensure that any conditions in relation to another disposition by the registered proprietor are complied with. For example, a notice may be entered to protect the priority of a right of pre-emption and at the same time a restriction entered to ensure that there is no disposition of the land to a third party without the written consent of the person having the benefit of the right of pre-emption.

The right to apply for the entry of a restriction must not be exercised without reasonable cause (LRA 2002 section 77(1)). This duty to act reasonably is owed to any person who suffers damage in consequence of its breach (LRA 2002 section 77(2)).

Application for Restriction

A person may apply for the entry of a restriction if he is the registered proprietor or entitled to be so registered, or if he has the consent of the registered proprietor or the person entitled to be so registered, or if he otherwise has a sufficient interest in the making of the entry (LRA 2002 section 43(1)). The Land Registration Rules 2003 ("LRR 2003") rule 93 sets out twenty-two different classes of person who are regarded as having sufficient interest in the making of an entry. These are dealt with in the appropriate sections of this book.

An applicant for a restriction should deliver to the registry:

(a) an application in form RX1 (full details of the restriction appear in panel 10. If the restriction requires notice to be given to a person, requires a person's consent or certificate, or is a standard form restriction that refers to a named person, that person's address for service must be stated);

(b) (if the application is made with the consent of the registered proprietor or person entitled to be so registered) the relevant consent unless this is given in panel 15 of form RX1 or the applicant's conveyancer certifies that he holds such consent. The certificate may be given in panel 11 of form RX1;

(c) (if the application is made by or with the consent of a person entitled to be registered as proprietor) evidence to satisfy the registrar of his entitlement. This may take the form of a certificate by the applicant's

conveyancer that he is satisfied that the applicant, or person consenting to the application, is entitled to be registered as proprietor and that he holds the originals of the documents that contain evidence of that person's entitlement, or an application for registration of that person as proprietor is pending at the Land Registry. The certificate may be given in panel 12 of form RX1;
- (d) (if the application is made by a person who claims that he has a sufficient interest in the making of the entry) a statement signed by the applicant or his conveyancer either giving details of the applicant's interest in the making of the required restriction or, if the interest is one of those specified in LRR 2003 rule 93, stating which of them. The statement may be given in panel 13 of form RX1; and
- (e) the fee payable. A fee calculator for all types of application is on the Land Registry's website at www.landregistry.gov.uk/fees.

An application for a restriction need not be in form RX1 provided it is for a standard form of restriction and the application is instead made in the additional provisions panel of form TP1, TP2, TP3, TR1, TR2, TR3, TR4, TR5, AS1, AS2, or AS3, or in panel 7 of form CH1, or in a charge which has first been approved by the registrar.

Notice of the application for a restriction and of the right to object to it is given to the registered proprietor, unless the application was made by him or with his consent, or the application was required to be made by LRR 2003 rule 94. Notice is also not given where the restriction reflects a limitation under an order of the court or the registrar, or under an undertaking given in place of such an order (LRA 2002 section 45). The registrar may not determine the application before the end of the specified period unless each person notified has indicated that he is not objecting or his objection has been disposed of. The specified period is the period ending at 12 noon on the fifteenth business day after the date of issue of the notice or, if more than one such notice is issued, after the date of issue of the latest notice. A business day is a day when the Land Registry is open to the public, that is every day except Saturdays, Sundays, Christmas Day, Good Friday or any other day either specified or declared by proclamation under the Banking and Financial Dealings Act 1971 section 1 or appointed by the Lord Chancellor.

For the position where the registered proprietor objects to the entry of the restriction, see *Disputes*, page 120.

Forms of Restriction

Standard forms of restriction are set out in LRR 2003 Schedule 4. Where an application is made for a non-standard restriction, the registrar may approve the application only if it appears to him that the terms of the restriction are reasonable and that applying the restriction would be straightforward and would not place an unreasonable burden on him. Before the terms of a non-standard restriction are formally agreed between parties, it is prudent to check with the registry that an application for such restriction will be approved. For example, it is unlikely that the registrar will accept an application for a restriction that expressly prevents the entry of a notice.

The standard forms of restriction are:

Form A (Restriction on dispositions by sole proprietor)
No disposition by a sole proprietor of the registered estate (except a trust corporation) under which capital money arises is to be registered unless authorised by an order of the court.

Form B (Dispositions by trustees – certificate required)
No disposition [*or specify details*] by the proprietors of the registered estate is to be registered unless they make a statutory declaration, or their conveyancer gives a certificate, that the disposition [*or specify details*] is in accordance with [*specify the disposition creating the trust*] or some variation thereof referred to in the declaration or certificate.

Form C (Dispositions by personal representatives – certificate required)
No disposition by [*name*], the [executor *or* administrator] of [*name*] deceased, other than a transfer as personal representative, is to be registered unless he makes a statutory declaration, or his conveyancer gives a certificate, that the disposition is in accordance with the terms [of the will of the deceased *or* the law relating to intestacy as varied by a deed dated *specify details of deed or specify appropriate details*] or [some variation *or* further variation] thereof referred to in the declaration or certificate, or is necessary for the purposes of administration.

Form D (Parsonage, church or churchyard land)
No disposition of the registered estate is to be registered unless made in accordance with [the Parsonages Measure 1938 *(in the case of parsonage land) or* the New Parishes Measure 1943 *(in the case of church or churchyard land)*] or some other Measure or authority.

Form E (Non-exempt charity – certificate required)
No disposition by the proprietor of the registered estate to which section 36 or section 38 of the Charities Act 1993 applies is to be registered unless the instrument contains a certificate complying with section 37(2) or section 39(2) of that Act as appropriate.

Form F (Land vested in official custodian on trust for non-exempt charity – authority required)
No disposition executed by the trustees of [*charity*] in the name and on behalf of the proprietor shall be registered unless the transaction is authorised by an order of the court or of the Charity Commissioners, as required by section 22(3) of the Charities Act 1993.

Form G (Tenant for life as registered proprietor of settled land, where there are trustees of the settlement)
No disposition is to be registered unless authorised by the Settled Land Act 1925, or by any extension of those statutory powers in the settlement, and no disposition under which capital money arises is to be registered unless the money is paid to *(name)* of *(address)* and *(name)* of *(address)*, *(the trustees of the settlement, who may be a sole trust corporation or, if individuals, must number at least two but not more than four)* or into court.
Note: If applicable under the terms of the settlement, a further provision may be added that no transfer of the mansion house (shown on an attached plan or otherwise adequately described to enable it to be fully identified on the Ordnance Survey map or title plan) is to be registered without the consent of the named trustees or an order of the court.

Form H (Statutory owners as trustees of the settlement and registered proprietors of settled land)
No disposition is to be registered unless authorised by the Settled Land Act 1925, or by any extension of those statutory powers in the settlement, and, except where the sole proprietor is a trust corporation, no disposition under which capital money arises is to be registered unless the money is paid to at least two proprietors.
Note: This restriction does not apply where the statutory owners are not the trustees of the settlement.

Form I (Tenant for life as registered proprietor of settled land – no trustees of the settlement)
No disposition under which capital money arises, or which is not authorised by the Settled Land Act 1925 or by any extension of those statutory powers in the settlement, is to be registered.

Form J (Trustee in bankruptcy and beneficial interest – certificate required)
No disposition of the [registered estate *or* registered charge dated [*date*]] is to be registered without a certificate signed by the applicant for registration or his conveyancer that written notice of the disposition was given to [*name of trustee in bankruptcy*] (the trustee in bankruptcy of [*name of bankrupt person*]) at [*address for service*].

Form K (Charging order affecting beneficial interest – certificate required)
No disposition of the [registered estate *or* registered charge dated [*date*]] is to be registered without a certificate signed by the applicant for registration or his conveyancer that written notice of the disposition was given to [*name of person with the benefit of the charging order*] at [*address for service*], being the person with the benefit of [an interim] [a final] charging order on the beneficial interest of *(name of judgment debtor)* made by the *(name of court)* on *(date) (Court reference ...)*.

Form L (Disposition by registered proprietor of a registered estate or proprietor of charge – certificate required)
No disposition [*or specify details*] of the registered estate [(other than a charge)] by the proprietor of the registered estate [, *or* by the proprietor of any registered charge,] is to be registered without a certificate [signed by [*name*] of [*address*] (or [his conveyancer] *or specify appropriate details*)] *or* [signed on behalf of [*name*] of [*address*] by [its secretary or conveyancer *or specify appropriate details*]] that the provisions of [*specify clause, paragraph or other particulars*] of [*specify details*] have been complied with.

Form M (Disposition by registered proprietor of registered estate or proprietor of charge – certificate of registered proprietor of specified title number required)
No disposition [*or specify details*] of the registered estate [(other than a charge)] by the proprietor of the registered estate [or by the proprietor of any registered charge] is to be registered without a certificate signed by the proprietor for the time being of the estate registered under title number [*title number*] [(or his conveyancer *or specify appropriate details)*] or, if appropriate, signed on such proprietor's behalf by [its secretary or conveyancer *or specify appropriate details*], that the provisions of [*specify clause, paragraph or other particulars*] of [*specify details*] have been complied with.

Form N (Disposition by registered proprietor of registered estate or proprietor of charge – consent required)
No disposition [*or specify details*] of the registered estate [(other than a charge)] by the proprietor of the registered estate [or by the proprietor of any registered charge] is to be registered without a written consent [signed by [*name*] of [*address*] (or [his conveyancer] *or specify appropriate details*)] *or* [signed on behalf of [*name*] of [*address*] by [its secretary or conveyancer *or specify appropriate details*]].

Form O (Disposition by registered proprietor of registered estate or proprietor of charge – consent of registered proprietor of specified title number required)
No disposition [*or specify details*] of the registered estate [(other than a charge)] by the proprietor of the registered estate [or by the proprietor of any registered charge] is to be registered without a written consent signed by the proprietor for the time being of the estate registered under title number [*title number*], [(or his conveyancer, *or specify appropriate details)*] or, if appropriate, signed on such proprietor's behalf by [its secretary or conveyancer *or specify appropriate details*].

Form P (Disposition by registered proprietor of registered estate or proprietor of charge – consent of proprietor of specified charge required)
No disposition [*or specify details*] of the registered estate [(other than a charge)] by the proprietor of the registered estate [or by the proprietor of any registered charge] is to be registered without a written consent signed by the proprietor for the time being of the charge dated [*date*] in favour of [*chargee*] referred to in the charges register [(or his conveyancer *or specify appropriate details)*] or, if appropriate, signed on such proprietor's behalf by [its secretary or conveyancer *or specify appropriate details*].

Form Q (Disposition by registered proprietor of registered estate or proprietor of charge – consent of personal representative required)
No disposition [*or specify details*] of [the registered estate *or* the registered charge dated [*date*] (referred to above)] by the proprietor [of the registered estate *or* of that registered charge] is to be registered after the death of [*name of the current proprietor(s) whose personal representative's consent will be required*] without the written consent of the personal representatives of the deceased.

Form R (Disposition by registered proprietor of registered estate or proprietor of charge – evidence of compliance with club rules required)
No disposition [*or specify details*] of the registered estate [(other than a charge)] by the proprietor of the registered estate [or by the proprietor of any registered charge] is to be registered unless authorised by the rules of the [*name of club*] of [*address*] as evidenced [by a resolution of its members *or* by a certificate signed by its secretary or conveyancer [*or specify appropriate details*]].

Form S (Disposition by proprietor of charge – certificate of compliance required)
No disposition [*or specify details*] by the proprietor of the registered charge dated [*date*] (referred to above) is to be registered without a certificate [signed by [*name*] of [*address*] (or [his conveyancer] *or specify appropriate details*)] *or* [signed on behalf of [*name*] of [*address*] by [its secretary or conveyancer *or specify appropriate details*], that the provisions of [*specify clause, paragraph or other particulars*] of [*specify details*] have been complied with.

Form T (Disposition by proprietor of charge – consent required)
No disposition [*or specify details*] by the proprietor of the registered charge dated [*date*] (referred to above) is to be registered without a written consent [signed by [*name*] of [*address*] (or [his conveyancer] *or specify appropriate details*)] *or* [signed on behalf of [*name*] of [*address*] by [its secretary or conveyancer *or specify appropriate details*].

Form U (Section 37 of the Housing Act 1985)
No transfer or lease by the proprietor of the registered estate or by the proprietor of any registered charge is to be registered unless a certificate by [*specify relevant local authority*] is given that the transfer or lease is made in accordance with section 37 of the Housing Act 1985.

Form V (Section 157 of the Housing Act 1985)
No transfer or lease by the proprietor of the registered estate or by the proprietor of any registered charge is to be registered unless a certificate by [*specify relevant local authority or housing association etc*] is given that the transfer or lease is made in accordance with section 157 of the Housing Act 1985.

Form W (Paragraph 4 of Schedule 9A to the Housing Act 1985)
No disposition (except a transfer) of a qualifying dwellinghouse (except to a qualifying person or persons) is to be registered without the consent of the Secretary of State given under section 171D(2) of the Housing Act 1985 as it applies by virtue of the Housing (Preservation of Right to Buy) Regulations 1993.

Form X (Section 81 or 133 of the Housing Act 1988 or section 173 of the Local Government and Housing Act 1989)
No disposition by the proprietor of the registered estate or in exercise of the power of sale or leasing in any registered charge (except an exempt disposal as defined by section 81(8) of the Housing Act 1988) is to be registered without the consent of the Secretary of State to that disposition under the provisions of (*as appropriate* [section 81 of that Act] *or* [section 133 of that Act] *or* [section 173 of the Local Government and Housing Act 1989]).

Form Y (Section 13 of the Housing Act 1996)
No transfer or lease by the proprietor of the registered estate or by the proprietor of any registered charge is to be registered unless a certificate by [*specify relevant registered social landlord*] is given that the transfer or lease is made in accordance with section 13 of the Housing Act 1996.

Form AA (Freezing order on the registered estate)
Under an order of the *(name of court)* made on *(date) (claim no)* no disposition by the proprietor of the registered estate is to be registered except under a further order of the Court.

Form BB (Freezing order on charge)
Under an order of the *(name of court)* made on *(date) (claim no)* no disposition by the proprietor of the charge is to be registered except under a further order of the Court.

Form CC (Application for freezing order on the registered estate)
Pursuant to an application made on *(date)* to the *(name of court)* for a

freezing order to be made under *(statutory provision)* no disposition by the proprietor of the registered estate is to be registered except with the consent of *(name of the person applying)* or under a further order of the Court.

Form DD (Application for freezing order on charge)
Pursuant to an application made on *(date)* to the *(name of the court)* for a freezing order to be made under *(statutory provision)* no disposition by the proprietor of the registered charge dated *(date)* (referred to above) is to be registered except with the consent of *(name of the person applying)* or under a further order of the Court.

Form EE (Restraint order or interim receiving order on the registered estate)
Under *(as appropriate* [a restraint order] *or* [an interim receiving order]) made under *(statutory provision)* on *(date) (claim no)* no disposition by the proprietor of the registered estate is to be registered without the consent of *(name of the prosecutor or other person who applied for the order)* or under a further order of the Court.

Form FF (Restraint order or interim receiving order on charge)
Under *(as appropriate* [a restraint order] *or* [an interim receiving order]) made under *(statutory provision)* on *(date) (claim no)* no disposition by the proprietor of the registered charge dated *(date)* (referred to above) is to be registered without the consent of *(name of the prosecutor or other person who applied for the order)* or under a further order of the Court.

Form GG (Application for restraint order or interim receiving order on the registered estate)
Pursuant to an application for *(as appropriate* [a restraint order] *or* [an interim receiving order]) to be made under *(statutory provision)* and under any order made as a result of that application, no disposition by the proprietor of the registered estate is to be registered without the consent of *(name of the prosecutor or other person applying)* or under a further order of the Court.

Form HH (Application for restraint order or interim receiving order on charge)
Pursuant to an application for *(as appropriate* [a restraint order] *or* [an interim receiving order]) to be made under *(statutory provision)* and under any order made as a result of that application no disposition by the proprietor of the registered charge dated *(date)* (referred to above) is to be registered without the consent of *(name of the prosecutor or other person applying)* or under a further order of the Court.

Court Order for Entry of Restriction
If it appears to the court that it is necessary or desirable to do so for the

purpose of protecting a right or claim in relation to a registered estate or charge, it may make an order requiring the registrar to enter a restriction in the register (LRA 2002 section 46(1)). Such an order may not be made for the purpose of protecting the priority of an interest which is, or could be, the subject of a notice. It is not necessary to use form RX1 to apply for the entry of the restriction; instead the court order and form AP1 should be delivered to the registry. No fee is required.

The court may include in such an order a direction that the entry of the restriction made in pursuance of the order is to have overriding priority. Where this is done an entry is made in the register to ensure that the priority of the restriction ordered by the court is apparent. Since such a direction of the court overrides an existing priority protection given by an official search with priority, the registrar gives notice of the entry to the person who applied for the official search (or the conveyancer or agent who applied on his behalf), unless the registrar is satisfied that such notice is unnecessary (LRR 2003 rule 100).

Obligatory Restrictions

In addition to the making of a court order made under LRA 2002 section 46(1), there are certain other circumstances where a restriction must be entered by the registrar without an application in form RX1.

Where two or more persons are registered as proprietors of registered land, the registrar must enter a restriction in Form A unless the survivor will be able to give a valid receipt for capital money (LRA 2002 section 44(1) and LRR 2003 rule 95(2)(a)).

Certain statutes require a restriction to be entered, for example the Housing Act 1996 section 13 (see *Registered Social Landlords*, page 254). Details of some of these statutory provisions and the appropriate restrictions to be entered are set out in LRR 2003 rule 95(2). These restrictions are dealt with in the appropriate sections of this book.

A bankruptcy restriction is required to be entered under LRA 2002 section 86(4). See *Bankruptcy*, page 34.

Application for an Order that a Restriction be Disapplied or Modified

An applicant who appears to the registrar to have a sufficient interest in a restriction may apply for the registrar to make an order disapplying or modifying the restriction (LRA 2002 section 41(3)). For example a restriction might require the consent of a person who has transferred his responsibility to a third party and an application then be made to modify the restriction by substituting the name of the third party in the entry.

An applicant should deliver to the registry an application form RX2 setting out:
  (a) whether the application is to disapply or modify the restriction and, if the latter, the details of the modification sought;

(b) why the applicant has a sufficient interest in the restriction to make the application;
(c) details of the disposition or the kind of disposition that will be affected by the order; and
(d) why the applicant considers that the registrar should make the order.

The application may be made prior to, or at the same time as, an application to register a disposition caught by the restriction.

The registrar may make such enquiries and serve such notices as he thinks fit and he may require the applicant to supply further evidence.

Cancellation of a Restriction

Any person may apply to cancel a restriction that is no longer required. The application must be made in form RX3 and no fee is payable. The application must be accompanied by evidence to satisfy the registrar that the restriction is no longer required. Where the restriction gives an address for service for any person who is not the applicant for cancellation, notice of the application is sent to that person.

When registering a disposition of a registered estate, the registrar must cancel a restriction entered for the purpose of protecting an interest, right or claim arising under a trust of land if he is satisfied that such estate is no longer subject to that trust of land (LRR 2003 rule 99).

The registrar may cancel a restriction without an application being made where he is satisfied that the entry is superfluous (LRA 2002 Schedule 4 paragraph 5(d)). For example, a restriction requiring the consent of the proprietor of a registered charge is cancelled when the charge is discharged, or a restriction may reflect a limitation on the powers of a previous proprietor.

Withdrawal of a Restriction

A person with the benefit of a restriction may apply for it to be cancelled without regard to the question of whether it still serves any purpose. The application must be made in form RX4 and no fee is payable. The application must be made by, or with the consent of, all persons appearing to the registrar to have an interest in the restriction. Where the restriction specifies a person whose consent or certificate is required or to whom notice is required to be given, that person may make the application without the consent of any other person interested in the restriction who is not so specified (LRR 2003 rule 98). A certificate may be given by a conveyancer that he holds any consents required. This certificate may be given in panel 11 of form RX4

No application may be made to withdraw a restriction that:
(a) is entered to prevent invalidity or unlawfulness in relation to dispositions and reflects some limitation on the registered proprietor's powers of disposition imposed by statute or the general law;

(b) is entered by someone who was under an obligation to apply under LRR 2003 rule 94;
(c) the registrar is obliged to enter;
(d) reflects a limitation under an order of the court or of the registrar, or an undertaking given in respect of such an order; or
(e) the court has ordered the registrar to enter.

Restrictions Entered under the Land Registration Act 1925

LRA 2002 applies to restrictions entered in the register prior to 13 October 2003 in the same way that it applies to restrictions made under LRA 2002. The effect of a restriction under the 1925 Act is preserved. For example, a restriction preventing the noting of a disposition is not treated as preventing the entry of a unilateral notice, since the restriction would not have prevented the entry of a caution against dealings.

Restrictive Covenants

Restrictive covenants usually require to be protected by way of notice in the register. For restrictive covenants between lessor and lessee, however, see *Restrictive Covenants in Leases*, page 178.

Where the restrictive covenants are revealed in the title lodged on an application for first registration or are contained in a transfer of part, notice of them is entered in the register without the need for a separate application. The fact that an interest is the subject of a notice does not necessarily mean that the interest is valid (Land Registration Act 2002 section 32(3)). The entry on first registration of a restrictive covenant which was void for non-registration as a land charge does not therefore confer any fresh validity on such covenant.

Where the registered proprietor enters into restrictive covenants in a deed of covenant, an application should be made for an agreed notice or a unilateral notice.

Agreed Notice

An applicant should deliver to the registry:
(a) an application in form AN1;
(b) the deed of covenant or a certified copy of it;
(c) the consent of the registered proprietor of the land where this is not contained in form AN1; and
(d) the fee payable. A fee calculator for all types of application is on the Land Registry's website at www.landregistry.gov.uk/fees.

The entry made in the register will give details of the interest protected.

Where a deed has been entered into varying the restrictive covenants, that variation may be the subject of an agreed notice in the same way. In that case the entry must give details of the variation. The same applies to a variation effected by an order made by the Lands Tribunal under the Law of Property Act 1925 section 84.

Where the registered proprietor does not consent to the entry in the register of an agreed notice, an application for entry of a unilateral notice may still be made.

Unilateral Notice
An applicant should deliver to the registry:
    (a) an application in form UN1;
    (b) a plan of the affected land (where the restrictive covenant affects only part of the land in the registered title); and
    (c) the fee payable. A fee calculator for all types of application is on the Land Registry's website at www.landregistry.gov.uk/fees.

Form UN1 should be completed on the following lines to show the interest of the applicant:
"person having the benefit of restrictive covenants contained in a Deed dated ... made between (*parties*) [as varied by a Deed dated ... made between (*parties*)]."

The unilateral notice will give brief details of the interest protected and identify the beneficiary of that notice.

Right to Buy and Right to Acquire under the Housing Acts

Many tenants of local authorities and certain other public sector landlords have the right to buy their houses or flats under the Housing Act 1985 ("HA 1985"). Many other tenants of registered social landlords have the right to acquire their houses or flats under the Housing Act 1996 ("HA 1996"). In the case of a freehold house the freehold is transferred to the tenant when he exercises his right to buy, and in the case of a flat or leasehold house a lease is granted to him, usually for 125 years. The tenant is given a discount on the purchase price.

The tenant must continue to be a secure tenant until the time of the transfer to him. The exercise of the right to buy does not create a proprietary interest in the land prior to that transfer and so does not form part of the tenant's estate on death (*Bradford City Council v McMahon* [1994] 1 WLR 52, [1993] 4 All ER 237 (CA)). Where death occurs, there may however be a new secure tenant within the meaning of HA 1985 section 136.

Charges on Landlord's Title
Where the right to buy is exercised, no discharge or releases are required in respect of any registered or noted charge, nor is the consent of any chargee under a restriction required (HA 1985 Schedule 6 paragraphs 20 and 21). In the case of the exercise of the right to acquire from a registered social landlord, the procedure in the Housing (Right to Acquire) Regulations 1997 Schedule 1 paragraph 41(g) applies. The tenant receives either evidence of the release from the charge provided by the chargee or a certificate from the landlord given under the HA 1985 Schedule 6 paragraph 23(1) or 23(3) (inserted by the Housing (Right to Acquire) Regulations Schedule 1 paragraph 41(g)). Such a certificate is effective to release the house or flat from the charge.

Rentcharges
A transfer under the right to buy or right to acquire is made subject to any existing rentcharge. Where the property being transferred is, with other land, subject to the rentcharge, the transfer must contain a covenant by the landlord to indemnify the tenant and his successors in title in respect of any liability arising under the rentcharge (HA 1985 Schedule 6 paragraph 21(3)). A lease granted under the right to buy or right to acquire is not affected by any rentcharge on the landlord's interest (HA 1985 Schedule 6 paragraph 20).

Statutory Easements
Unless excluded or modified, a transfer or lease under the right to buy or right to acquire is deemed to include a grant and reservation of the easements contained in HA 1985 Schedule 6 paragraph 2. These include rights of support, rights of light and air, and rights of drainage and other domestic services. An entry in respect of these statutory easements is automatically made in the register when the transfer is registered.

Discount Charges
Where a tenant exercises the right to buy or right to acquire, he is entitled to a discount on the purchase price. The tenant covenants in the transfer to repay the discount if there is a sale within three years. Certain disposals do not result in the repayment of discount (HA 1985 section 160). The covenant takes effect as a charge (HA 1985 section 156) and an entry is made automatically on registration of the transfer.

Acquisition on Rent to Mortgage Terms
Where the tenant exercises the right to buy on rent to mortgage terms under HA 1985 section 143, the provisions of Schedule 6A to that Act (as inserted by the Leasehold Reform, Housing and Urban Development Act 1993 section 117) apply. It is not possible to exercise the right to acquire from a

registered social landlord on rent to mortgage terms.

The landlord's share is secured by a legal charge in favour of the landlord which should be lodged for registration at the same time as the transfer to the tenant is registered. That charge has priority over the discount charge. The transfer to the tenant contains provisions relating to the paying off of the landlord's share.

Property to which HA 1985 Section 37 or 157 Applies
Where the sale to the tenant is of a house in a National Park, an area of outstanding natural beauty or an area designated as a rural area, the transfer or conveyance may contain a covenant limiting the freedom of the purchaser to dispose of the property. In such case where the sale is under the right to buy, a restriction in Form V is entered automatically in the proprietorship register (Land Registration Act 2002 ("LRA 2002") section 44(2) and the Land Registration Rules 2003 ("LRR 2003") rule 95(2)(c)). Form V is:

"No transfer or lease by the proprietor of the registered estate or by the proprietor of any registered charge is to be registered unless a certificate by [*specify relevant local authority or housing association*] is given that the transfer or lease is made in accordance with section 157 of the Housing Act 1985."

Where the sale is a voluntary sale to which HA 1985 section 37 applies, a restriction in Form U is entered automatically in the proprietorship register (LRA 2002 section 44(2) and LRR 2003 rule 95(2)(b)). Form U is:

"No transfer or lease by the proprietor of the registered estate or by the proprietor of any registered charge is to be registered unless a certificate by [*specify relevant local authority*] is given that the transfer or lease is made in accordance with section 37 of the Housing Act 1985."

Preserved Right to Buy
Where public sector landlords dispose of their housing stock, the tenant's right to buy may be preserved, even though the new landlord is not one which would otherwise be subject to the right to buy. Where this occurs, the transfer to the new landlord must contain a statement that the transfer is, so far as it relates to dwelling-houses occupied by secure tenants, a transfer to which the Housing Act 1985 section 171A applies. It must also contain a list of the dwelling-houses transferred which are occupied by secure tenants.

A transfer of unregistered land, or a lease out of unregistered land, to which the Housing Act 1985 section 171A applies is subject to compulsory registration (LRA 2002 section 4(1)(b) and (f)). See *First Registration*, page 133.

On registration of a transfer containing a statement that the Housing Act 1985 section 171A applies, a notice of the rights of the qualifying tenants and a restriction in Form W are entered automatically in the register. Form W is:

"No disposition (except a transfer) of a qualifying dwellinghouse (except to a qualifying person or persons) is to be registered without the consent of the Secretary of State given under section 171D(2) of the Housing Act 1985 as it applies by virtue of the Housing (Preservation of Right to Buy) Regulations 1993."

The rights of the tenant having the preserved right to buy are not overriding interests within LRA 2002 Schedule 3 and so are liable to be postponed under LRA 2002 section 29 unless protected by a notice in the register. Where the tenants are moved to another registered property, the landlord should apply for the notice and restriction to be entered in respect of that registered title, if there is no entry on that title. In respect of the notice, the landlord should deliver to the registry:

(a) an application in form AN1;
(b) a statement giving details of the preserved right to buy; and
(c) the fee payable. A fee calculator for all types of application is on the Land Registry's website at www.landregistry.gov.uk/fees.

In respect of the restriction, the landlord should deliver to the registry:

(a) an application in form RX1; and
(b) the fee payable. A fee calculator for all types of application is on the Land Registry's website at www.landregistry.gov.uk/fees.

Panel 10 of form RX1 should be completed with the restriction in Form W set out above.

Where the registered proprietor delivers to the registry a certificate that the registered title, or a specified part of it, is not subject to any rights of a qualifying person under the preserved right to buy, the notice and restriction may be cancelled or modified, as appropriate.

In certain circumstances a transfer by a local authority, a new town corporation, or a housing action trust requires the consent of the Secretary of State or the National Assembly for Wales. A transferee of housing stock following such consent may itself be subject to a requirement for similar consent on a subsequent transfer. A statement to this effect should be made in the transfer and a restriction in Form X is entered automatically in the proprietorship register. Form X is:

"No disposition by the proprietor of the registered estate or in exercise of the power of sale or leasing in any registered charge (except an exempt disposal as defined by section 81(8) of the Housing Act 1988) is to be registered without the consent of the Secretary of State to that disposition under the provisions of (*as appropriate* [section 81 of that Act] *or* [section 133 of that Act] *or* [section 173 of the Local Government and Housing Act 1989])."

Rights of Light and Air

Rights of light and air may subsist as legal easements; see *Legal Easements*, page 190.

The existence of an agreement which prevents the statutory period of prescription beginning to run does not create an incumbrance on the property (*Smith v Colbourne* [1914] 2 Ch 533 (CA)). The benefit of an agreement preventing the acquisition of rights of light or air will not therefore be entered as appurtenant to a registered estate.

If it appears to the registrar, either on first registration or on the registration of a registrable disposition, that an agreement prevents the acquisition of rights of light or air for the benefit of the registered estate, he may make an entry in the property register of that estate (Land Registration Rules 2003 rules 36 and 76).

Rights of Pre-emption

Following the decision of the Court of Appeal in *Pritchard v Briggs* [1980] Ch 338, [1979] 3 WLR 868, [1980] 1 All ER 294, the status of a right of pre-emption as an interest in land has remained doubtful. In the case of rights of pre-emption created on or after 13 October 2003, the Land Registration Act 2002 ("LRA 2002") section 115 provides that a right of pre-emption in relation to registered land has effect from the time of creation as an interest capable of binding successors in title, subject to the rules about the effect of dispositions on priority. For the rules about the effect of dispositions on priority, see *Priorities*, page 239.

A right of pre-emption in respect of registered land may be protected by the entry in the register of an agreed notice, a unilateral notice and/or by a restriction. A notice does not necessarily mean that the right of pre-emption is valid but does mean that the priority of that right will be protected on any registered disposition (LRA 2002 sections 32, 29 and 30). A restriction does not confer any priority; it simply prevents an entry being made in the register if it is not permitted under the wording of the restriction.

Agreed Notice
An applicant should deliver to the registry:
    (a) an application in form AN1;
    (b) the original document granting the right of pre-emption or a certified copy of it;
    (c) the consent of the registered proprietor of the land where this is not contained in form AN1; and

(d) the fee payable. A fee calculator for all types of application is on the Land Registry's website at www.landregistry.gov.uk/fees.

The entry made in the register will give details of the interest protected.

Where the registered proprietor does not consent to an agreed notice being entered in the register, an application for entry of a unilateral notice may still be made. A unilateral notice may be preferred where the applicant does not wish the terms of the pre-emption to be open to public scrutiny.

Unilateral Notice

An applicant should deliver to the registry:
  (a) an application in form UN1;
  (b) a plan of the affected land (where the right of pre-emption affects only part of the land in the registered title); and
  (c) the fee payable. A fee calculator for all types of application is on the Land Registry's website at www.landregistry.gov.uk/fees.

Form UN1 should be completed on the following lines to show the interest of the applicant:

"having the benefit of a right of pre-emption contained in a [*name of document*] dated ... made between ... ."

The unilateral notice will give brief details of the interest protected and identify the beneficiary of that notice.

Restriction

As a result of LRA 2002 section 42(2) no restriction may be entered for the purpose of protecting the priority of an interest which is, or could be, the subject of a notice. This does not necessarily prevent a restriction from being entered in addition to the notice of the right of pre-emption. Although the notice will protect the priority of the right of pre-emption, a restriction may be used to ensure that any conditions in relation to another disposition by the registered proprietor are complied with. The consent of the registered proprietor to the entry of the restriction is required.

An applicant should deliver to the registry:
  (a) an application in form RX1;
  (b) full details of the required restriction;
  (c) the consent of the registered proprietor of the land (unless this is given in panel 15 of form RX1 or the applicant's conveyancer certifies that he holds such consent. The certificate may be given in panel 11 of form RX1); and
  (d) the fee payable. A fee calculator for all types of application is on the Land Registry's website at www.landregistry.gov.uk/fees.

A possible form of restriction based on Form N in Schedule 4 to LRR 2003 is:

"No disposition of the registered estate by the proprietor of the registered estate is to be registered without a written consent signed by [*person*

having benefit of right of pre-emption] of *[address]* or his conveyancer."
A restriction in this form would not require the approval of the registrar under LRA 2002 section 43(3).

Rights of Reverter under the School Sites Acts

Where the School Sites Acts provide for land to revert to the ownership of the original grantor on the land ceasing to be used for the particular purposes set out in those Acts, the Reverter of Sites Act 1987 section 1 has effect. The School Sites Acts are those of 1841, 1844, 1849, 1851 and 1852. Section 1 has the effect of leaving the land vested in the trustees who hold the land immediately prior to the event which gives rise to the reverter. They will hold on a trust of land; accordingly a sale by two or more trustees or a trust corporation would overreach the beneficial interest of the revertee.

If there is no restriction in Form A on the register, a person who has a right of reverter has a sufficient interest for the purposes of Land Registration Act 2002 section 43(1)(c) to apply for a restriction in Form A to ensure that a survivor of the joint proprietors (unless a trust corporation) will not be able to give a valid receipt for capital money (Land Registration Rules 2003 rule 93(a)). Form A is:

"No disposition by a sole proprietor of the registered estate (except a trust corporation) under which capital money arises is to be registered unless authorised by an order of the court."

A restriction does not confer any priority; it simply prevents an entry being made in the register if it is not permitted under the wording of the restriction.

If applying for a restriction in Form A, the person who has a right of reverter should deliver to the registry an application in form RX1. No fee is payable where the application is in respect of a restriction in Form A only.

Panel 13 of RX1 should be completed on the following lines:

"The interest is that specified in rule 93(a) of the Land Registration Rules 2003."

Panel 10 should be completed as to Form A set out above.

Once a revertee becomes beneficially entitled, he should take a transfer of the land from the trustees and apply for registration in the usual way; see *Transfers*, page 298. The application should be accompanied by a letter confirming, if such be the case, that the land is not affected by anything done by the revertee prior to 17 August 1987, the validity of which is preserved by the Reverter of Sites Act 1987 section 1(4).

The Reverter of Sites Act 1987 also applies to rights of reverter under the Literary and Scientific Institutions Act 1854 and the Places of Worship Sites Act 1873. Everything said above applies equally to those Acts.

Sequestrators

Sequestrators appointed by the court under a writ of sequestration have a duty to enter on the property of the contemnor and take possession of all his estate. No notice of an order appointing a sequestrator may be entered in the register (Land Registration Act 2002 ("LRA 2002") section 87(2)).

An order appointing a sequestrator is treated as an interest affecting an estate or charge for the purposes of LRA 2002 (LRA 2002 section 87(1)). It cannot, however, be an overriding interest belonging to a person in actual occupation for the purposes of paragraph 2 of Schedule 1 or 3 to LRA 2002 (LRA 2002 section 87(3)).

The sequestrator may be treated as a person having a right or claim in relation to a registered estate or charge for the purposes of LRA 2002 section 42(1)(c) if he is applying for a restriction in Form L or Form N (Land Registration Rules 2003 rule 93(s)). The registrar must give notice of such an application to the proprietor of the registered estate or charge concerned (LRA 2002 section 42(3)).

A restriction does not confer any priority; it simply prevents an entry being made in the register if it is not permitted under the wording of the restriction.

Restriction

The sequestrator should deliver to the registry:
  (a) an application in form RX1; and
  (b) the fee payable. A fee calculator for all types of application is on the Land Registry's website at www.landregistry.gov.uk/fees.

Panel 13 of RX1 should be completed on the following lines:

"The interest is that specified in rule 93(s) of the Land Registration Rules 2003, the applicant being the sequestrator appointed by ... Court on [*date*]."

Panel 10 should be completed as to the appropriate restriction. Form L is:

"No disposition [*or specify details*] of the registered estate [(other than a charge)] by the proprietor of the registered estate [or by the proprietor of any registered charge] is to be registered without a certificate signed by [*name*] of [*address*] (*or* [his conveyancer] [*or specify appropriate details, for example* signed on behalf of [*name*] of [*address*] by its secretary or conveyancer]) that the provisions of [*specify clause, paragraph or other particulars*] of [*specify details*] have been complied with."

Form N is:

"No disposition [*or specify details*] of the registered estate [other than a charge] by the proprietor of the registered estate [or by the proprietor of any registered charge] is to be registered without a written consent signed by [*name*] of [*address*] (or [his conveyancer] [*or specify appropriate details, for example* signed on behalf of [*name*] of [*address*] by its secretary or conveyancer])."

Settlements

Registered land which is settled land must be registered in the name of the tenant for life or the statutory owner. The rights of beneficiaries, which are overreached by dispositions under the Settled Land Act 1925 ("SLA 1925"), are protected by the entry of appropriate restrictions in the register. An interest under a settlement under SLA 1925 is not an unregistered interest which overrides first registration or registered dispositions even where the interest belongs to a person in actual occupation of the land (Land Registration Act 2002 ("LRA 2002") Schedule 1 paragraph 2 and Schedule 3 paragraph 2). A notice cannot be entered in the register in respect of an interest under a SLA 1925 settlement (LRA 2002 section 33(a)).

No new SLA 1925 settlement can be created after 31 December 1996 (Trusts of Land and Appointment of Trustees Act 1996 section 2). Problems with unintentional settlements, as in *Costello v Costello* [1996] 1 FLR 805 (CA), cannot therefore arise where the settlement would be created after 1996.

Settled Land Forms of Restriction

Applications for first registration of settled land must be accompanied by an application in form RX1 for a restriction in Form G, H, or I as appropriate. There is a similar requirement where registered land is transferred into settlement or bought with capital money of the settlement. In addition to those restrictions the registered proprietor of settled land is under a duty to apply for such other restrictions as may be appropriate. In that case panel 13 of form RX1 should be completed to show that the restrictions applied for are required for the protection of the beneficial interests and powers under the settlement in accordance with the Land Registration Rules 2003 Schedule 7 paragraph 7(2).

Forms G, H and I are set out in the Land Registration Rules 2003 as follows:

Form G (Tenant for life as registered proprietor of settled land, where there are trustees of the settlement)
No disposition is to be registered unless authorised by the Settled Land Act 1925, or by any extension of those statutory powers in the settlement, and no disposition under which capital money arises is to be registered unless the money is paid to (*name*) of (*address*) and (*name*) of (*address*), (*the trustees of the settlement, who may be a sole trust corporation or, if individuals, must number at least two but not more than four*) or into court.

Note: If applicable under the terms of the settlement, a further provision may be added that no transfer of the mansion house (shown on an attached plan or otherwise adequately described to enable it to be fully identified on the Ordnance Survey map or title plan) is to be registered without the consent of the named trustees or an order of the court.

Form H (Statutory owners as trustees of the settlement and registered proprietors of settled land)
No disposition is to be registered unless authorised by the Settled Land Act 1925, or by any extension of those statutory powers in the settlement, and, except where the sole proprietor is a trust corporation, no disposition under which capital money arises is to be registered unless the money is paid to at least two proprietors.
Note: This restriction does not apply where the statutory owners are not the trustees of the settlement.

Form I (Tenant for life as registered proprietor of settled land – no trustees of the settlement)
No disposition under which capital money arises, or which is not authorised by the Settled Land Act 1925 or by any extension of those statutory powers in the settlement, is to be registered.

A house is not a mansion house if it is usually occupied as a farmhouse or where the site of the house and grounds does not exceed twenty-five acres (SLA 1925 section 65).

Transfer of Land into Settlement
A transfer of registered land into settlement must include the following provisions, with any necessary alterations and additions:
"The Transferor and the Transferee declare that –
(a) the property is vested in the Transferee upon the trusts declared in a trust deed dated ... and made between (*parties*),
(b) the trustees of the settlement are (*names of trustees*),
(c) the power of appointment of new trustees is vested in (*name*),
(d) the following powers relating to land are expressly conferred by the trust deed in addition to those conferred by the Settled Land Act 1925: (*insert additional powers*).
or, if the tenant for life is a minor and the transferees are the statutory owner–
(a) the property is vested in the Transferee as statutory owner under a trust deed dated ... and made between (*parties*),
(b) the tenant for life is (*name*), a minor, who was born on (*date*),
(c) the trustees of the settlement are (*names of trustees*),
(d) during the minority of the tenant for life the power of appointment of new trustees is vested in the Transferee,

(e) the following powers relating to land are expressly conferred by the trust deed in addition to those conferred by the Settled Land Act 1925: (*insert additional powers*)."

An application must also be made for a restriction in Form G, H, or I as appropriate.

Registered Land Bought with Capital Money

Where registered land is acquired with capital money the transfer must include the following provisions, with any necessary alterations and additions:

"The Transferee declares that –
(a) the consideration has been paid out of capital money,
(b) the property is vested in the Transferee upon the trusts declared in a trust deed dated ... and made between (*parties*),
(c) the trustees of the settlement are (*names of trustees*),
(d) the power of appointment of new trustees is vested in (*name*),
(e) the following powers relating to land are expressly conferred by the trust deed in addition to those conferred by the Settled Land Act 1925: (*insert additional powers*)."

An application must also be made for a restriction in Form G, H, or I as appropriate.

Registered Land Brought into Settlement

Where registered land has been settled and the existing registered proprietor is the tenant for life under the settlement, the registered proprietor must make a declaration in Form 6 and apply for a restriction in Form G modified as appropriate. This arises only where the settlement is a variation of a settlement created before 1 January 1997, or derives from such a settlement, and falls within the Trusts of Land and Appointment of Trustees Act 1996 section 2(2).

Form 6 is:

(*Date*). Pursuant to a trust deed of even date herewith, [made between A.B. (*name of tenant for life*) and C.D. and E.F. (*names of trustees of the settlement*)], I, the said A.B. hereby declare as follows –
(a) The land is vested in me upon the trusts from time to time affecting it by virtue of the said trust deed.
[(b) The said C.D. and E.F. are the trustees of the settlement.
(c) The following powers relating to the land are expressly conferred by the said trust deed in extension of those conferred by the Settled Land Act 1925 (*fill in the powers, if any*).]
(d) I have the power to appoint new trustees of the settlement.
(To be executed as a deed)

Proprietor Ceasing in his Lifetime to be Tenant for Life
Where a registered proprietor ceases in his lifetime to be a tenant for life and has not become absolutely entitled, he must transfer the land to his successor in title, or, if the successor is a minor, to the statutory owner. On the registration of the successor in title or statutory owner, the trustees of the settlement, if the settlement is continuing, must apply for any necessary alteration in the restrictions in the register.

Transfer on Death of Tenant for Life
Where the settlement continues after the death of the registered proprietor who was tenant for life, the personal representatives will transfer the land using form AS1 or AS2 to the person entitled. The applicant should deliver to the registry:
- (a) an application in form AP1;
- (b) form AS1 or AS2, as appropriate;
- (c) the grant of probate or letters of administration limited to, or including, settled land;
- (d) an application for restriction in Form G or H, as appropriate. This may be in the additional provisions panel of AS1 or AS2 or in form RX1;
- (e) the fee payable. A fee calculator for all types of application is on the Land Registry's website at www.landregistry.gov.uk/fees.

The assent in AS1 or AS2 must contain the following provisions with any necessary alterations or additions:

"The Personal Representatives and the Transferee declare that –
- (a) the property is vested in the Transferee upon the trusts declared in [a trust deed dated ... and made between (*parties*)] [the will of (*name of deceased*) proved on (*date*)],
- (b) the trustees of the settlement are (*names of trustees*),
- (c) the power of appointment of new trustees is vested in (*name*),
- (d) the following powers relating to land are expressly conferred by the [trust deed] [will] in addition to those conferred by the Settled Land Act 1925: (*insert additional powers*)."

Where the settlement ends on the death of the proprietor, an application by the personal representatives to register a transfer to the person entitled should be accompanied by the grant of probate or letters of administration and form RX3 for cancellation of the restriction relating to the settlement.

End of Settlement Other than on Death
Where the settlement comes to an end otherwise than on the death of the registered proprietor, the trustees of the settlement may enter into a deed of discharge in accordance with SLA 1925 section 17. An application to cancel the restriction relating to the settlement should be made in form RX3 accompanied by the deed of discharge.

Severance of a Beneficial Joint Tenancy

A registered proprietor may sever a beneficial joint tenancy. The severance may be effected by a deed of declaration entered into by the joint proprietors, but more often one of the joint proprietors serves notice on the other joint proprietors under the Law of Property Act 1925 section 36(2). Where there has been severance, the proprietors of a registered estate must apply for a restriction in Form A since the estate is held on a trust of land and, as a result of a change in the trusts, the survivor of joint proprietors will not be able to give a valid receipt for capital money (Land Registration Rules 2003 rule 94(1)(b)).

An applicant for such a restriction should deliver to the registry an application in form RX1. No fee is payable where the application is in respect of a restriction in Form A only.

Panel 10 should be completed as to Form A. Form A is:

"No disposition by a sole proprietor of the registered estate (except a trust corporation) under which capital money arises is to be registered unless authorised by an order of the court."

This ensures that a survivor of the joint proprietors (unless a trust corporation) will not be able to give a valid receipt for capital money and that the beneficial interests will be overreached on a sale under the Law of Property Act 1925 section 27.

A restriction does not confer any priority; it simply prevents an entry being made in the register if it is not permitted under the wording of the restriction.

For the position where the beneficial joint tenancy has been severed as a result of the bankruptcy of one of the joint proprietors, see *Bankruptcy of a Joint Proprietor*, page 39.

Shared Ownership Leases

A shared ownership lease allows a person who cannot afford to buy a property to purchase a share in the property. The purchaser is granted a lease of the property at a premium which represents the value of the share purchased. The rent is calculated to take account of the value of the share in the property that has not been purchased. Provisions in the lease allow the lessee to purchase further shares in the property, a procedure called "staircasing". The rent is reduced when further shares are purchased. There may also be further provisions allowing the lessee the option to call for a transfer of the lessor's interest in the property or, in the case of a flat, to call for a conventional lease of the flat.

Tenants who had the right to buy under the Housing Act 1985 but who did not qualify for the maximum mortgage had the right to be granted a shared ownership lease. That right was abolished by the Leasehold Reform, Housing and Urban Development Act 1993 section 107.

A shared equity lease sometimes contains a discount charge, for example under the Housing Act 1996 section 11 where the lessor is a registered social landlord. A notice of the discount charge is entered in the charges register.

Registration of the Lease
An application for registration of a shared ownership lease is made in the same way as for a conventional lease. Where the lease is granted out of a registered estate, an applicant should deliver to the registry:
  (a) an application in form AP1;
  (b) the lease;
  (c) a certified copy lease (if the original lease is to be returned);
  (d) any consent required under a restriction on the lessor's title;
  (e) any consent by a chargee on the lessor's title;
  (f) form DI giving the information as to overriding interests required by the Land Registration Rules 2003 ("LRR 2003") rule 57, including any documentary evidence of the interest; and
  (g) the fee payable. A fee calculator for all types of application is on the Land Registry's website at www.landregistry.gov.uk/fees.

On registration of the lease, it is allotted its own title number. Notice of the registered lease is entered on the lessor's registered title without any need for a separate application or further fee. Where the lease contains an option for the lessee to call for a transfer of the lessor's interest or to call for the grant of a lease in conventional form, notice of the option is entered in the lessor's title. No entry as to such option is made in the lessee's title.

Where the lease contains a provision requiring the lessee to offer a surrender to the lessor if the lessee wishes to assign before he has purchased all the equity in the property, a note of this obligation is made in the property register of the lessee's title.

Where the lease is granted out of unregistered land, an applicant should deliver to the registry:
  (a) an application in form FR1;
  (b) sufficient details, by plan or otherwise, so that the land can be clearly identified on the Ordnance Survey map;
  (c) the lease and a certified copy;
  (d) all deeds and documents relating to the title that are in the control of the applicant;
  (e) a list in duplicate in form DL of all the documents delivered;
  (f) form DI giving the information as to overriding interests required by LRR 2003 rule 28; and
  (g) the fee payable. A fee calculator for all types of application is on the

Land Registry's website at www.landregistry.gov.uk/fees.
Where the lease contains an option for the lessee to call for a transfer of the lessor's interest or to call for the grant of a lease in conventional form, no entry as to such option is made in the lessee's title. A C(iv) land charge should be registered in respect of the lessor's unregistered title.

Where the lease contains a provision requiring the lessee to offer a surrender to the lessor if the lessee wishes to assign before he has purchased all the equity in the property, a note of this obligation is made in the property register of the lessee's title.

The lessee may assign the benefit of any options in the lease granted in his favour. This may be done when the lessee mortgages the leasehold estate. No entry is made in the register of any such assignment.

Staircasing

The acquisition by the lessee of further shares in the property does not require any entry to be made in the register unless, at the same time, a deed is entered into varying the terms of the lease, usually by reducing the rent, or a discount charge arises on such acquisition.

Where there is a deed of variation of the lease, the lessee should deliver to the registry:

(a) an application in form AP1;
(b) the deed of variation;
(c) a certified copy deed (if the original is to be returned);
(d) the fee payable. A fee calculator for all types of application is on the Land Registry's website at www.landregistry.gov.uk/fees.

Where the further shares are acquired at a discount and the liability to repay the discount takes effect as a charge, for example under the Housing Act 1996 section 11 where the lessor is a registered social landlord, the applicant to enter an agreed notice of the discount charge in the lessee's title should deliver to the registry:

(a) an application in form AN1;
(b) the document creating the discount charge;
(c) a certified copy of the document creating the discount charge (if the original is to be returned); and
(d) the fee payable. A fee calculator for all types of application is on the Land Registry's website at www.landregistry.gov.uk/fees.

Souvenir Land

The Land Registration (Souvenir Land) Rules 1972 provided that the registrar could declare an area of land to be subject to a souvenir land scheme if that area consisted wholly or mainly of land which had been, or

was proposed to be, disposed of in souvenir plots. A plot of souvenir land was defined by the Land Registration and Land Charges Act 1971 section 4(5) as:
"any piece of land which being of inconsiderable size and little or no practical utility, is unlikely to be wanted in isolation except for the sake of pure ownership or for sentimental reasons or commemorative purposes."

The effect of that declaration was that disposals of individual plots within the designated area took effect as if the title were not registered. An entry on the following lines appears in the property register of the affected title:
"The land [edged and numbered ... in blue on the filed plan] is subject to a Souvenir Land scheme.
NOTE: Declaration dated ... filed."

It is no longer possible to make a souvenir land declaration.

Where a souvenir land declaration has been entered in the register and any unregistered transaction with that land has been made, the proprietor must not dispose of that land otherwise than in a manner which gives effect to the interests of any third parties who have become entitled to apply to be registered as proprietor of any part of that land (Land Registration Act 2002 (Transitional Provisions) Order 2003 ("LRA(TP)O 2003") article 11).

The particulars of the declaration entered in the register take effect as a restriction and the registrar may amend the register to substitute for the declaration in the property register a restriction in the proprietorship register (LRA(TP)O 2003 article 11(4) and (5)). The restriction is:
"No disposition is to be registered without the consent of the person or persons (if any) entitled to apply to be registered as proprietor of the land disposed of, or any part of it, as the result of any unregistered transaction effected since [*the date of the declaration as noted in the register*]."

Cancellation of Entries Relating to Souvenir Land

Where the registered proprietor can establish to the satisfaction of the registrar that there has been no unregistered transaction with the souvenir land after the declaration was made, so that no third party has become entitled to be registered as proprietor of it, he may apply using form AP1 for cancellation of the entry on the register relating to the souvenir land. The application may be made in respect of a particular part of the souvenir land only.

Application for Registration by a Third Party

A third party may apply to be registered as proprietor of part of the souvenir land using application form AP1 if he is able to establish to the satisfaction of the registrar that one or more unregistered transactions have been effected since the declaration was made and that, as a result of them and any other events that have taken place:
   (a) the legal estate in the land is vested in him; or

(b) a legal estate granted out of the land is vested in him; or
(c) a legal estate such as is referred to in (a) or (b) has been transferred to him, directly or indirectly, by the person in whom it has become vested.

The registrar gives notice of such application to the registered proprietor.

Special Powers of Appointment

A special power of appointment is a power under which the donee of the power, who may not be the registered proprietor, is able to appoint the property among a limited class of persons. Such a power of appointment takes effect in equity (Law of Property Act 1925 section 1(7)) and allows the donee of the power to transfer an equitable interest only.

A power of appointment cannot be noted in the register but the donee of a special power of appointment may apply for the entry of a restriction in relation to the registered land affected by the power (Land Registration Rules 2003 rule 93(e)). The applicant should deliver to the registry:

(a) an application in form RX1; and
(b) the fee payable. A fee calculator for all types of application is on the Land Registry's website at www.landregistry.gov.uk/fees.

Panel 13 of RX1 should be completed on the following lines:

"The interest is that specified in rule 93(e) of the Land Registration Rules 2003, the applicant being the donee of a special power of appointment which affects the land."

A possible form of restriction is:

"No disposition of the registered estate by the proprietor of the registered estate is to be registered without a written consent signed by [*name of donee of power*] of [*address*]."

A restriction in this form would not require the approval of the registrar under the Land Registration Act 2002 section 43(3). The registrar gives notice of the application and of the right to object to it to the registered proprietor unless his consent accompanies the application.

Sporting Rights

Sporting rights which are *profits a prendre* mainly exist in gross rather than as appurtenant to land. *Profits a prendre* in gross may be the subject of a voluntary application for first registration. For the protection of *profits a prendre* in gross and appurtenant profits, see *Profits a Prendre*, page 242.

As a result of the Twelfth Schedule to the Law of Property Act 1922 there are preserved to the lord in relation to copyhold land enfranchised under that Act, the rights, franchises, royalties or privileges of the lord in respect of any rights of chase or warren, piscaries or other rights of hunting, shooting, fishing, fowling, or otherwise taking game, fish or fowl. The Copyhold Act 1852 section 48 and the Copyhold Act 1894 section 23 excepted similar rights in respect of enfranchisement under those Acts. Any franchises of forest, free chase, park or free warren were abolished by the Wild Creatures and Forest Laws Act 1971 section 1(1). For the protection of franchises and manorial rights see *Franchises*, page 143 and *Manors*, page 202.

Corporeal Fisheries
There is a presumption that the owner of a several fishery in a non-tidal river is the owner of the bed of the river (*Hanbury v Jenkins* [1901] 2 Ch 401). This presumption prevails over the better known presumption that the owner of the land abutting a non-tidal river owns the bed to the middle of the stream. Both presumptions are rebuttable on the particular facts of a case. A similar presumption arises in the case of a several fishery in a tidal river that ownership of the fishery includes the soil under the fishery. Such a fishery must have been created by a grant of the Crown before Magna Carta 1297; see for instance *Duke of Beaufort v John Aird and Co* (1904) 20 TLR 602 where the evidence commenced with an extract from the Domesday Book. After Magna Carta such a fishery would have to have been created by statute.

A corporeal fishery, being land, is subject to compulsory first registration in the usual way; see *First Registration*, page 133. For the period of two years from 13 October 2003 the owner of an unregistered corporeal fishery may register a caution against first registration in respect of that land. Such caution will, however, cease to have effect at the end of that period of two years, except in relation to applications for first registration made before the end of that period. The applicant for the caution should deliver the following documents to the registry:
(a) an application in form CT1;
(b) a plan (or other sufficient details) to allow the land to which the caution relates to be identified clearly on the Ordnance Survey map; and
(c) the fee payable. A fee calculator for all types of application is on the Land Registry's website at www.landregistry.gov.uk/fees.

Form CT1 should be completed on the following lines to show the interest of the applicant:
"owner of the land and corporeal fishery by virtue of a Deed dated ... made between [*parties*]."

Statutory Charges

Some charges created by or under a statute have effect to postpone a charge which at the time of registration of the statutory charge is entered in the register or is the basis for an entry in the register. In practice the only likely examples are charges in favour of the Legal Services Commission on property recovered or preserved (Legal Aid Act 1988 section 16(6) and Access to Justice Act 1999 section 10(7)). In such cases the registrar gives notice of the statutory charge to the proprietor of any registered charge appearing on the affected title at the time of registration of the statutory charge. He also gives notice to any person who appears to be entitled to a charge protected by a notice in the register where that person's name and address appear in the register of the title in question. A person who suffers loss by reason of the registrar's failure to give such notice may be entitled to indemnity; see *Indemnity*, page 161.

A statutory charge which is not a local land charge must be completed by registration and does not operate at law until the registration requirements are met (Land Registration Act 2002 section 27).

An applicant to register a statutory charge should deliver to the registry:
(a) an application in form AP1;
(b) a statement of charge (for example in the case of a charge under the Access to Justice Act 1999 section 10(7), a statement is given by a person stated to hold the rank of, or equivalent to, Civil Service Grade 7 or above);
(c) a certified copy of the statement of charge (if the original statement is to be returned);
(d) (where the charge has priority over existing charges) an application in form SC; and
(e) the fee payable. A fee calculator for all types of application is on the Land Registry's website at www.landregistry.gov.uk/fees.

Where application form SC is lodged and the registrar is satisfied that the statutory charge has the priority specified in that form, an entry is made in the charges register showing that priority. If the applicant does not satisfy the registrar that the statutory charge has that priority but the registrar considers that the applicant has an arguable case, an entry may be made in the charges register that the applicant claims that priority. The proprietor of the statutory charge or the proprietor of another affected charge may apply to have any such entry of claimed priority removed or replaced by an entry guaranteeing the priority (Land Registration Rules 2003 rule 105).

Subrogation

Subrogation is a remedy not a cause of action. It is available in a wide variety of situations to reverse the defendant's unjust enrichment (*Boscawen v Bajwa* [1996] 1 WLR 328, [1995] 4 All ER 769 (CA)).

Where a lender makes a loan and that money is used to pay off an existing registered charge on the property, that lender may be subrogated to the rights of the original chargee, even though the entry in respect of the registered charge has been removed from the register. This may even be the case where the lender contemplated making only an unsecured loan, if otherwise a third party would be unjustly enriched at the lender's expense (*Banque Financière de la Cité v Parc (Battersea) Ltd* [1999] 1 AC 221, [1998] 2 WLR 475, [1998] 1 All ER 737 (HL)).

An example might be when a lender makes a loan to be secured by a first charge and part of the money advanced is used to discharge an existing charge. Unfortunately the application to register the lender's charge is not made during the priority period of its official search and, before its application for registration is lodged, an application to register another charge is lodged by a third party. The third party's charge will therefore have priority over the lender's charge (Land Registration Act 2002 section 29). The lender may be entitled to be subrogated to the original charge to the extent that its loan was used to redeem the original charge.

Where it is considered that a person has an interest in land as a result of subrogation, an application to protect that interest by a notice may be appropriate, although this is often a matter of locking the stable door after the horse has bolted. In practice, the fact that documentation to support an application for an agreed notice is usually not immediately available means that a unilateral notice is likely be applied for.

The applicant should deliver to the registry:
(a) an application in form UN1;
(b) the fee payable. A fee calculator for all types of application is on the Land Registry's website at www.landregistry.gov.uk/fees.

The statutory declaration in panel 11 of form UN1 or the conveyancer's certificate in panel 12 should set out the nature of the interest claimed and how it has arisen by subrogation.

The unilateral notice will give brief details of the interest protected and identify the beneficiary of that notice.

Supervisor of an Individual Voluntary Arrangement

An individual voluntary arrangement under the Insolvency Act 1986 sections 252 to 263 does not necessarily create an interest in land. Whether or not it does so depends on the particular arrangement approved by the meeting of creditors. For example an arrangement to pay sums out of future income to the supervisor of the individual voluntary arrangement does not lead to the making of any entry in a registered title.

Where the supervisor is being given a charge on the debtor's beneficial interest in a registered estate or that beneficial interest is being assigned to the supervisor, the supervisor should apply for the entry of a restriction. This is also the case if there is a declaration of trust by the debtor in favour of the supervisor.

Where the supervisor is applying for a restriction he should deliver to the registry:
 (a) an application in form RX1;
 (b) the consent of the registered proprietor of the land (unless this is given in panel 15 of form RX1 or the applicant's conveyancer certifies that he holds such consent. The certificate may be given in panel 11 of form RX1); and
 (c) the fee payable. A fee calculator for all types of application is on the Land Registry's website at www.landregistry.gov.uk/fees.

Where the consent of the registered proprietor is not available, the supervisor may apply on the basis that he has a sufficient interest in the making of the restriction (Land Registration Act 2002 ("LRA 2002") section 43(1)(c)). In this case panel 13 of form RX1 should be completed to show that the applicant is the supervisor of an individual voluntary arrangement and a copy of the individual voluntary arrangement should be lodged in support. Panel 10 should be completed to show the appropriate restriction or restrictions. The restrictions depend on what arrangement is in place. Form A and Form N are possible restrictions. Form A is:

"No disposition by a sole proprietor of the registered estate (except a trust corporation) under which capital money arises is to be registered unless authorised by an order of the court."

Form N is:

"No disposition [*or specify details*] of the registered estate [(other than a charge)] by the proprietor of the registered estate [or by the proprietor of any registered charge] is to be registered without a written consent signed by [*name of supervisor*] of [*address*]."

Where the consent of the registered proprietor is not available, the registrar gives him notice of the application and of his right to object (LRA 2002 section 45(1)).

Time Share

In a time share lease the right to possession under the lease is discontinuous. Such a lease may be the subject of an application for first registration no matter how short a period of the term is unexpired (Land Registration Act 2002 ("LRA 2002") section 3(4)). First registration, on the grant of such a lease out of unregistered land or the transfer or first mortgage of such an unregistered lease, is compulsory only where the term at the time of the grant, transfer or mortgage has more than seven years to run. A grant is also subject to compulsory registration where it is out of an unregistered freehold, or leasehold with more than seven years to run, and it is to take effect in possession after the end of the period of three months beginning with the date of the grant (LRA 2002 section 4).

A time share lease takes effect as a lease for a single term equivalent to the aggregate of the individual periods during which the tenant is entitled to occupy the demised premises (*Cottage Holiday Associates Limited v Customs and Excise Commissioners* [1983] QB 735, [1983] 2 WLR 861).

A grant of a term of years absolute out of a registered estate in land under which the right to possession is discontinuous is required to be completed by registration (LRA 2002 section 27(2)).

Prior to the coming into force of LRA 2002, leases granted for a term not exceeding twenty-one years were overriding interests under the Land Registration Act 1925. A lease which was an overriding interest under the Land Registration Act 1925 immediately before 13 October 2003 continues to be an unregistered interest overriding both first registration and registered dispositions (LRA 2002 Schedule 12 paragraph 12).

For applications for first registration of leases see *First Registration*, page 133 and for applications for registration of leases which are registrable dispositions, see *Leases which are Registrable Dispositions*, page 171.

Town or Village Greens

As a result of the Commons Registration Act 1965, all town or village greens in England and Wales were required to be registered with the appropriate council specified in that Act during a period ending on 31 July 1970. After that date no land capable of being registered under the Commons Registration Act is deemed to be a town or village green unless so registered. "Town or village green" is defined in that Act as land which has been allotted by or under any Act for the exercise or recreation of the inhabitants of any locality; or on which the inhabitants of any locality have a customary right to indulge in lawful sports and pastimes; or on which the inhabitants of any locality have indulged in such sports and pastimes as of right for not less than twenty years.

Registration under the Commons Registration Act 1965 was of town or village greens, rights of common over such land, and of the persons claiming to be or found to be owners of that land. For the position concerning rights of common over a town or village green, see *Commons*, page 99. No person was to be registered as owner of any land already registered at the Land Registry. Once ownership had been registered under the 1965 Act, the land was subject to compulsory registration at the Land Registry on sale, even in areas which at that time were not compulsory areas. The application had to be made within two months of the sale. Where this requirement has been overlooked, an application may be made to the registrar for an order under the Land Registration Act 2002 ("LRA 2002") section 6(5) extending the period for registration. The application may be made by letter and should explain the reasons the period for registration should be extended. See *Pinekerry Ltd v Needs (Kenneth) Contractors Ltd* (1992) 64 P & CR 245 (CA) (a case referring to the similar section 123 of the Land Registration Act 1925) as to the inability of a purchaser to show a good title to a sub-purchaser when an application for first registration had not been made within two months and no order under section 123 had been made.

Once a town or village green is registered at the Land Registry, the registrar notifies the appropriate council accordingly. The council then deletes the registration of ownership and indicates that the land is registered at the Land Registry.

The Commons Registration Act 1965 section 11 exempts from the effect of that Act the New Forest, Epping Forest and the Forest of Dean and any land exempted by an order of the Minister. See *Commons*, page 99, for details of land in respect of which such orders were made.

Where a town or village green was registered under the Commons Registration Act 1965 and the Commons Commissioner, following inquiry, was not satisfied that any person was the owner of the land, he could direct the registration authority to register as owner the parish council or other appropriate local authority as set out in section 8 of that Act. On registration under that section, the land vested in that local authority. Any such direction should be revealed on a subsequent application for first registration of the land.

Where, after 2 January 1970, any land becomes a town or village green, an application for that land, and for the rights of common over it and claims of ownership to it, to be entered in the appropriate registers maintained under the Commons Registration Act 1965 should be made in accordance with the Commons Registration (New Land) Regulations 196. For an example of a new town or village green being established by twenty years user as of right by the inhabitants, see *R v Oxfordshire County Council ex parte Sunningwell Parish Council* [2000] 1 AC 335, [1999] 3 WLR 160,

[1999] 3 All ER 385 (HL). For the position where there are any rights of common over such a town or village green, see *Commons*, page 99.

The Common Land (Rectification of Registers) Act 1989 made provision for removal from the register of town or village greens, on application by the owner, of dwellinghouses and land ancillary to dwellinghouses. Any such application had to be made by 22 July 1992. A copy of any order made under that Act should be lodged with any application for first registration of the land in question.

First Registration of a Town or Village Green
An applicant should deliver to the registry:
 (a) an application in form FR1;
 (b) sufficient details, by plan or otherwise, so that the land can be clearly identified on the Ordnance Survey map;
 (c) all deeds and documents relating to the title that are in the control of the applicant;
 (d) a copy of the entries in the Commons Registration Act registers;
 (e) a list in duplicate in form DL of all the documents delivered;
 (f) form DI giving the information as to overriding interests required by the Land Registration Rules 2003 ("LRR 2003") rule 28; and
 (g) the fee payable. A fee calculator for all types of application is on the Land Registry's website at www.landregistry.gov.uk/fees.

Rule 28 of LRR 2003 provides that a person applying for first registration must provide information to the registrar in form DI about any of the overriding interests (other than local land charges or public rights) set out in Schedule 1 to LRA 2002 that affect the estate to which the application relates and are within the actual knowledge of the applicant, but are not apparent from the deeds and documents accompanying the application. The registrar may enter a notice in the register in respect of any such interest.

The applicant is not required, however, to provide information about interests that, under section 33 or 90(4) of LRA 2002, cannot be protected by notice. Such interests are:
 (a) interests under a trust of land or under a Settled Land Act 1925 settlement;
 (b) a leasehold estate in land granted for three years or less from the date of the grant and which is not required to be registered;
 (c) a restrictive covenant between lessor and lessee, so far as relating to the demised premises;
 (d) an interest which is capable of being registered under the Commons Registration Act 1965;
 (e) an interest in any coal or coal mine, or the rights attached to any such interest, or the rights of any person under the Coal Industry Act 1994 section 38, 49 or 51; and
 (f) leases created for public-private partnerships relating to transport in

London, within the meaning given by the Greater London Authority Act 1999 section 218.

The applicant is also not required to provide information about a leasehold estate in land which falls within paragraph 1 of Schedule 1 to LRA 2002 but, at the time of the application, has one year or less to run.

In examining the title the registrar has regard to any examination by a conveyancer prior to the application and to the nature of the property. He may make searches and enquiries and give notice to other persons, direct that searches and enquiries be made by the applicant, and advertise the application (LRR 2003 rule 30).

Where there is a discrepancy between the town or village greens ownership register and the deeds, this must be accounted for. Registration as owner under the Commons Registration Act 1965 is not conclusive proof of ownership; a good documentary title must be produced to the Land Registry in the normal way. An exception to this is where the land has been vested in a local authority under section 8 as mentioned above.

Transfers

A transfer of a registered estate must be in form TP1, TP2, TP3, TR1, TR2, TR5, AS1 or AS3, as appropriate (Land Registration Rules 2003 ("LRR 2003") rule 58). Forms AS1 and AS3 are transfers by way of assent; see *Assents*, page 30.

Form TP1 is a transfer of part of one or more registered titles and TP2 is a similar transfer by the proprietor of a registered charge under the power of sale. Form TP3 is a transfer of a portfolio of titles where at least one is a transfer of part; form TR5 is used where the portfolio contains only whole registered titles. Form TR1 is a transfer of whole of one or more registered titles and TR2 is a similar transfer by the proprietor of a registered charge under the power of sale.

A transfer affecting two or more registered titles may, on the written request of the applicant, be registered as to some or only one of the registered titles (LRR 2003 rule 56). The applicant may later apply to have the transfer registered as to any other of the registered titles affected by it.

A transfer of part of the land in a registered title must have attached to it a plan signed by the transferor and clearly identifying the land transferred (LRR 2003 rule 213). If the land transferred is clearly identified on the title plan it may instead be described by reference to the title plan.

Where any registered estate is transferred wholly or partly in consideration of a transfer of another estate it must still be effected by a transfer in TR1 or TP1 as appropriate. A receipt for any equality money must be given in the receipt panel and the following provision must be

included in the additional provisions panel (LRR 2003 rule 59):
"This transfer is in consideration of a [transfer] [conveyance] of [*brief description of property exchanged*] dated today [(*if applicable*) and of the sum stated above paid for equality of exchange]."

A transfer of a registered estate is required to be registered and does not operate at law until the transferor or his successor in title is entered in the register as the proprietor (Land Registration Act 2002 ("LRA 2002") section 27 and Schedule 2). In the case of a transfer of part the following entries are also made in the registered title of the retained land (LRR 2003 rule 72):

(a) an entry in the property register referring to the removal of the estate comprised in the transfer; and

(b) entries relating to any rights, covenants, provisions, and other matters created by the transfer which the registrar considers affect the retained registered estate.

Instead of making the entry referred to at (a) above, the registrar may make a new edition of the registered title out of which the transfer is made and, if he considers it desirable, he may allot a new title number to that title.

Entries are also made on the new registered title relating to any rights, covenants, provisions, and other matters created by the transfer which the registrar considers affect the transferred part.

A person applying to register a transfer of a registered estate must provide information to the registrar in form DI about any of the overriding interests (other than local land charges or public rights) set out in Schedule 3 to LRA 2002 that affect the estate to which the application relates and are within the actual knowledge of the applicant. For details see *Overriding Interests*, page 223. The applicant must produce to the registrar any documentary evidence of the interest which is under his control (LRR 2003 rule 57). The registrar may enter a notice in the register in respect of any such interest.

The applicant is not required, however, to provide information about interests that, under section 33 or 90(4) of LRA 2002, cannot be protected by notice. Such interests are:

(a) interests under a trust of land or under a Settled Land Act 1925 settlement;

(b) a leasehold estate in land granted for three years or less from the date of the grant and which is not required to be registered;

(c) a restrictive covenant between lessor and lessee, so far as relating to the demised premises;

(d) an interest which is capable of being registered under the Commons Registration Act 1965;

(e) an interest in any coal or coal mine, or the rights attached to any such interest, or the rights of any person under the Coal Industry Act 1994 section 38, 49 or 51; and

(f) leases created for public-private partnerships relating to transport in

London, within the meaning given by the Greater London Authority Act 1999 section 218.

The applicant is also not required to provide information about a leasehold estate in land which falls within paragraph 1 of Schedule 3 to LRA 2002 but, at the time of the application, has one year or less to run.

The transferee should deliver to the registry:
(a) an application in form AP1 showing the application as "Transfer";
(b) a transfer in the appropriate form;
(c) form DI giving the information as to overriding interests required by LRR 2003 rule 57, including any documentary evidence of the interest; and
(d) the fee payable. A fee calculator for all types of application is on the Land Registry's website at www.landregistry.gov.uk/fees.

Trusts of Land

A trust of land is any trust of property which consists of or includes land. The trust may be of any description, whether express, implied, resulting or constructive and including a bare trust or a trust for sale, but not a settlement under the Settled Land Act 1925 (Trusts of Land and Appointment of Trustees Act 1996 ("TLATA 1996") section 1). Land which is held on a trust of land should be vested in the trustees. The registrar is not affected with notice of a trust (Land Registration Act 2002 ("LRA 2002") section 78).

It is not possible to enter a notice in the register to protect an interest under a trust of land (LRA 2002 section 33(a)). The trustees should apply for appropriate restrictions to reflect any limitations on their powers of disposition contained in the trust deed.

If the registrar enters two or more registered proprietors of a registered estate, he must enter a Form A restriction where the survivor of them will not be able to give a valid receipt for capital money. Form A is:

"No disposition by a sole proprietor of the registered estate (except a trust corporation) under which capital money arises is to be registered unless authorised by an order of the court."

Where a registered estate becomes subject to a trust of land under which a sole or last surviving trustee will not be able to give a valid receipt for capital money, the registered proprietor must apply for a restriction in Form A (Land Registration Rules 2003 ("LRR 2003") rule 94(1) and (2)). If such an application is not made, any person who has an interest under the trust of land may apply for the restriction in Form A.

Where the trust imposes limitations on the powers of the trustees under

TLATA 1996 section 8, for example the requirement to obtain a consent before sale, the registered proprietors must apply for a restriction in Form B (LRR 2003 rule 94(4)). This does not apply if the land is held on charitable, ecclesiastical or public trusts, but does apply where the legal estate is vested in the personal representatives of a sole or last surviving trustee. If such an application is not made, any person who has an interest under the trust of land where the powers of the trustees are limited under TLATA 1996 section 8 may apply for the restriction in Form B. The applicant should deliver to the registry:

(a) an application in form RX1; and
(b) the fee payable. A fee calculator for all types of application is on the Land Registry's website at www.landregistry.gov.uk/fees.

Where the applicant is a person who has an interest under a trust of land, panel 13 of RX1 should be completed on the following lines:

"The interest is that specified in rule 93(c) of the Land Registration Rules 2003, the applicant being a person who has an interest in the registered estate held under a trust of land where the powers of the trustees are limited by section 8 of the Trusts of Land and Appointment of Trustees Act 1996."

Panel 10 should be completed as to the restriction in Form B. Form B is:

"No disposition [*or specify details*] by the proprietors of the registered estate is to be registered unless they make a statutory declaration, or their conveyancer gives a certificate, that the disposition [*or specify details*] is in accordance with [*specify the disposition creating the trust*] or some variation thereof referred to in the declaration or certificate."

Where personal representatives hold the registered estate on a trust of land created by the deceased's Will, or on a trust of land arising under the laws of intestacy which is subsequently varied and their powers have been limited by TLATA 1996 section 8, they must apply for a restriction in Form C (LRR 2003 rule 94(3)). If such an application is not made, any person who has an interest in the due administration of the estate may apply for a restriction in Form C (LRR 2003 rule 93(d)). The applicant should deliver to the registry:

(a) an application in form RX1; and
(b) the fee payable. A fee calculator for all types of application is on the Land Registry's website at www.landregistry.gov.uk/fees.

Panel 13 of RX1 should be completed on the following lines:

"The interest is that specified in rule 93(d) of the Land Registration Rules 2003, the applicant being a person interested in the due administration of the estate of [*name*] deceased."

Panel 10 should be completed as to the restriction in Form C. Form C is:

"No disposition by [*name*], the [executor] [administrator] of [*name*] deceased, other than a transfer as personal representative, is to be registered unless he makes a statutory declaration, or his conveyancer gives a certificate, that the disposition is in accordance with the terms [of the will of the deceased *or* the law relating to intestacy as varied by a deed dated *specify details of deed or specify appropriate details*] or [some variation *or* further variation] thereof referred to in the declaration or certificate, or is necessary for the purposes of administration."

TLATA 1996 section 6(6) provides that the powers of an absolute owner of land conferred by that section shall not be exercised in contravention of, or of any order made in pursuance of, any other enactment or any rule of law or equity. TLATA 1996 section 6(8) provides that where any enactment other than that section confers on trustees authority to act subject to any restriction, limitation or condition, trustees of land may not exercise the powers conferred by that section to do any act which they are prevented from doing under the other enactment by reason of the restriction, limitation or condition. Any person who has a sufficient interest in preventing a contravention of TLATA 1996 section 6(6) or (8) may apply for a restriction in order to prevent such a contravention (LRR 2003 rule 93(b)).

Vesting Registered Land in New Trustees
Where new trustees have been appointed in place of existing trustees the simplest course is to proceed by way of a transfer in form TR1 from the registered proprietors to the new trustees. The additional provisions panel of the transfer should include a statement that the transfer is made for the purpose of giving effect to the appointment of new trustees. The legal estate passes to the new trustees when they are registered as proprietors (LRA 2002 section 27). See *Transfers*, page 298.

Where a deed of appointment or retirement of trustees has an express or implied vesting declaration to which the Trustee Act 1925 section 40 applies, an application may be made to register the disposition by operation of law without executing a transfer. This might be appropriate, for example, where a person other than the existing registered proprietors has the power of appointing new trustees. The limitations on using this procedure in respect of charges and leases requiring a consent to alienation should be noted (Trustee Act section 40(4)). The applicants to register such a disposition should deliver to the registry:

(a) an application in form AP1;
(b) the deed of appointment or retirement;
(c) a certified copy of the deed of appointment or retirement (if the original deed is to be returned);
(d) a certificate from the conveyancer acting for the persons making the appointment or effecting the retirement that they are entitled to do so, or other evidence to satisfy the registrar that the persons making the appointment or effecting the retirement are entitled to do so;
(e) form DI giving the information as to overriding interests required by LRR 2003 rule 57, including any documentary evidence of the interest; and

(f) the fee payable. A fee calculator for all types of application is on the Land Registry's website at www.landregistry.gov.uk/fees.

Where the court has made a vesting order the applicants should deliver to the registry:

(a) an application in form AP1;
(b) the vesting order;
(c) a certified copy of the vesting order (if the original is to be returned);
(d) form DI giving the information as to overriding interests required by LRR 2003 rule 57, including any documentary evidence of the interest; and
(e) the fee payable. A fee calculator for all types of application is on the Land Registry's website at www.landregistry.gov.uk/fees.

Unincorporated Associations

Where an unincorporated association holds land the legal estate must be vested in trustees. For the position where the unincorporated association is a charity, see *Charities*, page 69. The following restriction in Form A is entered in the proprietorship register in accordance with the Land Registration Act 2002 ("LRA 2002") section 44(1):

"No disposition by a sole proprietor of the registered estate (except a trust corporation) under which capital money arises is to be registered unless authorised by an order of the court."

If no other restriction is entered, the proprietors' powers of dispositions are taken in favour of any disponee as being free from any limitation affecting the validity of a disposition (LRA 2002 section 26). The trustees should therefore consider applying for any further restriction, for example to ensure compliance with club rules. The applicants for such a restriction should deliver to the registry:

(a) an application in form RX1; and
(b) the fee payable. A fee calculator for all types of application is on the Land Registry's website at www.landregistry.gov.uk/fees.

An appropriate restriction is Form R which is:

"No disposition [*or specify details*] of the registered estate [(other than a charge)] by the proprietor of the registered estate [or by the proprietor of any registered charge] is to be registered unless authorised by the rules of the [*name of club*] of [*address*] as evidenced [by a resolution of its members *or* by a certificate signed by its secretary or conveyancer [*or specify appropriate details*]]."

For the position where the registered estate is to be vested in new trustees of an unincorporated association, see *Vesting Registered Land in New Trustees*, page 302. In the case of trustees holding for a trade union or an unincorporated employers' association, a vesting declaration is implied in a memorandum or written record of the resolution of a meeting appointing or discharging trustees; a deed is not required (Trade Union and Labour Relations (Consolidation) Act 1992 sections 13 and 129).

Upgrading Titles

Where a registered estate has been awarded a class of title which is less than absolute, an application to upgrade it may be made under the Land Registration Act 2002 ("LRA 2002") section 62. The registrar has power to upgrade the class of title where he is satisfied as to the title, applying the same standards as on an application for first registration. This usually means that the defect that resulted in the grant of the particular class of title on first registration has been remedied.

A possessory title to freehold land may be upgraded to absolute after twelve years if the registrar is satisfied that the proprietor is in possession of the land (LRA 2002 section 62(4)). In the case of leasehold land, a possessory title may be upgraded to good leasehold after twelve years if the registrar is satisfied that the proprietor is in possession of the land (LRA 2002 section 62(5)). A proprietor is in possession if the land is physically in his possession, or in that of a person who is entitled to be registered as the proprietor of the registered estate. Land in the possession of a tenant is treated as being in the possession of the landlord. Land in the possession of a mortgagee is treated as being in the possession of the mortgagor. Land in the possession of a licensee is treated as being in the possession of the licensor. Land in the possession of a beneficiary is treated as being in the possession of the trustee. (LRA 2002 section 131.)

An application to upgrade the class of title of a registered estate may be made by the proprietor of that estate or a person entitled to be registered as proprietor. Such an application may also be made by the proprietor of a registered charge affecting that estate or a person interested in a registered estate which derives from that estate.

None of the powers to upgrade the title in LRA 2002 section 62 is exercisable if there is outstanding any claim adverse to the title of the registered proprietor which is made by virtue of an estate, right or interest the enforceability of which is preserved by virtue of the existing entry about the class of title (LRA 2002 section 62(6)).

Where a registered freehold or leasehold estate is upgraded to absolute, the proprietor ceases to hold the estate subject to any estate, right or interest the enforceability of which was preserved by virtue of the previous entry about the class of title. This also applies where the title is upgraded to good leasehold, except that then the upgrading does not affect or prejudice the enforcement of any estate, right or interest affecting, or in derogation of, the title of the lessor to grant the lease (LRA 2002 section 63).

Upgrading Possessory or Qualified Freehold to Absolute
An applicant should deliver to the registry:
   (a) an application in form UT1;
   (b) documentary evidence to satisfy the registrar as to the title (this is not required where the title has been registered as possessory for at least twelve years and panel 9 of form UT1 has been completed to show the proprietor is in possession);
   (c) where the application is by a person entitled to be registered as the proprietor of the estate sought to be upgraded, evidence of that entitlement;
   (d) where the application is by a person interested in a registered estate which derives from the estate sought to be upgraded, evidence of the applicant's interest where this is not apparent from the register (panel 8 of form UT1 must also be completed with details of the interest claimed); and
   (e) the fee payable. A fee calculator for all types of application is on the Land Registry's website at www.landregistry.gov.uk/fees.

Upgrading Possessory or Qualified Leasehold to Good Leasehold
An applicant should deliver to the registry:
   (a) an application in form UT1;
   (b) documentary evidence to satisfy the registrar as to the title (this is not required where the title has been registered as possessory for at least twelve years and panel 9 of form UT1 has been completed to show the proprietor is in possession);
   (c) where the application is by a person entitled to be registered as the proprietor of the estate sought to be upgraded, evidence of that entitlement;
   (d) where the application is by a person interested in a registered estate which derives from the estate sought to be upgraded, evidence of the applicant's interest where this is not apparent from the register (panel 8 of form UT1 must also be completed with details of the interest claimed); and
   (e) the fee payable. A fee calculator for all types of application is on the Land Registry's website at www.landregistry.gov.uk/fees.

Upgrading Good Leasehold to Absolute
An applicant should deliver to the registry:
   (a) an application in form UT1;
   (b) documentary evidence to satisfy the registrar as to any superior title which is not registered;

(c) where any superior title is registered with possessory, qualified or good leasehold title, documentary evidence to satisfy the registrar that that title qualifies for upgrading to absolute title;

(d) evidence of any consent to the grant of the lease required from any chargee of any superior title and any superior lessor;

(e) where the application is by a person entitled to be registered as the proprietor of the estate sought to be upgraded, evidence of that entitlement;

(f) where the application is by a person interested in a registered estate which derives from the estate sought to be upgraded, evidence of the applicant's interest where this is not apparent from the register (panel 8 of form UT1 must also be completed with details of the interest claimed); and

(g) the fee payable. A fee calculator for all types of application is on the Land Registry's website at www.landregistry.gov.uk/fees.

Upgrading Possessory or Qualified Leasehold to Absolute

An applicant should deliver to the registry:

(a) an application in form UT1;

(b) documentary evidence to satisfy the registrar as to the title to the estate sought to be upgraded (this is not required where the title has been registered as possessory for at least twelve years and panel 9 of form UT1 has been completed to show the proprietor is in possession);

(c) documentary evidence to satisfy the registrar as to any superior title which is not registered;

(d) where any superior title is registered with possessory, qualified or good leasehold title, documentary evidence to satisfy the registrar that that title qualifies for upgrading to absolute title;

(e) evidence of any consent to the grant of the lease required from any chargee of any superior title and any superior lessor;

(f) where the application is by a person entitled to be registered as the proprietor of the estate sought to be upgraded, evidence of that entitlement;

(g) where the application is by a person interested in a registered estate which derives from the estate sought to be upgraded, evidence of the applicant's interest where this is not apparent from the register (panel 8 of form UT1 must also be completed with details of the interest claimed); and

(h) the fee payable. A fee calculator for all types of application is on the Land Registry's website at www.landregistry.gov.uk/fees.

Vendor's Lien

A vendor's lien arises when a binding contract for sale of the land is made, and subsists until the purchase money is paid. It can continue even though the vendor has executed a transfer of the land and given possession to the purchaser. If the vendor has agreed that he will take some other form of security for the purchase money then the lien does not arise.

If a registrable disposition of a registered estate is made for valuable consideration, completion of the disposition by registration has the effect of postponing to the interest under the disposition any interest affecting the estate immediately before the disposition the priority of which is not protected at the time of registration (Land Registration Act 2002 ("LRA 2002") section 29(1)).

Since a vendor's lien is an interest affecting the estate before the transfer (as it arises on creation of the contract), on registration of the transfer the purchaser of the registered estate takes free of the vendor's lien unless the vendor has already protected the lien before registration of the transfer. The vendor should therefore protect his lien by entering a notice against his own title before completing the transfer. For liens arising under the Leasehold Reform, Housing and Urban Development Act 1993 section 32(2), see *Collective Enfranchisement*, page 91.

Agreed Notice
The vendor should deliver to the registry:
   (a) an application in form AN1;
   (b) the contract or a certified copy of it; and
   (c) the fee payable. A fee calculator for all types of application is on the Land Registry's website at www.landregistry.gov.uk/fees.
The entry made in the register will give details of the interest protected.
   A unilateral notice may be preferred where the applicant does not wish the terms of the agreement giving rise to the lien to be open to public scrutiny.

Unilateral Notice
An applicant should deliver to the registry:
   (a) an application in form UN1;
   (b) a plan of the affected land (where the vendor's lien affects only part of the land in the registered title); and
   (c) the fee payable. A fee calculator for all types of application is on the Land Registry's website at www.landregistry.gov.uk/fees.
Form UN1 should be completed on the following lines to show the interest of the applicant:
   "having the benefit of a vendor's lien arising under an agreement for sale dated ... made between [*registered proprietor*] and [*purchaser*]."

The unilateral notice will give brief details of the interest protected and identify the beneficiary of that notice.

Writs or Orders Affecting Land

A writ or order of the kind mentioned in the Land Charges Act 1972 section 6(1)(a) is treated as an interest affecting an estate or charge for the purposes of the Land Registration Act 2002 ("LRA 2002") (LRA 2002 section 87(1)). It cannot, however, be an overriding interest belonging to a person in actual occupation for the purposes of paragraph 2 of Schedule 1 or 3 to LRA 2002 (LRA 2002 section 87(3)). Such a writ or order is one affecting land issued or made by any court for the purposes of enforcing a judgment or recognisance.

Such a writ or order may be protected by the entry on the register of a notice or a restriction or both of these. The application may be made by the person who has obtained such a writ or order, or his assignee or chargee (Land Registration Rules 2003 ("LRR 2003") rule 172). In practice, an application for an agreed notice or a unilateral notice will be the usual course of action. In the case of an application for an agreed notice, the registrar may approve the application without the consent of the proprietor where he is satisfied of the validity of the applicant's claim.

Agreed Notice
An applicant should deliver to the registry:
 (a) an application in form AN1;
 (b) the writ or order or a certified copy of it; and
 (c) the fee payable. A fee calculator for all types of application is on the Land Registry's website at www.landregistry.gov.uk/fees.
The entry made in the register will give details of the interest protected.

Unilateral Notice
An applicant should deliver to the registry:
 (a) an application in form UN1;
 (b) a plan of the affected land (where the writ or order affects only part of the land in the registered title); and
 (c) the fee payable. A fee calculator for all types of application is on the Land Registry's website at www.landregistry.gov.uk/fees.
Form UN1 should be completed on the following lines to show the interest of the applicant:
 "person having the benefit of a [*writ or order in question*] of the ... Division of the High Court] [... County Court] dated ... [*set out full court reference and parties*]."

The unilateral notice will give brief details of the interest protected and identify the beneficiary of that notice.

Restriction
The applicant should deliver to the registry:
  (a) an application in form RX1; and
  (b) the fee payable. A fee calculator for all types of application is on the Land Registry's website at www.landregistry.gov.uk/fees.

The form of restriction sought will depend on the nature of the writ or order. One possibility based on Form N in Schedule 4 to LRR 2003 is:

"No disposition of the registered estate by the proprietor of the registered estate is to be registered without a written consent signed by [*applicant*] of [*address*] or his conveyancer."

A restriction in this form would not require the approval of the registrar under LRA 2002 section 43(3). The registrar must give notice of such an application to the proprietor of the registered estate or charge concerned (LRA 2002 section 42(3)).

Index

Absolute title........................20, 32, 86–87, 88–89, 151, 304–306
Access, neighbouring land, to................1–3
Accretion.................................3–4
Acquire, right to............................274–277
Acquisition order..............................96–98
Adjacent land, access to........................1–3
Adjudicator to Her Majesty's Land Registry............................120–122, 213
Administration order............................4–6
Administrative receiver..........................6–8
Administrator...4–6
Adverse possession........8–21, 87, 90, 121, 131, 206, 226, 228, 256–260
Advowson..21
After-acquired property.....................42–43
Agreement–
    further consideration, for..............25–26
    lease, for..21–23
    mortgage, for................................23–25
Air, rights of..278
Airspace..26
Alteration, register, of........26–28, 114, 161
Amalgamation, titles, of....................28–29
Annuity..29–30
Applicant for registration, death of 116–117
Application–
    outline............33, 66–67, 106, 126–127, 140, 152, 222–223
    priority of...................................241–242
Appointment, special powers of........... 290
Appurtenant right..................................138
Area of outstanding natural beauty.......................................255, 276
Assent...30–33
Association, unincorporated..........303–304
Attorney, power of........................236–238

Bankruptcy...34–47
    discharge from..............................41–42
    inhibition...36
    joint proprietor, of........................39–40
    matrimonial home, and.................44–46
    notice................................34–35, 40, 42
    restriction..........................35–36, 41, 42

    sale by trustee in...........................38–39
    trustee in.......................................36–47
    vesting of estate following.......... 36–37, 39, 41
Bare licence...................................193–194
Bare trust.......................................47–48
Benefice, incumbent of....................81–83
Beneficial interests, joint proprietors, of 49–50, 286
Bona vacantia....................................50–51
Boundaries........................ 10, 51–55, 233
Buy, right to................................ 274–277

Care, lack of................................ 161, 162
Cathedrals....................................... 84–85
Cattlegates...100
Caution–
    alteration of register, against........ 64–66
    conversion, against......................55–56
    dealings, against..........................56–59
    first registration, against...... 59–66, 112, 119–120
    franchise, in respect of......................143
    manorial rights, in respect of....112, 203
    matrimonial home rights, in respect of.. 188
    non-statutory rights, in respect of.. 123–124
    notice of deposit or intended deposit, in respect of...................................214
    order vacating.....................................59
Cautioner–
    notice to............................. 56, 61, 64, 65
    showing cause...............................58–59
    successor to...................................64–66
Chancel repair... 66
Charge–
    apportionment of............................... 17
    created by company, registration of......................... 103, 117, 184–184
    created by limited liability partnership, registration of............. 117, 194–195
    discount, in respect of..............275, 288
    effect of disposition of on priority of interests.. 240
    equitable.................................... 126–129

Charge, continued–
   floating..140–141
   legal.. 184–190
   limited owner's...........................195–196
   matrimonial home, in respect
      of...44–45, 188
   minor, in favour of............................80–81
   statutory...292
Chargee, sale of property by.................. 188
Charging order....................... 45–46, 66–69
Charity..69–79
   disposition by.................... 73–75, 76, 77
   disposition in favour of..................69–72
   exempt........................ 70–71, 79, 83–84
   incorporation of............................. 78–79
   non-exempt....................... 74–76, 79, 81
   trustees of...................................... 77–79
Children...79–81
Church Commissioners......................83–84
Church of England............................ 81–86
CIT form... 215
Classes of title................................... 86–90
Club 303–304
Coal 90–91
Coal mines.. 90–91
Collective enfranchisement..............91–98
Commons....................... 99–101, 295–297
Companies......................................102–104
Compulsory first registration... 75, 99, 105, 119, 134–136, 150, 295
Compulsory purchase....................104–108
Consideration, further, agreement to
   pay.. 25–26
Constructive trust........................... 108–109
Contract for sale............................. 109–111
Contractual licence........................193–194
Conversion, caution against...............55–56
Copies, official...............................214–217
Copyhold................................111–113, 291
Corporations..................................102–104
Corporeal fisheries................................291
Correction, mistake, of......26–28, 113, 161
Costs 27, 28, 114–116
Covenant–
   implied............................ 157–161, 180
   indemnity... 163
   positive....................................... 234–235
   restrictive.................. 178–179, 273–274
Credit union... 116
Creditors' notice......................................36
Crown–
   land, adverse possession of................ 18
   passing of property to, by

   escheat....................................50–51
   rent, overriding first registration...... 225
Customary right..................................... 224

Dealings, caution against..................56–59
Death–
   applicant for registration, of..... 116–117
   registered proprietor, of............231–233
Debenture.............................117, 140, 250
Deed–
   arrangement, of..........................118–119
   enlargement of.........................125–126
   execution of..... 103–104, 131–132, 195, 236, 237–238, 250
   lost.. 201–202
   memorial of............................... 201–202
   poll.. 104–106
   right to rectification of.............206–207
Demesne land.......................50, 119–120
Deposit, notice of..................................214
Diluvion... 3–4
Diocesan Board of Finance...............81, 95
Disclaimer........................46–47, 198–200
Discount, on exercise of right to
   buy.......................................275, 288
Dispute.. 120–122
Division of titles....................................122
Document–
   edited information.................... 215, 216
   executed by attorney.........................236
   exempt information.................. 215–217
   transitional period............................217

Easement–
   enter land, to... 1
   equitable........................... 130–131, 191
   legal.......... 130, 190–193, 224, 227–228
   parsonage or church land, appurtenant
      to.. 86
   statutory...275
Edited information document........ 215, 216
Effluxion of time, determination of
   lease by... 182
Embankment........................ 123–124, 225
Enfranchisement–
   collective.. 91–98
   copyhold, of...................... 111–112, 291
   leasehold.................................... 167–169
Enlargement, long lease, of...........124–126
Equality money.............................298–299
Equitable–
   charge.. 126–129
   easement........................... 130–131, 191
Equity, estoppel, by...............................248

Index

Equity, mere....................206–207
Erosion, land, of...........................3
Escheat..............................50–51
Estate–
   disposition of, effect of on
      priority of interests..............239–240
   right, conveyance of......................... 131
   rentcharge – see *Rentcharge*
Estoppel................................248
European Economic Interest
   Grouping....................131–133
Exclusive use........................ 133
Exempt–
   charity................... 70–71, 76, 79, 83–84
   disposal............................154–155
   information document............ 215–217
Extortionate credit transaction........ 44, 250

Filed plan – see *Title plan*
First registration............................133–139
   caution against....... 59–66, 112, 119–120
   compulsory.................. 75, 99, 105, 119,
              134–136, 150, 295
   easement arising prior to.......... 190–191
   evidence in support of...................... 137
   following assent............................30–32
   franchise, of............................. 144–145
   interests which override............224–226
   legal profit a prendre arising prior
      to............................... 242–243
   mines and minerals, of..............207–208
   objection to.................................. 61–63
   person in adverse possession, by.. 18–20
   procedure for............................ 136–139
   town or village green, of...........297–298
   unregistered land, of................. 133–139
Fisheries, corporeal............................. 291
Floating charge...............................140–141
Flying freehold.............................. 141–142
Foreclosure......................................188–189
Foreshore.............................15, 18, 142
Forfeiture, lease, of............................... 182
Forgery............................. 145–146, 161
Franchise....................................... 143–145
   affecting...........................60, 144, 219
   caution against first registration
      of... 59–66
   first registration of.... 133–139, 144–145
   overriding first registration...............225
   registered, lease of............................ 145
   relating.......................60, 144, 219–220
Fraud 145–146, 153, 161, 162, 163

Freehold–
   collective enfranchisement of.......91–98
   enlargement of long lease to.....124–126
   flying....................................... 141–142
   transfer of pursuant to enfranchisement
      of lease................................ 168–169
Freezing order............................... 147–148
Friendly society..............................148–149
Full title guarantee........................ 157–158

General vesting declaration...........106–108
Gift 150–153
Glebe land.. 85–86
Good leasehold title.. 32, 89, 151, 304, 305
Grant-aided land......................155–156
"Hedge and ditch" rule...........................52
Historical information........................... 153
Housing action trust...................... 153–155
Housing association,
   unregistered...................... 102, 155–157

Implied covenant............................157–161
Implied trust................................. 108–109
Indemnity–
   covenant...163
   fraud, in respect of.................... 146, 153
   mines and minerals, in respect of..... 209
   registrar, by....... 114–115, 161–163, 214
Index–
   map, search of.....................................219
   official search of........................219–220
Individual voluntary arrangement..........294
Industrial and provident society............. 164
Inheritance tax charge............................241
Inhibition–
   abolition of... 164
   bankruptcy..36
   cancellation of........................... 164–165
   freezing order, in respect of..............147
   incumbent of a benefice, in respect
      of.. 81–82
   modification of........................ 164–165
Insolvency – see *Administration order;*
   Administrative receiver; Bankruptcy;
   Bona vacantia; Deed of arrangement;
   Individual voluntary arrangement;
   Insolvency administration order;
   Liquidator; Overseas Insolvency
   proceedings; Receiver; Sequestrator.
Insolvency administration order....... 40–41
Intended deposit, notice of....................214
Interest–
   costs or indemnity, on.............. 114, 162

Interest, continued–
   overriding................................ 223–228
   priority of.................................239–241
Interim receiving order................. 260–262
Internal waters...165

Joint proprietor(s)..........................166, 286
   bankruptcy of...................................39–40
   beneficial interests of.............49–50, 286
   death of..166
Joint tenancy, severance of................... 286

Land charge, local.........................200–201
Land, trust of......... 108–109, 232, 300–303
Lease 169–184
   acquisition of............................. 173–174
   agreement for................................21–23
   back.. 96
   covenants implied in.........159–160, 180
   determination of....................... 181–183
   disclaimer of....................................... 199
   expiry of... 182
   extension of 173–174, 180–181
   first registration of..................... 133–139
   forfeiture of...182
   grant of, effect of on priority of
      interests.. 240
   long, enlargement of................. 124–126
   not exceeding seven years........ 170–171
   not exceeding three years. 170–171, 209
   option to renew................. 170, 220–222
   registered franchise, of...................... 145
   registered manor, of...........................204
   registration of disposition of.....171–172
   registration of, required............. 169–170
   restrictive covenants in.............. 178–179
   right to determine.............................. 183
   shared ownership......................286–288
   surrender of.................................180, 181
   time share... 295
   unregistered, determination of..........183
   variation of............... 172–173, 211, 288
Leasehold enfranchisement...........167–169
Legal aid charge.....................................292
Legal charge..................................184–190
Legal easement............130, 190–193, 224,
       227–228
Licence............................. 1, 2–3, 193–194
Lien, vendor's...................... 25, 95–96, 307
Light, right of..278
Limitation periods, adverse possession
   and...... 8–9, 11, 14–15, 18–19, 131, 142
Limited liability partnerships........ 194–195
Limited owner's charge............. 195–196

Limited partnership............................... 197
Limited title guarantee......................... 158
Liquidator......................................197–200
Local authority, right to buy
   from.. 274–277
Local land charge...................200–201, 225
Long lease, enlargement of........... 124–126
Lost deed..201–202
Lost modern grant, doctrine of.............. 192

Manorial rights..............112–113, 202–203
Manors....................... 202–204, 219–220
Maps 52, 233–234
Matrimonial home.....44–46, 188, 204–205
Mental disability, registered proprietor,
   of 11–12, 206
Mental Health Act 1983, patients
   under..205–206
Mere equity...................................206–207
Merger..181
Minerals.............................. 161, 207–209
Mines and minerals........ 29, 161, 207–209,
       225
Minor..79–81
Mistake, correction of....... 26–28, 113, 161
Monetary local land charge...........200–201
Mortgage.......................... 23–25, 129, 135

National Park............................... 255, 276
Neighbouring land, access to................ 1–3
Non-exempt charity.............. 74–76, 79, 81
Non-statutory right................................225
Notice..209–214
   access order, of............................2, 211
   acquisition order, of.....................97–98
   administration order, of........................ 4
   agreed....................................... 210–211
   agreement for lease, of................ 21–22
   agreement for mortgage, of......... 23–24
   application for acquisition order, of... 96
   appointment of liquidator, of....197–198
   bankruptcy..................................... 34–35
   cancellation of............................ 211, 212
   charge, of... 45
   charging order, of................. 45, 67–68
   claim to vesting order, of.............93–94,
       175–176
   contract for sale, of................. 109–111
   creditors'..36
   deposit, of.. 214
   easement, of..............................191, 192
   entry of.. 210
   equitable charge, of........................ 127
   equitable easement, of..................... 130

Index

Notice, continued–
    floating charge, of..............................140
    former copyhold, of..........................112
    franchise, of......................................143
    freezing order, of......................147–148
    inheritance tax...................................210
    interests which cannot be protected
        by......................................5, 209–210
    interests, of...............................138–139
    interim receiving order, of.........260–262
    lease, determining......................182–183
    lease, of...170
    local land charge, of..................200–201
    manorial rights, of.................... 112, 203
    matrimonial home rights, of............ 188,
        204–205, 210
    mere equity, of...........................206–207
    non-statutory rights, of...............123–124
    option, of..................................220–221
    pending charging order, of................. 67
    pending land action, of............ 2, 92, 230
    preserved right to buy, of................. 277
    profit a prendre, of............ 194, 243–244
    property adjustment order, of... 246–247
    restraint order, of......................260–262
    restrictive covenant, of............ 178–179,
        273–274
    right of collective enfranchisement,
        of... 91–92
    right of pre-emption, of............ 278–279
    right to acquire new lease, of....174–175
    right to extended lease, of.................173
    right to leasehold enfranchisement,
        of.......................................167–168
    subrogation, of..................................293
    unilateral.........................210, 211–213
    vendor's lien, of................................307
    vesting order, of............93–94, 176–177
    writ or order, of........................ 308–309

Objection–
    application, to................................... 120
    cancellation of notice, to.................. 213
    entry of restriction, to....................... 264
Occupation, person in................... 224, 227
Official copies..............................214–217
Official custodian for charities....71–72, 77
Official search..............................217–220
    index, of....................................219–220
    priority, with....................217–218, 241
        unavailable.......... 32–33, 66–67, 106,
        126–127, 140, 152
    priority, without................................218

Option–
    purchase, to...............................220–222
    renew lease or purchase reversion,
        to................................ 170, 220–222
    shared ownership lease,
        under................................... 287, 288
Order–
    affecting land............................308–309
    court, of, to rectify register................27
    sale, for.. 129
Ordnance Survey.....................52, 233–234
Outline application.............33, 66–67, 106,
    126–127, 140, 152, 222–223
Overage.. 25–26
Overriding interest........................223–228
    coal or coal mine, in..................... 90–91
    duty to provide information about........5,
        7–8, 19, 31, 33, 38, 101, 105, 106,
        107, 125, 137, 150, 152, 171,
        250–251, 297–298, 299–300
    transitional provisions in respect
        of.. 20–21
Overseas insolvency proceedings.........228

Parsonage land................................. 82–83
Partnership..229
    limited..197
    limited liability......................... 194–195
Party wall.. 52–53
Pending action, notice in respect
    of 34–35, 67
Pending land action......................229–230
    access order constituting..................... 1
    protecting priority of......... 1, 2, 92, 147,
        175–176
Personal representatives................116–117,
    231–233, 301
Plans 233–234
Positive covenant..........................234–235
Possession–
    adverse.......................8–21, 87, 90, 121,
        131, 206, 226, 228, 256–260
    defences to action for................... 17–18
    enforcement of judgment for........ 17–18
Possessory title.......20, 87–88, 89–90, 304,
    306
Postponement, deed of......................... 186
Power of attorney..........................236–238
Pre-emption, right of.....................278–280
Prejudicial information.................215–216
Priority–
    application, of............................241–242
    charge, of......................... 129, 186–187

Priority, continued–
   interest, of.................................239–241
   reserving period of....217–218, 222–223
Profit a prendre............................ 242–246
   caution against first registration
      of... 59–66
   first registration of............ 133–139, 245
   licence to enter land in exercise of... 194
   overriding first registration.......224, 244
   overriding registered
      disposition........... 227–228, 244–245
   registration of........... 243–242, 245–246
Property adjustment order.............246–248
Proprietary estoppel.............................. 248
Proprietor, registered, death of......231–233
Proprietors' names, search of index
   of 220
Public right, overriding first
   registration......................................225
Public sector landlords, right to buy
   from.. 274–277
Public-private partnership lease... 134, 226,
                            238–239
Purchase, option to........................220–222

Qualified title.............. 20, 87, 89, 305, 306
Qualifying estate, meaning of................. 59

Receiver.. 249–251
   address for service of........................249
   administrative.................................. 6–8
   court, appointed by................... 251–253
   Court of Protection, appointed
      by..205–206
Rectification, register, of,....... 26, 145–146,
                    161, 162, 253–254
Registered disposition, interests which
   override......................226–228, 244–245
Registered social landlord.... 154, 254–255,
                            274–277
Rent–
   apportionment of....................... 179–180
   exoneration from....................... 179–180
   to mortgage................................275–276
Rentcharge.................................... 255–260
   adverse possession of............... 256–260
   caution against first registration
      of... 59–66
   covenants implied in................. 160–161
   creation of................................. 235, 256
   first registration of..................... 133–139
   indemnity in respect of.................... 275
   life, for, annuity constituting........ 29, 30
   release or redemption of.............. 76–77

Restraint order..............................260–262
Restriction....................................262–273
   acquisition order, in respect of........... 98
   agreement for lease, in respect
      of... 21, 23
   agreement for mortgage, in respect
      of... 23, 24–25
   agreement to pay further consideration,
      in respect of............................25–26
   annuity, in respect of.................... 29–30
   application for...........................263–264
   bankruptcy order, in respect of....35–36,
                                             41
   cancellation of.................................. 272
   cathedral, in respect of........................84
   charge, in respect of..........................185
   charging order, in respect of.........68–69
   claim to vesting order, in respect of. 176
   collective enfranchisement, in respect
      of.. 92, 93
   constructive, implied or resulting trust,
      in respect of...................................109
   contract for sale, in respect of.. 109, 111
   court order for entry of............. 270–271
   deed of arrangement, in respect
      of.. 118–119
   Diocesan Board of Finance, in respect
      of... 85
   disapplication of....................... 271–272
   EEIG, in respect of........................... 132
   entry of...................................... 262–263
   equitable charge, in respect of.. 128–129
   form A..... 40, 48, 49, 68, 69, 72, 79, 80,
      109, 128, 149, 166, 197, 229, 247,
      265, 271, 280, 286, 294, 300, 303
   form B.................48, 232–233, 265, 301
   form C......................232, 265, 301–302
   form D.. 82, 265
   form E................. 72, 74, 75, 76, 77, 265
   form F..................... 71–72, 77, 265, 270
   form G..................... 266, 282, 284, 285
   form H.............. 196, 266, 282, 283, 285
   form I................ 196, 266, 282, 283, 284
   form J...40, 266
   form K................................ 68, 69, 266
   form L...94, 98, 118, 235, 252, 267, 281
   form M......................................235, 267
   form N..... 93, 94, 97, 98, 111, 118, 119,
      176, 177–178, 222, 230, 247, 249,
      252, 267, 279–280, 281, 294
   form O... 267
   form P.. 268
   form Q..................................... 197, 268

Index

Restriction, continued–
form R, S, T...268
form U, V................................. 269, 276
form W.............................. 269, 276–277
form X.. 269, 277
form Y.. 255, 269
form AA, BB..................................... 269
form CC....................................269–270
form DD.. 270
form EE................................... 262, 270
form FF..262
form GG, HH............................261, 270
forms of..................................... 264–270
fraud or forgery, in respect of............146
freezing order, in respect of...... 147, 148
grant-aided land, in respect of.......... 156
housing action trust, in respect of.....154
individual voluntary arrangement,
   in respect of..................................294
interim receiving order, in respect
   of 260–262
joint proprietors, in respect of.......... 166
limited owner's charge, in respect
   of... 196
limited partnership, in respect of...... 197
local land charge, in respect
   of.. 200–201
Mental Health Act patient, in respect
   of.. 205–206
modification of......................... 271–272
nature of..262
non-standard form of................. 264–265
obligatory..271
option, in respect of.......... 220, 221–222
partnership, in respect of.................. 229
pending land action, in respect of.....230
positive covenant, in respect of........ 235
preserved right to buy, in respect
   of... 277
property adjustment order, in respect
   of.. 246–247
receiver, in respect of............... 249, 252
registered social landlord, in respect
   of....................................... 154, 254
rentcharge for life, in respect of... 29–30
restraint order, in respect of......260–262
right of pre-emption, in respect of...278,
                            279–280
sequestrator, in respect of.................281
settled land, in respect of............. 29–30,
                            282–283
souvenir land, in respect of...............289

special power of appointment, in
   respect of......................................290
trust, in respect of....... 48, 232, 300–301
vesting order, in respect of......... 94, 176,
                            176–177
withdrawal of............................272–273
writ or order, in respect of........ 308, 309
Restrictive covenant...... 178–179, 273–274
Resulting trust............................... 108–109
Reverter, right of.................................. 280
Right–
acquire, to................................ 274–277
air, of... 278
buy, to....................................... 274–277
common, of.................................99–101
light, of... 278
pre-emption, of......................... 278–280
reverter, of...................................... 280
way, of, vehicular..................... 191–192
River–
bed... 291
wall................................ 123–124, 225
Rural area...................................... 255, 276

School sites... 280
Sea wall................................ 123–124, 225
Search, official.............................. 217–220
Sequestrator.................................. 281–282
Settled land........................... 231, 282–285
Settlement............................ 185, 283–284
Severance, joint tenancy, of................. 286
Shared ownership lease.................286–288
Souvenir land................................ 288–290
Special powers of appointment............. 290
Sporting rights................................290–291
Squatters – see *Adverse possession*
"Staircasing"............................... 286, 288
Statutory charge................................... 292
Statutory declaration–
adverse possession, in support
   of...................... 13–14, 16, 258–260
enlargement of long lease, in support
   of.......................................125, 126
Statutory easement............................... 275
Sub-charge................................... 189–190
Subrogation...293
Surrender, lease, of...................... 180, 181

T marks... 53
Tacking.. 186
Tenancy–
common, in... 49
joint..49, 286

317

Tenant for life–
　death of 285
　proprietor ceasing to be 285
Time share 295
Tithe, right to payment in lieu of 226
Title–
　amalgamation of 28–29
　classes of 86–90
　division of 122
　plan 51–52
　upgrading .. 55–56, 87, 89, 161, 304–306
Town or village greens 295–298
Transfer 298–300
　declaration of trust, on 49–50
　forms of 298
　part, of 298, 299
Transitional period document 217
Transitional provisions–
　adverse possession, in respect of 18, 20–21
　cautions, in respect of 55–56, 60
　corporeal fisheries, in respect of 291
　Crown rents, in respect of 225
　demesne land, in respect of 112
　easements, in respect of 193
　franchises, in respect of 143
　legal easement, in respect of 228
　manorial rights, in respect of 112, 203
　non-statutory rights, in respect of 123–124
　overriding interests, in respect of 20–21
　profits a prendre, in respect of .. 228, 245
　right to payment in lieu of tithe, in respect of 226
Trust–
　bare 47–48
　constructive 108–109
　declaration of, on transfer 49–50
　implied 108–109
　land, of 108–109, 232, 300–303
　minor, for 79, 80
　resulting 108–109
Trustee–
　application by, for registration 81
　bankruptcy, in 36–39, 42–43, 45–47
　charity, of 77–79
　new, vesting land in 302–303
Undervalue, transaction at 43–44, 250
Unincorporated association 303–304
Unjust enrichment 293
Unregistered interest, overriding .. 223–228

Unregistered land–
　first registration of 133–139
　gift of 150–151
Upgrading title 55–56, 87, 89, 161, 304–306
Vehicular right of way 191–192
Vendor's lien 25, 95–96, 307
Vesting–
　declaration 302–303
　declaration, general 106–108
　disclaimed property, of 46–47
　estate, of on bankruptcy 36–37, 39
　order 92–95, 129, 175–177, 199–200
Village greens 295–298
Voidable transaction 43–44
Water, boundary with 3–4
Waters, internal 165
Writ, affecting land 308–309